Allen Ginsberg's Buddhist Poetics

Allen Ginsberg's Buddhist Poetics

Tony Trigilio

Southern Illinois University Press
Carbondale

Copyright © 2007 by the Board of Trustees,
Southern Illinois University
All rights reserved
Printed in the United States of America

10 09 08 07   4 3 2 1

Library of Congress Cataloging-in-Publication Data
Trigilio, Tony, date.
  Allen Ginsberg's Buddhist poetics / Tony Trigilio.
    p. cm.
  Includes bibliographical references and index.
  ISBN-13: 978-0-8093-2755-3 (alk. paper)
  ISBN-10: 0-8093-2755-4 (alk. paper)
  1. Ginsberg, Allen, 1926–1997—Religion. 2. Buddhism in
literature. I. Title.
  PS3513.I74Z94 2007
  811'.54—dc22   2006034378

Printed on recycled paper. ♻

The paper used in this publication meets the minimum requirements of American National Standard for Information Sciences—Permanence of Paper for Printed Library Materials, ANSI Z39.48-1992.∞

For Shelly

Contents

Preface: Four Faces of Ginsberg's Buddhism   ix
Acknowledgments   xix

1. Ginsberg's Spiritual Fathers   1
2. Queer Dharma, Anxiety, and Fantasy in "Angkor Wat"   30
3. The Two Truths of "The Change"   62
4. Language and the Limits of Romanticism   85
5. Strategies of Retreat   118
6. Language, Dream, Self-(Dis)Closure   156
7. On the Devotional   187

Notes   199
Works Cited   239
Index   249

Preface: Four Faces of Ginsberg's Buddhism

It is usually difficult to trace the origins of a book to any single source. Still, I know that this one began several years ago during a debate on the old Contemporary American Poetry (CAP-L) Internet listserv. A fellow scholar had derided Allen Ginsberg as a poet of "hysterical loudmouthedness," and another dismissed Ginsberg's poetics as mere "ranting." I felt compelled to reply, not necessarily to defend Ginsberg, because such defenses prevail to excess in Beat fandom, and these defenses don't always help us read the poems. But at the time, I was working on my first book, *"Strange Prophecies Anew": Rereading Apocalypse in Blake, H. D., and Ginsberg*, and from my research on Ginsberg and the Anglo-American prophetic tradition, it seemed just too easy to dismiss him in this way without at least a glance at how hysteria and loudmouthedness (not to mention the potential value of poetry as ranting) could be read as deliberate strategies, as actual crafted prophetic utterance rather than mere spectacle.

I composed a response that described his intentions as a mode of Western prophetic speech and explicated the Buddhist framework from which they came. I argued that much of what was at stake in his presumed ranting was whether or not the ramble and ruckus of his chanting could be taken seriously as manifestations of his particular "Buddhist poetics." To do so, I had to take his Buddhism as a serious vehicle of his craft. I was reading Ginsberg as a religious writer. And I was surprised that hardly any models existed in the scholarly community for such a reading. Just as his revision to the opening line of "Howl" from "starving mystical naked" to "starving hysterical naked" seeks to realize the "mystical" in the material, more specifically in the "hysterical," Ginsberg's emphasis on the "breath-unit" is an attempt to fuse the visionary consciousness of Biblical prophecy with what was for him the sacred space of human consciousness learned through his study and practice of meditation and mantra chanting. The revisionary strategy Ginsberg brought to this first utterance of "speech-breath-thought" in "Howl"—of the breath as a unit of the poetic line—dramatizes in miniature the structural impetus of the poem to combine immanent and transcendent representation so that the secular art of poetry might also represent sacred experience. I reasoned in my posting that if we dismiss Ginsberg's stylistic and thematic concerns as only contradictory or as insubstantial (ranting), then we should proceed to Walt Whitman and work backwards, dismissing all poets who make claims to the visionary. As I wrote my listserv response, I kept in mind the anecdotes I'd heard from other writers over the years about their experiences with Ginsberg and his conception of a Buddhist poetics. "I saw Ginsberg read once, and he chanted straight through the first thirty minutes," they'd say. Yes, it seemed to me, of course a Buddhist poet would be inclined to incorporate the sacred speech of mantra chanting within the secular framework of a poetry reading. As I wrote to the listserv: "Ginsberg's emphasis on the breath-unit is so strongly rooted in his reading of the Bible within and against Buddhist practice that we might need to start a holy war to resolve the blurred boundary between literary poetry and meditative poetry in Ginsberg."

While writing this listserv message, I realized that in order to read Ginsberg's poetic strategies as fully as possible—without recourse to holy war—I had approached him as if he were a Buddhist poet. More intriguing, my reading of Ginsberg as a Buddhist poet did not seem as unusual to me as it did to the many scholars I knew (especially the two on the list to whom I was responding). We usually take poets at their word when they profess themselves, for instance, as Christians; we do not question the religious commitment of, say, poets as diverse as T. S. Eliot, W. H. Auden, Robert Lowell, or Denise Levertov. But, often, we do not extend such a reading strategy to Ginsberg—and it is easy to understand why. Ginsberg questioned the seriousness of his own Buddhist commitment, often describing himself as a "flaky Buddhist"; those around him, from well-known Beat colleagues to his student apprentices, did much the same.[1] To complicate matters further, Ginsberg's first and most well-known Buddhist teacher was Chögyam Trungpa Rinpoche, whose alcoholism and sexual excesses were as well known to the Western Buddhist community as were his skillful and popular methods of making ancient Buddhist texts relevant to the contemporary world. Ginsberg became a student of Trungpa's version of Buddhism—the "Crazy Wisdom" lineage—and on the surface, their student-guru relationship would not seem to support the idea that Ginsberg was a serious Buddhist. As I discuss later in this book, the impulse of Crazy Wisdom to claim the authority of a lineage (so crucial as a form of currency in Tibetan Buddhism) and simultaneously work actively to undermine the authority of lineage-making can create a crippling paradox in any discussion of the authenticity of Ginsberg's Buddhist practice. This book examines how Ginsberg struggled with this paradox as he cast Trungpa's Buddhism within a familiar conceptual framework traceable to the Anglo-American visionary poetry of Blake and to Dada and Surrealism.

This book is the first sustained scholarly effort to take (and to test) Ginsberg's poetry at its word as Buddhist poetry. I also will draw from Ginsberg's extensive prose work, which has received little commentary to date, and from his journals and teaching transcripts housed at the Stanford University Library. This book examines what Ginsberg meant when he called himself a Buddhist poet and examines the cultural contexts—especially the politics of gender, sex, sexuality, and the Cold War—from which this self-identification emerged. As I will discuss further in chapter 1, it is crucial to keep in mind the critical silence that met Jay Dougherty's 1987 argument that Ginsberg's later poems are best read by readers with some recognition of the poet's Buddhist lexicon and spiritual practice (81). Dougherty's remarks were a call to action in the scholarly community, but no one responded. To be sure, readers cannot ignore Michael Schumacher's reliable 1992 biography *Dharma Lion: A Critical Biography of Allen Ginsberg*. Schumacher's book rightly places Ginsberg's Buddhism at the center of his career—from the poet's early autodidactic forays into the dharma through his formalized study with Trungpa—yet the book's biographical heft is not matched by a similarly substantial critical or scholarly eye. The book is an invaluable document of Ginsberg's life but does not offer anything resembling close readings of the poetry or the Buddhist principles and practices that often frame the poetry. With Schumacher's biography and three years earlier Barry Miles's useful *Ginsberg: A Biography*, the biographical contexts for the poems are available for analysis and discussion, but little work exists that combines Ginsberg's texts and contexts with the depth one would expect from a scholarly book.

My argument in this book is quite simple. Ginsberg's struggle with Buddhism is central to understanding his post-"Kaddish" visionary work; and only through an understanding of his maturation as a Buddhist can we consider the scope of his career in detail. It is important that words such as *struggle* and *maturation* are used in this context in this book. Ginsberg did not formalize his Buddhist practice, that is, did not take vows with a teacher/guru, until 1972, more than fifteen years after he began explicitly acknowledging the debt of Buddhism to his poetry. Even then, after he took his bodhisattva vows[2] in 1972 and began study with Trungpa, he struggled to reconcile the autodidactic roots of his Buddhism with a newfound mode of practice firmly established within a hierarchical Tibetan lineage, represented by Trungpa, whose highly individualized conception of Crazy Wisdom was framed nonetheless by his understanding of Tibetan Buddhist resources that had been handed down for centuries from one guru to the next. Jack Kerouac was Ginsberg's first Buddhist teacher, as I discuss in more detail in chapter 2, but the force of Kerouac's Catholic conversion at the end of his life problematizes the long-range extent of his influence on Ginsberg's Buddhism.[3] Before Trungpa, from Ginsberg's first readings in Buddhism in the mid-1950s through his early incorporations of Buddhist terminology in *Howl and Other Poems* and *Kaddish and Other Poems* and through his travels to India in 1962 through 1963, his Buddhist practice was autodidactic and, as such, was eccentric and erratic. After "Kaddish" in 1961 and through the 1960s, his Buddhist practice still was not formalized, but the influence of Buddhism on the range of his poetics was narrowed to include mantra and chant speech as vectors of his fluctuating trust in referentiality. He began formal teaching with Trungpa in 1972, including readings of the major texts of the Tibetan Mahayana (and Vajrayana) traditions, those that taught the Tibetan graduated path to enlightenment, or *lam rim*, in which the practitioner endeavors to achieve enlightenment in this lifetime to help others reach the same goal in their current lifetimes.[4] His teachings with Trungpa continued through Trungpa's death in 1987; the poet became a student of Gehlek Rinpoche after meeting him in 1989. Even though Ginsberg's commitment to study with Gehlek Rinpoche was also a move away from the Crazy Wisdom school, the poet's study and practice of Buddhism with Gehlek Rinpoche were a continuation of the Vajrayana tradition's emphasis on the embodied immediacy of Tantra[5] that Ginsberg first learned about from Trungpa. For both Trungpa and Gehlek Rinpoche, the path to enlightenment was a matter of Tantric practice. At any given moment, Ginsberg's teachings with Trungpa or Gehlek Rinpoche could be on specific texts, such as Shantideva's seventh-century Mahayana classic, *The Way of the Bodhisattva*, or on specific, advanced Tantric pedagogical tools, such as Trungpa's Shambhala training or Gehlek Rinpoche's translations in Western, contemporary language of the Tibetan *lam rim*. During this time, when Ginsberg's teachings in Tibetan Buddhism ran a recursive gamut back-and-forth between beginning and advanced texts, he also formed the Jack Kerouac School of Disembodied Poetics within Trungpa's Naropa Institute (now Naropa University) in 1974, which would become the first accredited Buddhist college in the United States. Ginsberg ran Naropa's poetics department, the academic name for the Kerouac School, and taught there and at Brooklyn College through the end of his life. His classes ranged through Blake, the Beat Generation, Spiritual Poetics, Meditation and Poetics, and Spontaneous and Improvised Poetics. He planned to publish transcripts of his Naropa classes, and, as such, his student assistants tape-recorded and transcribed his lectures, now archived in the Ginsberg collection at Stanford University.

No matter how easy it might seem to trace this basic time line of Ginsberg's Buddhism, it is another thing entirely to apply it to the poetry, given the circuitous path of Ginsberg's Buddhist commitment and its effects on his poems. Still, I argue in this book that no matter how circular his Buddhist practice might seem, several important patterns of influence can be traced from the nonlinear narrative of his spiritual practice. Ginsberg's struggles with sex and sexuality, his use of drugs, his neoromanticism and its resultant ambivalence on matters of transcendence and visionary experience, his protest poetry, his final poems of sickness and dying—all cannot be seen in full detail without an understanding of how they shaped and were shaped by his Buddhist practice. The structure of this book reflects Ginsberg's movement from the fits and starts of autodidactic instruction to the linearity of formal teachings with Trungpa and, later, with Gehlek Rinpoche.

This book is organized according to the four faces of Ginsberg's maturation as a Buddhist after his early famous works, "Howl" and "Kaddish": these "faces" make themselves visible in his poetry as manifestations of anxiety, romanticism, performativity, and linguistic experimentation. Chapter 1 discusses Ginsberg's earliest fusions of Western and Eastern conceptions of mind in the context of his psychological struggles as a poet and gay man. Chapter 1 also explores how the complexities of transference and countertransference might be applied both to his relationship with his father, his first guide in spiritual matters, the poet Louis Ginsberg, and to his relationship with his father-guru, Trungpa, also a poet. Chapters

2 and 3 read Ginsberg's two most notable Buddhist long poems "Angkor Wat" and "The Change" as nervous religious pilgrimages necessary to the development of his nascent Buddhist poetics. These chapters also contextualize the poems with Ginsberg's prose statements on Buddhism and poetics, material often overlooked in discussions of Ginsberg's work. Written within just one month of each other in 1963, these poems taken together demarcate the boundaries of Ginsberg's early Buddhist poetics, a period of experimentation when the poet adopts, paradoxically, both asceticism and ecstasy as models for prophetic poetry. Such influences were tentative, not surprisingly, insofar as this was a period of significant, sometimes clashing, modes of experimentation for Ginsberg, writing in the aftermath of the enormous success of both "Howl" and "Kaddish." He found the language, imagery, and conceptual framework of Eastern religious thought inspirational and in this early ecumenical period of his practice was comfortable with his deliberate conflation of Hinduism and Buddhism in the early- to mid-1960s. He crafted from Buddhism a political urgency for his poetry. At the same time, he was taught by Buddhism not to be attached even to his own political beliefs, including his belief, for a time, that his 1948 vision of Blake reciting "Ah Sunflower!" in Harlem united the political and artistic exigencies of his poetics of prophecy. Chapters 4 and 5 explore the greater role language itself takes as politicized subject matter in Ginsberg's Buddhist poetry from the mid-1960s through the early-1970s. During this period, his Buddhist poetics is characterized by experiments in language with the mantra and the asemantic breath-unit as a foundation for meaning-making. As I discuss in chapters 4 and 5, Ginsberg's one speech-breath-thought poetics functions at this time as a model of sacred speech that might unite Western neoromantic ideals of the integrity of the individual utterance with Eastern ideals of fluctuating, unstable subjectivity. This fusion of Western and Eastern ideas of the subject was located, for Ginsberg, in a tripartite conceptual framework, Buddhist body-speech-mind, which only marginally trusted the power of language to represent sacred experience.

Chapter 6 proceeds from this fusion and explores how Ginsberg's Buddhist poetics leads him to a Buddhist humanism that evades the dangerous universalizing potential of humanism. The challenges to this Buddhist humanism, discussed in chapters 1 through 5, are strongest during the period of the poet's career discussed in chapter 6, when Ginsberg's Buddhist poetics was shaped by scandal and by communal and familial fragmentation. Chapter 6 examines the virtues and limitations of the experimentalist urgency of Ginsberg's Buddhist poetics as they manifest within three distinct cultural and philosophical contexts: first, the political controversy surrounding the early years of Naropa Institute, specifically the violence of the 1976 Vajrayana retreat attended by poet W. S. Merwin and his companion Dana Naone; second, Ginsberg's continual reexamination of the figure of his mother, Naomi, as an authorizing maternal figure for a language of the sacred that revises the language Ginsberg inherited from his poetic fathers Louis Ginsberg, William Carlos Williams, and Trungpa; and third, his efforts in the poems of his late career to forge a Buddhist poetics that merges oppositional tendencies of humanist urgency and postmodern self-diffusion.

Chapter 7 attempts to trace the tendencies of Ginsberg's Buddhist poetics as vectors of contemporary innovative poetry and suggests further study of the varied practices of contemporary "Buddhist poetics" in the West. As such, this book continues the arguments of scholars such as David Loy and Jay L. Garfield, among others, that Buddhism sounds many of the same philosophical notes as does poststructuralism. Chapter 7 speculates on the shape of Buddhist-inspired poetics in the U.S. in an era when American Buddhism—in the practices of both recent immigrants and of converts—is increasingly assimilated in the panoply of the country's major religions.[6]

Just as the story of a book's origins also is the story of its shape and structure, so, too, is it a story of methodology. My approach is to study Ginsberg's poems and their contexts with the usual scholarly distance. I employ various levels of diction in this book—multiple modes of discourse that, I hope, alert readers to the variety of Ginsberg's thought and development as a Buddhist-inspired poet and emphasizes the need to approach his work from various frames of reference. The sometimes specialized terminology of this book borrows often from the terms of art in philosophy, which is to be expected, insofar as Buddhism is usually studied within the field of philosophy. Issues of language and levels of usage are important to all scholarly work and are questions of accessibility and good writing. However, these are especially important issues in the newly formed field of literary criticism called Beat Studies—a field that presumes that the literature of the Beat Generation, like all literature, yields to greater understanding when approached through the interdisciplinary lens of contemporary critical theory rather than only through the lenses of formalist or biographical criticism.

The question one often is asked when discussing a manuscript-in-progress, especially someone like myself who is also a poet and just as likely to be sharing work with fellow artists as with fellow scholars, is whether the book will be a "theory book." Of course, all critical response is "of theory": that is, responses from nineteenth-century biographical criticism through mid-twentieth century New Critical formalism are all responses informed by a template that is "theoretical." The more urgent question is to consider what sort of theory one proceeds from. In the case of Ginsberg's eclectic thought, the answer requires various angles of vision and requires a range of theoretical perspectives, old or new ones, to create more complete readings of Ginsberg texts than have been proffered in the past. Those theoretical perspectives that seem the most abstruse appear so because they borrow heavily from other disciplines. That is, their presumed difficulty is a serious issue for those of us who are literary scholars, because they borrow from fields such as philosophy, psychology, sociology, and history, to name four, rather than just from literary studies itself. Or to put it another way, to forecast material that appears later in this book: to speak of the "performative" in language and literature is to invoke the admittedly pyrotechnic language of Judith Butler—but, more important, this is to invoke Butler by way of the nervous, nerdy humor of her antecedent in linguistic performativity, J. L. Austin. Moreover, to speak of "reification" is to borrow not only from the Marxist critique of capitalist mystification systems but also from the terms of art of religion and philosophy—especially the study of Buddhism and its efforts to explain the "middle way" (Madhayamaka School of thought) as a space between reification and nihilism. To speak of the psyche as a "territoriality," as do Gilles Deleuze and Félix Guattari, is to reimagine the challenge of the postwar antipsychiatry movement as a postcolonial challenge, one that demands, for Deleuze and Guattari, a move toward deterritorialization. The subject is "territorialized" by a colonizing regime that maintains power by making those territories seem "normal"—by rendering them normative. I discuss later in this book how for Ginsberg the colonizing territory of what Adrienne Rich later calls "compulsory heterosexuality" was the regime of Moloch who parcelled out the mind and body into territorialities based on a heteronormative imperative. This imperative simply enforced the "hetero" as "normative" and pathologized any other sexual practice as dissent from this norm.

The implicit argument of my methodology, as it is for most contemporary scholars, is that we do ourselves a disservice, as writers and readers, when we describe such language as the lexicon of a monolith called "theory." It is, instead, the variegated language of multiple disciplines, and, as such, it is a reminder that, of course, the "fields" we study are separated at best by porous boundaries.

A final note is necessary on methodology. Too often, the scholar's interest in the admittedly engaging biographical details of Beat writers' lives substitutes for an actual discussion of the work itself and its contexts. Beat biography can cast an obscuring shadow on matters of textuality and craft. I will use biographies as source material: Schumacher's *Dharma Lion* and the letters in *Family Business*, along with Miles's *Ginsberg: A Biography*. Still, I will move beyond biographical criticism—at one time the dominant mode in Beat Studies—in order to render a narrative of discovery of the many modes of Ginsberg's particular Buddhist poetics.

Acknowledgments

This book was completed with the help of a Faculty Development Grant from Columbia College Chicago. My thanks to David Krause, Jan Garfield, and the members of the Faculty Development Committee. Special thanks to Joris Soeding for his valuable research assistance in the writing and preparation of this manuscript. Thanks also to Lindsay Bell for her administrative help. I owe special thanks to the students in my Whitman and Ginsberg seminar at Columbia College Chicago for their many inspiring ideas over the years. My gratitude to the staff of the Green Library Department of Special Collections at Stanford, especially Margaret Kimball, Steven Mandeville-Gamble, and Michael G. Olson, for their energetic assistance with this project. My thanks to Karl Kageff and the editorial staff at Southern Illinois University Press for their interest in this project from the beginning and for their sharp eyes and patience during the editing and production process. Special thanks to Mary Lou Kowaleski for her careful copyediting of the manuscript.

I owe deep gratitude to colleagues and friends for their advice, encouragement, and good cheer. As always, the faults of this book, whether many or few, are mine and not theirs. Thanks to Jean Petrolle, for commentary on chapter drafts; Karen Osborne, for discussing the Beats, gender, and sexuality with me when this book was in its earliest stages; Arielle Greenberg, for turning my attention to the Stanford "Practitioners of Reality" symposium; and David Trinidad, for our discussions of exploratory poetics that became vital to chapter 7. Thanks to Michael McClure for suggestions that also influenced the final chapter of the book. I owe deep gratitude to John Whalen-Bridge for his thorough reading of the manuscript and for his astute revision suggestions on literary and Buddhist history. I wish to thank Kurt Hemmer, Kirby Olson, and Andrew Wilson for their helpful, detailed readings of the manuscript. I am grateful to Diane Putnam for our inspiring discussions of Ginsberg's Congressional testimony. My thanks to Douglas Kerr for his help with the recordings of the "Practitioners of Reality" symposium. Warm thanks to Diane di Prima for encouraging this book at such an early stage and for her confidence that I could write it. I owe deep gratitude to Guy Rotella, Stuart Peterfreund, and Mary Loeffelholz, whose lessons on writing, research, and good sense are always with me. Thank you, Geshe Tsultrim Chöphel, for your living examples of *bodhicitta*. To Michael Trigilio, special thanks for your critical and artistic inspiration—and for being a dear family member.

Of course, as always, heartfelt thanks to Shelly Hubman for patience through all the stages of this project and for her help sorting the dharma wheat from chaff. And for her deep, abiding love.

Parts of chapters 4 and 5 appeared originally as the essay "'Will You Please Stop Playing with the Mantra?': The Embodied Poetics of Ginsberg's Later Career" in *Reconstructing the Beats* (ed. Jennie Skerl).

For permission to quote from Allen Ginsberg's unpublished notebooks, journals, and teaching transcripts, I am grateful to the Department of Special Collections, Stanford University Libraries and Peter Hale and Bob Rosenthal of the Allen Ginsberg Trust. My thanks to Harold Collen and the estate of Louis and Edith Ginsberg for permission to quote from Louis Ginsberg's correspondence. Special thanks to Larry Keenan for permission to reprint his photograph on he cover. For permission to quote from the poetry of Allen Ginsberg, my gratitude to HarperCollins Publishers, the Allen Ginsberg Trust, and the Wylie Agency: Copyright © 1984, by Allen Ginsberg; Copyright © by the Allen Ginsberg Trust.

Allen Ginsberg's Buddhist Poetics

1

Ginsberg's Spiritual Fathers

> There is another world, and it is in this one.
> —Louis Ginsberg, 1975

Against Interpretation

Allen Ginsberg's earliest and most famous works in *Howl and Other Poems* and *Kaddish and Other Poems, 1958–1960* document his struggles with his mother's mental illness, his disappointment with his father's eventual middle-class artistic and political quietism, and his efforts to understand his homosexual identity in pre-Stonewall America. He was raised in an early-twentieth-century Jewish socialist-communist household in Paterson, New Jersey, and his Hebraic background frames his self-representation as a poet-prophet in the same sense that Blake and Milton, among others in Anglo-American poetry, envisioned themselves as inheritors of a lineage of prophecy traceable to the Bible. As much as he identified with Hebraic prophecy, he equally was compelled to rewrite Judaism, as in his revisionary engagement with the traditional Hebrew prayer for the dead in "Kaddish." To borrow a phrase from John Rodden's influential work on the rhetoric of literary reputation, Ginsberg's "reputation formation" becomes vexed at this point where his Hebraic background leads him, restlessly, to study and practice of Eastern sacred tradition.[1] After

"Kaddish," Ginsberg continues to fashion his poetic project as one that is indebted to Western prophecy, but he does so with increased emphasis on how Western prophecy might be modified, even radically revised, by traditions such as Hinduism and Buddhism. As I will discuss later in this book, Ginsberg's East-West prophetic poetry poses problems for religious and literary scholars as the result of the inevitable eccentricities of his early, autodidactic study of Eastern sacred practice. It is important to note in these early pages that as Ginsberg's poetry becomes identified more with his Buddhist practice than with his Jewish background, the inconsistencies of his self-taught Buddhism come into greater relief. As a later critic writes of the volume *Mind Breaths: Poems 1972–1977*, which was published five years after Ginsberg began formal study with Trungpa, these poems are less than accessible to Western audiences who do not possess "a knowledge of Ginsberg's Buddhist-Trungpa teachings and vocabulary" (Dougherty 84).

Ginsberg's wide range of deftness with his Buddhist source material creates difficulties for scholars and casual readers alike. As poetry written with the cultural and historical urgency of the Biblical prophetic line, his Buddhist poems invite energetic readings as experiments in cultural-religious hybridization and as poetry of political action (or what has come to be termed "socially engaged Buddhism"). However, as a Beat Generation icon and a Buddhist, his reputation for spontaneity and his distrust of New Critical aesthetic unity and finish would seem to resist the sustained interpretative acts of scholars. It is the goal of this book to sustain interpretation while mindful of Ginsberg's efforts to reconceive this Beat improvisatory aesthetic as a Buddhist one. I wish to map Ginsberg's competing, and at times eccentric, Buddhisms into something that might be called his "Buddhist poetics." I do not mean to suggest that the poet crafted a systematic poetics of Buddhism; to do so would foolishly run counter to the documented distrust of systemization in Ginsberg's body of work. What I term throughout this book as Ginsberg's Buddhist poetics is, instead, a constellation of major philosophical positions and sacred physical and textual practices that Ginsberg appropriates with such increased emphasis in his career that eventually a more complete reading of his poems demands a greater understanding of his Buddhism.

The poet's divergent, at times vexing, appropriation of Eastern sacred practice might be exemplified best by an iconic photograph of the poet dancing at the 1967 Human Be-In at Golden Gate Park in San Francisco.

This music, art, and poetry festival, with its equally neoromantic subtitle, "A Gathering of the Tribes," was attended by twenty-five thousand people and included significant Beat Generation poets such as Gary Snyder, Lawrence Ferlinghetti, and Diane di Prima. One of the most frequently reproduced images from the festival is the photograph of an enchanted Ginsberg consumed in feral dance—full beard and garment flowing, love beads whirling around his neck. It is a useful icon for Ginsberg's paternal contribution to 1960s' youth culture: the primitivism of the hippie movement given the enraptured imprimatur of the previous decade's Beat icon, Ginsberg, now at age forty-one a father to the new, self-appointed counterculture. For readers familiar with Ginsberg's religious influences, the image, too, evokes the tradition of Hebrew ecstatic prophecy that he took as his religious inspiration for his poetics of prophecy. However, before arriving at this place—1967, enraptured dance, flowing garments, recitation of poems and mantras—Ginsberg passed through a significant period of anxiety and difficult asceticism. As much as the Ginsberg of the 1967 Human Be-In seems to channel Wordsworth's famously articulated "spontaneous overflow of powerful emotion," the romantic-pantheistic, liminal experience of this gathering of tribes was part of a larger, contentious period of contradiction, doubt, and experiment in his religious practice and in his forging of what he would come to describe as a spiritual poetics.

Because it seems to signify only a self-evidently ecstatic, countercultural spiritual practice—what I would contend is a seductive but incomplete reading at best—the image of Ginsberg from the Human Be-In is an important place from which to launch my study of his Buddhist poetics. The ecstatic Ginsberg from the Human Be-In is the Ginsberg who comes to us as a Dionysian hipster icon in the cultural imaginary; this is the Ginsberg who seems only orientalist, who for years played the harmonium and finger symbols and chanted mantras at poetry readings.[2] My book does not shy from these versions of the Ginsberg myth, nor does it fully trust the charge that they are fraudulent gestures of religiosity. In the chapters that follow, I examine Ginsberg's career-long efforts to craft a language for the sacred in his poetry that would reflect the philosophical framework of his increasingly serious—or, at the least, serious enough—Buddhist practice.

As the Human Be-In image suggests, part of the problem in assessing the role Buddhism played in Ginsberg's poetics is in Ginsberg's self-fashioned hipster mythos, which tends to valorize Ginsberg's Dionysian pose, a media-savvy construction suitable for consumption by postwar social revolutionary youth subcultures, but a figure that resists scrutiny of the depth of religious feeling, if any, behind it. After all, the event was a "be-in," suggesting that to be a "human being," all one does is "be": critical consciousness, then, is potentially elided in this ecstasy of "being" that dominates the image of Ginsberg's self-abandoned dance. Interpretive difficulties arise, too, even when one addresses the critical implications of the photograph itself. More specifically, this particular issue of interpretation manifests as a question of how "authentic" religiosity was defined in the late-twentieth-century United States. To approach the religiosity behind the Ginsberg image from the Human Be-In, the choice would seem either to fix a sober, critical eye only on the image as a cultural icon, an eye that the image itself seems to resist in its orgiastic excess, or to persist and read the image as a product of East-West syncretism in a period, the 1960s, marked by a contradiction between widespread religiosity, on one hand (including large numbers of Buddhist converts drawn from Judaism), and eccentric appropriations of religious source material on the other.[3]

I have chosen the latter in this book—a persistence amid the syncretic and eccentric alike—as a way of reading Ginsberg's East-West convergence. No matter how much the image resists critical appropriation, it nevertheless suggests the importance of further study of Ginsberg as a poet and media figure in the ongoing cultural synthesis of East and West. By dint of his extraordinary (for a poet) artistic popularity, Ginsberg became one of the most significant symbols of the turn to religions of the East in the late-twentieth-century United States. He accomplished this position as cipher for American Buddhism first through his autodidactic reading of major Buddhist texts in translation; second, through his active, documented desire to find qualified Buddhist teachers with whom to study and his eventual active engagement with such teachers as Trungpa and, after Trungpa's death, Gehlek Rinpoche; third, through his regular meditation practice, an important complement for any Buddhist to the theoretical components of Buddhist teaching and textuality; and, finally, through his significant work as one of the early founders of Naropa University, the only accredited Buddhist institution of higher learning at the time in the United States. To avoid sectarian arguments, those that would privilege, say, the viewpoint on emptiness held by Middle-Way (Madhyamaka) School of Tibetan Buddhism over the view of the Mind-Only (Cittamatra) School, I define *authenticity* in terms of the most fundamental definitions of Buddhism that frame American Buddhists' definition of themselves as indeed

Buddhist: taking refuge in the Three Jewels of Buddhism (the Three Jewels are discussed in detail in chapter 2 in the context of Ginsberg's invocation of this refuge practice in "Angkor Wat"); studying Buddhism with a recognized teacher or lama; and disciplining oneself to a regular meditation practice. As Rick Fields asserts in *How the Swans Came to the Lake: A Narrative History of Buddhism in America*, such a definition of "authenticity" is precisely that to which American Buddhists as far back as the nineteenth century aspired, even when thwarted by the lack of recognized teachers in the U.S. This definition, too, reflects the authentic practice that late-twentieth-century U.S. practitioners have been able to maintain in a cultural climate in which teachers from Tibet, Vietnam, India, and elsewhere regularly offer instruction in the U.S., either as visiting teachers or as immigrants teaching at established Buddhist centers.[4]

Buddhism and Modern Poetry

As his major prose statement on the religiosity of poetry, Ginsberg's essay "Meditation and Poetics" can serve as an introduction to what I call his Buddhist poetics throughout this book. As a poet working within the Western prophetic tradition and one who shaped this tradition to include Eastern practices of the sacred, Ginsberg is foremost concerned in the essay with how the secular art of poetry might accommodate spiritual concerns at all. The intersection of literary artifice and sacred experience is for him, as for Jack Kerouac, a matter of textual and spiritual "Beatitude." Ginsberg frames this question of secularism and spirit in terms of the artificial division between high and low cultures that has been present in commentaries on Beat literature from Norman Podhoretz's early accusations of the Beats as "know-nothing bohemians" to John Tytell's assertion of nakedness as a pivotal Beat literary trope for liberation from the language of containment enforced by high-culture elites. As Elizabeth Wilson argues, any understanding of bohemian counterculture is incomplete without an exploration of its role in mediating high and low culture: "The figure of the bohemian personifies the ambivalent role of art in industrial society; and Bohemia is a cultural *Myth* about art in modernity, a myth that seeks to reconcile Art to industrial capitalism, to create for it a role in consumer society" (3). Wilson's description of the dual insider/outsider role of the bohemian artist is useful in historicizing Ginsberg's spiritual poetics as a negotiation of the artificial divide between high and low culture: "The myth of the bohemian [. . .] seeks to resolve the role of art as both inside and outside commerce and consumption, and to reconcile the economic uncertainty of the artistic calling with ideas of the artist's genius and superiority" (3).

Ginsberg begins "Meditation and Poetics" with an engagement of the high-culture/low-culture divide, and in turn, he creates his own division and classification system for high and low art. He reminds readers, "It's an old tradition in the West among great poets that poetry is rarely thought of as 'just poetry'" (262). As if rediscovering an ancient tradition always already there, Ginsberg argues, "Classical poetry is a 'process,' or experiment—a probe into the nature of reality and the nature of the mind." High poetry, classical verse in this formulation, is that which explores consciousness; low verse, in contrast, is written for consolation or publication—"mere picturesque dilettantism or egotistical expressionism" (262). For Ginsberg, classical verse, or "real poetry," as he also describes it, is a poetry of meditation and mindfulness. In this usage, *mindfulness*, or Buddhist *samathi* practice, can be defined as a form of lucid, self-conscious wakefulness or lucid self-consciousness of phenomena in which past and future are considered as constructions, and the only trustworthy time designation is, to borrow from romanticist terminology, the continuous present. In such a setting, real poetry is for Ginsberg characterized by its tendency to take as its subject the exploration of the mind in its immediate apprehension of phenomena. In a formulation that recasts Western phenomenological aesthetics as a mode of meditative poetics, Ginsberg argues, "Major works of twentieth-century art are probes of consciousness—particular experiments with recollection or mindfulness, experiments with language and speech, experiments with forms" (263).

Thus, Ginsberg's Buddhist poetic strategies are predicated on memory ("recollection or mindfulness"), representation ("experiments with language and speech"), and containment ("experiments with forms"). Memory, speech, and containment also are significant to late-twentieth-century postmodern practices, often tracing their contemporary origins to the diverse practices of the Language movement, in which (to risk oversimplification) language and structure—representation and containment—function as both poetic form and content. As I discuss in the subsequent chapters, memory and mindfulness exist in tension with each other in Ginsberg's Buddhist poetics; and, more important, these subsequent chapters demonstrate that such a strategy mirrors the same tension between the reification of selfhood and the impermanence of selfhood in a major Buddhist concept, the Two Truths, that frames much of Ginsberg's Buddhist-inspired poetry.[5] Memory and memorializing are important for Ginsberg, from his early confessional work that reshapes family memory through his career-long tendency to date his works, along with their time and place of composition, at the bottom of each finished poem. Ginsberg's emphasis on the importance of memorializing emerges from humanist tendencies that otherwise exist in seeming opposition to the innovative urge of late-twentieth-century experimental Language-inspired poetics, in which greater emphasis is bestowed on representations of memory as such—and with memorializing as a process—than on actual memories themselves. Thus, Ginsberg's Buddhist-inspired poetic strategies might be considered paradoxically both experimental and safe. This assertion, which I develop further in chapters 6 and 7, is not meant to denigrate experimentalists or traditionalists—or to stand as a tautology—but instead is meant to imply that the opposing poles of what we deem avant-garde or conventional do not offer an adequate vocabulary for discussing work, such as Ginsberg's Buddhist poetry, that depends on cultural and aesthetic hybridization.

Ginsberg's Buddhist study and practice inhabit this space between humanist and posthumanist notions of subjectivity as this space negotiates Western and Eastern ways of knowing. In terms of literary history, this negotiated space borrows both from Ginsberg's inheritance of Anglo-American romanticism and from twentieth-century experimentalist poetics. Ginsberg argues that the spiritual poet requires "a certain deconditioning of attitude—a deconditioning of rigidity and unyieldingness—so that you can get to your own thought." Such is the romantic revival at the core of Ginsberg's spiritual poetics: the poet needs a deconditioning of reificatory states of consciousness in favor of a privileging of originality that promises a return to a transhistorical, romantic individual—that is, a return "to your own thought." For Ginsberg, this romantic mobility takes its cue from both Keats's idea of negative capability and from what Ginsberg describes as Whitman's "acceptance of the mind's raw contents." It is, too, a Buddhist poetic impulse, where the deconditioning process operates "parallel with traditional Buddhist ideas of renunciation—renunciation of hand-me-down conditioned conceptions of mind." Yet at the same time, Ginsberg describes twentieth-century poetry as a radical, even bohemian, corrective to the essentializing extreme of this romantic position. He describes a "few Buddhist *dharma* phrases" that "correlate charmingly with the process of Bohemian art of the twentieth-century," one of which seems especially suited to Ginsberg's career-long work with improvisatory composition: "'Don't conform to your idea of what is expected but conform to your present spontaneous mind, your raw awareness.' That's how *dharma* poets 'make it new'—which was Pound's adjuration" ("Meditation and Poetics" 264–65). The transcendental impulse of romanticism and its preoccupation with heroic originality are commingled with the modernist sensibilities that come to Ginsberg by way of Ezra Pound. Together the two become part of Ginsberg's focus on what he describes as "the process of Bohemian art of the twentieth century." Ginsberg's vision of spiritual poetics is one in which process-oriented compositional strategies such as improvisation intersect with the radical freeplay of language and subjectivity that characterizes postmodern poetry. The urge to "make it new" is positioned quite tenuously against the human tendency to reify and continually re-reify its perceptions.

Ginsberg's emphasis on language and form as modes of potentially sacred, "decondition[ed]" speech puts his Buddhist project at risk all the same. Insofar as Buddhism teaches that enlightenment, or *satori*, is a nondualistic state of mind outside the parameters of language, Ginsberg's efforts to create a sacred language inspired by Buddhism might seem relegated to failure from the start. Ginsberg asserts nevertheless that a spiritual poetics must concern itself with *satori* perception: "As part of 'purification' or 'de-conditioning' we have the need for clear seeing or direct perception—perception of a young tree without an intervening veil of preconceived ideas; the surprise glimpse, let us say, or insight, or sudden Gestalt, or I suppose you could say *satori*, occasionally glimpsed as esthetic experience" (265). Thus, Ginsberg writes, in the absence of "'purification' or 'deconditioning,'" perception hardens into abstraction. All the same, language itself can never achieve *satori*; language can trigger it as "occasionally glimpsed [. . .] esthetic experience." Ginsberg's Buddhist poetics, then, is not necessarily concerned with achieving *satori* as it is with representations of *satori*—that is, with the process of mind trying to understand itself. This effort at direct perception depends less on romantic transcendentalism and more on twentieth-century tactics invoked by Pound, specifically on his imagist dictum of "direct treatment of the thing."

Ginsberg remakes Pound's imagism as a Buddhist mode of perception. Pound's imagism is embodied—recalling, for Ginsberg, the Buddhist sacred triad of body, speech, and mind—and it is materialist as it insists on blurring the boundary between immanence and transcendence in its effort to conceive a language for sacred experience. Invoking William Carlos Williams's poem "Thursday," Ginsberg remakes Williams into a poet-father whose artistic practice vocalizes embodied Buddhist speech. At the same time, he constructs a Williams who is a precursor poet-father of Buddhist mindfulness; and, more important, the materiality of Williams's poetic vision anticipates the same in Ginsberg's first Buddhist teacher, Trungpa. Williams's poem invokes a metaphysics of dream-life only to return squarely to material, everyday lived experience. Gazing at the sky, the speaker of "Thursday" revises this traditionally neoplatonic visionary search as an internal, embodied quest:

> [. . .] feeling my clothes about me,
> the weight of my body in my shoes,
> the rim of my hat, air passing in and out
> at my nose—and decide to dream no more.
> (qtd. in Ginsberg, "Meditation and Poetics" 267)

For Ginsberg, this poem is located at the juncture of meditative poetics and twentieth-century modernism: "that one single poem is the intersection between the mind of meditation—the discipline of meditation, letting go of thoughts—and the Yankee practice of poetry after William James, where the poet is standing there, feeling the weight of his body in his shoes, aware of the air passing in and out of his nose" (267–68). Pound's "direct treatment of the thing," then, is transformed by Ginsberg so that the thing in question includes not just an external object of awareness but also the body as an inwardly sought object of its own mind's awareness. That such a mode of apperception is sacred, recasting the extensional logic of vision as intensional, is for Ginsberg a function of breath itself. Breath is a sacred locus of action in Buddhist meditation practice and is significant, too, in the West as the etymological root of the word *spirit* (which of course comes from the Latin *spiritus*, for "breath"). For Ginsberg, language spoken from the breath—spoken with a mindful awareness of breath—is sacred language.

Just so, Ginsberg writes that one must be mindful, too, of poetic history; not Eliot's vision of the great monuments of Tradition but instead the history of twentieth-century experimentalist traditions: "To catch the red wheelbarrow [. . .] you have to be practiced in poetics as well as practiced in ordinary mind" ("Meditation and Poetics" 269). This "ordinary mind," or a mind steadied by the "deconditioning attitude" of spiritual poetics, is found, according to Ginsberg, in a lineage of innovative verse that in the West stretches from William Blake, through the modernism of Pound and Gertrude Stein, and through Charles Olson's projective verse, other Black Mountain poets, and the San Francisco Renaissance. Ginsberg claims Trungpa, too, for this tradition. Thus, it is a tradition of experimentation with the sacred: it is materialist, spoken from the breathing body and the mind probing itself, at Ginsberg would term it, at the same time that it vocalizes dissatisfaction with the secular boundaries of art and artifice. The mind probes the nature of itself in Ginsberg's formulation—a rhetoric of vision inspired by Buddhist notions of nonattachment and ultimately by the sacred possibilities of material experience.

Ginsberg's perception of a similarity between East and West is evidence, for him, of a poetic tradition in itself. For instance, quoting from one of the most important passages in Olson's "Projective Verse," Ginsberg writes, "I interpret that set of words—'one perception must move instanter on another'—as similar to the dharmic practice of letting go of thoughts and allowing fresh thought to arise and be registered, rather than hanging onto one exclusive image and forcing Reason to branch it out and extend it into a hung-up metaphor" ("Meditation and Poetics" 271). Ginsberg's hipster language aside, this yoking of Olson with "letting go of thoughts" and preventing "hung-up metaphor" indeed reflects the Buddhist ideal of nonattachment.[6] Earlier, nonattachment was phrased as Keats's negative capability; later in the essay, it is the Buddhist notion of renunciation, where the term represents for Ginsberg "a way of avoiding a conditioned art work, or trite art, or repetition of other people's ideas" (271-72). Nonattachment and renunciation re-envision Pound's dictum to "make it new"; they resist the urge to reify by commingling the groundlessness of Eastern *shunyata* with the flux of Western modernist experimentation. (*Shunyata*, often translated as *emptiness*, is a core Buddhist doctrine that holds that all phenomena are empty of essentialist existence and that the reality of all phenomena emerges instead from interrelation and interdependence.) Borrowing from stories of the Buddhist saint Milarepa's "Hundred Thousand Songs of Milarepa," Ginsberg emphasizes, too, that such a poetics depends on both ordinary mind and "spontaneous mind," where the "on-the-spot improvisation" of the latter is undertaken "on the basis of meditative discipline" (272-73).

The parameters of Ginsberg's Buddhist project are thus far sketched with special emphasis on his construction of a literary historical lineage for his Buddhist work and its aesthetic and spiritual concerns. As described in "Meditation and Poetics," Ginsberg's Buddhist poetics depends on an interplay of memory, speech, and formal containment, where form is just as often experimental as it is beholden to the past; it depends on a conjunction of the solidity of romantic humanist selfhood and the diffusion of postmodern, and often Buddhist, subjectivity; and it depends on a conceptual framework in which the immanent body is the locus of visionary, sacred experience often represented otherwise in the West as transcendental. The issues introduced thus far are developed in greater depth throughout this book, allowing, I hope, for readers to see where the boundaries of Ginsberg's Buddhist poetics are both clarified and challenged as his own Buddhist practice becomes more formalized.

Describing his vision of the language of meditative poetics, Ginsberg closes "Meditation and Poetics" with the assertion, "If you allow the active phrase to come to your mind, allow that out, you speak from a ground that can relate your inner perception to external phenomena, and thus join Heaven and Earth" (273). If, for Ginsberg, meditation can be seen as the action of the mind aware of itself, then a poetics of meditation must include an active language that takes the mind as its object and, as in his early prophecies such as "Howl" and "Kaddish," commingles immanent and transcendent representation in an effort to create a language that will join Heaven and Earth. This project resembles Blake's effort in *Milton* to envision the second coming of Christ as a vision of "Jerusalem" built "[i]n Englands green & pleasant Land" (1: 15-16). As I discuss later in this book, the most important Western influence in Ginsberg's construction of a Buddhist poetics is Blake, who reinforces for Ginsberg the importance of Whitman's expansive visionary poetics but with a materialist rather than transcendentalist impulse that exerts more influence on Ginsberg's Buddhist study and practice than does Whitman's vision. As Ginsberg comes to terms with his earlier obsession with his 1948 vision of Blake reciting "Ah Sunflower!" in Ginsberg's Harlem apartment, the influence of Blake as a spiritual poet—in the definition of *spiritual poet* articulated in "Meditation and Poetics"—becomes increasingly central to Ginsberg's East-West poetics of prophecy.

"Confrontation with Louis Ginsberg's Poems"

At the same time that Ginsberg constructs a lineage of experimental poetics that, conveniently, also might be deemed spiritual, his development of a spiritual poetics is fraught with complications that arise from his psychological and familial relationships. Ginsberg's aptly titled essay "Confrontation with Louis Ginsberg's Poems," an introduction to his father's 1970 volume *Morning in Spring*, Louis's third collection of poetry and the first since 1937, suggests that visionary experience, family dynamics, and literary production combine to form a relational rather than hierarchical pattern of influence that for the son is crucial in the construction of a spiritual poetics. Influence does not proceed solely as an Oedipal enterprise (as in Harold Bloom) or as a burden inherited by each new generation of artists (as in Walter Jackson Bate). Ginsberg's description of the minute epiphanies of his father's pastoral lyric verse echoes what he might say of his own poetry from his 1948 Blake vision onward: "Would that all sons' fathers were poets! for the poem and the world are the same, Place imagined by Consciousness, and the squared exact forms of these poems are tiny models of Hebrew-Buddhist Universes rhyming together in Imagination" (18–19). The tiny models of Hebrew-Buddhist Universes affirmed therein are as much extracted from his father's texts as they are projected upon them: for Ginsberg, the poems are at once both texts of "agnostic compassion" as they are representations of "an Evanescent Eternity as Weir'd as any invented by Poe (or mapped in the Zohar or unhexed after Avelokiteshvara's Prajna Paramita Sutra)" ("Confrontation" 17, 19). At one level, Ginsberg imagines his father as a fellow poet in the prophetic line, echoing the Book of Numbers in a statement of both lament and celebration: "Would that all sons' fathers were poets!"[7] Still, his father is at times cast as only a typological figure in this line, a writer of "agnostic compassion emotionally dense as any deity-faith" whose work is notable primarily as a precursor for his son's—insofar as it merely creates the conditions for his son to surpass him.

In this way, the strong poet of Bloom's formulation is replaced by the strong tradition of Judaism, which Ginsberg reenvisions as part of his Buddhist study and practice: Louis's poetry "completes a cycle of generations and is transmitted through myself in *Kaddish* as a litany of praise of Oblivion that buries mortal grief" ("Confrontation" 17–18). As biographer Barry Miles reports, Louis literally provided his son with an English-language translation of the traditional Hebrew Kaddish prayer with a note that both affirmed and authorized his son's desire in "Kaddish" to revise the visionary history of the prayer. Of the translation, Louis wrote, "Those chants therein have a rhythm and sonorousness of immemorial years marching with reverberations through the corridors of history" (qtd. in Miles 207). Of course, Louis's influence extends further than just his bestowal of a figural, enabling litany for "Kaddish." Interviewed for the *Jerusalem Post Magazine* in 1971, Louis points up "Kaddish" as evidence of both his son's sense of continuity with Judaism and his own disapproval of his son's attraction to Buddhism. On his contribution to "Kaddish," Louis explains, "When his mother died in the sanatorium, he called me up from California and asked me to get him a *Siddur* (prayerbook), and he wrote his famous '*Kaddish*'" (11). However, his son's incorporation of Buddhism as a revision of religious exceptionalism represents for Louis an unproductive destabilization of racial and religious identity. Immediately after describing his role in the origin of "Kaddish," Louis says, "People ask him why he, as a Jew, follows the Buddhists, and he says he wants to preach idealism of the human race, to take the best of all religions. I say that's a good idea, but before I do that, I want to study more and explore more of my own Jewish heritage" (qtd. in Gefen 11).[8]

Ginsberg's conception of himself as an American Buddhist poet-prophet emerged from a productive, tangled confluence of Louis's authority as father who bestowed the Hebraic tradition on his son and of Louis's influence as poet. This tangle in turn generates the joint readings that Ginsberg and his father gave from 1966 through 1975. As the *Jerusalem Post Magazine* feature on Louis describes them, these Allen-Louis readings themselves were complex stagings of an unlikely alliance between "establishment" fathers and countercultural sons in which audiences comprised "two groups: Hippies and their fathers" (Gefen 9). Louis observes that audience members come to the readings "to see how a father and a son, who seem so different, can get along."[9] A 1968 account in the Passaic, New Jersey, *Herald-News* of a joint reading at Rutgers University suggests, too, the complexity of familial ardor in the elder Ginsberg's pattern of influence: "Allen appeared, at times, worried while standing under the garish lights and looking out the auditorium doors into the Newark night. [. . .] While Louis kept the spectators chuckling, Allen sat on the floor before the speaker's platform, gazing up at his father like a boy entranced by his teacher" ([Bishop] 11).[10] This comment on the Rutgers reading demonstrate the depths of Louis's artistic and psychological influence on his son. Moreover, their emphasis on Ginsberg's response to his father as "a boy entranced by his teacher" suggests that such influence is pedagogical rather than adversarial for Ginsberg. This model of influence, I argue, anticipates the literary and spiritual qualities of the student-guru relationship that Ginsberg later forms with Trungpa and Gehlek Rinpoche.[11] For Ginsberg, Buddhism is at once a revision of Western ontology and an occasion for the transference of his father, as both poet and Jewish patriarch, onto his gurus.[12]

Considered, then, as part of the context of Ginsberg's study and practice of Buddhism, "Confrontation with Louis Ginsberg's Poems" offers a vocabulary with which to explore how the burden and inspiration of his father are commingled with the son's efforts to craft a distinctly Buddhist poetics. The entire essay is framed by Ginsberg's opening assertion of the burden of his fathers, where he states, with some affected aesthetic fatigue, that he has been "[l]iving a generation with lyrics wrought by my father." This exhaustion is affirmed by William Carlos Williams's early, paternal critique of "my own idealised iambic rhymes sent him for inspection" (11). Thus, Ginsberg's introduction to Louis's poetry serves to remind readers that he is the product of two spiritual and poetic fathers, both Louis and Williams. More important, too, is the context that nags the conceptual margins of the introduction, in which Ginsberg, famous at the time as one of the earliest progenitors of postwar open forms, now finds himself praising his father's early-century closed forms. Neither his praise nor criticism of his father is energetic; instead, both reveal the complexities of influence. On one hand, his invocation of Williams's critique of his own work serves to comment on his father's, too, rejecting Louis's work as too close to his son's earliest efforts; at the same time, Ginsberg reminds readers of his father's steady accretion of accolades, especially his inclusion in Louis Untermeyer's famous *Modern American and Modern British Poetry*.[13] Ginsberg, then, is left with a dilemma of his own making in the essay. Louis's poetry is represented as the mirror of his son's less mature work; the son nevertheless reminds readers that, in Untermeyer's words, Louis's "lyric touch" enables him "to make words sing something as well as say something" (11). Still, Ginsberg reminds readers, with some critical judgment, that "no literal music was intended" by his father (11). In Ginsberg's reading of the modernist era, his father's language was like much of twentieth-century verse, indebted to the lyre while hobbled by a culture in which "lyric words had parted company from music a century or centuries before" (12). The language of the fathers, then, is complicated by the son's projection of himself into their poetic lineage. Their words are musical, with an engaging "lyric touch," yet only as "rote degenerate lyric meter," a dominant postwar modernism whose "stingy Rhythm" dominated poetics until, in Ginsberg's heroicizing narrative of literary history, an "ampler-bodied and more naked breath'd tradition began to sound freely Prophetic" a new contemporary song (13).

The poet's rhetorical strategy here, of course, is to argue for his father's relevance in this introduction without at the same time rendering his own poetic project deadened and equally "stingy." He praises his father's well wrought lines only to later disentangle them from those of Ginsberg's own era. Yet, for a poet of more than one literary father, Ginsberg must make sure he never quite submerges Louis's poetic mode. Contemporary open forms, even those that blur popular music with poetry, are those that, for Ginsberg, "had broken thru the crust of old lyric forms like my father's" only to find themselves "evolved back to the same forms refreshed with new emotions and new subtleties of accent and vowel articulated in consequence of deep-breath'd song" (14). Of course, this complicated lineage—where older forms are both a "crust" that must be broken at the same time that they are, paradoxically, forms into which new modes "evolv[e] back"—seems to confirm that poetic influence is a source of a son's anxiety over his competition with his father and that the past is a burden. But Ginsberg's literary-spiritual lineage was as much recursive as it was Oedipal or hierarchical.[14] Reading his father's work, he eventually asserts, "I won't quarrel with his forms here anymore: by faithful love he's made them his own [. . .]" (15). As such, a more complex psychological model is needed to describe the recursive relationship of influence with his fathers, Louis and Williams.

Discussions of Ginsberg's poetic, and eventually Buddhist, influences must allow for a complicated dialectic of transference that can recast Oedipal competition and usurpation into the embodied, relational language that Ginsberg prefers in his affirmation of the need for "deep-breath'd song." A new schema of influence also must account for Ginsberg's eventual abandonment in the introduction to *Morning in Spring* of his "quarrel" with Louis's poetics in favor of an introduction that valorizes his father's aesthetics as a form of "faithful love." This recursive turn to "faithful love" follows from Ginsberg's reenvisioning in mid-essay of his "confrontation" with his father's poetics—a struggle so important that it becomes the title of his essay. Once Ginsberg asserts influence as recursive rather than hierarchical, he also recalls and revises his essay title: "Confronting my father's poems at the end of his life, I weep at his meekness and his reasons, at his wise entrance into his own mortality and his silent recognition of that pitiful Immensity he records of his own life's Time, his father's life time, & the same Mercy his art accords to my own person his son" (14–15).

I do not mean to suggest that Ginsberg's motives in the essay only are to reconfigure notions of influence. Instead, I wish to emphasize that for Ginsberg these questions of influence equally are questions of relationality as they are, in Bloom's terms, of competition and usurpation. Ginsberg indeed describes his father's poetics as "outworn verse" and an "anachronism" (14); however, Ginsberg's essay also emphasizes that his own poetics emerges from his relationship with his father's. Ginsberg's essay serves a dual purpose: first, to clear a space for a contemporary lineage of open-form poetics, demonstrating the past as a burden not of belatedness but one that must be corrected of its reiterative, anachronistic utterance that risks "jaded music," and second, in its invocation of a transcendent, romanticist impulse he is both influenced by and seeks to revise—that of Shelley, in the below instance—the essay aims to reconceive his resistance as a mode of faithful doubt in the past:

> All poets from Shelley to Housman knew that melancholy immortality, their body impulses, sensations, consciousness & feelings embedded like flies in amber verse. I have resisted this mode as an anachronism in my own time—the anachronism of my own father writing the outworn verse of previous century voices, reechoing the jaded music and faded affect or sentiment of that music in a dream-life of his own sidestreet under dying phantom elms of Paterson, New Jersey [. . .]. ("Confrontation" 14)[15]

Ginsberg invokes his poetic fathers selectively. Williams corrects Louis's "faded affect"; and from Ginsberg's relationship with Louis—both his resistance to and eventually awe of it when faced with Louis's construction of "tiny models of Hebrew-Buddhist Universes"—the son's relational model of spiritual poetic influence is shaped. As I discuss later, relationality is crucial in Ginsberg's spiritual practice as a Buddhist. Moreover, it is important in his efforts to create a language for vision that, in its evocation of both materiality and ontological uncertainty, would reflect Buddhist teachings on shunyata and the Two Truths and would justify his invocation of mantra speech. As I discuss in the following section, such an emphasis on relationships rather than singularity is emphasized most of all in Tantric Buddhism, the variation Ginsberg practiced as a

Buddhist in the traditions of his primary teachers, Trungpa and Gehlek Rinpoche. Indeed, as Ann Weinstone argues, "Tantra is a practice of relationality par excellence. Nothing happens outside of relationship; all practices are practices within and of intensified relationality." The matrix of embodied relationality in Tantra is in the guru-student relationship: "The guru provides the disciple with an experience of and a model for unconditional relationality with everything" (Weinstone 34).

Father Trungpa

Given the significance of relationality in Tantric Buddhism, it is important to discuss Ginsberg's critical commentary on the poetry of his first guru, Chögyam Trungpa Rinpoche—an unsuccessful effort to create a wide readership for Trungpa, a poet whose work appealed to few outside of Crazy Wisdom Buddhist circles. In 1983, only seven years after his father's death and twenty years after Williams's, Ginsberg wrote the introduction for Trungpa's *First Thought, Best Thought: 108 Poems*.[16] As with Louis's introduction, Ginsberg found himself trying to place a father-poet into the tradition he himself popularized. Of course, the introduction to Trungpa's book was one more instance of Ginsberg promoting friends—from his successful advocacy for Kerouac and William S. Burroughs through the outrage he caused when he tried to bring in Peter Orlovsky to the Academy of Arts and Letters. Still, what is important in the Trungpa introduction is not whether Ginsberg's assessments of his guru's poetic talent were correct or nepotistic but instead how his appropriation of literary history frames his Buddhist project. In his Trungpa introduction, poetic tradition is perceived again by Ginsberg as relational, even recursive, rather than competitive. In this instance, however, the process of lineage-making is a matter of Tantric Buddhist relationality, suggesting that Ginsberg's transference of his father onto Trungpa is one of his most significant literary efforts since "Kaddish" to augment the strong tradition of his father's Judaism with Buddhism. Just as in the introduction to *Morning in Spring*, Ginsberg confronts the issue of belatedness: the essay seeks to honor the past without abandoning Beat, neoromantic impulses to continually "make it new" through a poetics of spontaneity, embodied breath-forms, and candor. Indeed, Ginsberg's introduction to *First Thought, Best Thought* and his revisions of this introduction demonstrate that his relationship with his poetic fathers enacts a poetics in which the past is reshaped to fit the concerns of Beat sensibility. In the process of reenvisioning the past to fit a Beat counterculture narrative of the continuous present, Ginsberg, of course, also is trading on his reputation; that is, his introduction of his poetic fathers, Louis and Trungpa, legitimizes these fathers' poetic efforts. Just as Ginsberg served as an unofficial publicist for Beat Generation literary efforts—helping with the publication of Kerouac's and Burroughs's early works, especially—so, too, does he contribute to the publications of his poetic fathers. The critical narrative of influence popularized by Bloom as an Oedipal competition is complexified by Ginsberg in these introductions. Indeed, as Ginsberg describes in a 1969 letter to his father, his effort to help find a publisher for *Morning in Spring* is as much a result of the quality of Louis's poems as it is from "reverse nepotism" of the son on behalf of his father (*Family Business* 293).[17]

The difference, of course, between poetic fathers Louis and Trungpa is the guru-student relationship between Ginsberg and Trungpa. This relationship itself is transferential, as I discuss later in this chapter, and is therefore predicated upon a simultaneous recognition and repression of the traditional Oedipal family romance. What is more important to Ginsberg's introduction to *First Thought, Best Thought* is his efforts to reconceive Trungpa's poetic identity as one that contributes to the literary-historical legacy carved by the Beats, rather than one that places Trungpa as a Tibetan other in Anglo-American literary discourse. As he did with Louis, Ginsberg engages Trungpa's role as a bearer of the past and reconceives it as a legacy important to the present. This task is easier with Trungpa than with Louis, insofar as Ginsberg does not have to revise an aesthetic he previous has disdained in his work, the closed-form lyric; instead, he can construct a Trungpa who represents, as a Tibetan lama, a mysterious, ancient lineage—in itself already "made new" by its own otherness in the West. For Ginsberg, Tibetan antiquity represents a spiritual force that might enhance contemporary poetics. Thus, he constructs a Trungpa who, problematically, possesses an idealized Absolute Truth that is necessary for contemporary poetry because, in Ginsberg's words, it is "too late to go back and clothe the skeleton of God, tho Eliot, Claudel & others yearned nostalgic for such divine certainty" (introduction xiii, xiv).[18] Ginsberg asserts that Trungpa voices a previously inaccessible vocabulary for contemporary poetic prophecy, one that is spoken, specifically, through the Vajrayana lineage (the accelerated, Tantric form of Mahayana Buddhism) that he represents. For Ginsberg, a Buddhist poetics is one steeped in the Buddhist principle of the Two Truths, where representations of the sacred are both Absolute and, paradoxically, materialist in their doubt of divine certainty. Moreover, Ginsberg's statement of poetics places Trungpa in, as Ginsberg describes it, an "unusual" position as "a contemporary poet who's master of an ancient 'system'" (xiii). This "system," for Ginsberg, rewrites traditional notions of literary history, especially the lineage of poetic prophecy that traces itself to Dante: "Within my memory, it was Academically fashionable to say that the XX Century lacked the culture for great Poetry, not possessing, as Dante's time did, a 'system' of cultural assumptions on which to hang an epic" (xiii). Tibetan Buddhism offers such a system for Ginsberg. This distinction between past and present, West and East, is also a function of Ginsberg's continual quarrel with the academy. In his earliest drafts of the introduction, his assertion that "the XX Century lacked a culture for great Poetry" stood on its own; later, in the published version, he qualifies this lack, attributing it to mistakes made by "Academically fashionable" notions of periodization. Trungpa represents a possibility for Ginsberg to forge a Buddhist poetics from a Western academic critical framework—to continue Ginsberg's career-long "correction" of academic critical discourse at the same time he seeks to enhance the academic legitimacy of his own reputation.[19]

As Ginsberg accommodates, uneasily, the academic establishment in his introduction to Trungpa's *First Thought, Best Thought*, he suggests that the middle-way teachings of Madhayamaka Buddhism are exemplified in both his own poems and in the work of his precursor fathers.[20] Indeed, his invocation of the Two Truths to explain Trungpa's poetry might just as well be a statement on Ginsberg's own work. Trungpa's June 1972 compositions, for instance, "approach the theme of personal love using open Western forms and 'first thought best thought' improvisatory technique—statements which mediate between the formality of Dharma Master and a man immersed in Relative Truth" (introduction xiv). Ginsberg proclaims Trungpa to be a poet who constructs subjectivity as both diffuse and singular, a reflection of Ginsberg's similar commitment in his own work. Ginsberg argues that Trungpa enters into "the American idiom as it's been charmed into being by Williams, Kerouac, Creeley and others," and the result "is a ravishing combination of Total Anarchy & Total Discipline" (introduction xvii–xviii). Ginsberg concludes that Trungpa mediates between "Absolute Truth expressed thru symbols" and "Relative Truth nail'd down in devotional commitment to the American Ground he's set out to transvalue and conquer" (introduction xviii). As he has said of Louis's poetry, this "commitment" also is to a poetics in which "the poem and the world are the same"—where the poet is guided by a literalism of the imagination that makes poems whose "squared exact forms" become "tiny models of Hebrew-Buddhist Universes" ("Confrontation" 18–19). As Ginsberg writes of Trungpa, in material from his original 1976 draft of the introduction: "[T]his lama writes like a western fish peddler who writes primitive manner poetry & is a natural rabbi without a beard" ("Comments" 11). Louis's legacy authorizes Ginsberg's own reenvisioning of it; indeed, Ginsberg conceives of a naturalized mode of Hebraic authority only insofar as such authority can be revised by the Tibetan Buddhist lama, Trungpa, who stands as a natural rabbi without a beard.

As often is the case for Ginsberg, his sensibilities as a Buddhist poet are shaped as much by Buddhist practice as by his commitment to Blake. In the original draft of the introduction, Ginsberg deploys the Two Truths as a trope for what Ginsberg sees as Trungpa's revival of transatlantic romanticism. He argues that Trungpa is "some kind of incarnation of Absolute Truth" who "has been invoked by previous decades—a century—of American poetic karma"; he compares the challenges of reading Trungpa in a secular world to the same difficulties that occur when reading Blake's prophecies. Ginsberg's final question to his readers, in the published version of the introduction, also maps the boundaries of his own East-West prophetic poetry, in which, as I discuss in further detail in chapter 4, the confluence of Blake and Buddhism recall and modify Whitman's visionary urgency. He asks, "What will Walt Whitman's expansive children do faced with such a Person?" (xviii). As I imply in chapter 3, the question actually is a self-reflexive one for Ginsberg and is a reminder that the important romantic inheritance of Whitman eventually is revised by Ginsberg as he increasingly incorporates a Buddhist conceptual framework in his poetry. Ginsberg melds Blake and Buddhism into this gap that arises from his differences with Whitman. Thus, when Ginsberg suggests in his earlier draft of the introduction that readers must contend with Trungpa's poetry as analogues of Blake's prophecies, he also is stating the precedence of his 1948 Blake vision in authorizing both his contemporary poetics of prophecy and, as I discuss in chapters 2 and 3, his increasingly Buddhist-influenced poetics that takes Blake as a primary Western source.

It should come as no surprise that Blake, who reenvisioned divine madness in his prophecies so that his prophetic bard's madness was the perfection of a divine wisdom, is Ginsberg's Western model for what he sees as the revolutionary energy of Trungpa. Blakean divine madness was Ginsberg's analogue for Trungpa's Crazy Wisdom Buddhism. The early story of Ginsberg's Buddhism is framed by the Crazy Wisdom lineage promulgated most famously by Trungpa. Everything that one might expect, stereotypically, from Buddhism—the quiet discipline of meditation, the asceticism of mindfulness, the respect for the authority of past traditions of masters—is turned upside-down in a method of Buddhist practice that represents itself as a revisionary Buddhism. Such is the difficult contrariety one must engage when studying or practicing in Crazy Wisdom, which demands that the practitioner both submit to teachings on the renunciation of desire and, crazily, also fight the tendency to renounce. Crazy Wisdom takes the law of karma, the certainty of cause-and-effect relationships in Buddhism, and challenges its inherent authority as law. In his book *Crazy Wisdom*, Trungpa claims that the enlightened mind of Crazy Wisdom exists on the boundary between altruism and "the legality of karma" (30). For Trungpa, practitioners in the Crazy Wisdom school seek to achieve a state of mind paradoxically both untamed and awakened. Such an approach would appear to be a distinct contrast to the otherwise axiomatic, for Buddhists, words of wisdom by the eleventh-century saint Atisha, who wrote in *The Bodhisattva's Jewel Garland*: "When among many, watch your words, / When remaining alone, watch your mind." Taking as its starting point the "infantlike mind" of "playful aggression," Crazy Wisdom is a revisionist Buddhism—yet at the same time, its goal is, much as Atisha's, to tame the mind" (Trungpa, *Crazy Wisdom* 28–29).

In Trungpa's discussion of the root guru of his Crazy Wisdom version of Tibetan Buddhism, the ancient Indian figure Padmasambhava, Trungpa makes it clear that Crazy Wisdom gets its name from the awakened yet potentially terrifying aspects associated with Padmasambhava. During the 1960s and 1970s, when the hushed Buddhist environment stereotypically associated with Zen was the normative conception of Buddhism in the U.S. cultural imaginary, Trungpa instead introduced Padmasambhava as a figure of deterritorializing uncertainty. Describing the narrative of Padmasambhava's enlightenment as an allegory for that of his own students' awakening, Trungpa says: "Having experienced the awakened state of mind, and having had experiences of sexuality and aggression and all the pleasures that exist in the world, there is still uncertainty about how to work with those worldly processes" (*Crazy Wisdom* 37). As a mode of Tantric Buddhism, where desire is a component of spiritual practice rather than a hindrance, Trungpa's Crazy Wisdom school introduces "worldly processes" to be integrated into one's spiritual pilgrimage; "uncertainty" comes from how to devise strategies to engage such processes, not from how to renounce them. In this sense, as Ginsberg's notes to Trungpa's Buddhist teachings indicate, Trungpa argued that the undomesticated dharma practice of Crazy Wisdom could be achieved properly only through rigorous study and practice. In his notes to a 29 August 1975 lecture by Trungpa, Ginsberg writes, crucially: "Wisdom comes before crazy. Shd be Wisdom-Crazy [not Crazy Wisdom]" (Notebooks).

Fields reports that Trungpa's "appearance was disquieting and puzzling to many, for he presented an entirely different picture from other teachers. He ignored health food and ate whatever he wanted [. . .]. He also smoke and drank without apology [. . .]" (*How* 309). Fields and others, including Stephen T. Butterfield, have noted that Trungpa's hedonism was an effort to enact the very spiritual materialism in which his students unwittingly framed their practice and thereby to demonstrate how to absorb this materialism into Tantric practice. As Fields writes, "There was nothing, [Trungpa] liked to point out, more boring than meditation. 'In order to follow the spiritual path,' he wrote in *Meditation in Action*, 'one must first overcome the initial excitement'" (*How* 310). Trungpa adapted the Padmasambhava legend to the sociocultural experimentation of the Vietnam era, staging American orientalist exoticism in his personal presentation, then incorporating such excitement in defamiliarizing gestures that would bring students face-to-face with the dharma once they had, as one student said, "exhausted the resources of their own self-entertainment" (Fields, *How* 310). As compatible as such an approach might be with Tantra's emphasis on using desire as a vehicle for diminishing attachment to desire, Crazy Wisdom also risks sheer anarchy.[21] In chapter 6, I will discuss in greater depth how what Trungpa calls the "playful aggression" of Crazy Wisdom reached its limit for Ginsberg, and for other Western Buddhists, in the late 1970s and early 1980s.

Psychoanalysis as a Practice of the Sacred

As enabling patriarchs, Ginsberg's poetic fathers influence his work on an important psychological level, too. Ginsberg's self-professed commitment throughout his career to psychoanalysis is well documented, including his early professional analysis during and after college, and his amateur analysis with Burroughs from 1945 to 1946.[22] For Ginsberg, psychoanalysis also is a practice of the sacred, and as such, Trungpa becomes an object of transference who combines Louis's art (in the form of Trungpa's poetry) and Naomi's divine madness (in the form of Trungpa's Crazy Wisdom Buddhist tradition).[23] A foremost example of Ginsberg's belief that the exploration of mind in psychoanalysis entails a concomitant spiritual exploration of mind is his 3 September 1947 letter to Louis, detailing his decision to ship to France instead of returning to Columbia University for the fall semester. Ginsberg explains to his father that he wishes to save money from his work at sea for psychoanalysis rather than for this final semester at Columbia. He assures his father that he will complete his studies at Columbia, adding, "[D]on't worry about me becoming a permanent wastrel just because I'm trying to 'save my soul' as scientifically as possible" (Ginsberg and Ginsberg 15). Ginsberg asks his father's blessing of this psycho-spiritual project without particularly asking at all. This implicit rather than explicit request for blessing is couched in an elliptical confession of the young poet's homosexuality: "The analysis is important to me, and if you knew [. . .] my sexual and soul-ful difficulties you would bless my efforts" (Ginsberg and Ginsberg 15). This important letter, on the eve of Ginsberg's trip overseas, frames the primary concerns of what would become his spiritual poetics: he represents his psychoanalytic and religious quests as one, and he frames both of these quests with a request for his father's blessing rather than position himself in an iconoclastic relation to his father's Judaism. For Ginsberg, Buddhism fuses psychic and material experience, and it is "blessed" by the originary Hebraic influence of his father (even if it eventually swerves from this influence). As further evidence of this relational instead of singularist conception of his father's influence, Ginsberg asks Louis, too, to bless his struggles to understand his sexual identity rather than adopt the subject position of Oedipal competitor or prohibitive father. His own sexual identity still was not narratable to the young Ginsberg—hence, his implicit "if you knew" phrasing rather than any direct statement about desire. Ginsberg's letter suggests that he might be able to name, hence to know, himself only through a practice, psychoanalysis, that he sees as both scientific and sacred. Thus, Ginsberg's construction of the sacred was based on a conceptual framework that privileged an embodied psychospiritual pilgrimage in which desire is a key component of spiritual development, just as desire functions for him later, too, in his Tantric Buddhist practice. Ginsberg's effort to forge this psychospiritual dynamics of relationality was affirmed emotionally and economically by his father. On 15 September 1947, Louis writes back to assure his son that after graduation he had planned to contribute money toward his son's psychoanalysis—"to help you out for the doctor"—but that in light of the letter of 3 September, Louis would help sooner rather than later. "Save your money," he writes, "and what additional you'll need, I'll provide later" (Ginsberg and Ginsberg 18).

These questions of help and influence were mutual ones for Ginsberg and his father, rather than just instances of traditional paternal providing. Significantly, at the level of Ginsberg's poetic influence, Louis serves as a countertransferential figure, in which Louis projects onto his own son the desire to have a paternal figure who can "provide." As I have discussed earlier in this chapter, Ginsberg served as a de facto literary agent for his father, especially seeing *Morning in Spring* to publication and legitimizing it with his introduction. The Louis-Allen correspondence shows that from the publication of *Howl and Other Poems* onward, their letters increasingly involve the sharing and critiquing of each other's poems, suggesting an initial relationship in which poetic influence is conversational instead of rigidly hierarchical. Yet, this relationship reinvokes a hierarchical impulse, a countertransference of sorts, when Louis's relative lack of literary reputation is factored into it. Schumacher observes, "In time, there was almost a complete reversal of position" between father and son, with Louis seeking the advice of his son on both the work itself and the promotion of it" (Ginsberg and Ginsberg 27). It is no surprise that, in light of Ginsberg's literary reputation and Louis's difficulties publishing his work in the 1960s, often their critiques of each other's poetry in the letters proceeds as a one-way artistic relationship. To cite one of several available examples, Louis provides detailed commentary on "September on Jessore Road" in his correspondence, but his remarks do not produce any changes in the poem. This undated letter from December 1971 continues the quarrel between the two over what might best be called issues of New Critical unity—a disagreement seen throughout their correspondence—where Louis suggests that "the poem is too long and taxes one's patience" and adds, "I'd omit at least two pages including the 3 stanzas on p. 4, as these mar the general unity of the poem" (Ginsberg and Ginsberg 325–26). Anticipating Louis's need for formal unity, Ginsberg wrote the following instruction at the top of the typescript before he sent the letter: "Dear Louis—Please note any flaws—some lines irregularly long can still be *sung*—that's the criteria."

I emphasize Ginsberg's relationship with Louis to introduce the psychological and spiritual shadings of Ginsberg's Buddhist poetics that will be elaborated in the following chapters. Their literary relationship proceeds from a productive tension between relationality and hierarchization, and Ginsberg's Buddhism develops in much the same way. Their literary relationship often was conversational—marked by the passing back and forth of poems in the mode that would be called workshopping in contemporary parlance—in their efforts to shape each other's work. At the same time, this relationship was inflected by the power imbalance in their literary reputations. Their vastly uneven literary reputations further complicate and subvert the workings of the traditional Oedipal drama—the "complete reversal of position" between father and son that Schumacher describes, in which Ginsberg serves as parent bringing forth his father's poems into the contemporary literary arena. Ginsberg's poetic "fathers" represent a complicated relational rather than wholly competitive lineage. Ginsberg "fathers" Louis's poetry in his letters and his introduction to *Morning in Spring*, and the particular circumstances of Ginsberg's increasingly revered literary reputation during this period create the conditions for a complete reversal of position that is both a literary and Oedipal reversal.

As seen in the introduction to *First Thought, Best Thought*, Ginsberg also "fathers" Trungpa's poems into print, yet no similar reversal of position occurs with Trungpa. That is, the transference relationship between student and teacher in Tibetan Buddhism does not produce the attendant countertransference that it would in psychoanalytic practice. As Polly Young-Eisendrath writes, teacher-student relationships across Buddhist traditions expand the traditional childhood emotional dynamics of transference to include the Buddhist practitioner's "projection of the perfected spiritual nature (Buddha Mind or true nature) that the student cannot initially find within herself. The student experiences or sees this quality in the [Buddhist] teacher and wants to attain it" (311).[24] Yet the countertransferential relationship so important in psychoanalysis does not generally apply to Buddhist student-teacher relationships. Young-Eisendrath's description of the Zen teacher-student relationship also can explain the guru-student relationship in Tibetan Buddhism. She explains that "the Zen teacher and student are understood to be fundamentally unequal, spiritually speaking," insofar as Zen tradition teaches that "[t]he developed teacher has mastered his or her own mind and not merely the knowledge of Buddhism" (312). Understood this way, the Buddhist teacher-student relationship depends upon the student's transference; at the same time, as a result of rigidly hierarchical Buddhist instruction on the role of teachers—that, unlike the analyst in the dialogic relationship of psychoanalysis, gurus "*do* know their own motives *and* what is best for their students"—a corresponding countertransferential element is not present in such relationships. The hierarchical quality of the teacher-student relationship is amplified when applied to the Tantric practices of Tibetan Buddhism. Mark Finn's description of Tantra is useful here: Tantra is a practice in which "nothing is excluded, and the whole tendency of the mind to exclude is challenged." This effect of Tantra to include all mental and phenomenal experience subverts the division and classification gestures of the mind, destabilizing "the whole tendency of the mind to exclude." The goal of this destabilization process is to induce the mind to see its frame of reference, the self, as a fiction. As Finn notes, such is the need for a guru to guide the practitioner through this unstable terrain. This subversion of exclusionary thinking creates a "lack of conceptual reference points" that potentially "puts sanity and morality up for grabs." The need for student dependence on a teacher, known in Tibetan Buddhism as guru devotion, arises from such potentially harmful chaos. Finn concludes that the "hazards" of Tantra "are mitigated by a relationship to the spiritual teacher" in which "[d]evotion to the teacher reduces pride"; as such, the guru-student relationship "'contains' the intense experience of the student, and the teacher offers both guidance and interpretations" (109).

As I discuss in chapter 6, in the examination of the effects of the 1976 Naropa Snowmass scandal, the otherwise-enabling possibilities of guru devotion actually disrupted Ginsberg's creative process for a time in the late 1970s and early 1980s. In this regard, too, it is important to consider how Ginsberg's development of a poetics influenced by Tibetan Buddhism emerge from the Oedipal negotiations between Ginsberg and his father. On one hand, Trungpa represents, in Ginsberg's words, "[m]y extremely delicate love life, my relations with my teacher" (Clark 53). For Ginsberg, such questions of desire always are political, from his earliest incorporations of queer desire in "Howl" through his final poems, such as "Dream," from *Death and Fame*, in which he and Peter Orlovsky conceive a child together. Indeed, questions about his guru are politicized for Ginsberg at the level of desire, invoking the complex negotiations of queer identification that mark his work. As he explained to Tom Clark in a 1979 interview published in *Boulder Monthly* and reprinted in Clark's

Great Naropa Poetry Wars, questions about guru devotion are difficult to answer, because "I feel too defensive. Like a fairy being asked if he's a fairy" (53). At the same, Ginsberg expresses a need to extricate desire from politics, because, in the transference relationship that would superimpose Louis Ginsberg upon Trungpa, the impulse to historicize only reduces the power of mythic transference. Indeed, guru devotion, as interpreted by Ginsberg, is the space where desire and family relations meet. Ginsberg resists when asked to describe his guru-student relationship with Trungpa, emphasizing that "the very nature" of such a relationship is so imbricated with "personal relations" that, he protests, repeating: "you're talking about my love life."[25] Ginsberg's study and practice in a tradition, Tibetan Buddhism, that encourages a transference relationship between guru and student in the form of guru devotion enact, too, the struggle between material politics and his tendency to mythologize political relations in his poems.

As I will explore later, discussing "Wichita Vortex Sutra" in chapter 3, Ginsberg incorporates the political possibilities of desire in ways that are alternately historical or mythologized, depending on the cultural and aesthetic circumstances of their composition. In this instance, where Clark is grilling the poet on the potential abuses of unconditional guru devotion in light of the Snowmass incident at Naropa, Ginsberg chides Clark for what he considers a reductive effort to critique guru devotion "with reference to cultural artifacts like the Bill of Rights" (53). When pressed further by Clark to explain in a Western historical context the personal, even familial, parameters of guru devotion, Ginsberg contextualizes guru devotion in terms of Freud's primal scene. Ginsberg refuses, with some anxiety, to take a position on allegations of Trungpa's abusiveness. Instead, he admits simply that he does not want to act on curiosity, for fear he might actually expose primal taboo: "I don't want to know about Trungpa. [. . .] You know, just like you don't want to ask your father about the night he fucked your mother and made you" (58). To further illuminate how the intersection of Ginsberg's familial relationships inflect his Buddhist relationships—what I have recast herein as a question of poetic influence—Ginsberg's particular Tibetan Buddhist practice with Trungpa can be seen in light of what Finn has described as the "flexible relationship to the Oedipus complex" in Tibetan Buddhist mythos (111). This "flexible relationship" comes to bear most of all in the mythic narrative of the enlightenment of the Buddhist saint Naropa, the figure so important in Trungpa's lineage that Trungpa named his educational institution after him.

As Finn describes it, in a discussion framed by Trungpa's interpretation of Tantric practice, Naropa's story is framed by a sexual conflict with his parents: required by his royal parents to marry and propagate the royal line of descent, Naropa complied with their wishes but refused to consummate the marriage (110). This "sexual standoff" lasted eight years, after which Naropa was permitted to study Buddhism in a formal, scholastic setting. However, after experiencing a vision that told him he only understood Buddhism in a cursory manner, he undertook a pilgrimage to seek the Buddhist master Tilopa, who eventually becomes his primary teacher, or root guru. Under guidance from Tilopa, Naropa was taught that "[h]is practice was to regard enlightenment as identical with sex and aggression" (110). Such a pedagogical approach, Finn writes, pushed Naropa to consider suicide. This strain on Naropa caused Tilopa to engage his student more directly, and the resulting practice says much about how the psychoanalytic framework of the Oedipal drama is useful in understanding the history of Tibetan Buddhism as taught by Trungpa:

> The penultimate teaching required Naropa to remember the moment of his conception and feel hatred toward his father and longing toward his mother. Tilopa cautioned him that some meditators may become too frightened of an original primal scene to proceed. [. . .] The result of this 'working through' for Naropa was a new experience of his body and sexuality. He consummated a relationship with a young woman and went on to become a teacher living in the forest. Although many conventional practitioners once considered him disreputable and unsavory, Naropa is now known as a great master. (Finn 110–11)

These complementary prehistories, Trungpa-Buddhist and psychoanalytic, present a pattern of ideas around which the prehistory of Ginsberg's prophetic poetry can be framed.

Discussing Ginsberg's creative and competitive energies in an Oedipal context, family romance, is useful for two primary reasons. First, Ginsberg's assurance in his 3 September 1947 letter to his father that his desire to become an analysand was an effort "to 'save [his] soul' as scientifically as possible" suggests that for Ginsberg psychoanalysis was a legitimate response to both psychic and spiritual malaise. Ginsberg's effort to save his money to seek the unorthodox analysis of a Reichian suggests, too, that his own relationship to the Oedipus complex, like his relationship with psychoanalysis in general, was "flexible," to recall Finn's language. Second, the institution Ginsberg founded, the Jack Kerouac School of Disembodied Poetics, is, of course, located within a university named after Naropa, whose mythic story of enlightenment depends on a prehistory wherein he successfully negotiates what Western psychoanalysis would call an Oedipal family drama. Thus, for Ginsberg as for the patron saint of his Buddhist lineage, Naropa, the prehistory of sacred practice includes significant continuity and revision of the dominant metaphors of sex and aggression in the conventional psychoanalytic narrative of family romance.[26] Real poetry is for Ginsberg a spiritual practice, as he argues in "Meditation and Poetics"; as this introductory chapter has attempted to demonstrate, the reality of such poetry depends upon a complexity of psychic, familial, aesthetic, and sacred forms. It depends, especially, on an Oedipal prehistory that includes the poet's early artistic and sexual awakening—from his quarrels with Louis's forms, to Louis's support of psychoanalysis as a sacred practice, to Ginsberg's transference onto Trungpa of his indebtedness to Louis's aesthetic and spiritual practices. The following chapter demonstrates the sexual and spiritual conflicts that arise in the poetry from these complicated prehistories.

2

Queer Dharma, Anxiety, and Fantasy in "Angkor Wat"

> In other words, the spiritual life is determined by the physical world presented.
> —Allen Ginsberg, 1978

Authenticity, Authority, and Refuge

At a critical moment in "Angkor Wat" (1963), Ginsberg's long collage-voice poem of his pilgrimage to the Angkor Wat temples in Siemreap, Cambodia, the speaker interrupts his interior monologue to invoke the Buddhist refuge prayer. The prayer is a concise statement of sacred purpose in which the Buddhist practitioner vows to step outside the privatizing interiority of his/her spiritual practice and join the larger community of past, present, and future Buddhists. The practitioner asserts in sanctified speech his/her commitment to Buddhism and accepts this commitment as a mode of sanctuary: the disciple takes refuge in the inspirational deeds of the historical Buddha, in the dharma (the teachings of the Buddha), and the sangha (technically, the community of monks and nuns but commonly translated as the community of fellow Buddhist practitioners). The refuge prayer offers the practitioner the solace of a spiritual community, while urging the practitioner to transform his/her quotidian commitments from self to other. As speech recited during major Buddhist teachings and ceremonies and in private meditation, the refuge prayer enacts this movement from self to other in language.

In "Angkor Wat," the authenticity of the speaker's prayer—and his conception of sacred language—is at stake as the poet questions whether homosexual desire is compatible with Eastern spiritual practice. At first glance, he seems to reject the question outright, responding with a troubled asceticism found only in popular stereotypes of Buddhism, not in the actual refuge prayer as it is transmitted by teachers adhering to past lineages of study and practice. In addition to this unusual asceticism, Ginsberg's refuge prayer in "Angkor Wat" conflates Buddhism and Hinduism, precisely the sort of commingling characteristic of the new formations of religiosity that emerged in the United States in the 1960s—what Robert S. Ellwood terms a postwar "glossolalia" of religious discourse as the country transitioned from modern to postmodern modes of sacred practice (6). It is within such a context, then, that Ginsberg's speaker proclaims:

> I'm not going to eat meat anymore
> I'm taking refuge in the Buddha Dharma Sangha
> Hare Krishna Hare Krishna
> Krishna Krishna Hare Hare
> Hare Rama Hare Rama
> Rama Rama Hare Hare
>
> (*Collected* 309)

Ginsberg's refuge prayer renounces the eating of meat, an asceticism not required in Buddhism. The speaker's prayer suggests, however, that Ginsberg's sensitivity to the location of the poem, its cultural specificity, is accurate: the possibility that the Buddhist refuge prayer and the Hindu Hare Krishna mantra might be equivalent is supported historically by the side-by-side coexistence of Buddhist and Hindu practices at Angkor Wat through the fourteenth century, when Buddhism became the dominant religious and cultural force at the temples.

Still, the almost breezy interchangeability of the two religious traditions could seem facile in this section of the poem, considering the history of Buddhism is predicated on a separation from its Hindu past. Ginsberg's potential misreading of the refuge prayer can be understood in its cultural context without disparaging the poet's commitment to Buddhism: it is an instance of what Ellwood would describe as postwar glossolalia, and this particular manifestation of glossolalia itself can be traced to the decidedly informal practices of U.S. Buddhists decades earlier. It is useful, then, to keep in mind the divergent practices and autodidactic necessities of Western Buddhist instruction in the early- to mid-twentieth-century. Ginsberg's eccentric rendering of Buddhism in "Angkor Wat" reflects the lack of qualified teachers in the West in 1963 who could offer instruction in Buddhism. U.S. Buddhism in the postwar era was, at best, nascent. However, Buddhist religiosity was not a new phenomenon in the United States in the twentieth century. It dates back, at the least, to the creation of the Theosophical Society in New York in the mid-1870s. Richard Hughes Seager describes the Theosophical Society founders, Henry Steel Olcott and Helena Petrovna Blavatsky (Madame Blavatsky), as most likely "America's first convert Buddhists" (35). Yet, American Buddhists often were forced to look outside the United States for qualified Buddhist teachers. Thomas A. Tweed has explained how the 1965 repeal of immigration quotas based on national origins was a crucial development in U.S. Buddhism, bringing both Asian practitioners and qualified Asian teachers to the country. Tweed compares U.S. interest in Buddhism in the late-nineteenth century with similar interest after World War II and concludes, "Unlike in the Victorian period [. . .] Caucasian sympathizers and adherents in the second half of the twentieth century could find [Buddhist] institutions to support their interest and teachers to nurture their development" (*American Encounter* 159). As Tweed asserts, this availability of teachers "had an effect on the nature of Buddhist conversions and the sources of its appeal" in the mid- to late-twentieth century U.S. (*American Encounter* 159). In contrast, Fields observes in *How the Swans Came to the Lake* that qualified teachers were difficult to find in the postwar United States More existed in the post–World War II United States. than during the Victorian era, to be sure, but few still were available at all. Fields's divergence here is noteworthy, because his account of American Buddhism is strongest in its narrative of Buddhists from the postwar U.S. counterculture, especially the Beats. Noting the exception of Gary Snyder's formal Buddhist education in Japan, Fields observes that Beat enthusiasm for Buddhism led to a "mostly literary" and at times "idiosyncratic" Buddhism (214). For instance, Fields explains, in these early years Ginsberg "was still looking backward to the kind of visionary experience [his 1948 Blake vision] that had overwhelmed him in Harlem years before" (214). According to Fields,

Ginsberg lamented the lack of Buddhist teachers available in the 1950s. Describing his early experiences with the Zen tradition, Ginsberg tells Fields, "'Nobody knew much about zazen [. . .]. It was a great tragedy. If somebody had just taught us how to sit, straighten the spine, follow the breath, it would've been a great discovery" (214).

I begin this chapter with Ginsberg's use of the Buddhist refuge prayer not just to illustrate the idiosyncrasies of his early Buddhist study—these do not need much energy to unearth. Indeed, as John Tytell has observed, Beat Buddhism can be seen as "eccentric, inconsistent, and most of all eclectic" (26). Of course, Ginsberg's early Buddhism would be a struggle, as is any autodidactic undertaking. Instead, I wish to foreground these idiosyncrasies from the start, in their cultural context, so that the development of Ginsberg's early Buddhism can be seen as part of the spiritual and cultural conflicts of the early 1960s, especially as the U.S. increased its military commitment to South Vietnam and as part of the poet's own efforts to reconcile homosexuality and sacred experience. Early Buddhist poems such as "Angkor Wat" and "The Change: *Kyoto-Tokyo Express*" emerge from such conflicts. The spiritual crisis that led to "Angkor Wat" and "The Change"—and his effort to write himself out of this crisis in the poems themselves—is as important to the development of Ginsberg's Buddhist poetics as is the early success of "Howl" and "Kaddish." In "Angkor Wat" and "The Change," he crafts a set of consistent formal and thematic strategies that fuse Eastern and Western conceptual practices and forms of the sacred. As significant products of his early Buddhist study and practice, these poems represent Ginsberg's earliest interventions in debates over language, subjectivity, sexuality, and the politics of sacred speech in contemporary U.S. poetry.

For literary and cultural critics, Ginsberg's Buddhist-Hindu conflation in the "Angkor Wat" refuge prayer seems to articulate an inauthentic Buddhist sensibility. My emphasis on Ginsberg's early "eccentric" Buddhism affirms the extent to which these commentaries are accurate. In a 1970 review of Ginsberg's *Indian Journals*, Reed Whittemore describes the post-World War II U.S. Buddhist impulse in which Ginsberg participated as part of a generalized "easy Easternness" in which all things Eastern were necessary accessories for the hipster mythos. In this argument, the historical and conceptual particulars of the East, especially the major difference between the theism of Hinduism and the nontheism of Buddhism, were elided in the contemporary orientalist gestures of Ginsberg and fellow alternative religious seekers. Whittemore's comment would seem to confirm the remarks of many commentators who have seen Ginsberg's Buddhism as mere dabbling, or, in Tytell's estimation, as an effort primarily to expand his artistic breadth.[1] Yet, perhaps it is too easy to ascribe an "easy Easternness" to someone such as Ginsberg, whose study and practice of Eastern tradition grew into a lifelong commitment only after eccentric, autodidactic beginnings. A poet well known for his embrace of the improvisatory, Ginsberg eventually developed a Buddhist practice characterized by a self-reflexive and revisionary impulse encouraged by Buddhism's supple phenomenology.

Buddhism was, for him, a crucial third term between Judeo-Christian transcendentalist discourse and the postwar materialist discourse of an emergent U.S. "military-industrial complex." Ginsberg incorporated Buddhism in the construction of a poetic language that would be mindful of the limits of both political materialism and religious transcendentalism: his early major poems, "Howl" and "Kaddish," deployed Buddhist conceptions of what the contemporary critical community would call a deconstructive sense of self and language to forge a poetics of prophecy situated between the poles of materialist and transcendentalist discourse. His prose accounts of his earliest study of Buddhism with Jack Kerouac, published in *"Howl": Original Draft Facsimile* and *Deliberate Prose* (edited by Bill Morgan), suggest that Ginsberg's early study of Buddhism in the 1950s was an attempt at a syncretic understanding even though few trained Buddhist teachers from the East actually lived and practiced in the West. In a 1954 letter to Ginsberg, Kerouac posited that the study of Buddhism was consistent with the systematic study of science or the writing process: "For your beginning studies of Buddhism, you must listen to me carefully and implicitly as tho I was Einstein teaching you relativity or Eliot teaching the Formulas of Objective Correlation on a blackboard in Princeton" (qtd. in Schumacher 194). Later, in the 1990 essay "Kerouac's Ethic," Ginsberg describes with admiration Kerouac's intelligence as a Buddhist teacher, noting that he possessed, too, an "almost intuitiv[e]" command of the "substratum" of Buddhism. Ginsberg suggests that Kerouac's intuitive mastery of dharma strengthened his abilities as a Buddhist teacher but simultaneously limited him: "Unfortunately, Kerouac had no teacher in the lineage of Zen or classical Buddhism" (369).

Despite Ginsberg's conflation of Hinduism and Buddhism in the "Angkor Wat" refuge prayer, his poetry and prose of his early career suggest, in contrast, that Buddhism was an influence taking shape for him in its traditionally distinct form from Hinduism. Ginsberg's own notes to "Angkor Wat" complicate even further the refuge prayer conflation. His 1984 notes suggest that his interpretation of the refuge prayer itself was incomplete when the poem was published in 1968. "Angkor Wat" originally appeared in the 1968 collection *Planet News*. However, the poem also was published in a stand-alone edition by London's Fulcrum Press in 1968, titled *Ankor Wat*, with Alexandra Lawrence's photos from the Angkor temples and detailed explanatory endnotes by Ginsberg. These notes were reprinted verbatim in Ginsberg's *Collected Poems, 1947–1980*. The only difference between the notes as they appear in *Ankor Wat* and in *Collected Poems* occurs in Ginsberg's notes to the refuge prayer section. In his 1968 unpaginated notes to the poem's refuge prayer in *Ankor Wat*, Ginsberg identifies the prayer as "The three refuges, which the author interprets as: I take my refuge in my Self, I take my refuge in the nature of my Self, I take my refuge in the company of my fellow Selfs." Yet, Ginsberg's 1984 reprint of the notes in *Collected Poems* contains a curious addition to this note. After reproducing his original 1968 interpretation of the refuge prayer, Ginsberg added: "[Non-Self interpretation.—A.G., 1984.]" (771).[2]

The corrective impulse of the revision is significant to understanding how Ginsberg's readings of Buddhism in "Angkor Wat" contribute crucially to the development of his Buddhist poetics. Elsewhere, in *"Strange Prophecies Anew,"* I have discussed how Ginsberg's autodidactic early reading and study of Buddhist source material shaped his early, major Buddhist-influenced poems, "Howl" and "Kaddish." This chapter extends this discussion to encompass the combined effects on Ginsberg's poetry of both his autodidactic Buddhist studies and his search, especially in the early 1960s, for a qualified Buddhist teacher. This search for a guru coincides with Ginsberg's desire to abandon his attachment to his 1948 Blake vision, an extranatural experience that, as he argued throughout his career, launched and gave shape to his early prophetic poetry. In this early period of his career, Ginsberg's Buddhist poetics takes its shape for him from his reading in Blake; at the same time, Eastern religiosity rescues him from an overarching dependence on Blake. This intersection of Anglo-American interests (his Blake vision) and Buddhist interests (his search for a guru) leads to the creation of one of his most important early statements of a Buddhist poetics, "Angkor Wat," the first of a long two-poem sequence that culminates with "The Change."

Although "Angkor Wat" and "The Change" are companion poems, written just a month apart in 1963 and paired in their subject matter, critical attention tends to focus primarily on "The Change." This emphasis is understandable: in its title alone, "The Change" offers readers a clear sense of a spiritual crisis overcome within the interiority of the poem; in contrast, "Angkor Wat" requires extratextual attention to the exotic ruins of Cambodia's Angkor temples themselves and an understanding of Buddhist practice itself that do not come easily without explanatory notes. Moreover, "Angkor Wat" is cast in a cut-up collage monologue, a discursive strategy framed by hermetic references to fragmented, autobiographical material. "Angkor Wat" presents difficulty for readers not familiar with Buddhist history or practice and for readers accustomed to the autobiographical transparency familiarized in more well-known long poems such as "Howl" and "Kaddish." To be sure, the confessional material in "The Change" is more accessible than in "Angkor Wat," insofar as the private experience of Ginsberg's Blake vision was part of the public lore of contemporary poetry through Ginsberg's repeated invocation of it at the time in his writing and interviews. Still, the "change" recorded in these poems cannot be understood substantively without an exploration of Ginsberg's early Buddhist practice in "Angkor Wat."

Ginsberg's remarks in "Kerouac's Ethic" emphasize the importance of the refuge prayer in the poet's earliest instruction in Buddhism by Kerouac. Ginsberg notes that "the first direct Buddhist word I heard from Kerouac's mouth after [his] letters, was his singing of the Three Refuges" (363). This early encounter was foundational. Kerouac "introduced me to Buddhism in the form of song" (363). Thus, the refuge prayer is crucial to Ginsberg's earliest Buddhist instruction—the "first direct Buddhist word" he heard from Kerouac—and this early Buddhism came to him, as a poet, through the aesthetic medium of song. "Kerouac's Ethic" offers a way of understanding the complications that emerge from Ginsberg's understanding of Buddhist subjectivity in his early career. Ginsberg writes that Kerouac's singing of the refuge prayer "first introduced me to the delicacy and softness of his Buddhism aside from the tough truth of suffering, transitoriness, and no permanent Allen Ginsberg or permanent Jack Kerouac" (364). Between Ginsberg's mid-1950s' understanding of Buddhism and the period during which he composed "Angkor Wat," the "delicacy and softness" of Buddhism and his belief in "no permanent Allen Ginsberg" gave way to a decidedly different conception of Buddhist subjectivity, one in which Ginsberg valorized, in the Fulcrum Press notes, an unproblematically reified "Self" which resided "in the company of [its] fellow Selves."

This shift from a fluctuating subjectivity to a reified one is dramatized in the spiritual crisis that launches "Angkor Wat." Ginsberg's 1984 revision to the 1968 "Angkor Wat" endnote functions much like his words in the 1990 essay on Kerouac and Buddhism. As a revision, the 1984 commentary suggests a twofold means of understanding Ginsberg's early Buddhist poetics. First, it is a reminder that Ginsberg's Buddhism was never a static entity and was always in a recursive process of vision and revision subject to the poet's shifting cultural contexts (like Buddhism itself, which always shifts to reflect the cultural norms and practices of its host country even as it participates in historical shifts in these same norms and practices in the host country). Second, it suggests that "Angkor Wat" is a crucial poem for understanding the early development of his Buddhist poetics; the poem is significant enough to Ginsberg that in his 1984 *Collected Poems*, he felt the need to correct his original notes on Buddhism in the poem itself so that the speaker of the poem takes refuge in both the illusory self—of course, his only tactile, pragmatic point of contact with the sense world—and the fully realized nondual Non-Self that, ideally, frames the Buddhist practitioner's utterance of the refuge prayer.[3]

Indigestible Collage

"Angkor Wat" demonstrates how personal and political anxiety was the first challenge Ginsberg faced in his development of a Buddhist poetics. Like most of Ginsberg's early prophecies, "Angkor Wat" dramatizes a pilgrimage to find a material language for sacred experience. It does this within the bounded physical space of the speaker's desiring body and, figurally, within the bodies of the sacred Angkor temple statuaries. As is "Howl" and "Kaddish," "Angkor Wat" is skeptical of the power of language to transparently convey reality at the same time that, paradoxically, the poem keeps in the offing a wish-fulfillment for a primordial language. Prophetic language in "Angkor Wat" is primordial, as poetic speech authorized by the Buddhist statuary in the Angkor temple complex; but for Ginsberg, the authority of prophecy always is subject to revision, and this revisionary urge is represented in the poem by the famous banyan trees that snake through, and undermine, the authority of the venerable walls and roofs of Angkor. Prophetic language, a personal language for

Ginsberg, is located in the anxious body of the speaker of the poem, as it is located, too, in the bodies of the "secret heroes" of "Howl" and of Naomi in "Kaddish"—bodies that transgress the corporeal boundaries that authorize desire and sanity in the postwar United States.

"Angkor Wat" is shaped by Ginsberg's desire to create a sacred language within otherwise obsessive, secularized anxieties about desire, aging, illness, and death. The speaker's pilgrimage in the poem conceives Buddhism as a force that redeems anxieties over sickness and aging. Thus, he vows to take refuge the Three Jewels of Buddhism as they are physically manifest in the temple of Angkor Wat itself.[4] In "Angkor Wat," a cause-and-effect relationship is suggested by the speaker's bodily sickness and the disciplinary presence of American servicemen in the poem; political and religious illness is created by the univocal, coercive authority of covert military advisors. Yet, something has changed for the poet between his last major Buddhist-influenced long poem, "Kaddish," and "Angkor Wat." In "Kaddish," Naomi is blessed "in sickness," but in "Angkor Wat," sickness is something indigestible—a phantasmic condition the speaker wishes his body would reject.

Written as a product of extensive international travel in the 1960s in an effort to understand the globalist import of his poetry, the poem is a hinge between an earlier, domestic Williams and Whitman-inspired American exceptionalism and a later hybrid internationalist impulse. "Angkor Wat" also is the first of a series of poems in Ginsberg's career that attempt to merge Williams's poetics with one inspired by Buddhist *vipassana*[5] practice—a poetry grounded in concrete particularity but also in Ginsberg's belief, inspired by vipassana meditation, that an inextricable connection between perceiving body and perceiving mind creates sacred speech and, therefore, sacralizes the imagination. In a 1978 interview with Paul Portugés, Ginsberg explains that his Buddhist poetics owes much to Williams's "elemental observations" (*Visionary Poetics* 148). Ginsberg cites such elemental observations as an important influence on his Buddhist poetics throughout his career. As his Naropa teaching transcripts demonstrate, his focus on how Williams transformed ordinary observation into vision was a major point of emphasis in Ginsberg's poetics much earlier in his career, even before the Portugés interview:

> Williams's phrase is that the mind should be clamped down on objects [. . .]. I think that's the condition of [. . .] arriving at your awareness of what's around you, writing it all down, articulating it,

writing poems, the mind being clamped down on objects, and William Blake, visionary and elevated and romantic as he was, oddly had exactly the same recipe: His practical rule was 'Minute Particulars.' ("Complete" 13-14)

Ginsberg's Naropa transcripts allow him a space—the autonomous professorial zone of the classroom—from which to theorize his Buddhist poetics and his Blake-Williams-Buddhist fusion. The "visionary and elevated and romantic" impulse of Blake's vision finds its pragmatic equivalent in Williams. Ginsberg asserts, more specifically, that Williams's vision represents a crucial, materialist vector of a Buddhist poetics. As he explains in a 1978 "Meditation and Poetics" Naropa lecture, "the spiritual life is determined by the physical world presented" ("Complete" 6). He argues later in the same lecture that Williams's attentive poetics was part of a larger movement in early-twentieth-century art toward a "Samatha-Vipassana: poetics characterized by "focus, concentration, simplification, mindfulness, realization of present space, non-imposition of fantasy on the object in space, but clear perception of sight, sound, smell, taste, touch, and thought ("Complete" 9). In 1976 at a poetics lecture at Naropa, Ginsberg elaborates on this convergence of vipassana and the work of Williams. He asserts that both represent the act of "paying attention to ordinary mind detail and a sharpening of focus and finer clearer Zenish perception of a black scrape on the floor where a chair has been pulled. In other words, one detail indicating a whole previous activity" ("Complete" 62). He describes this mode of perception as "seeing what's in front of the eyes, or seeing where the eye strikes" and argues that a source also can be found in the objectivist poetics of Louis Zukofsky. In a 1989 interview with Lewis MacAdams, Ginsberg asserts that this sacred particularity emerges from a visionary poetry suffused with the experience of shunyata, in which the absolutist value of the logos is suffused instead with a situational language based on materialist relationality rather than logocentric transcendentalism.

This focus on sacred physicality is troubled, of course, in a poem such as "Angkor Wat" where the sick physical body is a trope for the nationalist illness Ginsberg perceives in the impulse to colonize. In "Angkor Wat," Ginsberg conceives a samatha-vipassana attentive language for representing the early history of American involvement in Vietnam. This recourse to his Buddhist study merges, too, with Ginsberg's deepening interest in the objectivist inheritance of poets such as Williams, Zukofsky, and Charles Reznikoff. However, commentators have tended to read past the cultural contexts of "Angkor Wat," focusing on nevertheless important questions of surrealist stylistics and patterns of metaphor in ways that bracket the East-West convergence in the poem. Such a reading, focusing exclusively on the formalist interiority of the poem, neglects that Ginsberg's samatha-vipassana language is positioned outside the poem, too: that Ginsberg's obsessions with the illnesses of his physical body and the American body politic enact narcissism as the nationalist illness that samatha-vipassana might cure.

The most detailed formalist reading of the poem is from David Lehman, who emphasizes the "montage effect" of the poem in discussion in which the body is never more than a metaphor for technique: the insatiable bodily appetite in "Angkor Wat" is a figure, for Lehman, of the poet's relentless accumulation of bricolage. Whittemore focuses on Ginsberg's appropriation of Buddhism in the poem, yet his response lingers on a critique of Ginsberg's Buddhism as a formal trope without investigating the significance of Buddhism as a dynamic, conceptual schema for Ginsberg. I would argue, instead, that collage is an extension of religious content, in which otherwise incompatible conceptual frameworks for sacred experience are yoked together. Indeed, the effort to enact surrealistic form within a Buddhist framework is for Ginsberg precisely a question of content, one that suggests that the poem begins to stage Ginsberg's poetics of a hybridized American Buddhism.

What has changed, perhaps most of all, between "Kaddish" and "Angkor Wat" are public circumstances as much as private ones. "Angkor Wat" anticipates the significance of the U.S. war in Vietnam and reconceives the growing military presence there in 1963 as a symptom of imperialism. Colonial conquest is figured as an illness that for Ginsberg parallels his own self-attachment and his obsession with reproduction. Early in the poem, the speaker articulates his obsessions:

> meat, smoking, ganja
> sex, cannibal spies, Prop-
> agation of this Skin, thin
> vegetable soups [. . .]

(Collected 307)

Political, religious, and libidinous obsessions recur throughout the poem. In their manifestations of anxiety neurosis, they affirm a contentious intersection of Buddhism and self-consciousness in the poem. To recall and revise Whittemore's commentary, such a conflict calls to question whether the poem is "easy" in its "Easternness" at all. These obsessions disrupt the articulation of a redemptive Buddhism for Ginsberg in "Angkor Wat," a Buddhist-influenced poetics of possibility that might emerge from the ruins of Angkor Wat in the same way that the end of suffering emerges from ruin in the Four Noble Truths. According to the Four Noble Truths, suffering ceases when the Buddhist disciple realizes shunyata—that is, when the disciple realizes that intersubjective experience is empty of an essentialized, reified frame of reference. In the shadow of the ruins of the Angkor temple complex, the speaker of "Angkor Wat" seeks redemption through shunyata. He attempts to guide his pilgrimage by multiplicitous frames of reference that emerge when the self is emptied of its absolutist point of view, but the bodily obsessions that emerge from his anxiety neurosis obscure this effort to craft such a subjectivity.

As a response to the univocal authority of U.S. expansionism, the poem takes shape in disjunctive, collage lines whose multiple voices at times are at cross-purposes with each other. Significantly, this collage form voices itself as counterstatements to U.S. policies at the same time that the speaker doubts the authority of his own poetics. With the imperial appetites of the country reinscribed as an individualist digestive disorder, Ginsberg frames the poem with individual self-obsession—a form of self-indulgence in direct contrast to the poet's own commitment to social engagement. The subjective, diary-like lineation of the poem, too, contradicts its authorizing Buddhist influence in its failure to extend beyond the inward-seeking self to engage the social and material conditions that presumably are the sources for the poem itself.

Thus, when seen only at the level of language, the depth of Ginsberg's engagement with U.S. policy in the poem is debatable. Lehman has described the surrealist form of "Angkor Wat" as Ginsberg's response to U.S. militarization of Southeast Asia with a nonlinear ethics of alterity. As I suggest in chapter 3, such a reading illuminates "The Change" more fully than it does "Angkor Wat." Lehman argues that the poem is structured "[l]ike an Eisenstein film," where a "montage effect" is produced from "a series of basic oppositions" (193). The oppositions Lehman identifies can be summarized, productively, in a familiar enough schematic in which the individual poet-prophet speaks against the grain of what he would term the "military-industrial complex" as it takes shape in the military itself, its authorizing politicians, and the country's complicit (for Ginsberg) journalistic media. Lehman hesitates, correctly, to praise the poem, implying that the poet's Surrealistic technique does not quite create a Surrealist ethos: "Even in the snatches of dialog, we are never really hearing anyone other than the poet, his interpretation, characterization, and embodiment of all that he describes" (193). Of course, Surrealism conventionally evades the hierarchizing tendency of reason in favor of a fragmented, nonrational multiplicity of voices produced when the censoriousness of the conscious mind is relaxed. In this way, the unquestioned monovocal authority of military hierarchies stand in opposition to the speaker's collage voice. Military speech is emphasized as a dangerous, delimiting discourse, one in which the poet's fear of change is equivocal with the fears of an ordinary solider "just doing [his] / Professional duty," the General "scheming / murders," and the journalist simply "chasing a story" (*Collected* 309). Yet, militarized hierarchies actually are reinforced by the use of collage-voice in the poem, insofar as one speaker's voice controls the circulation of what is proffered as multivocal speech—an environment that, as Lehman aptly puts it, becomes no more than the "embodiment of all he [the speaker] describes." In such a discursive landscape, the voice of the conqueror, in this case the U.S. military, silences dissenting voices. Even the speaker mutes himself, as when he protects himself hitchhiking: "I hitched / get polite when you'se a hiker / 'I going to take *both* sides'" (309–10). This minor shift in linguistic usage—grounded, too, in the fact that one indeed must be polite "when you'se a hiker"—forecasts issues of language and imperialism that will overwhelm later poems such as "Wichita Vortex Sutra" and "Angkor Wat." Ginsberg's deliberately clumsy colloquialisms when representing discourses that underwrite the war suggest a recasting of univocal authority as ironic detachment. Nevertheless, it remains questionable whether the incorporation of multiplicitous voices in "Angkor Wat" creates a counterdiscourse to militaristic language that otherwise would mute dissent or whether the poem actually stifles such a discourse. This issue of poetic form and political resistance is not quite resolved until the speaker embodies his desire for the sacred later in the poem, a process that leads to the transformative vision of "The Change."

"Angkor Wat" is not Ginsberg's first foray into Surrealist poetics, of course. Ginsberg often invokes Surrealism as a figure for the failure of the politics of resistance against the hyperreal logic of industrial capitalism—a technique that promises liberation at the same time that it imagines its own defeat.[6] As he renders failure narratable in collage-voice, Ginsberg searches for an embodied language that might resist coercive military discourse. His language of resistance combines nonlinear representation, queer identity, and Buddhist study and practice. Where Surrealism, for instance, presumes desire and convulsive eroticism as its *telos*, so, too, does Tantric Buddhism presume that attachment to desire is diminished only by an eschatological embrace of desire. In a 15 June 1958 letter to Peter Orlovsky cited by Schumacher in *Dharma Lion*, Ginsberg describes a useful interconnection he saw among Buddhism and the nonlinearity of Dadaism. As Schumacher describes Ginsberg's letter, the poet "believed Tzara to be 'in a way the best writer' of the Dadaists because Tzara saw a similarity between Dadaist art and Zen koans. Both, Tzara believed, were riddles aimed at freeing the human mind" (286). This relationship between Dada and Zen survives as a trace in the larger relationship between Eastern thought and the European Surrealist/Dadaist avant-garde that Ginsberg establishes in "Angkor Wat." Eventually in the poem, Buddhism becomes a larger force than just Zen koaning. Buddhist tradition moves instead beyond "riddl[ing]" and becomes an important conceptual frame for the poem, as it is staged in a tense setting in the Southeast Asian Buddhist-Catholic convergence of South Vietnam and Cambodia—a bull's-eye, as Ginsberg sees it, targeted for Western military action in the early 1960s.

Earlier, in the Orlovsky letter, Ginsberg characterizes Buddhism and Dadaism as liberating forces, "freeing the human mind" from the tyranny of self-consciousness. Such a focus depends, too, on his use of spontaneity. In his endnotes to "Angkor Wat," for instance, he explains that it "was written in one night half-sleeping and waking, as transcription of passages of consciousness in the author's mind made somnolent by an injection of morphine-atrophine [*sic*] in a hotel room in the town of Siemreap, adjacent to the ruins of Angkor Wat" (*Collected* 772).[7] The virtues and limitations of Ginsberg's early, autodidactic Buddhism are manifest in "Angkor Wat," as the poem's experimental, improvisatory technique collides, unevenly, with the religious framework of Ginsberg's early Buddhist study. This fusion also launches Ginsberg's earliest efforts to forge a prophetic poetry of both body and mind, in which his emerging queer political conscience might intersect with the internationalist political activism that marks his poetic career from the mid-1960s until his death.[8]

Poetry and the sacred, surrealist collage and referentiality, body and mind, are framed by tropes of consumption. Specifically, as Lehman writes, the poem is marked by "the continued use of the metaphor of digestion"

(193). The poet's fixation with bodily experience, which prompts him to pronounces himself "obsessed / with meat, smoking, ganja / sex," suggests the only way he can absorb the splendor of the temples of Angkor Wat is to ingest them (*Collected* 307). Language mediates consumption and digestion, staging a situational ethics in which thought and experience intersect in the body:

> words meat / death
>   mind-soup
> eaten last night, greedily fried macaroni
>   with rare beef—all the children
>   scream at my long awkward hair [. . .]
>
>   (*Collected* 315)

Yet, language is inadequate to represent the experience, insofar as "words" are just "meat / death" in the poem; they are a "mind-soup" the poet devours, then disgorges in haste. Sexually, too, the body is represented in a condition of detached or even debased corporeality. As in "This Form of Life Needs Sex," the poem is riven by a need to affirm, on one hand, the exigencies of homoerotic desire, and on the other hand, a building fixation to have children—resulting in Ginsberg's assertion that he is "obsessed" with "Prop- / agation of this Skin" (*Collected* 307). The conceptual framework of the poem might best be understood instead through recourse to tropes of *indigestion*: for every moment that the body is brought into play, it reacts with a violent disincorporation of experience, a nausea that stalks him through the poem.

    In "Angkor Wat," the body alternately rejects what it consumes, producing nausea, or consumes nothing corporeal except its own naked fantasy. Ginsberg's "greedily" consumed fried pasta does not go down well. The poet's indigestion is dramatized by an image of children; not the procreative images for which he longs in "This Form of Life Needs Sex" but instead children who mock his long hair as a visible representation of his privileged American otherness. The stanza breaks immediately, and Ginsberg vision of the foreign landscape of the Angkor temples shifts to fantasy:

> On the bed [. . .] I ached and strained my
> sphincter opened hoped
> to get next time befucked by
> a Cambodian sweet policeman
>
>   (*Collected* 315–16)

Food leads to nausea, and eating itself never quells Ginsberg's fears of death and illness; sex, the poet's figural act of ingestion and incorporation, never extends beyond masturbation, where the poet's open, hopeful sphincter "strain[s]" toward unfulfilled fantasy.[9] Language, of course, intensifies the problem of desire in the poem. Speech forecloses the production of desire, even as language seeks to articulate its multiplicitous pleasures in collaged discourse. As the poet speaks his desire, agency recedes from his voice. Digestion and nausea, then, are matters of both form and content. The poet's appetites are autoerotic; however, his food is indigestible, and sexual intercourse is thereby experienced in the abstract contiguities of the imagination rather than the body. In its effort to anatomize ecstasy in collage language, the poem only heightens its own fragmentation as a language that maps anxiety and unrequited desire.

The body in "Angkor Wat" is the locus for ecstatic visionary experience, yet also for spiritual crisis—a condition that calls to question standard readings of Ginsberg as a vatic voice of ecstasy and sexual liberation.[10] Ginsberg's conflation of digestion and indigestion localizes in the body his conflation of Buddhist and Hindu tradition. The result, of course, is in part the "easy Easternness" Whittemore finds in the early Buddhist work, an easeful orientalism that pervades the poem. "Angkor Wat" exudes exoticism, to be sure, at times reading as a poet-prophet's long-awaited grand tour, offering him a chance to eat soup and drink tea among the natives and "salut[e] the Buddha-baby in / the cloth flowered pram / sucking its chubby plum [. . .]" (*Collected* 307). Yet, the poem also dramatizes the beginning of Ginsberg's internationalist consciousness, his Beat jeremiad of the 1960s that took him through India, Cuba, and Czechoslovakia with an urgency to extend his Whitman-influenced optimism beyond the boundaries of the United States and craft a redemptive reenvisioning of American sexual and spiritual politics. In this way, "Angkor Wat" is poised between Ginsberg's earlier work, such as "Howl" and "Kaddish," and the trajectories his career take later in his construction of an embodied Buddhist poetics of prophecy. Ginsberg's Buddhist poetics leads to his earlier trials with the form in "Howl" and "Kaddish"; in "Angkor Wat," he visits the ruins of early Cambodian Buddhism in order to create a Buddhist poetics that fuses the particulars of physical impermanence, sexuality, and the languages of war and pacifism. In response to discursive practices that would underwrite war, he composes a fragmented, multiperspective poem. Yet, his collage style valorizes his own singularist voice, a univocal authority that is consistent with the hierarchizing discourses the poem ostensibly would resist.

The way out of this conundrum, perhaps, lies in Ginsberg's assertion of a homosexual identity congruent, for him, with the potential of Buddhism to revise hegemonic heterosexuality as a Queer Dharma.[11] That Ginsberg eventually could find in Buddhism a discourse that would authorize homosexuality is not surprising, given the historical complexities and contradictions in Buddhism's response to homosexuality and given Buddhism's admonitions against attachment to *desire*, per se, instead of an outright condemnation of homosexuality as a so-called transgression. Jeffrey Hopkins offers a scholarly perspective on the appeal Buddhism might have for a practitioner such as Ginsberg: "The Indo-Tibetan perspective that conceptual thought and orgasmic bliss have the same inner nature and that, in fact, the state of orgasmic bliss is more subtle than conceptual thought might help undermine the warped need to attack homosexuals out of fear that they have not assumed the 'proper' male perspective of dominance ("Compatibility" 382–83). The interchangeability of cultural definitions of masculinity and femininity that contributes to homophobia is, for Hopkins, precisely the interchangeability found in Tibetan Buddhist teachings on identitylessness and Tantric sexual yoga. He offers the reminder that the purpose of sexual yoga is "not mere repetition of an attractive state [of sexual pleasure] but revelation of the basic reality underlying appearances"—and, more important, he argues that this sexually realized "revelation" is compatible with both heterosexual and homosexual desire ("Compatibility" 378).[12] Indeed, as Peter A. Jackson has demonstrated, "Buddhism is a complex tradition and there is no single canonical or scripturally sanctioned position on homosexuality" (84). According to José Ignacio Cabezón, this lack of an identifiable scriptural or rhetorical position on homosexuality "has made Buddhism flexible in its accommodating to the [sexual] mores and societal attitudes of the different cultural areas to which it spread" (43).

Thus, Ginsberg could imagine, in a decade that would culminate in the Stonewall uprising, a Queer Dharma that might not distinguish between heterosexuality and homosexuality in its teachings on the usability of desire in sacred practice. Specifically, the Queer Dharma that emerges from Angkor Wat's ruins is, for Ginsberg, one that substitutes a performative language for a language of transcendentalism. In doing so, the poem reenvisions sacred language as a mode of representation in which the human body takes the shape of spiritual signification—rather than construct that body as that which is elided by spirit in a conventional transcendentalist discourse that reifies the body as a topos for that which is spiritually fallen.

Queer Dharma on Theme by Whitman

Ginsberg's representation of the body, then, is more complicated than the celebratory liberationism implied by his Beat reputation-making and codified in readings, such as those by Portugés and Tytell, suggesting that candor and nakedness in and of themselves relieve the coercive burden of the past. While the pleasures of the body indeed are celebrated in "Angkor Wat" and "The Change," Ginsberg portrays the body in these poems as an object of simultaneous histrionics and anxiety. Mine is perhaps an unusual statement to make, given that Ginsberg, of course, became one of the United States's most visible post-Stonewall gay civil rights advocates and that such advocacy depends upon a crucial transvaluation of the gay body as an accepted, often celebrated vehicle of spirit. However, I would argue that Ginsberg's queer activism is marked as much by celebration as by the anxieties evident in poems such as "Angkor Wat" and "The Change."

Thus, I briefly will guide this discussion away from "Angkor Wat" in this section, exploring instead his poems "Love Poem on Theme by Whitman" and "This Form of Life Needs Sex" in order to examine how Ginsberg's queer poetics contextualizes the cultural politics and individualist anxiety that undergirds the Buddhist impulse of "Angkor Wat." As Gregory Woods observes, many early critical reactions to Ginsberg's work fail to mention his open, explicit representations of homosexuality or imply such representations "only reluctantly, and by indirect means" (194). To be sure, as far back as 1979, Robert K. Martin's *Homosexual Tradition in American Poetry* places Ginsberg in a continuum of gay male writers ranging from Whitman through Thom Gunn. Yet, Martin's discussion of "A Supermarket in California" stands in contrast to Frederick Eckman's commentary on the poem, which acknowledges the phantasmic Whitman who cruises grocery stockboys but does not comment on the particularities of this central homoerotic encounter in the poem. In a similar fashion, Stephen Stepchanev's 1965 examination of "America" and "Love Poem on Theme By Whitman" points to specific queer experience in both poems but does not elaborate on the significance of such experience in Ginsberg's poetry; and Ihab Hassan's 1973 survey of Ginsberg notes in passing the influence of homosexuality, drug use, and mental illness in his work but does not comment on their significance in his poetry. Despite Ginsberg's iconographic image as a gay poet, pre- and post-Stonewall, it has taken the major shifts in literary criticism produced by queer studies to acknowledge the gay tradition in which Ginsberg writes.

For Ginsberg, the originary American writer in this tradition is, of course, Whitman, as seen in his numerous public commentaries on Whitman and in poems from "A Supermarket in California" (1956) through "I Love Old Whitman So" (1986).[13] Yet, Ginsberg's early representations of homosexuality influenced by Whitman also are characterized by self-doubt, as in "Love Poem on Theme by Whitman." This poem echoes Whitman's unease; it reflects the same impulse that urges Whitman to celebrate the male body while, in contrast, encoding desire in displacement and synecdoche, as in, respectively, "Trickle-Drops" and "I Saw in Louisiana a Live Oak Growing." In "Love Poem on Theme By Whitman," Ginsberg recapitulates the twenty-ninth-bather sequence from section 11 of Whitman's "Song of Myself" but ends the poem with wistful loneliness rather than the seemingly vigorous solitude of Whitman's poem.[14] He "lie[s] down between the bridegroom and bride," a "naked and restless" couple whose receptivity suggests they might be waiting precisely for the speaker's polymorphic, phantasmic intrusion into their bedroom (*Collected* 115). In section 11 of "Song of Myself," the speaker's voyeuristic gaze is displaced into the central figure of a woman who surveils a group of male bathers. Ginsberg's persona, by contrast, does not mediate the sexual encounter of "Love Poem on Theme by Whitman": the speaker nestles himself between the bride and groom in a polyamorous threesome of bodies portrayed as variously sexed objects of desire. Yet, the poem, like Whitman's, extends only as far as the speaker's fantasy; all sexual activity operates as a projection of the speaker's unconscious. The poem is spoken entirely in the future tense as a wish fulfillment enacted by the speaker's desire to "bury my face in their shoulders and breasts, breathing their skin, / and stroke and kiss neck and mouth and make back be open and known." The act of burying himself in "their" bodies accelerates into the next line of the poem, where its possessive pronouns recede into an ecstatic, polysexual wrangle.

What is at stake in the central fantasy of each poem is the hegemonic primacy of heterosexual desire. The identity of the sexed subject who speaks each poem is elusive. The governing fantasy in Whitman's poem is authorized by heteronormative desire; the voyeuristic male gaze is coded female at precisely the moment that the subject splashes with the twenty-eight male bathers who formerly were the objects of her vision. In contrast, "Love Poem on Theme by Whitman" heightens the ambiguity of desire at the precise moment when normative activity would be proscribed—that is, when the speaker enters the cultural sanctity of the marriage bed. Heteronormativity is staged so that its primacy might be emptied. Ginsberg's poem, then, is the politically contestatory version of Whitman's fantasy. Homoerotic desire irrupts within hegemonic heterosexuality, represented by the marriage union and, in turn, questions the normative primacy of heterosexuality. Polyamorous activity in Ginsberg's poem is rendered in narrative, as realist discourse, suggesting that the phantasm of the poem might not be found in the boundary between the ghostly speaker and the married couple but instead in the materialist boundary that separates the heterosexual from the homosexual. The poem furthermore implies that as this boundary is breached, the ensuing rupture asserts a familiar narrative in which the naturalization of the heterosexuality depends on the pathologization of homosexuality. Culturally coded norms of femininity and masculinity, too, collapse into a "throbbing contraction" of particularly anonymous "bellies" (*Collected* 115). The normative boundaries of gender and sexuality collapse. In their wake, the poem stages what Judith Butler would describe as subversive sexual parody—a tactic that, in her words, "depriv[es] the naturalizing narratives of compulsory heterosexuality of their central protagonists: 'man' and 'woman'" (146). The poem openly confronts the naturalization of heterosexual desire as it revels in its secretive, ambisexual pleasures. Pleasure is dramatized as an erosion of the hierarchies that privilege male-coded subjects over female-coded subjects and that are circumscribed by the naturalization of heterosexuality.

Just so, as a poem predicated upon a sexual-political gesture that is secret—hence, privatizing—the poem is not in itself an emancipatory avowal of a queer imperative. Specifically, on the politics of gender and sexuality, Butler offers the reminder of the political potential of narrating the failure to transgress: "The injunction *to be* a given gender produces necessary failures, a variety of incoherent configurations that in their multiplicity exceed and defy the injunction by which they are generated" (145).[15] The speaker's omnivorous fantasy stages itself "all before the mind wakes, behind shades and closed doors in a darkened house" (115). The fantasy might be no more than an isolated, masturbatory awakening, a solitary gesture that cannot exceed, for Ginsberg, the pressures of heterosexual desire because it never makes itself known in a public, communal arena.[16] The poem takes place in the dark, and its actions are shrouded. The speaker awakens in a setting seethed, moreover, in gloom: "[. . .] the mind wakes, behind shades and closed doors in a darkened house / where the inhabitants roam unsatisfied in the night, / nude ghosts seeking each other out in silence" (115). This is a poem in which ambisexual anonymity—a threesome of "hot hips and buttocks screwed into each other"—would seem itself an act that screws matrimony's hegemony. Yet, the speaker nevertheless awakens in a world where his transgressive fantasy occurs only in secret. The ghost who once stole himself between a naked bride and groom is consigned to the role of wandering shade at the end of the poem. This love poem revises the discourse that authorizes it, engaging more explicitly and politically Whitman's "theme" from "Song of Myself." However, like the section from "Song of Myself" that it echoes, the self sung in this poem fails to enact unmediated nonnormative desire, and a heterosexual imperative still reigns beyond the poet's imagination (Whitman) and the poet's "shades and closed doors" (Ginsberg).

Heterosexual hegemony is recast as a capitalist version of Whitman's "procreative urge" in Ginsberg's 1961 poem "This Form of Life Needs Sex," where Whitman's theme again is revisited and found lacking. Crucially, the poem anticipates the role of Buddhism and desire in "Angkor Wat"; anxiety and fear of death dominate "This Form of Life Needs Sex." The poet turns to a marketplace lexicon, representing himself as a "homosexual capitalist afraid of the masses" whose fear of death creates a wish to reproduce himself despite his overwhelming fear of women (*Collected* 284). As a "homosexual capitalist afraid of the masses," he is a potential supplier who fears the very demand he wishes to create, a capitalist Quixote doomed to failure from the start. He, nevertheless, seeks a "woman Futurity" from whom might issue forth "my own cockbrain replica Me-Hood" as a way of evading death, his "fear of the Blot" (*Collected* 284). This mythic futurity recalls and revises the painful, quasi-incestuous past with his mother, Naomi, depicted in "Kaddish," revisiting the most abject images of feminity in Ginsberg's body of work and not, as in "Kaddish," to elegize someone else but instead to elegize his own futurity, to mourn the children he never will have. The mythic woman in "This Form of Life Needs Sex" is a "living meat-phantom" whose "hang of pearplum / fat tissue" the speaker finds "abhorr[ent]" (*Collected* 284)." For Whitman, lived experience is the sum of each individual's "procreative urge."

Writing within this tradition, Ginsberg asks what can be produced from male-male desire; this is a problematic question for Ginsberg, as a poet, inasmuch as procreation falls outside the boundaries of the lineage he inherits from Whitman. To be sure, poems as cultural productions can themselves become figures of gestation and reproduction. Yet, the solitary, unsettling ending of "This Form of Life Needs Sex" suggests that, as in "Love Poem on Theme by Whitman," a cultural artifact is an unsatisfying, bloodless representation of the productions of desire.

Whitman's exuberant procreative urge is sexually unsatisfying for the speaker in these early poems that fuse lust and anxiety. Desire is represented as a capitalist sum of sperm produced, all of which leads to nothing, in a solitary cosmos whose pleasures fade overnight into "trickle[s]" and leave, as their remainder, an unfulfilled romanticist wish for a "replica Me-Hood" that might be generated from same-gender sexual union:

> You can fuck a statue but you can't
>   have children
> You can joy man to man but the Sperm
>   comes back in a trickle at dawn [. . .]
>
>   (*Collected* 285)

As mentioned earlier, Ginsberg reaches back to Whitman as a model for a Buddhist poetics in which both body and mind are engaged with equal emphasis. Yet, the intertextual echoes of Whitman's enthusiasm are threatened by the cultural pressures of a heterosexual, procreative imperative that asserts, "You can fuck a statue but you can't have children."

Thus, despite Ginsberg's self-fashioned Beat liberationist mythmaking—iconographically communicated, for example, in the ecstatic "Human Be-In" image—the embodied spiritual poetics he crafts in "Angkor Wat" is suffused, nevertheless, with anxiety. Ginsberg described in "Kaddish" that his unrequited desire for his high-school classmate Paul Roth brought him to study at Columbia University, where Roth was a student and where, of course, the literary and cultural counterstatements of the Beat Generation were launched. Roth recurs as a symbol of unfulfilled desire in "Angkor Wat." Roth is an untouchable fantasy, a flashback as the speaker flies from India to Cambodia. However, in this poem, Roth's inaccessibility is the product of the poet's quarrel with Western religious prohibition. "Jumping in and out of space," the poet is inspired to return to the "Graham Avenue past, and stare out the / window happily at

Paul R—/ passing down the 1942 Broadway [. . .]" (*Collected* 322). From the memory of Roth, the poet leaps to a critical juncture in his religious development, where desire and sacred experience are crucially interconnected. Immediately upon envisioning Roth walking down Broadway, the speaker recalls "the gothic church, the alleys and / Synagogues of Mea Shearim [. . .]" (*Collected* 322). This conjunction of his desire for Roth and his emphasis on Mea Shearim, contemporary Jerusalem's Orthodox Hasidic section, implies that for Ginsberg homosexual desire is inextricable from the efforts of traditional Western religion to contain such desire. Ginsberg's notes are more than just gloss on the poems. They also serve a didactic purpose; in this instance, a specific rhetorical emphasis on the allure of the religious traditions that both authorize his spiritual poetics and exert coercive pressure on such poetics to de-emphasize desire. In his 1986 annotations to "Howl," his footnotes are more than explanatory, and instead they are meant as hints to inspire his younger readers to investigate the same source material that inspired him; his notes are "hints" that are "dropped" for his most favored readers, as Whitman, too, dropped such hints to his "fancied" readers (*Howl* 126).[17] His notes on "Angkor Wat" suggest that his juxtaposition of memories of Roth and the Mea Shearim synagogues echoes the "hymnless" and "Heavenless" heresy that frames his revisionary Kaddish prayer in "Kaddish" (*Collected* 212).

Yet, as often is the case in Ginsberg's revisionary poetics of prophecy, his studies in the spiritual traditions of the East reenvision his assertions of Western sacred experience:

>   Jerusalem's hated Walls—
> I couldn't get over to the Holy Side and weep
>   where I was supposed to by History
>   Laws got confused stamped
>   in my passport, lost in the refugee
>   Station at Calcutta.
>
>   (*Collected* 322)

Jerusalem's "hated Walls"—memories of his first visit to Israel, taken that same year—are erected in the poem as soon as the Broadway fantasy image of Paul Roth is articulated. These walls prevent him from acting on his fantasy, thereby blocking his desire to "get over to the Holy Side" of sexual expression "and weep." Bureaucratic mistakes send him instead to a scene that enacts the refuge prayer of "Angkor Wat, as the speaker finds himself in the "refugee / Station at Calcutta." As in "Kaddish," the religiosity of Western "refugees" is engaged in a revisionary gesture underwritten by Eastern ways of knowing and crafted specifically to account for the politics of desire (*Collected* 214). But Ginsberg's Buddhist study in the early 1960s did not necessarily help him create a language for Queer Dharma. Indeed, the revelatory "saintly motorcyclists" of "Howl" become "Motorcyclists crying together" in the sexless fantasies of the speaker in "Angkor Wat." As in "This Form of Life Needs Sex," the urge to *recreate* is stalled by the protagonist's vain urge to *procreate*. Ginsberg speaks of a reenvisioned Buddhism that might admit queer desire in "Angkor Wat"; yet, as the poem progresses, his syncretic vision is undermined every time that the phrase "give up desire for children" is uttered. To abandon the wish to have children is, for the speaker, tantamount to an urge to "give up—this Prophesy": the impossible choice of the poem requires either an abandonment of Whitman's procreative urge or an abandonment of his Buddhist poetics.

Asceticism and Desire

Parenthood is another challenge in Ginsberg's development of a Buddhist poetics—parenthood is a figure for death anxiety in "Angkor Wat," as it is in "This Form of Life Needs Sex." "Angkor Wat" demonstrates that Ginsberg's spiritual quest in the early 1960s was grounded in a newfound asceticism, a response to his fear of death—a marked departure from poems such as "Howl" and "Kaddish," in which self-dissolution was imperative in the rhetorical strategies of the poems. Equally important, Ginsberg's confluence of mythology and history is crucial to the construction of a language for vision in the poem. For Sitaram Onkar Das Thakur, an Indian teacher and proponent of asceticism he met in the holy city of Benares in December 1962, just months before the composition of "Angkor Wat," Ginsberg's desire to procreate represented an overdetermined emphasis on selfhood—an attachment to Me-hood that needed to be overcome rather than embraced as part of the poet's spiritual quest. Based as it was on Das Thakur's teachings, the renunciation of desire was anything but a gesture of easy Easternness as Ginsberg's anxieties accumulated after "Howl" and "Kaddish." Das Thakur's asceticism becomes a model, albeit a difficult one, for Ginsberg at the time; and eventually the teacher appears in Ginsberg's premantra "invocation" in "Wichita Vortex Sutra," where Das Thakur is described as one of the

"Lords / of human kingdoms," specifically as he "who commands / give up your desire" (*Collected* 406).

In his 1968 dedication to *Indian Journals*, Ginsberg refers more specifically to Das Thakur in language that suggests the guru's relevance to a poem such as "Angkor Wat," written within a year of the India travels documented in *Indian Journals*. The dedicatory remarks to Das Thakur include:

> [Das Thakur] advised quitting onions meat sex cigarettes in order to find a Guru by repeating the mantra Guru Guru Guru Guru Guru Guru three weeks continuously (and also said, "Give up desire for children,") which led to conversation on bamboo platform in Ganges with Dehorava Baba who spake "Oh how wounded, how wounded!" after I fought with Peter Orlovsky.

Ginsberg's invocation of mantra speech here is both mythologizing and historical, which might be expected, given his eventual tendencies toward a Tibetan version of Buddhism. As James Burnell Robinson notes of Tibetan hagiography, the Tibetan emphasis on both historiography and myth produces a textual history unlike that seen in India: in Tibetan sacred biography, language functions as a representation of both immanence and transcendence. The transhistorical emphasis of biographies of Tibetan masters is matched by the "claim of these stories to historicity" (67). As such, for Robinson, the Buddhist saints in these narratives "represent continuity; they bind the great [sacred] figures of the past to our own history-bound humanity," which results in an "affirmation of the sacred in the processes of history in which we all live" (67). Much the same is at work in Ginsberg's modulation of Indian and Buddhist legacies of mantra speech for his own Buddhist spiritual and poetic practice. As language passed down from one spiritual master to another in an unbroken lineage, the mantra is considered a sacred speech act in Hinduism and Buddhism. Yet *as language*, the mantra is ostensibly materialist—and, as repetitive language, the mantra is for Ginsberg a resignifying practice. This confluence of sacred history and material language emerges from Ginsberg's own words in the dedication, where the sheer repetition of "Guru" over a three-week period is portrayed as a speech act that, Ginsberg is told, would create the conditions for the poet to find a teacher.

Das Thakur further counsels him to adopt ascetic bodily habits and in doing so invokes archetypal notions of a guru-student relationship, in which the hierarchy between guru and student is rigidly demarcated and is authorized by the obedient student's willingness to choose the renunciatory over the worldly. At the same time, Das Thakur's asceticism is curiously never quite separated from desire in Ginsberg's dedication. Das Thakur's ascetic declarative, along with Ginsberg's claim of three weeks of mantra chanting, leads to a decidedly materialist "conversation" with Dehorava Baba, another of the "Lords / of human kingdoms" in "Wichita Vortex Sutra." Dehorava Baba privileges the productions of desire; rather than advise Ginsberg to "qui[t]" his sexual restlessness, Dehorava Baba simply commiserates with the poet's resulting lovesick, wounded condition. The archaic "spake," of which Ginsberg is fond of using to elevate the ordinary to the mythic, suggests that Baba's language for desire is as sacred as Das Thakur's admonitions against desire.

Ginsberg's definitive accounts of his early-career spiritual pilgrimage to Asia, recounted in prose in *Indian Journals* and in poetry in "Angkor Wat," are framed by a contradictory language of both asceticism and desire, with both tendencies mythologized. Buddhism still is foreign to Ginsberg at this time; and he experiences its otherness through contradiction just as often as coherence, in which the mythopoetic is invoked even as Buddhism's relentless materialism is articulated. In later poems such as "Wichita Vortex Sutra" and "Guru Om," the remarks of Das Thakur and Dehorava Baba return as an authoritative language for the spiritual pilgrimages of Western Buddhist students. Eventually, by the early 1970s, Ginsberg's contradictory deployment of asceticism and desire is portrayed by the poet as a dialectical framework in the Tantric mode of Buddhism taught to the poet by Trungpa and, later, Gehlek Rinpoche.[18]

Ginsberg's struggle to reenvision Buddhism as a Queer Dharma is one of the most significant influences "Angkor Wat" exerts on his development of a Buddhist poetics. What remains as a stubborn residue of his mix of asceticism and desire in "Angkor Wat" is Das Thakur's admonition to "Give up desire for children." Undertaken under the duress of this admonition, "Angkor Wat" faces the paradox of creating a Queer Dharma from the ruins of the Cambodian temple, while it undertakes this task of recreation within a sacred teleology of asceticism. With the body in "Angkor Wat" cast as the locus of spiritual crisis, Das Thakur's ascetic message does not induce vision and instead creates the conditions for the speaker's obsessive paranoia. Das Thakur and by extension the Hindu tradition that authorizes him as guru serve as a force of delimitation against which the speaker's appetites collide. The speaker of "Angkor Wat" internalizes Das Thakur's disciplinary "warnings in dream" at the same time that he fixates on vegetable pleasures. This confluence of discipline and pleasure results in paranoid obsession "with meat, smoking, ganja / sex, cannibal spies" (*Collected* 307). Rather than encourage an expansive vision, the teachings of Das Thakur lead Ginsberg to fear, discipline, and inaction borne of obsessive fantasy. These anxieties subsequently influence Ginsberg's language for embodied, sacred experience in "The Change."

By the time of "Angkor Wat," Ginsberg already had established himself as a poet of candor; the success of the confessional mode of "Howl" and "Kaddish," as well as his victory in the "Howl" obscenity trial, would suggest that by the composition of "Angkor Wat," he viewed his utterances as anything but hesitant or anxious. Yet, a procreative imperative suffused his work during this period; and where prophecy once was a matter of proclaiming the world "Holy," ugliness and all, in "Footnote to Howl," the anxious pilgrimage of "Angkor Wat" suggests that visionary experience was no longer a question of simply naming the world visionary and summarily being done with it, especially in a world where the poet's sexual identity conflicted with his religiosity. Even Naomi, "from whose pained head [he] first took Vision" in "Kaddish," is now reduced to a disciplinary reminder that Ginsberg's refusal to participate in a heterosexual procreative economy in "Angkor Wat" brings him closer to an anxious void: "Ever Naomi in my ear—a sad case of refusing to / grow up give birth to die" (*Collected* 223; 313). When he views the beatific smile of Angkor Wat's gigantic statue of Avalokiteshvara, the Buddha of compassion, he sees nothing redemptive. Instead, he is reminded of the anxieties of his attraction to men, leading him to ask himself why he does not "even faintly desire those / black silk girls in the alley of this / clean new tourist city" (*Collected* 313).[19]

Failure as Redemption

Thus far, I have explored how the inspiration of Whitman's procreative urge reaches a troubled apex in "Angkor Wat," a poem vexed by coercive heterosexuality and fear of death. Despite these anxieties, the poem is important to Ginsberg's development of a Buddhist poetics that would not reject desire and appetite. Ginsberg's rhetoric of vision in the poem is framed by a dialectic of asceticism and desire. Responding to the difficulties of this uneasy fusion, the poem dramatizes the speaker's effort to obey Das Thakur's ascetic imperative and his subsequent struggles with parallel impulses toward both renunciation and desire. Even though the poet's reputation is that of a liberating hedonist, asceticism and desire exist in a crucial dialectical relationship in his work, a dyad that resembles that of sobriety and drug use in his poetry of the mid-1960s. Ginsberg's drug experiments function as explorations of subjectivity and poetic composition rather than only as recreational indulgence. In his notes to "Angkor Wat," which appear in the original Fulcrum Press edition (1968) and are reproduced in *Collected Poems, 1948–1980*, Ginsberg informs readers that the poem was composed with the aid of morphine as an attempt to evade the censoriousness of self-consciousness. More important, these notes suggest that Ginsberg's attempt to evade self-censorship is inspired and authorized by his Buddhist practice; he even implies that the composition of his drug-influenced improvisatory poem was blessed by his presence at the Angkor Wat complex. As quoted earlier in this chapter, he tells readers that the poem was written as "a transcription of passages of consciousness in the author's mind made somnolent by an injection of morphine-atrophine [*sic*]" and "adjacent" to Angkor Wat. According to Ginsberg's notes, the only section of the poem not written under the influence of morphine was an impressionistic account of Angkor Thom, one of the adjacent temples in the Angkor Wat complex; this account was composed from "notes taken earlier that day high on ganja (pot) on the roof of the temple of Angkor Thom" (*Collected* 772).

As such, the poem continues the cultural work of "Howl" and "Kaddish," in which an adjacent Buddhism plays a central role in creating an apocalyptic selfhood. That is, these poems create a rhetoric of vision in which the belief in an independent, essentialist subjectivity is reenvisioned as an experience of shunyata consciousness as a model of Buddhist subjectivity, one continually created and re-created from the fluctuations of intersubjective experience. "Angkor Wat" dramatizes a rhetoric of vision in which the ancient Buddhist ruins of the Angkor complex adjacent to the poet underwrite a poetics of "transcription[s] of passages of consciousness" rather than a poetics of craft, wit, or finish. Adjacency is preferred over precision; "passages of consciousness" preferred to ontological trust. In Dwight Goddard's translation of the Four Noble Truths, one of Ginsberg's earliest Buddhist textual sources, the Buddha asserts that a precondition for enlightened experience is an apocalyptic consciousness, an "extinction of consciousness"—i.e., an "extinction" of a self-consciousness otherwise

Queer Dharma, Anxiety, and Fantasy in "Angkor Wat"

grounded in essentialist subjectivity. The Buddha states in Goddard's translation of the sutra that "one may rightly say of me, that I teach annihilation, that I propound my doctrine for the purpose of annihilation . . . the annihilation namely of greed, anger, and delusion" (41–42).

Despite the influences of Goddard's translation, "Angkor Wat" is troubled by the adjacency, rather than direct engagement, of its Buddhist sources. The primary influences of "Angkor Wat"—morphine, marijuana, and Buddhism—are consistent with Ginsberg's efforts in his career to meld his social and aesthetic experiments into a poetics in which the boundaries among art, vision, and consciousness are porous. Yet, the poem suggests that its own poetic strategies fail. The poem is riven by its emphasis on an alteration of consciousness through a process of "annihilation," to quote Goddard's translation of the Four Noble Truths, in which drugs and Buddhism fail to perform as transformative "technologies of the self"[20] for Ginsberg at this period in his career. Indeed, as evidence of failure, in the Angkor Thom section, Ginsberg exclaims, "Buddha save me, what am / I doing here / again." If the poem's speaker were not already so self-obsessed, this moment would seem an ironic counterstatement to Judeo-Christian metaphysics. Instead, this passage of the poem misreads Buddhism, a result of the limitations of Ginsberg's autodidactic study of the tradition. One of the more well-known stories in Buddhist mythos recounts the Buddha's inability to "save" even his own cousin Devadatta from a terrifying rebirth in a "hell realm" that resulted from a careless life.[21] In short, to proclaim "Buddha save me" is for Buddhists to state the impossible. This misreading of Buddhist tradition in "Angkor Wat" emerges from the speaker's paranoid attention to the physical solidities of selfhood. Yet, the speaker's paranoia is critical to his transformative experience in "The Change." Anxiety is an influence that produces in this instance linguistic confusion for the speaker—what he describes as a lurching "meat/death/mind-soup," a clumsy locution that enacts the speaker's confusion at the moment it is articulated. As the poet attempts to evade the univocal perils of self-consciousness in a fragmented, surreal form, he simultaneously is "confus[ed]" by this same process.

As I discuss in the following chapter, the perils of collage language—confusion and fragmentation—are transformed in "The Change" as part of Ginsberg's construction of a performative language for sacred experience. Thus, "The Change" confirms Lehman's analysis of the role of Surrealist collage in "Angkor Wat" but extends such a reading so that Surrealism becomes a mode of sacred practice; the poem performs the Surrealist ethos that Lehman finds lacking. Ginsberg's most well-known example of such poetics is the metapoetic declaration at the end of part I of "Howl" that the poem is shaped by the deliberately absurdist production of "incarnate gaps in Time & Space through images juxtaposed" (*Collected* 130). Still, "Angkor Wat" is suffused with a crippling "meat/death" anxiety, a "mind-soup" of obsessive paranoia unlike the famous "images juxtaposed" of the post–World War II politics in "Howl," whose protagonists suffer as they listen to a similarly confused "hydrogen jukebox" (*Collected* 126). Thus, the topoi of "Angkor Wat"—the recovery of an embodied spiritual practice (for Ginsberg, a Queer Dharma) and the expansion of consciousness through drug use—are also the very elements that threaten to disable the poem. Ginsberg's revision of Buddhism as a Queer Dharma is troubled by his speaker's fixation on propagation of the skin, and this procreation anxiety is worsened by morphine and marijuana. Death anxiety is, he writes, "[w]hat happens to me when I get high" (*Collected* 306).

Read within the poem's wartime historical context, this failure of a Surrealist Queer Dharma ironically sustains Ginsberg's rhetoric of vision in the poem and anticipates the redemptive spiritual journey of "The Change." U.S. involvement in Vietnam repeatedly interrupts the speaker's pilgrimage. War, in this instance, represents figurally the limits of privatizing self-consciousness. Amid the banyan trees branching around the Avalokiteshvara statue at the Angkor complex, Ginsberg's speaker is acutely aware of "american husbands in sportshirts [. . .] / on holiday from US Army Saigon" who snake around the streets of Siemreap and inhabit its hotels (308–9). As he performs the *abhaya mudra*, a Buddhist hand-gesture to invoke calmness that later appears in "The Change," he sees himself as "[n]othing but a false Buddha afraid of / my own annihilation" (*Collected* 310).[22] Immediately following this anxious admission, he acknowledges that the legacy of Amiri Baraka's racial politics—and Baraka's break with his fellow Beats over their inattention to race—as an extension of the speaker's fear of death. As discussed earlier, Ginsberg's estimation of himself as a public figure, his emerging internationalist consciousness, circumscribed his work during the composition of "Kaddish" and authorized the international travel that led to the pilgrimage of "Angkor Wat." However, faced with the realities of sickness and aging, Ginsberg adopts a public persona of failure in "Angkor Wat," describing himself as a poet running in cowardice from the war machine—one whose social activism is inadequate when compared to that of fellow artists such as Baraka, whose life-changing trip to Cuba had occurred just three years earlier in 1960.

These anxieties of influence, a past heritage of avant-garde poetics from Apollinaire to contemporary representations in Baraka and the work of fellow Beats, are themselves reconceived in a Buddhist poetics that highlights the influence of anxiety. As I discuss in chapter 4, Ginsberg's poetics of anxiety in "Wichita Vortex Sutra" describes the Vietnam War's fragmented bodies in language that is itself fragmented. The improvisatory, tapevoice composition technique of "Wichita" shatters linearity—a mimetic strategy that reveals the wartime complicity of a mass media whose images of "boys with sexual bellies aroused" are subjected to "bomb blast terrific in skull & belly" and become "shrapneled throbbing meat" (*Collected* 404, 402). It is important to note that this technique in "Wichita" is anticipated in "Angkor Wat": the body in "Angkor Wat" is one route to a sacred discourse, yet it also is a fragile instrument of war always already marked by impermanence. The speaker of the poem fantasizes about procreation as a means of establishing himself as permanent, an ultimately failed proposition in the poem. This fantasy forecasts "Iron Horse," the companion poem to "Wichita," in which Ginsberg's failure to create a multivocal communitarian vision is articulated as a failure borne of solipsistic masturbation fantasies. In the "meat/death" of "mind-soup," Ginsberg's speaker in "Iron Horse" eventually surrenders his desires "wet handed by meat sex" (*Collected* 311). Amid his efforts to meet a Cambodian boy in "Angkor Wat" and his efforts to voice collaged, multivocal sacred poetics, the speaker is haunted by conflicting impulses of desire and asceticism in a country where U.S. forces are covertly launching a war: soldiers on holiday in "sportshirts" are superimposed on Angkor Wat's Avalokiteshvara, and the speaker's sexual fantasies are reduced to images of bodily destruction represented in monologic language and framed by masturbation. As the poem ends with these failures of voice and desire, the speaker worries over "which bullet which airplane which nausea / be the dreadful doomy last / begun" (*Collected* 323). The poem never evades self-consciousness. Its authorizing linguistic form is the internal monologue, and the best the speaker can accomplish is a solitary "cold coffee at / Midnight" (*Collected* 323). Unlike Ginsberg's earlier apocalyptic epics, "Howl" and "Kaddish," apocalypse in "Angkor Wat" does not produce the promise of rebirth through a multivocal, conversational language for prophecy. Instead, the poem prophesies destruction. It stages the annihilation of the "meat" body in language underwritten by a nervous metaphysics of presence; its annihilation of self-consciousness is a fantasy framed by variously vocalized representations of the Buddhist notion of nonduality.

Significantly, this frail coexistence of Western teleology and Eastern beginninglessness creates a liminal, transformative experience for the speaker of "The Change." Read as paired poems of a singular spiritual pilgrimage, "Angkor Wat" and "The Change" blur the boundary between Western thought, seen in the traces of Ginsberg's authorizing Blake vision, and Eastern thought, represented in his emerging Buddhist practice. This East-West collision produces anxiety in "Angkor Wat" and a nightmare vision in "The Change." However frightening the visionary experience of "The Change" might be for its speaker, the poem is more than just an expression of terror. As I discuss in the following chapter, "The Change" is a deliberate experiment to merge otherwise incompatible notions of Western ontological certainty and the shunyata experience of selfhood that marks Buddhist teachings on nonduality.

3

The Two Truths of "The Change"

> One wants to have visions because one thinks that one's ordinary reality, ordinary consciousness is not visionary enough. Which is a big stink everybody has about themselves—everybody—that their body is awful, their mind is awful. Being who you are is awful enough without being *that* awful!
>
> —Allen Ginsberg, 1978

Truths of the Body

In "The Change," Ginsberg recasts the anxieties of "Angkor Wat" as a problem of creating an embodied, sacred language that does not lapse into hedonism or escape into transcendentalism. Michael Schumacher, Barry Miles, and Paul Portugés have observed that Ginsberg's 1963 visit to India helped him shake his obsession with using drugs to reexperience his Blake vision of 1948. Critics are in consensus that Ginsberg's Eastern influence at the time proffered an embodied alternative to the corporeal evasions of the poet's drug use. Schumacher describes the "change" of the poem as a substantial reenvisioning of spiritual purpose for Ginsberg: "For fifteen years, Ginsberg had been trying to find *God*—in death, in poetry, in other forms of consciousness" (*Dharma Lion* 394-95). "The Change," he argues, represents Ginsberg's eventual desire "to find God in the self and accept what he discovers" (*Dharma Lion* 395). This quest is both a continuation and revision of Ginsberg's self-fashioning as a poet-prophet begun in "Howl": "Despite a substantial ego that led him to make prophetic statements in his poetry that led him to believe that he possessed a voice worth hearing, Ginsberg had never accepted himself—not entirely, at least, not in a way that ended his quest" (*Dharma Lion* 395). Ginsberg turned to drugs in the past to create a language for prophecy; his trip to India, in contrast, redirected his poetic and spiritual experiments inward. Miles notes that while in India "he had questioned the validity of his search for a means to higher consciousness, and by the time he reached Japan he had already changed his position a good deal" (326). This change amounted to a reconsideration of the role of drug use in his prophetic poetry. According to Miles, "Joanne Kyger, in her journals, noted that [Ginsberg] no longer spoke about the significance of his drug visions when he stayed with them [Kyger and Gary Snyder] in Kyoto" (326). As Portugés notes in *The Visionary Poetics of Allen Ginsberg*, the poet met with Swami Shivananda in India, where the Swami "direct[ed] Ginsberg to his heart" as an effort to instruct the poet to "stop trying to transcend the body" (93). Ginsberg reports to Tom Clark in his famous 1966 *Paris Review* interview that he was "reassure[d]" by the swami's assertion, "Your heart is your guru" ("Art" 47).[1] Indeed, Schumacher argues, "Returning to the body meant being aware of it, and in India and the Orient [Ginsberg] had found two practical ways of accomplishing this: mantra chanting and meditation" (396).

At the same time, Ginsberg's reading of Blake—specifically, with attention to Blake's embodied representations of the divine—was inextricable from his experiences in India, Cambodia, and Japan. In the *Paris Review* interview, Ginsberg explains to Clark that the swami's words, like those of other holy men the poet met in India, brought him back to an aspect of Blake's influence that his drug use at this stage had obscured. The affirmative rhetoric of "Howl" and "Kaddish"—the embodied mercy and sacred physicality of vision important to Ginsberg in both poems—anticipates what the poet realized in India in 1963: both poems enact Blake's famous "human form divine," in which the human (immanent) and the divine (transcendent) are united in one form. As Ginsberg describes to Clark, these Indian teachers "pointed back to the body—getting *in* the body rather than getting out of the human form. [. . .] living in and inhabiting the human form. Which then goes back to Blake again, the human form divine" ("Art" 48). "Howl" and "Kaddish" inaugurated an embodied poetics that Ginsberg could not sustain at this point in his career. However, his 1963 Asian travels produced a period of corrective transition portrayed in the spiritual journeys of "Angkor Wat" and "The Change." As he says to Clark, "the Asian experience kind of got me out of the corner I painted myself in with drugs. [. . .] It finally would get so if I'd take the drugs I'd start vomiting. But I felt that I was duly bound and obliged for the sake of consciousness expansion, and this insight, and breaking down my identity, and seeking more contact with primate sensation, nature, to continue" ("Art" 46-47). Drugs were both an obstacle and obligation in Ginsberg's effort to expand his range of consciousness. While in India, Ginsberg re-envisioned his past drug influences in terms of a Blake-Buddhist fusion of body-speech-mind poetics rather than a flight into transcendentalism. The obsession with the Blake vision forced him out of his body, looking for an external technology for expanded consciousness—in drug use, especially LSD, peyote, mescaline, and psilocybin; this disembodied pilgrimage was, as he describes to Clark, a search for a "technique for experimenting with consciousness" ("Art" 44). As I argued earlier, this experience with drugs was not just recreational; it was part of a pilgrimage for him, a "duly bound" obligation to explore the frontiers of consciousness while, paradoxically, reducing consciousness to "primate sensation." In this way, Ginsberg's use of drugs as a "technique" to combine disembodied transcendentalism and sensate experience echoes his search for a primal language for vision in "Howl" and "Kaddish"—that is, a language both "mystical" and "commonsensical," as in "Howl," or "Backroom metaphysics" and schizoid babble, as in "Kaddish." His experiences with Indian teachers convinced him that he should not abandon his efforts to craft a poetics of embodied representations of the sacred. The India journey affirmed his desire to develop a Buddhist poetics in which the metaphysical might be experienced in concrete, particular, immanent lived experience; eventually, this poetics emerges as one that proceeds from the emphasis on body, speech, and mind taught by Buddhism.

As important as Blake is in Ginsberg's prophetic lineage, Ginsberg would assert later that "The Change" dramatizes the means by which he eventually shook his attachment to the Blake vision and whereby he cautioned himself, more importantly, against the impulse to re-reify this vision. Describing his drug experiences after the Blake vision to a 1976 Naropa Poetics class, Ginsberg says that his drug use from 1948 to 1963 constituted an effort to "get back into" the "eternity" he had experienced during the Blake vision ("Complete" 42). Ginsberg notes that his drug experiences during this time were unsatisfactory, often addled with anxiety, because of his persistent fears that the drugs would not allow him to return to the "eternity" of the 1948 vision. His encounter during the 1963 Asia trip with Tibetan lama Dujom Rinpoche, soon after the visit with Swami Shivananda, was crucial in this regard. Dujom Rinpoche is one of the many dedicatees in *Indian Journals*. Ginsberg writes in the dedication that Rinpoche "sucked air through his teeth in sympathy calming my fears of LSD hallucination and advised 'If you see anything horrible don't cling to it if you see anything beautiful don't cling to it.'" Rinpoche's admonition on "cling[ing]" was important enough to Ginsberg that he repeated it frequently in interviews and lectures, applying it equally to discussions of drug use and to Buddhist doctrinal questions. Such advice inspired Ginsberg to reenvision his poetics to reflect a rhetoric of vision more consistently focused on the body as a sacred intersection of both immanent and transcendent experience. Ginsberg tells the Naropa classroom that Rinpoche's comment "actually cut the Gordian knot of my mind," allowing him the chance to see how he "had been clinging constantly to the memory of a vision," a clinging that, in turn, had alienated him "from direct perception, whether it was visionary or ordinary" (43). Thus, according to Ginsberg, as his Buddhist practice deepened, the body eventually became a central trope where visionary (transcendental) and ordinary (immanent) experience were staged coequivalently.

Still, mindful of the body anxieties of "Angkor Wat," it is tempting to read a transcendentalist impulse into "The Change." Portugés, the only critic who has written extensively on "The Change," argues that the poem is "Ginsberg's attempt at mystical exorcism" (*Visionary Poetics* 96). This remark is true enough, given Ginsberg's privileging of the immanent body over transcendentalism in the poem and in his commentaries on the poem. Nevertheless, Portugés's assertion does not engage fully the contradiction Ginsberg is working within: after all, if the poem indeed "exorcises" the mystical, then it must do so with the mystical sensibility inherent in exorcism itself, as a mystical practice conceived to purge demonic possession. The poem instead is notable most of all for its forging of a sacred language that reenvisions drug use, transforming its mystical representations in

"Angkor Wat" into an embodied obstacle and obligation that, eventually, is subsumed into the materialist rigors of Buddhist practice. Portugés usefully traces "The Change" to the Satipatthana Sutra, a Buddhist text that focuses on the materiality of the body, its impermanence, and its eventual death. Thus, the very conceptual framework that for Ginsberg launches the "exorcism" in the first place is the decidedly nonmetaphysical, immanent practice of Buddhism, represented in the poem by the Satipatthana practice and in the poem's echo of its companion piece, "Angkor Wat." Following so closely on the bodily anxiety of his Angkor experience, "The Change" is one of Ginsberg's first poems to document a shift from an anxious transcendentalist obsession to the concrete particulars that appealed to him as both a nascent Buddhist practitioner and a poet who represents himself as an inheritor of the Williams-Zukofsky-Reznikoff objectivist lineage.

"The Change" dramatizes what Ginsberg described in the 1976 lecture as a "continued churning over and over" of his early-career "insistenc[e]" that he could return to the "eternity" of the Blake vision. In this lecture, Ginsberg describes the composition of the poem on the Kyoto-Tokyo express, the setting of "The Change": he "just started crying," his tears a recognition that he "wasn't going to get into heaven." Of course, given his practice in the nontheistic cosmology of Buddhism, this realization was not that he somehow had been abandoned and that he wasn't going to get into a metaphysical location called heaven. Instead, the tears were part of a combined immanent-transcendent visionary experience dramatized in the poem—a heaven representable in language—much the same sort of experience dramatized in "Howl" and "Kaddish." Indeed, as he describes in the 1976 lecture, "the minute I began crying I found myself in heaven again, very briefly"; "The Change" is a poem that "records" this experience of an *immanent* heaven. He notes in the lecture that "The Change" dramatizes a "poignant moment of the slow process of getting the monkey [his reification of the Blake vision] off my back" ("Complete" 44). What is at stake at this point in Ginsberg's career is the construction of a language for vision that dramatizes both a desire for transcendence and a belief in the power of the human imagination to recreate a Blakean (and, significantly for Ginsberg, a Buddhist) human form divine in poetic language.[2] Earlier in his career, both "Howl" and "Kaddish" represented this rhetoric of vision in terms of lyric and narrative elegy, respectively. By 1963, however, after a period of transcendentalist drug use, it was the genre of the spiritual confession that deepened the reenvisioning impulse of Ginsberg's Buddhism: seen in this way, the confessions of "Angkor Wat" lead to the redemptive rhetoric of "The Change." Ginsberg's confessional autobiography, not surprisingly, both continues and revises the tradition of spiritual confessional literature in the West. As might be expected of the literature of spiritual confession tracing back to Augustine, Ginsberg's spiritual confession is one in which autobiography is allegory. But the Western teleological impulse in spiritual confession is reconceived so that the locus of "conversion" is the mind's interaction with the material world—what Buddhism terms the "dependent arising" of phenomena—not the soul's interaction with a metaphysically present God.

The interpretations proffered by Schumacher, Miles, and Portugés of a self-evident, redemptive return to the body in "The Change" require, nevertheless, a greater attention to the nuances of Ginsberg's language. Ginsberg's culminating linguistic gesture is expressed in performative speech; as in his later poems, sacred speech is made representable in the spell-like illocutionary gesture of the performative utterance.[3] Influenced by the power of such language, Ginsberg proclaims, as if uttering an incantation, "In my train seat I renounce / my power, so that I do / live I will die" (*Collected* 329). Moreover, this renunciatory moment in the poem depends for Ginsberg on an embodied poetic sensibility:

> In Russia the young poets rise
>   to kiss the soul of the revolution
>   in Vietnam the body is burned
>   to show the truth of only the
>   body in Kremlin & White House
>   the schemers draw back
>   weeping from their schemes—
>
> (*Collected* 329)

Ginsberg's return to the body is not simply a renewal of sensory experience; instead, it claims the body as both product and producer of political experience. The idealized, ineffable "soul" of the Russian Revolution is tangibly "kiss[ed]" by young Russian poets, and Cold War stratagems of the U.S.S.R. and United States are exposed as propaganda in Vietnam by the burning of bodies—seen exotically as a gesture of purity. Significantly, these burned bodies are part of both sacred ritual and political activism, echoing the Buddhist charnel grounds of the Satipatthana meditation and the political self-immolation of Buddhist monks in Vietnam protesting the

Diem regime. "The Change" was written just two months after the first of the famous self-immolation protests of Vietnamese Buddhist monks, Thich Quang-Doc's suicide on 8 May 1963. Given the strict prohibitions against murder and suicide in Buddhist scripture, the political self-sacrifice of these monks is paradoxical in its representation as a sacred act.[4] Churning as he is over the sacred possibilities of the body, Ginsberg does not seek to resolve the paradox but instead proclaims from the self-immolations that "the body is burned / to show the truth of only the / body." Even the line break, it seems, is uneasy with the idea that *ahimsa*, the Buddhist principle of nonviolence, might be suspended by the monks in this instance.

The body, as desired/desiring and as a sacrificial object, is the locus of imaginative vision in "The Change." The revisionary body politics of the poem are influenced, too, by Ginsberg's extensive reading of Blake, in which the creative imagination and corporeal energy of Poetic Genius transforms observation into vision. "The Change" ends with a vision of a material world both ensouled and embodied by the poetic imagination, much the same way Poetic Genius functions for Blake at the end of "A Vision of the Last Judgment." Ginsberg appropriates from Blake the image of a visionary sun to mediate the relationship between the body and the object of its vision—between seer and seen—and in turn to create a renovating vision of the natural world. At the close of Ginsberg's poem, the sun is described as the poet's "visible father / making my body visible / thru my eyes!" ("Complete" 330). The sun is paternalized but not as the metaphysical "Nobodaddy" of Blake's critique of Christianity; instead, the sun is the poet's "visible father" who enables an embodied visionary poetics.[5] Under the renovating father, Ginsberg's vision in "The Change" is, significantly, one in which the body is a vehicle of Buddhist ideas of nonattachment. The poet detaches from attachment to his 1948 Blake vision. Buddhist nonattachment is a detachment from attachment, not detachment from the self or its material world. Nonattachment constructs a middle-way between absolutism and nihilism and is crucial in the Buddhist notion of the Two Truths, which Ginsberg incorporates into his negotiation of transcendent and immanent modes of representation. As would be expected in Tantric discourse, his efforts to detach from the bodily anxieties produced by his attachment to the vision involve an engagement with the body itself. What becomes, for Ginsberg, a Tantric process of vision is indebted, too, to Blake's similar effort to forge a rhetoric of vision that is embodied at the same time that it keeps the limitations of the body—as an impermanent entity—in the offing. In "A Vision of the Last Judgment," Blake writes, "I question not my Corporeal or Vegetative Eye any more than I would Question a Window concerning a Sight I look thro it & not with it" (566). For Blake, the prophetic artist sees *through* the eye and not *with* it—that is, the prophet is guided by vision, not observation, and thereby reconstructs the natural world as visionary. The famous closing of "A Vision of the Last Judgment" stages this process of imaginative re-envisioning: "When the sun rises do you not see a round Disk of fire somewhat like a Guinea O no no I see an Innumerable company of the Heavenly host crying Holy Holy Holy is the Lord God Almighty" (565-66). Ginsberg explicitly affirms the attraction of "A Vision of the Last Judgment" in his *Paris Review* interview, where he explains how the 1948 Blake vision and the influence of Paul Cézanne combine in his early visionary poetics. Ginsberg argues that Cézanne's visionary "patience" of eye allowed him, like Blake, to "see through his eye," creating a relationship between artist and audience in which viewers might "see through his canvas to God" ("Art" 31). As a trope for religious experience first deployed in "Angkor Wat," the body in "The Change" is not a reificatory vehicle of either extreme of ecstasy or anxiety. Instead, corporeality sanctifies the body as a location between the quotidian and the sacred, creating an intersubjective relationship with the material world in which, as Ginsberg writes, his "Identity [is] now nameless / neither man nor dragon / or God" (*Collected* 330).

Yet, Ginsberg's effort to create an embodied poetics between attachment and aversion and one in which the subject in language is nameless, leaves behind an important residual question. That is, how can the desiring body be identified as such in sacred language without lapsing into an unproductive—and, for Ginsberg, neoplatonic—division of self and soul? An answer can emerge from a revisitation of the 1984 revisionary endnote to "Angkor Wat" discussed in chapter 2. "The Change" anticipates the issues raised by this later endnote, and in doing so, the poem mediates this presumptive split between body and spirit in Western metaphysics. "The Change" provides the "Non-Self interpretation" of the refuge prayer that is missing, according to the 1984 note, in the original 1968 published version of "Angkor Wat." The poem represents the desired and desiring body in a language of contrarieties indebted to the Two Truths. Seen in the context of Buddhist teaching on the Two Truths, the conflicting conceptions of self in the 1968 and 1984 notes coexist in tenuous contradiction with each other.

The doctrine of the Two Truths depends to some extent on the Buddhist practitioner's movement from the solitude of meditative practice and into a community of shared, lived experience with others. Otherwise, the beginningless continuities of mind in Buddhism, the ongoing rebirths of individual consciousness, risk nihilistic solipsism for the individual practitioner.[6] Ginsberg undertakes such a movement in "The Change," transforming the private anxieties of "Angkor Wat" into the social experience of two primary (and contradictory) truths. The body becomes a foundation for absolute truth, while the truth of the body lies in its impermanent foundation, one whose only predictable action is its own dissolution. The poem indeed stages the speaker's acceptance of death, in the tradition to which Portugés refers in his discussions of the poem and the Satipatthana Sutra. For Ginsberg, "the body is burned / to show the truth of only the / body." This singular truth of immanence and destruction is indebted to the Satipatthana Sutra and is of political importance as it rattles "the schemers" in Moscow and Washington. Thus, "the truth of only the / body" is a dyadic truth—a sacred combination, for Buddhists, of relativism and absolutism expressed in the Two Truths, the "heaven" on earth represented in the antimetaphysical conceptual framework encouraged by Buddhist practice.

As a doctrine first propounded by the second-century Indian philosopher Nagarjuna, the Two Truths offer a third term between singularist and mediated experience for Buddhists. The Two Truths also provide Ginsberg a framework from which to forge a middle-way between the tactile reality of the quotidian world and the experience of nonduality (the shunyata, or emptiness, of the world seen through the enlightened eyes of a Buddha). For Buddhist practitioners, the Two Truths suggest an opportunity to engage the reality of objects and persons of lived experience, "objects of knowledge" in Buddhism, rather than deny them as secularized illusion. Materialist, empirical objects of knowledge are a means by which Buddhist practitioners can engage quotidian objects and simultaneously reenvision their own human tendency to reify. The purpose of such engagement is to empty the object of the essentialized identity the subject has imputed on it; the subject transforms the experience of perception into a dialectical engagement between subject and object. Neither subject nor object is said to occupy an absolutist frame of reference. Thus, subject-object distinctions are called into question and revised in the seer-seen relationship presumed by the Two Truths. As Guy Newland describes it, a conscious effort to incorporate the Two Truths into Buddhist practice encourages Buddhists to resist "extremes of permanence," or, in short, to resist "any position that reifies phenomena." The Two Truths disavow nihilism, insofar as nihilism in the Buddhist tradition "deprecates phenomena" by refusing to acknowledge that phenomena exist at all (Newland 59). In short, the Two Truths force Buddhist practitioners from the solitary vicissitudes of contemplative practice into the world—into landscapes marked by desire, appetite, and conflict in "Angkor Wat" and "The Change"—so that practitioners might forge a path that disavows the extremes of both materialism and metaphysics.

The sexual frame of the 1948 Blake vision is recast immediately in the poem as a part of an ambisexual pilgrimage, the beginning of a complex vision of sacred experience that reenvisions Blake's human form divine in terms of queer sexual politics. Ginsberg opens "The Change" with the declarative statement that his speaker has "Come home" (*Collected* 324). However, "home" reiterates the procreation anxieties that undergird "Angkor Wat"—the obsession with "Prop- / agation of this Skin" in "Ankgor Wat" that leads to frustrated masturbation in which the speaker laments his solitary subject position "wet handed by meat sex" (*Collected* 307, 311). In the poem, home is "the pink meat image," a female-coded representation of a "silent soft open vagina / rare womb of new birth" (*Collected* 324). Yet, the female body is for Ginsberg, at best, a transient space upon which to project male-male desire. The poet is home, yet "home" is a female body that functions citationally as masculine rather than feminine. Proclaiming that he is gratified to be touched by another person again, no longer masturbating, the speaker shifts straightaway to images of male-male desire in which the speaker is "waiting for a sign, a throb / softness of balls, rough / nipples alone in the dark / waiting for a weird finger" (*Collected* 324). The act of being touched again brings the speaker to tears. Eventually, the poem creates a language of absolute and relative truth in both Biblical language and the language of pop psychology: "I am that I am" (*Collected* 324). The speaker's movement away from masturbation toward a redemptive, gratifying sexual encounter with another person is a figure for Ginsberg of his movement as a poet away from the solitary Blake vision and toward a conception of vision that includes a larger human community.[7] As he notes in the *Paris Review* interview, the Blake vision occurred while he was alone in his Harlem apartment, just after he had masturbated. Thus, in a poem in which the Blake vision itself is questioned as a reified metaphysical vision for Ginsberg in his construction of an embodied Buddhist poetics, it is crucial that the action that framed the original Blake vision, masturbation, is overwhelmed by "rough / nipples alone in the dark / waiting for a weird finger." The procreation obsession of "Angkor Wat" is bracketed off, and the "rare womb of new birth" in "The Change" becomes a "cock [. . .] touched by hands by mouths, / by hairy lips" (*Collected* 324). Thus, "The Change" opens with a reenvisioning of the body politics of "Angkor Wat"; this revision of its companion poem transvalues the heteronormative procreation anxieties of a poem such as "This Form of Life Needs Sex" into a queer poetics in which Buddhism and same-gender sexual desire are together crucial to the formation of sacred speech. For Ginsberg, Tantric Buddhism is inseparable from Queer Dharma. Such an embodied poetics is under stress by the Vietnam War, and it is this stress that underwrites the movement from "Angkor Wat" to "The Change."

Thus far, in this chapter and the previous one, I have argued that "Angkor Wat" and "The Change" should be read as two parts of the same spiritual pilgrimage because of the proximity of both their composition and their paired subject matter. The multiplicitous "change" the speaker undergoes in "The Change" can be understood substantively in such a reading, as can the influence the poems exert on Ginsberg's nascent Buddhist poetics of the early 1960s. This chapter also suggests that "The Change" creates a language of sacred experience through a valorization, rather than renunciation, of desire. The poem dramatizes the speaker's move from isolation to community, a process framed by Ginsberg's understanding of Buddhism's Two Truths but sexualized, too, as a movement from masturbation (in "Angkor Wat") to partnered sexual encounter (in "The Change"). Moreover, the sexual nature of movement from "Angkor Wat" to "The Change" is politically charged, wherein the speaker reconceives heterosexual procreation anxiety in terms of acceptance, at times celebration, of homosexual desire. Thus, for Ginsberg, "The Change" is articulated at the intersection of cultural, spiritual, and sexual vectors of a Buddhist poetics and serves as a hinge between his early- and mid-career Buddhist poetics.

Naming the Nameless Body

Ginsberg's reenvisioned sexual politics in "The Change" furthermore must contend with a critical paradox: namely, Ginsberg's assertion that the body can enable and sustain sacred experience, as it does in his Blake vision, while he remains mindful that the body cannot maintain its visionary power as it ages and ultimately dies. Thus, he must create a system by which the body is represented as sacred while acknowledging its corporeal reality—its impermanence and fragility, especially during wartime—and he must do so without claiming the metaphysicality usually ascribed to sacred phenomena in the West. "The Change" crafts such a system, recreating identity as an oscillating subjectivity framed by the Two Truths. The Jehovic symbology of Ginsberg's assertion, "I am that I am," eventually is destabilized as part of the "change dramatized in the poem. The unfixed subjectivity of Ginsberg's speaker is influenced by the Satipatthana Sutra's teachings on emptiness and identity—crucial, for Ginsberg, in a Buddhist poetics whose ontological authority privileges Eastern sacred practice over Western in its eschewing of transcendentalism. This exorcism of the mystical, to recast Portugés's formulation, purges not just the speaker's trust in metaphysics, the source of his obsession with the Blake vision but also casts off the authorizing power of the metaphysics of the exorcism ritual itself: the speaker asserts his distrust in Yahweh, whose "I am that I am" assertion offers a conventional glimpse of logocentric authority.[8] Thus, the poem not only changes the *I* at the center, the speaker, but also transforms the context that authorizes the speaker's reificatory subjectivity. Inspired, paradoxically, by the failure of Buddhist perception in "Angkor Wat," Ginsberg portrays the speaker's pilgrimage in "The Change" as a Buddhist one: as a drama of reification in which the speaker's identity eventually is destabilized and—as this process is framed by the Two Truths—resists its own re-reification.

As unusual as the term *re-reification* may sound, it is apt here. The Two Truths recognize the inevitability of the human tendency to reify; that is, they realize our impulse toward "extremes of permanence," as Newland puts it. This concept suggests that only by acknowledging the shunyata quality of human experience—in which subjects and objects exist as interdependent processes of cause and effect, or perception and action—can practitioners become comfortable with the dialogic, relational nature of Buddhist epistemology. Commenting on the Buddhist Middle-Way System's view of consciousness and phenomena epitomized in the Two Truths, Newland asserts that in such a system, "[c]onsciousnesses exist not in and of themselves, but only in relation to other phenomena—as knowers of their objects and as objects appearing to other consciousnesses" (73). Thus, in grappling with the idea of existence at all, the Buddhist practitioner must gradually acquaint him/herself with the idea that in Buddhism, what is called existence is not a privatizing concept but instead a relational one, and the language that creates subjectivity is not monologic but dialogic. Specifically, guided by the Two Truths, the practitioner struggles to reconceive his/her impulses toward singularist, absolutist modes of thought in order to transform them into a decidedly tense middle-way, a desirable though unstable position of conflict between reification and nihilism for Buddhists in which neither condition might assert itself permanently. As a Buddhist and poet, Ginsberg crafts a middle-way in his poetics that is not, then, mere middling indecisiveness cloaked, to recall Whittemore, in an "easy Easternness." Given Ginsberg's earlier remarks on the nightmare visions of his drug experiences, this tension between reification and nihilism is more than just a conceptual exercise, too, in "The Change." The movement from reificatory subjectivity to relational subjectivity in the poem is a tortured one for the speaker.

As section 2 of the poem opens, the speaker vomits, an action that recalls Ginsberg's remarks to Clark about his drug use immediately prior to the Asia trip. The speaker's awful vision continues unabated: a serpent appears crawling in his bed, a consistent trope for the speaker's death in the poem. As he imagines his own death, inspired by the charnel-ground recollections of the Satipatthana Sutra, the speaker sees no hope in the possibility of a redemptive afterlife. He sees a "metallic Bethlehem out the window" ("Complete" 325), which echoes the dehumanizing role of machinery in much of Ginsberg's early work, especially the Urizenic figure of Moloch in "Howl." Bethlehem's promise of redemption, then, is no more hopeful than the Nobodaddy Blake vehemently confronts in his work. The speaker, furthermore, imagines himself as a hungry ghost from Buddhist mythos, an apt image in the dialectic between asceticism and desire in "Angkor Wat" and "The Change": Buddhist hungry ghosts are spirits who have died in the throes of unquenched desire. In Buddhist mythos, hungry ghosts take their desire with them into rebirths as wandering shades, creatures doomed to see and touch their objects of desire but with no bodily means of consummating their appetites. Hungry ghosts often are portrayed as figures with large bellies whose mouths and throats are too small to take in any of the food and drink they desire.[9] As a hungry ghost, Ginsberg's speaker asks plaintively, "How can I / be sent to Hell / with my skin and blood[?]" (325). The speaker answers his own question, affirming that the debilitating power of his reificatory sense of self and his ravenous desires are themselves a figure for hell. He is there already.

These same unrequited cravings that lead to misery in "Angkor Wat" now embody the speaker, as hungry ghost, in "The Change":

> Gasping, staring at dawn over
> > lower Manhattan the bridges
> > covered with rust, the slime
> > in my mouth & ass, sucking
> > his cock like a baby crying Fuck
> > me in my asshole Make love
> > to this rotten slave [. . .].
>
> > > (*Collected* 325)

Ginsberg's oppositional strategy for envisioning a redemptive, sacred body seems facile: that is, by simply shifting from the other-world of the madly unrequited hungry ghost to the desired and desiring human being, naked in the bed with semen still in his mouth and anus, the poet seems to assert a self-evident liberatory desire, an anatomy of impossibly unfettered ecstasy. Thus, the language that portrays the speaker as a rotten slave might only be the ironic discourse of sadomasochism, in which *slave* is a theatrical honorific in the drama that is part of the pleasure of such intercourse. On the surface, this image might indeed represent the redemptive alternative to solipsistic masturbation. In poems such as "Many Loves" and "Please Master," Ginsberg portrays sadomasochistic sexuality precisely as a symbiotic relationship, with language, too, that is ironic in its erotic avowal of the master's dominance and slave's submission. Both poems are autobiographical accounts of Ginsberg's occasional romantic relationship with Neal Cassady. These poems represent Ginsberg-Cassady sexual encounters in such a way that Cassady seems self-evidently the controlling master having his way with a submissive Ginsberg. However, at closer reading, each poem dramatizes sexual activity that, of course, would not occur without the person in the slave subject position initiating intercourse. This strategy produces a submissive "confess[ion]" from the dominant Cassady in "Many Loves"; and, as in "Please Master," the slave takes control of the master's every sexual action with each iteration of "Please master." Indeed, language in "Please Master" is crucial to staging the erotic power relations central to the poem.[10] The speaker describes himself as "a dog on the table yelping with terror delight to be loved"; he demands that his master call him "a dog, an ass beast, a wet asshole" (*Collected* 495). These words produce exactly the "terror delight" the speaker seeks in sadomasochistic encounter, producing a situation in which the master is "bamming it in while I cry out your name I do love you" (*Collected* 495).

However, the symbiotic quality of this erotic master-slave relationship—its power equities in such discourse—is absent in "The Change." Historical power inequities fill this gap, suggesting that the speaker's recapitulation of the Satipatthana Sutra's charnel ground is a response to militarization in Vietnam and its Buddhist-Catholic conflict so that private experience might be revised in terms of intersubjective experience. Ginsberg's deployment of relative and absolute truths in the poem is too complex for a simple recasting of the hungry ghost as a satiated human being fed by his own abjection. The speaker, instead, seems to be representing himself unironically as a "rotten slave"; the semen still in his mouth and anus is equated, grammatically, with "bridges / covered with rust," and seems equally corrosive. Moloch, as a mythic demon who debases the city by mechanizing its citizens, might do much the same to the speaker's sexual community. Whereas language in "Please Master" triggers sexual activity, the words that convey desire in "The Change" are described as part of a "Black Mantra" that contributes the very rot that vexes the speaker in this section of the poem (*Collected* 326). The speaker moves in this section out of self-consciousness and into a nonironic, uncontained abjection. To imagine an intersubjective relationship with the world, he inhabits its deprecated victim spaces—as a soldier on the rampage, as a Vietnamese villager, and as an African American beaten by the Ku Klux Klan, who, uttering their own black mantras, are portrayed as "black magicians / in white skin robes," anticipating Ginsberg's representations of Pentagon war planners as "black magicians" in "Wichita Vortex Sutra" (*Collected* 326).[11] Ginsberg's rhetoric of vision produces an identification with what the poem later terms the "refused." Such a rhetorical strategy is significant, given that the poem can be seen as a companion to his search for refuge in "Angkor Wat." This solidarity, of sorts, with the refused and rejected is part of a shift from isolation to community that begins with his refuge prayer in "Angkor Wat." A conception of solidarity is important, too, in the Satipatthana Sutra, in which the practitioner is encouraged to visualize his/her dead body in charnel grounds; this vision is meant to recognize the terrifying consequences of identifying with one's body and the redemptive possibilities of identifying with the sensate experiences of others.

In this shift from isolation to community, the poem represents in mystical terms the speaker's pilgrimage from self-cherishing subject to one who submerges his sense of self in order to identify with others. This is, in fact, Ginsberg's fantasy for ending the Vietnam War, one that is revisited and elaborated as the mantric poetics of "Wichita Vortex Sutra." The mystical, then, threatens a shunyata identity formation; it is a mode of representation that threatens to negate the material body as much as worldliness might elide the sacred. The speaker seeks a materialistic form that can take the shape of his desire for the transcendental. This search for an immanent form of the mystical calls to question Portugés's notion that the poem is an "exorcism." Indeed, this culminating moment in "The Change" resembles the tendency of his two most famous poems, "Howl" and "Kaddish," to represent the sacred in a paradoxical fusion of immanent and transcendent signification. In this section of the poem, such a mode of signification takes the form of a superimposition of identities rather than a submersion of selfhood. The speaker imagines himself projected on one of the most visible iconographic images in Hindu mythos:

> Kali mother hung with
> nightmare skulls O Myself
> under her pounding
> feet!
>
> (Collected 327)

As an apocalyptic icon, the vanquishing Hindu mother-goddess Kali signifies rebirth, of course, as much as destruction. Kali functions in "The Change" in much the same way Naomi does in "Kaddish," in which Naomi is the mother of destructive hospitalizations who also "gave suck first mystic life" to the poet (*Collected* 223). For Portugés, the poem dramatizes Ginsberg's "exorcism" of the death obsession that grew from his attachment to the Blake vision and his subsequent effort to reexperience the vision with his drug use from 1948 to 1963. Portugés is correct, insofar as the poem records Ginsberg's effort to purge his attachment to the Blake vision. However, as I have argued, "The Change" is concerned, most of all, with exorcising the mystical as part of Ginsberg's construction of a Queer Dharma. The poem purges Ginsberg's attachment to the Blake vision as a mystical event—his purging of the vision as a reificatory moment that would remain somehow outside the immanent particulars of quotidian experience and especially outside the parameters of the body. It does so by deploying the mystical in dream-terror images but only to empty the mystical of its authorizing power, as does its Buddhist textual source, the Satipatthana Sutra.

The speaker emerges from under the feet of Kali to proclaim that he is a worm beneath "the heel of the daemon horses" (*Collected* 327). This is an allusion to Blake's "Proverbs of Hell" from "The Marriage of Heaven and Hell," in which Blake's heroic demon in the poem asserts, "The cut worm forgives the plow" (35). Ginsberg's speaker describes himself as a worm when he is crushed by Kali but, significantly, reborn in a decidedly human, rather than metaphysical, form. This human form is neither the anxious body of "Angkor Wat" nor the ecstatic form that opens "The Change." Instead, it oscillates between the two, a cut worm that seeks the ultimate bodhisattva change in the poem—to forgive "the heel of the daemon horses" who have trampled it.[12] In order for a Buddhist even to begin a bodhisattva path, s/he must at least understand conceptually the shunyata experience of his/her own identity. Ginsberg's speaker does so through what seems like self-abnegation in "The Change":

> Allen Ginsberg says this: I am
> > a mass of sores and worms
> > & baldness & belly & smell
> > I am false Name [. . .].
>
> (*Collected* 327)

If this indeed is a moment of self-abnegation, then it only celebrates the neurosis of appetite that pervades "Angkor Wat" and might serve little more than to acknowledge the influence of anxiety in both poems.[13] Yet, Ginsberg identifies himself as a "false Name" in precisely the only stanza where he names himself at all. Ginsberg's autobiographical poetics was familiar enough to readers in 1963 that the curious shift to the third person in this stanza actually serves to defamiliarize readers with an unwieldy redundancy. The stanza ends with a reassertion of the falsehood inherent in naming at the same time that it culminates in an act of naming. In its axiomatic assertion that the act of naming ("Allen Ginsberg says this: I am") only serves to reify identity ("I am false Name"), the poem's lone act of naming undermines reificatory language without lapsing into nihilistic silence. Ginsberg's speaker recognizes that the sacred truth of the body in his poetics is a necessary fiction spoken in a trope of doubling. An anatomy of ecstasy becomes an anatomy of disgust, just as semen becomes rust early in the poem. This transformation emphasizes the act of naming as a fiction that as the Two Truths teach—and as the body demonstrates—both threatens and encourages sacred experience.

When the redundantly identified "Allen Ginsberg," who stands as "a mass of sores and worms," emerges from the nightmare dream-vision, he renames himself in words that echo the Tetragrammaton, YHWH, the source for Blake's fourfold human form divine: "I am that I am I am the / man & the Adam of hair in / my loins" (*Collected* 327). Ginsberg adds an additional first person pronoun to Yahweh's proclamation "I am that am" from Exodus, suggesting that what is at stake in Ginsberg's Buddhist poetics is not just a materialist language to represent the sacred but also a language for the role of the individual mortal self in sacred experience—an embodied and desiring subjectivity, for Ginsberg, whose very assertion of an embodied sacred subjectivity is transgressive because the citationality of this body is figured as homosexual. The speaker describes himself as the "man & the Adam of hair in / my loins" and emphasizes that the Two Truths frame his corporeal spiritual pilgrimage: "This is my spirit and / physical shape I inhabit" (*Collected* 327).

In his 1984 annotations, Ginsberg felt compelled to add a "Non-Self interpretation" correction to his original endnotes to "Angkor Wat." I have argued that "The Change" enacts this revision; moreover, I contend that "Angkor Wat" and "The Change" together dramatize successive steps in an individual subject's spiritual pilgrimage and, as such, provide insight into the role of subjectivity in Ginsberg's early Buddhist poetics. "The Change" reconceives the "meat / death" anxiety of "Angkor Wat" as a necessary step on a path whereby the human subject can take part in sacred experience that is representable in sacred language. Such experience as it is reenvisioned in "The Change" would occur without a denial of the subject's impermanent, embodied form, and its fluid sexuality and without denying the oscillating intersubjective relationships that emerge from the instabilities of language and representation. This chapter also has demonstrated that both Blake's human form divine and Buddhism's notion of the Two Truths can offer useful conceptual frameworks for understanding Ginsberg's impulse toward a paradoxically materialist and transcendentalist Buddhist poetics. The visionary framework of "The Change," its superimposition of quotidian experience and dream-vision, offers an imagistic representation of his immanent-transcendent language and locates the speaker's specific corporeal anxieties and joys in same-gender desire.

"The Change" constructs a Queer Dharma sensibility that failed in "Angkor Wat." Stating that he no longer wishes to be imprisoned by "meat / death" anxieties, the speaker asks, "Who would deny his own shape's / loveliness in his / dream moment of bed[?]" (*Collected* 328). Ginsberg's speaker stages a bedroom scene in which he sees his own male-coded shape looking back at himself and one in which he finally, in the redemptive path staged in these two poems, questions his original "den[ial]" of his desire for same-same erotic unity. The sexual impulse of this moment is framed, too, by a category of understanding, influenced by his reading and practice of Buddhism, in which subject-object distinctions are collapsed. This moment from "The Change," then, contrasts with an earlier poem of body and spirit, "Love Poem on Theme by Whitman," in which unfixed gender distinctions were deployed in a dream-sex scene that ended unsatisfyingly for the speaker and his bedmates. As he writes in "The Change":

> In this dream I am the Dreamer
> and the Dreamed I am
> that I am Ah but I have
> always known
>
> (*Collected* 328)

As Dreamer and Dreamed in this vision, Ginsberg's speaker is both subject and object of desire, a formulation that questions the discriminatory power of language to distinguish experience by bestowing names upon it. This is an experience, he notes, that he has "always known," which suggests that the Blake vision of 1948 limited Ginsberg as much as it inspired him; the vision launched him into unproductive paths of inquiry for the primordial language of experience, such as his attachment to drug use, but also imaginative ones, such as the Cézanne-inspired "noun and dash of consciousness" that pervades the search for primal language in "Howl." Ginsberg's poetics is located in the search for a primordial language that also is supple enough to admit its own materiality—and, in turn, its own instability.

His Buddhist poetics at this stage of his career is based on a contrariety traceable to both the Two Truths and his reading in Blake. Both influences fuse contradictory absolutist and relativist truths into a tense framework that swerves from the often authoritative claims of propositional logic. That Ginsberg inherits a tolerance, even pleasure, from such contradiction is evident in his fusion of his Jehovic and Buddhist influences: "I am / that I am Ah." Of course, *Ah* can be read as an expletive that intensifies the statement that follows—the speaker realizes a truth he has always known. But the use of *Ah* in the context of two poems that so markedly fuse Judeo-Christian and Buddhist influence—"Angkor Wat" and "The Change"—should be seen, too, as an anticipation of the important role that the *Ah* articulation, as a breath utterance, serves later in Ginsberg's career: as a mantra, *Ah* is nonsignificatory speech that performs a sacred commingling of body, speech, and mind as it is spoken from the breath.[14]

Toward a Mantric Poetics

Sacred speech that invokes both Yahweh and the Buddha—both Hebraic and Eastern influence—is crucial to Ginsberg's Buddhist poetics in "Angkor Wat" and "The Change." Yet, as I have discussed earlier, Ginsberg's incorporation in "Angkor Wat" of the abhaya mudra, a Buddhist sacred hand-gesture of calm abiding, leads only to more anxiety—to his speaker's self-representation as a "a false Buddha afraid of / my own annihilation" (*Collected* 310). The abhaya mudra is revisited in "The Change," this time as a culminating physical gesture in the speaker's reenvisioning of the body as a locus of visionary pilgrimage rather than a source of anxiety neurosis. Toward the close of "The Change," the speaker contextualizes the mudra in his years lost "denying my image," a reference to Ginsberg's efforts to conceptualize a metaphysics of the body during the search to reexperience the Blake vision through drug use but also a reference, of course, to Ginsberg's previous conflicts over his sexual identity. Back "home" as both "the Dreamer/and the Dreamed," and with hands that caress the "throb/ softness of balls," the speaker offers a sexualized version of the abhaya mudra as a "great gesture of / Peace & acceptance" (*Collected* 324, 328). As it performs the abhaya mudra, the body—more specifically, the gay male body—is the intersection of the Two Truths and as such, is important to the speaker's pilgrimage rather than a source of deprecatory appetites. Ginsberg stages a dramatic conflict between the speaker performing the mudra hand-gesture and the abstract "war on Man" that the speaker is forced to confront (*Collected* 328). This conflict, of course, is particularized when seen in the context of how the increasing wartime presence of the United States in Vietnam frames the imagery, language, and action of "Angkor Wat" and "The Change." The abhaya mudra is an effort to still a conflict represented significantly in a double-voiced language: The mudra dramatizes the internal war of the speaker as a microcosm of the larger war effort in which he inevitably, as an American visiting the East, takes part. The mudra becomes his embodied statement of resistance to a war that daily sunders the bodies of soldiers and civilians. This double voice, commingling the sacred and material, is important as a trope in itself but is also significant in Ginsberg's continuing effort to craft a Buddhist poetics that negotiates reificatory absolutism and relativistic nihilism. This doubling takes on a larger role as a tense, oscillating discursive act in both poems, bringing together the autobiographical and the political—the gay male body of the individual and the imperial body of the state—at the same time that it forges an embodied, immanent language (a hand-gesture) for transcendentalism (a hand-gesture reconceived as a redemptive mudra).

This hand-gesture finds its equivalent language in performative speech. Ginsberg closes the poem with a famous spell-like exhortation, affirmed by Portugés, Miles, and Schumacher as evidence of the true change in the poem. Ginsberg's speaker proclaims: "In my train seat I renounce / my power, so that I do / live I will die" (*Collected* 329). For Portugés, this is the key moment in the "mystical exorcism" dramatized in the poem; the moment is, he says, Ginsberg's "head-on confrontation with the fears of cosmic doom and an announcement that he is abandoning his vows to Blake" (*Visionary Poetics* 96). As much as this section of the poem, especially, portrays the poem's primary conflict—that is, the confrontation between attachment to the body and the body's inevitable dissolution—the abstracted notion of "cosmic doom" seems less than helpful for a poem that takes up the decidedly concrete question of how sacred experience can be represented in materialist language without surrendering the particularity of the body. Such a focus on language and the sacred is also the same focus of much of Blake's poetry, as seen in Ginsberg's reenvisioning of "The Marriage of Heaven and Hell" as an expression of the bodhisattva ideal. Thus, what is renounced in the speaker's train seat on the way from Kyoto to Tokyo is less likely a "vo[w] to Blake" and more plausibly a renunciation of the poet's previous reification of the Blake vision. After the difficulties of looking to drug use to reexperience the Blake vision and after the ascetic admonitions of the Indian teachers Ginsberg met during the composition of "Angkor Wat" and "The Change," it would seem that the object of the speaker's renunciation is his reification of the Blake vision. As Buddhism teaches of attachment, Ginsberg is detaching from his attachment to the Blake vision, not disengaging himself from the inspiration proffered by the poet's reading of Blake in itself.

This distinction is significant, insofar as Ginsberg's Buddhist teachings demand an engagement with the quotidian world, not an abandonment of it. From this moment of renunciation, the body reemerges as an intersection of materiality and the sacred, an impermanent space where lived experience and death are no longer sources of anxiety but instead are recast as liminal visionary experiences. The language that represents this pilgrimage is suffused with shunyata. It is marked by the speaker's utterance of the name Allen Ginsberg only insofar as this name is described in terms of nonduality, as the presumably immutable assertion of a nevertheless "false Name." Indeed, as the poem closes, the power of naming cannot stabilize the speaker's fragmented subjectivity; he exists in neither human, demonic (represented by dragon and serpent images in the poem), or Godly representation: he describes his identity as "now nameless," an oscillating subjectivity that is "neither man nor dragon or / God" (*Collected* 330). Such a statement is crucial to reading the final moments of the poem, Ginsberg's intertextual weaving of Blake's "A Vision of the Last Judgment" into a moment of apocalyptic consciousness in which the speaker's annihilation of his reificatory self unveils a subjectivity marked by a vision of the Sun as his visible father. At this moment in the poem, Ginsberg's language for the sacred could lapse into reiterative, logocentric speech, the same name-of-the-father language for religious authority that Blake visualizes as Nobodaddy. But Ginsberg's speaker has renounced such language on the train as part of a search for a language that, paradoxically, privileges its own namelessness at the same time that it searches for a means by which to name the sacred. A vocabulary for this nameless trust in naming, as it were, can be found in Buddhism's Two Truths, in which the idea of an immutable selfhood is both asserted and distrusted as is the ostensibly self-evidentiary and illusory experience of the senses.

The body is represented in "Angkor Wat" as a locus for attachment to desire and aversion to death. As the speaker's pilgrimage continues in "The Change," the body is reenvisioned as a sacred, culturally specific space that is desired and desiring and is a source of neither ecstasy or disgust. For Ginsberg, the Two Truths, an organizing principle for

Buddhism as important as the Four Noble Truths, offers a language that can represent this idea of the body as a middle-way between attachment and aversion—without lapsing into a debilitating either/or division of self or soul, body, or spirit. The relative truth of the body, with its attendant desire and disgust, can be a physical space for the experience of Buddhist absolute truth—the realization of emptiness, itself a *nonabsolute absolute*—if the practitioner experiences the body with an eye toward forging a middle-way between the pleasure and anxiety of appetite, an experience the speaker himself charts in these poems.

In Ginsberg's emerging Buddhist poetics, the language for such experience is found in mantra speech. These poems forecast the importance of the mantra in later works such as "Wichita Vortex Sutra" and "Iron Horse." It is worth noting, too, that "The Change," "Wichita Vortex Sutra," and "Iron Horse" take place in moving vehicles. Allusions to jet travel are crucial, too, to "Angkor Wat"; and Ginsberg's assertion of himself as a "Buddhist Jew" occurs in the mediating "mid Heaven" air flight in "Kral Majales." Movement, in this case, travel, and more specifically modern mass travel, is more than just a coincidence of composition for Ginsberg. Movement enacts the constant flux of meaning-making that is crucial to his conception of an unfixed, anti-logocentric language for the sacred in his Buddhist poetics. Signifying semantic movement in forms of mass travel, moreover, suggests the populism of such a poetics.[15] Buddhism teaches that all practitioners can become Buddhas, and this is one of significant breaks the religion makes from Ginsberg's Hebraic background. As Newland notes, the otherwise difficult, even esoteric, concept of the Two Truths is taught as a "knowable" sacred tradition, as a complexity that nevertheless is "accessible to understanding." The Two Truths, he writes, "are two types of things that [practitioners] can know, and that [practitioners] should aspire to know" (15).

4

Language and the Limits of Romanticism

> I wanted the historical event to be the end of the war, and so I prepared the declaration of the end of the war by saying I hereby make my language identical with the historical event, *I here declare the end of the war!*
> —Allen Ginsberg, 1980

Song, Concentration, and Ambivalence

As Chicago police rushed the crowd in Lincoln Park the day before the 1968 Democratic National Convention, Ginsberg gathered himself into full lotus position and began chanting mantras. The audience had convened in the park for a concert by John Sinclair and MC 5. Earlier, Ginsberg led the crowd in fifteen minutes of chanting the Hare Krishna mantra; now, as police moved violently through the park, Ginsberg sat near the stage repeating the Sanskrit syllable "Om." Ginsberg's chanting spread, and before long, groups of fellow chanters formed around him. According to Michael Schumacher, the crowd's continuous chanting that day eased tension and prevented a full-blown riot in the park (511). As Ginsberg explained in 1969 to Paul Carroll, he had expected to chant for roughly twenty minutes to calm himself, "but the chanting stretched into hours, and a big circle surrounded me" (Allen Ginsberg, interview with Paul Carroll 92). The chanting eventually lasted eight hours. He told Carroll that the effect of chanting surprised him. The experience "felt like grace," he said, adding, "I was in a revolving mass of electricity. I was in a dimension of feeling other than the normal one of save-your-own-skin" (Allen Ginsberg, interview with Paul Carroll 92).

However visionary and politically productive this event was for Ginsberg, his experience of grace emerged from spontaneous religious feeling rather than authoritative religious practice. Indeed, as he explained to Carroll, the chanting that day in Chicago achieved its full potency only when "somebody passed me a note on which an Indian had written, 'Will you please stop playing with the mantra and do it seriously by pronouncing the 'M' in OM properly for at least five minutes?'" Ginsberg added, "I realized I'd been using the mantra as song instead of concentration, so I started doing it his way" (Allen Ginsberg, interview with Paul Carroll 92).

This moment in Chicago suggests a vocabulary for the shape of Ginsberg's Buddhist poetics after "Angkor Wat" and "The Change," in which he fuses "song" and "concentration" in his appropriation of mantra speech. As I have discussed earlier, Ginsberg's desire to blur the boundaries between oppositional conceptual frameworks—such as between song and concentration or between East and West—dates back to his 1948 Blake vision, which inspired his tendency in "Howl" and "Kaddish" to combine metaphysical and materialist modes of representation in revisionary poetic prophecy. During most of the 1960s, Ginsberg sought to live and practice the prophetic role written so largely in earlier poems such as "Howl" and "Kaddish" and reenvisioned in "Angkor Wat" and "The Change." His vows "to help mankind" from "Kaddish" (*Collected* 214) that frame his early life often centered in the 1960s on bringing the mantra from private Eastern religious practice into public, political view. The results were mixed, as in Chicago, when Ginsberg's own cultural authority as an East-West cultural translator was challenged, and he was chided to "stop playing with the mantra." His poetry and public life suggest that Ginsberg's incorporation of the mantra into his language for prophecy was, like his early Buddhism in general, an autodidactic pursuit that at times could be sophisticated in its approach to language and action. However, just as often, such language could be reductive in its understanding of the mantra as a Manichean manifestation of "magic language"—a language deployed in his poetry as a counterforce to the "black language" of disciplinary governmental institutions.¹ Ginsberg's poetic strategies fluctuate this way throughout his career, trusting containment as often as he expresses ironic ambivalence toward gestures of poetic containment. Yet, such fluctuation (however difficult to categorize) is important to the political impulse of his Buddhist poetics. More specifically, Ginsberg's continued study and practice of the mantra throughout his later career signals a shift in his poetics and suggests that an understanding of the role of the mantra can illuminate Ginsberg's contribution of a poetics of the sacred in late-twentieth-century American poetry.

Ginsberg deploys the mantra in the 1960s as a means of reenvisioning his one speech-breath-thought poetics—part of his continuing effort to write a poetry of sacred experience in an emerging contemporary, postmodern landscape that increasingly distrusted linguistic referentiality. To be sure, the breath always has been a crucial part of his work. As much as his career, for instance, is indebted to Whitman's experiments with the catalogue, only in the later poems does Ginsberg reenvision the role of *repetition* in the catalogue by studying and practicing the role of repetition in the mantra. Repetition remains in the later poems as in the early ones but this time in the service of a language that performs, rather than points to, its referents. The emphasis on "who" as a demonstrative base in "Howl" that points to and names the heroes of the poem becomes, as I discuss in chapter 5, the repetitious wind-breath of "Mind Breaths" and the repetitious "noticing" of "On Cremation of Chögyam Trungpa, Vidyadhara." Thus, an earlier emphasis on demonstrative naming, a trust in significatory relationships, is transformed into a trust in performance, in an effort to dramatize the "widening" of consciousness emphasized previously, for instance, in Ginsberg's epigraph to *Kaddish and Other Poems*.

Yet, as the previous chapter shows, Ginsberg's strategies for widening consciousness, as expressed in the *Kaddish and Other Poems* epigraph, are not marked by consistency or systematic conceptualization. Asceticism and desire converge, as do anxiety and ecstasy, and the result is at times a reificatory romantic transcendentalist subjectivity and at other times a Buddhist critique of self-presence. As this chapter discusses, this ambivalence is framed by the poet's engagement with various versions of what Michel Foucault would term governmentality: a system of state power in which discipline is internalized by each subject as a form of individual self-control that augments the external forms of discipline imposed by the state. Such disciplinary self-regulation is significant in "Wichita Vortex Sutra," a poem whose linguistic strategies anticipate his experiences with the mantra in Chicago in 1968 and then later in his 1966 U.S. Senate testimony on the Narcotics Rehabilitation Act, which for Ginsberg became a platform for propounding a notion that the care of the self proceeds from a seemingly contrarious fusion of Buddhist materiality and romantic transcendentalist drug use. This chapter also reads "Wichita" and the Senate testimony in the context of Ginsberg's increased awareness of his public reputation as artist and activist. As such, this chapter explores his attempt to craft a language for sacred experience that is both mindful of the integrity of autobiography—of the ego at the core of any construction of literary reputation—and supple enough to project a Buddhist-inspired notion of the self into the culture at large as a pacifist, reconstructive force.[2]

Into the Vortex

David R. Jarraway's work with "Wichita Vortex Sutra" implies that the poem contributes to a larger body of Vietnam War literature that identifies and engages a "crisis of knowledge" at the heart of late-twentieth-century American culture. Jarraway's focus on the "vortex" of language at the core of "Wichita" is important, but he does not explore the religious sensibility crucial to a poem whose title, a sutra after all, demonstrates its Buddhist influence. In the mid-1960s, Ginsberg began to trust language as a performative vehicle that undoes its own referential power—and, more important, he represented such undoing as a practice of the sacred. Performative speech offers a vantage from Western linguistics to read the Hindu and Buddhist influences in Ginsberg's language for sacred experience in his poetry. Linguist J. L. Austin describes performative speech as language that is "*doing* something rather than merely *saying* something [. . .]. [I]n saying what I do, I actually perform that action" (235). Indeed, Ginsberg's aesthetic attraction to performative language is consistent with what Michael Davidson has described as a general postwar turn from the high modernist well-wrought "artisinal" poem to a conception of poetry in which action is trusted over craft—a poetics of "doing rather than representing" (*Guys like Us* 29). Ginsberg writes in "Reflections on the Mantra" (1966) that a poetics of mantra speech presupposes a trust in words that extends beyond their referential function; he argues that mantra recitation produces a relationship between speech and action in which "the original thin-conscious association with meaning disappears and the words become pure physical sounds uttered in a frankly physical universe" (148). Mantra chanting becomes, for Ginsberg, "a vehicle for the expression of nonconceptual sensations of the worshiper" (148). Based on a conflation of Hindu metaphysics and Buddhist materialism—the sort of conflation that led to complaint in Chicago—Ginsberg argues that "the names of the Gods used in the mantra are *identical* with the Gods (or powers invoked) themselves" (149). The mantra is a mode of speech that, as Austin writes of the performative, operates on the boundary between speech and action, transferring attention from "what a certain utterance *means*" to "what was the *force* [. . .] of the utterance" (251). For Ginsberg, a performative, mantric poetics reaches beyond materialist language to the expressive body of the speaker, specifically the speaker's breath.

In his essay "Contemplation on Publications," Ginsberg writes that without a concomitant emphasis on the breath-unit, with which he first experimented in "Howl," a mantric poetics risks a language underwritten by an illusion of self-presence—speech that leads "to spiritual delusion of Godhood rather than breakthru [*sic*] of common awareness" (213). David Loy's conjunction of Mahayana Buddhism and poststructuralism might suggest a way of thinking through Ginsberg's embodied East-West poetics, in which a Mahayana-poststructuralist account of language and subjectivity can point, for Loy, "to an experience beyond language—or, more precisely, to a different way of experiencing language and thought" (60). Thus, as Loy offers a familiar critique of the potential for linguistic freeplay to lead to a deconstructive void, he also frames this critique with an argument for the critical possibilities of poststructuralism, asserting that Western radical thought limits poststructuralism in a celebration of freeplay that is "defective only because it is not radical enough" (59). Ginsberg's construction of a poetic language underwritten by Buddhist conceptions of the immanent sacredness of body and breath—where textuality can point to "a different way of experiencing language and thought," to borrow from Loy—is a crucial organizing principle for the direction of his Buddhist poetics from "Wichita" onward. His emphasis on a fluid, mediated subjectivity is circumscribed by a poetics that unravels the solidity of the Western human subject with the deconstructive impulse of Mahayana Buddhism. Yet, his poetics also tempers linguistic freeplay, containing subjectivity in a position of tremulous certainty, in the fluctuating inflows and outflows of the spoken breath.

"Wichita" was written during a 1966 poetry-reading tour of Kansas financed with a Guggenheim grant. The pacifist impulse of the poem is framed by Ginsberg's slow realization during this reading tour that he now was regarded, for better or worse, as a spokesperson for an emerging youth culture. In contrast, "Howl" was epic in its scope but private in its origins, as was "Kaddish."[3] With "Wichita Vortex Sutra," the vatic traditions of Blake and Whitman that inspired Ginsberg's early career now were staged against a deepening war effort in Vietnam and an emerging public relations struggle by the Pentagon to win public support for the escalation of this war effort. By 1965, Ginsberg recognized a need to continue and revise the prophetic language of "Howl," "Kaddish," "Angkor Wat," and "The Change" to address the deepening crisis in Vietnam. The trust in naming that marks "Howl" and "Angkor Wat" and the trust in nonreferential language that suffuses "Kaddish" and "The Change"—especially, in the latter poem, the speaker's navigation of questions of self-dissolution in the Satipatthana Sutra—represent both the limit and possibility of language, a boundary condition he engages in "Wichita." Ginsberg's concern in "Wichita" is to reawaken the creative potential of human desire, to remind readers that "ecstatic language" might be produced from human suffering, on the muted plains, "when our trembling bodies hold each other / breast to breast on a mattress." A new language is necessary to represent this confluence of desire and tenderness, even if it must be spoken in the poem by an aging poet ambivalent about his potency at a turn in his career. "I'm an old man now," he writes, "and a lonesome man in Kansas / but not afraid / to speak my lonesomeness in a car . . . " (*Collected* 405). Ginsberg constructs a mantra from which a language for pacifism might be shaped, a reflection of Ginsberg's increasingly public persona of the 1960s: "I lift my voice aloud, / make Mantra of American language now, / I here declare the end of the War!" (*Collected* 407). "Wichita" creates a language for prophecy that swerves from linguistic transparency, as he does in four significant earlier prophetic poems: in his use of the breath-unit line to supplement the integrity of individual utterances in "Howl"; in his incorporation of nonreferential prayers and cawing crows to bless Naomi's funeral in "Kaddish"; in his commingling of anxiety and ecstasy in "Angkor Wat," which simultaneously critiques and extols his emerging Buddhist poetics; and in his invocation and reenvisioning of the Satipatthana Sutra in "The Change."

"Wichita" functions as a sutra, as a Buddhist scripture, transforming wartime language with the same urgency that an earlier poem, "Sunflower Sutra," incorporated revisionary prophetic language to transvalue the human form's otherwise arid self-representation into an ecstatic figuration. Yet, "Wichita" evades history at the same time that it stages the historical as an occasion for political activism. In a 1968 interview with Michael Aldrich, Ginsberg argues that the mantric poetics of "Wichita" emerges from the poem's historical moment, an effort to "make a series of syllables that would be identical with a historical event" ("Improvised Poetics" 46):

> I wanted the historical event to be the end of the war, and so I prepared the declaration of the end of the war by saying 'I hereby make my language identical with the historical event, *I here declare the end of the war!*'—and set up a force field of language which is so solid and absolute as a statement and a realization of an assertion by my will, conscious will power, that it will contradict—counteract and ultimately overwhelm the force field of language pronounced out of the State Department and out of [Lyndon] Johnson's mouth. ("Improvised Poetics" 46–47)

The poem stages a mantra-based, performative opposition to the Vietnam War. Yet, as if to forecast his "playing" with the mantra in Chicago, Ginsberg's strategy in "Wichita" does not reach beyond a reductive mythologizing, one that recasts the language of the peace movement as "white magic" to Lyndon Johnson's "black magic" in a rhetorical battle for public opinion:

> Where they [Johnson and his military advisors] say "I declare—We declare war," they can say "I declare war"—their mantras are black mantras, so to speak. They pronounce these words, and then they sign a piece of paper, of other words, and a hundred thousand soldiers go across the ocean. So I pronounce *my* word, and so the point is, how strong is my word? ("Improvised Poetics" 47)

In "Wichita," the language of the Pentagon is mythic speech, even though the Pentagon's actions in history are circumscribed by the materialist language of wartime propaganda broadcast on the radio and documented by Ginsberg in the poem. The language of Johnson and his advisors is variously voiced as "language used / like magic for power," language that naturalizes imperialist power inequities, and voiced also as "Black Magic language" wielded "by inferior magicians with / the wrong alchemical formula for transforming earth into gold" (*Collected* 401).

Ginsberg's language reveals the burden of the very prophetic lineage that inspires the poem. His literary influence in "Wichita" traces, of course, back to Whitman's attempt in *Democratic Vistas* to revive American literature and democracy by throwing off what he saw as the materialist decadence of the U.S.'s European legacy. Ginsberg constructs a Whitman for "Wichita" who inspires as much as ruptures the Western prophetic lineage; and this Whitman-Ginsberg rupture is crucial, as I argue in chapter 2, to Ginsberg's revisionary poetics of prophecy. Whitman is evoked so that he might be modified in "Wichita."[4] Whitman's trust in the metaphysics of industrial progress, his hypostatic drama of manifest destiny in "A Passage to India," for instance, is undercut in Ginsberg's opening lines. "Blue eyed children" clasp Whitman at the beginning of "Wichita," and, alongside Whitman, these children "envision / Iron interlaced upon the city plain" in an echo of the visionary optimism of "Passage to India" (394). However, this romantic vision is overwhelmed by the persistent drone of banal, often propagandistic, radio commentary that Ginsberg incorporates in "Wichita" as a force that colonizes the imagination—as "language abused / for Advertisement" and deployed "like magic for power on the planet" (*Collected* 401). Commercial language is the language of conquest in the poem, in which newspapers in the poem confuse reportage and jingoism with headlines such as *"Vietnam War Brings Prosperity."* The technological sublime that sparked Whitman's optimistic "Iron interlaced" prophetic nationalism is subsumed into materialistic power relations that prop the war.

As much as *Democratic Vistas* inspires *The Fall of America*, the war fever of Whitman's own work, such as "Beat! Beat! Drums!" and "Song of the Banner at Daybreak," is rewritten in "Wichita." Whitman's trust in poetic language that heals the wounds of war, his universalist "Word over all" that unites the postbellum United States in "Reconciliation," is untenable for Ginsberg during the Vietnam War, no matter that Ginsberg has proclaimed, "Thy sins are forgiven, Wichita!" in this song of himself:

> What if I opened my soul to sing to my absolute self
>   Singing as the car crash chomped thru blood & muscle
>   tendon skull?
> What if I sang, and loosed the chords of fear brow?
>   What exquisite noise wd
>   shiver my car companions?
>   (*Collected* 397)

Ginsberg's poetics of possibility, his optimistic tenderness framed by a contradictory image of a "car crash chomped thru blood & muscle," falters in part 1 of the poem. Riding through a Great Plains plump from wartime propaganda, his "exquisite noise" echoes back to him in inert language. Talking back to a radio preacher whose sermonizing advocates tacit acceptance of the Pentagon's Vietnam policy, Ginsberg contrasts the kinetic path of his automobile traveling with the figurative stasis counseled by the religious establishment on the automobile's radio: "between Beatrice & Lincoln— / 'Better not to move but let things be,' Reverend Preacher?" Stasis underwritten by church authority, by a preacher who prefers "let[ting] things be" to the power of possibility, leads him to conclude, "We've all already disappeared." The problem in "Wichita" still is "Language, language"; and the force of candor, crucial for both Whitman and Ginsberg, is not enough to redeem without recourse to Ginsberg's Buddhist influences.

This song of self and nation rent by war also is a sutra, a Buddhist scriptural text, that takes Blake's vortex as a central figuration for consciousness. It is an artifact of both song and concentration, a poem divided in its attempt to redeem the language of Johnson's "inferior magicians" and of materialist radio propaganda. In "Wichita," language is the stage upon which song and concentration meet; a poem in which, as in "The Change," Ginsberg's Buddhism intersects with Blake's vortex. The vortex is Blake's agitated, violent image for apocalyptic consciousness, generating the movement from the "mundane shell" of human consciousness to the Fourfold Human Form Divine, where, as Blake writes in his annotations to Bishop Watson's *An Apology for the Bible*, "every man" might "converse with God & be a King and Priest in his own house" (615). "Wichita" intervenes in the rhetoric of war with a language suffused by the Buddhist conception of shunyata, which deconstructs Western metaphysics by recasting subjectivity as a constructed performance rather than an irreducible ontological essence. Ginsberg counters wartime language with the "Prajnaparamita Sutra over coffee" (*Collected* 395), an effort to render such language empty of an essentialist presence, as Blake's vortex does with representations of human consciousness. The Prajnaparamita Sutra, the definitive sutra on shunyata, appears casually—introduced "over coffee"—in the struggle over language in "Wichita":

> Prajnaparamita Sutra over coffee—Vortex
> of telephone radio aircraft assembly frame ammunition
> petroleum nightclub Newspaper streets illuminated by Bright
> EMPTINESS—
>
> (*Collected* 395)

These words, spoken early in part 1, lead to a call to action similar to the Bard's Song in Blake's *Milton*. However, if "Eternal salvation," a world redeemed by prophetic language in *Milton*, is to be represented in "Wichita Vortex Sutra," such redemption can occur for Ginsberg only at a point of contact between Blake's bardic voice and the Highest Perfect Wisdom sutra on emptiness, the Prajnaparamita Sutra. Ginsberg's Bard puns on misunderstandings of shunyata, the Buddhist conception of groundlessness that empties self-presence in a manner resembling contemporary Western poststructuralism. As such, shunyata functions not as mystic speech but as a form of common language, as sacred speech that might "overwhelm" the State Department's "force field of language."[5] Loy argues that a conceptual framework that would borrow from both Mahayana and Western poststructuralism "opens up the possibility of deconstructing another duality: that between Western philosophy, defining itself as rational inquiry, and its 'shadow' the mystical tradition" (80). Whether Ginsberg actually achieves such fusion or whether mantric speech in "Wichita" is merely a dualistic counterweight to Johnson's "black language" is a question Ginsberg begins to address, fatalistically, later in the poem and also in its companion poem, "Iron Horse." By the time of "Iron Horse," wartime rhetoric continues to "hurry" the country to war (*Collected* 445). Rather than craft a language to counter the words that prop the war, as he does in "Wichita," Ginsberg retreats in "Iron Horse" from the linguistic environments that inspire the revisionary impulse of these poems: "Better withdraw from the newspaper world / Better withdraw from the electric world / Better retire before war cuts my head off" (*Collected* 446).

As in "The Change," Ginsberg's Buddhist influences are rarely far removed from his Blakean ones. "On to Wichita to prophesy! O frightful Bard!" he writes, aware that the prophesying Bard careens "into the heart of the Vortex," where Blake's human form divine—crucial to the construction of a Buddhist poetics in "Angkor Wat" and "The Change"—is under attack by U.S. escalation in Vietnam. Young students caught in the poem's Vortex suspect their government lies to them as new draft notices, in the form of more "black language," arrive every day. These "boys with sexual bellies aroused" are "chilled in the heart by the mailman" (*Collected* 404-5). Selective service notices come "writ by machine," but the problem of the poem is not so much the machine—as Moloch the machine is the demonic Spectre of "Howl"—but instead the *language* of the machine. Speaking to his prophetic audience, Ginsberg's Bard asserts, "I search for the language / that is also yours— / almost all our language has been taxed by war" (*Collected* 406). Reenvisioning language taxed by war and taxed *for* war is the Bard's quest in the poem and might be considered the redemptive impulse of much of Ginsberg's later work.

Ginsberg's compositional process in "Wichita" forecasts the shape of his later poetics, especially in its embrace of a middle-way, Madhyamaka influence. The spacing and line breaks of "Wichita" re-create broken, fragmented language that is both the casualty and cause of war fever in the poem. "Wichita" was composed on a trip through Kansas, as Ginsberg spoke his immediate impressions into a tape recorder that also picked up passing sounds and radio news snippets, many of which were included later in the poem. The on-off clicking of the tape recorder determined the line breaks in the poem, extending Ginsberg's one speech-breath-thought poetics into an ambivalent compositional space framed by a tension between improvisation and craft: enjambment, then, becomes an effect of both multimedia spontaneity and reflective revision in the poem. Ginsberg later termed this compositional process "auto poesy," punning on *automobile*, *automatic*, and *autoerotic* to suggest the importance of transience, spontaneity, and desire in the poem's composition.

In his work on the role of tape recordings in contemporary literature, Davidson observes that the ability to record the human voice reduced notions of literary voice to artifice, to an illusion of self-presence that could shape new forms of political resistance. This "divided character of orality" in contemporary literature empties authentic speech at the same time that it, paradoxically, "posits self-presence as its ground" ("Technologies of Presence" 100). Framed by such a tension between the artificial and the genuine, this impulse in contemporary literature fashions itself as "authentic" in order to interrogate dominant discourses of authenticity in a Cold War culture of surveillance where "technology is capable of separating voice from speaker, conversation from community" ("Technologies of Presence" 103). Davidson observes that the tape recorder provided Ginsberg with a tool to recast prophetic language as a function of technological culture, in which prophecy "no longer emanates from some inner visionary moment but from a voice that has recognized its inscription within an electronic environment" ("Technologies of Presence" 106).[6]

"Wichita" dramatizes the ambivalence that characterizes Ginsberg's self-representation as a poet-prophet in the mid-1960s: his "midheaven" and "middleeuropean" naming of himself as a "Buddhist Jew" in "Kral

Majales"; his skepticism toward his increasingly public role and his embrace of this role; and his trust in both organic voice and tapevoice. Perhaps a way to think through the ambivalence of Ginsberg's approach to the mantra in the poem—without attempting to resolve the ambivalence with a thoroughgoing rationalism, a target itself of his war poetry—would be to understand his strategy in the poem as an extension of that which is deployed in "Kaddish." Ambivalence in "Kaddish" is alternately vexing and visionary; as a redemptive biography of Naomi, the poem recalls monovocal religious language and revises it with a prophetic language dependent on ambivalence and an ironic containment of ambivalence. In "Kaddish," as I have quoted earlier, Naomi is the figure "from whose pained head [the poet] first took Vision" and a figure against whom he summons "final cops of madness" and continues her debilitating institutionalization (*Collected* 223). Ginsberg describes Naomi as "beautiful Garbo of my Karma," invoking a Karmic debt that for the young poet includes his mother's dangerously incestuous sexuality and her visionary status as the muse who "gave suck first mystic life & taught me talk and music" (*Collected* 223). Divinity in "Kaddish" is represented not through a standard metaphysical mode, where the poet is touched by the extranatural hand of God, but by moving continually between representations of urban and pastoral, immanence and transcendence, and sense and nonsense.

As if a continuity of the poetics of ambivalence in "Kaddish" and Ginsberg's subsequent language for vision in his U.S. Senate testimony, Ginsberg's poetic war with the Pentagon in "Wichita" is portrayed as a metaphysical, Manichean battle between black karma and white karma. However, at the same time, this conflict hinges on the Pentagon's failure to honor the individual, material lived experience of combatants and citizens on both side of the war. It is both beholden to and wary of the human tendency to reify conflict in ahistorical, metaphysical terms that elide the exigencies of everyday lived experiences. The poem asserts that Robert McNamara's "bad guess" in 1962 about the escalation of the war contributed to the suffering of tens of thousands over a four-year period. The material reality of this bad guess is hypostatized into a magical realm that Ginsberg's Bard answers with more magic, responding to the Pentagon's "funky warlocks" with the language of his contemporary Bard's song. For Ginsberg, the poem is a response to Johnson's "Communion of bum magicians," his "Sorcerer's Apprentices who lost control / of the simplest broomstick in the world: Language." "Wichita" invokes a contemporary

Bard from the Blakean Vortex to rescue the Sorcerer's Apprentices from themselves: "O longhaired magician come home take care of your dumb helper / before the radiation deluge floods your livingroom." The "longhaired magician" answers Johnson's magicians with more magic—dramatizing his own version of dualistic otherness—as he wields a "good" broomstick to vanquish an evil one. This Bard comes to repair the damage wrought by Johnson, to "take care of" Johnson's "dumb helper" because Johnson's "magic errandboy's / just made a bad guess again / that's lasted a whole decade" (*Collected* 401).

"Wichita" anticipates the linguistic turn in contemporary U.S. poetry at the same time that, as Davidson suggests, it reenvisions Whitman's desire to "sing the body electric" in the surveillance culture of the Cold War ("Technologies of Presence" 106). For Ginsberg, the tape recorder he used to compose "Wichita" is the teleotechnological component of mantra speech; a means by which an authentic speech—and authentic speaker—could be constructed that would declare the end of the war. As he explains to Aldrich, the machine recorded the spontaneous composition of the poem: "these lines in 'Wichita' are arranged according to their organic time-spacing as per the mind's coming up with the phrases and the mouth pronouncing them." In Ginsberg's improvisatory poetics, the boundary between spontaneity and reflection is, respectively, a boundary between the organic-humanistic and the technological and serves as a critical location for imaginative speech. He notes that the "organic time-spacing" of the lines is predicated upon pauses "of a minute or two minutes between each line as I'm formulating it in my mind and the recording." The edge of improvisation, where its frame and end meet, is a location that simultaneously limits and produces speech in the poem with each click of the microphone's on-off switch. The ritualized boundary of this improvised voice emerges from Ginsberg's Hindu and Buddhist sources. He tells Aldrich that composition-by-tape-recorder "is like a form of Yoga: attempting to pronounce aloud the thoughts that are going through the head" (interview with Michael Aldrich 29). The poem forecasts the aesthetic turn that would become the Language movement in U.S. contemporary poetry in the following decade, where form *is* content rather than an extension of content. Innovations in contemporary poetry such as organic form and open-field poetics can be recast as "organic time-spacing" in "Wichita": the mind's thought and the mouth's utterance are coexistent in time, and the line itself performs the circumstances of its composition, with tape-recorder clicks reproduced as line breaks that climb down the page.

Buddhism and the technologies of Cold War culture combine to create a boundary site that produces pacifistic language in "Wichita." The mantra simultaneously summons and subverts the referential power of language. In its emphasis on spontaneity as a mode of production and containment, Ginsberg's mantric poetics reveals what Dick Hebdige calls, in his study of late-twentieth-century improvisation, "the illusory permanence of any enframed edge" (346). What Hebdige describes as "deliberate spontaneity," referring to a broad range of late-twentieth-century cultural practices, I instead would term "ritualized spontaneity" to represent Ginsberg's use of the mantra in his Buddhist poetics (340). This bounded condition of improvised speech is, as Hebdige describes, both "plain" and "secreted": "in its compound resistance to the self-evident logic of representation, [deliberate spontaneity] takes us to the very edge of language (the word *edge* referring here to 'the border or part nearest some limit; the commencement or early part; the beginning; as, the *edge* of a field; the *edge* of evening')" (340). For Ginsberg, a mantric poetics enables poet and audience to experience together this edge of representation; it is poetic language poised at the limit of a frame and beckoning past the point where that frame, as active, performative language, collapses into the beginning of a newly enframed structure. This edge of representation revises the isolated consciousness of "Howl," part 2—where the speaker's internalization of Moloch reduces him to "a consciousness without a body" (*Collected* 131)—with performative speech constructed as an embodied, redemptive language that blurs the boundary between poet and audience. As Ginsberg describes in his "Improvised Poetics" interview with Aldrich, mantric poetics "catalyze[s]" in the audience the "same *affects* or emotions" experienced by the poet during the composition of the poem. The form of the poem, then, is the content of the poem: "Doing mantra made me conscious of what I was doing in Poesy, and then made my practice a little more clear, because now I realize that certain rhythms you can get into, are . . . *mean* certain feelings" (36). Continuing his insistence on a primal language for prophecy, the "noun and dash of consciousness" in "Howl," Ginsberg asserts that the metrics of the Hindu Gayatri mantra represents a sacred "universal meter" for poetic prophecy. The Gayatri meter, he tells Aldrich, is "as complicated as the nature of the human body . . . or is fitted to the nature of the human body and touches all the key combinations" ("Improvised Poetics" 35).⁷ The improvised immediacy of the mantra elevates the individual utterance to the level of cultural memory and historical necessity. If Ginsberg's message all along has been to "widen the area of consciousness," this message has never been separate from Blake's idea that "the eye altering alters all." Buddhism offers Ginsberg a vocabulary for representing the visionary experience of that eye. Mantra language offers him a way between oppositional terms, a path that maintains the deconstructive turn of Buddhist language and ideas with Ginsberg's neoromantic belief in a stable self—one who breathes, one who notices, one who desires.

Yet, Ginsberg's belief in the magic of mantra chanting eventually confuses the terms of his engagement with materialist governmental rhetoric. The Vietnam War rages, of course, toward the Tet Offensive, and U.S. race relations continue to decay in a white supremacist culture. As the final lines of the poem sardonically caution, "The war is over now— / Except for the souls / held prisoner in Niggertown / still pining for love of your tender white bodies O children of Wichita!" Ginsberg's note to the poem explains "Niggertown" as "Area of Wichita between Hydraulic and 17th streets" (*Collected* 411; 780). Schumacher writes that this section of Wichita was segregated and impoverished as a result of racism and indifference, a significant cultural context for the relationship between mantric poetics and the poem's ending. Despite Ginsberg's attention to language and politics, Schumacher argues, "his words were not necessarily going to change the course of history—not as long as racists had hateful mantras of their own" (465). "Wichita" depends on a contradictory incorporation of the mantra, where magic is at odds with materiality. His belief in the magic of the mantra confuses the terms of his engagement with materialist governmental rhetoric; but at the same time, Ginsberg seemed to understand the antimetaphysical, performative roots of the mantra, a foundation he drew from as his Buddhist poetics continued to develop. Ginsberg's understanding of the mantra and of the materialist, empirical aims of Buddhism is deepened as the later poems fuse a mantra-based language with a poetics indebted to the vital role of the material body in Buddhist practice. Ginsberg's continued study of the mantra offers him a theory of language that might revive the romantic imagination's engagement with pacifism. In this way, the mantra underwrites a Buddhist and Western poetics of revision in his later career that reenvisions Blake's Human Form Divine, just as the "longhaired magician" of "Wichita" engages, amid the challenges of the poet's own tendency toward dualism, the damage done by sorcerer's apprentices in order to "tak[e] care of" these apprentices themselves.

Poetry and Confession

Ginsberg's appearance before the U.S. Senate in June 1966—between the composition of "Wichita" and its companion poem, "Iron Horse"—suggests much about the complex relationship between his romanticism and his Buddhism. Often for Ginsberg, the impetus for syncretic religiosity emerges in the secularized arena of legal testimony. As quoted note 14 of chapter 3, Ginsberg's testimony during cross-examination at the Chicago Seven trial in 1969 offers insight into how religious and juridical discourses are suffused for him with desire. Ginsberg cites Whitman in his testimony as both literary and spiritual father and portrays his work as a continuity of Whitman's. More important, he argues in this juridical setting that his work also revises his forefather's—as a "projecti[on]" of his own personality onto his literary inheritance—in a lineage of embodied poetics that does not produce "shame" and is "basically charming actually."

The most extensive convergence of Ginsberg's poetic and juridical discursive strategies occurred three years earlier, during his testimony before the U.S. Senate on the Narcotic Rehabilitation Act of 1966. The rhetorical purpose of Ginsberg's testimony was to deploy his public media persona to affect U.S. drug policy, specifically to prevent the criminalization of what were becoming known as "psychedelic" drugs. At the same time, his testimony illustrates how Ginsberg's personal drug experimentation affected his developing Buddhist poetics. As such, Ginsberg's testimony—with confessional and autobiographical modes of speech merging in the ritualized setting of the U.S. Congress—is important to understanding how his conception of sacred experience inflects his construction of a subjectivity mindful of both Buddhist materialism and Western metaphysics.

Foucault's discussion of confession, ritual, and meaning in his first volume of *The History of Sexuality* suggests a vocabulary for negotiating the complex intersection of individual agency and state authority in Ginsberg's testimony. Foucault writes, "Since the Middle Ages at least, Western societies have established the confession as one of the main rituals we rely on for the production of truth" (58). Referring to the codification of confessional discourse in the emergence of religion and law in the West, he argues that we "have become a singularly confessing society" (59).[8] Ginsberg's opening avowal in the halls of Congress commingles personal, autobiographical, and confessional modes of discourse, and in doing so, it significantly echoes the anxieties of "Angkor Wat" and "The Change":

> I am here because I want to tell you about my own experience, and am worried that without sufficient understanding and sympathy for personal experience laws will be passed that are so rigid that they will cause more harm than the new LSD that they try to regulate. [. . .]
>
> I hope that whatever prejudgment you may have of me or my bearded image you can suspend so that we can talk together as fellow beings in the same room [. . .] trying to come to some harmony and peacefulness between us. I am a little frightened to present myself, the fear of your rejection of me, the fear of not being tranquil enough to reassure you that we can talk together, make sense, and perhaps even like each other—enough to want not to offend, or speak in a way which is abrupt or hard to understand. (United States Senate 487)

After the poet uttered his anxious opening words, Senator Jacob Javits assured Ginsberg to speak freely, prompting Ginsberg to reaffirm the inward-seeking confessional tone of his forthcoming testimony: "Since I wish to speak personally, I want to speak about my own inside feelings, because that is in a sense what we will be discussing" (United States Senate 488). These words led to an immediate discussion of the poet's 1948 Blake vision, a reminder that ecstasy and anxiety are incorporated as a dialectic in Ginsberg's Buddhist rhetoric of vision.[9]

As personal as his testimony may be, Ginsberg was participating in a ritual of juridico-medical discourse designed to regulate the practices of the culture at large. According to the Senate Judiciary Committee, the hearings were meant to "usher in a whole new era in the Federal Government's approach to the problem of narcotic addiction" (1). The focus of the hearings was the Narcotic Rehabilitation Act of 1966, which would establish sentencing and rehabilitation guidelines for Federal drug offenses, and would offer to those convicted of violating federal drug laws the opportunity of "civil commitment for the purposes of medical and psychiatric treatment prior to and instead of a criminal trial" (1). In light of the disciplinary nature of the judicial setting, it is significant, then, that Ginsberg began his testimony at the level of the personal and confessional. His later assertion in the testimony that he was emphasizing his "direct experience of psychedelics under different conditions" is consistent with his poetics of concrete experience and candor (492); at the same time, it is consistent with an approach to knowledge and discipline that, as Foucault has observed, for centuries in the West has created the conditions whereby "truthful confession was inscribed at the heart of the procedures of individualization by power" (*History* 58–59). For Ginsberg during the Senate hearings, as for Foucault in his histories of discourse and power, self-knowledge is linked to the subject's internalization of state disciplinary mechanisms. These two disciplinary modes together produce, for Ginsberg, language that represents simultaneously the potential expansion of consciousness and its possible reinscription as a mechanism of power. In "Wichita" and later that same year in "Iron Horse," it is Buddhism that offers Ginsberg one possible means of interrupting this reinscription.

I would argue that a Foucauldian reading of Ginsberg's Buddhist poetics during this stage in his career suggests that Ginsberg's language was emboldened by the paradox between his confessionalism and his study of Buddhist nonduality. Such a reading can offer a vocabulary for how this paradox served as a screen for complex tensions between self and other—more specifically, between self and culture. Ginsberg deployed Buddhism to foreground political questions of agency in a liberatory, neoromanticist discourse that, by the 1960s, reached its eschatological limit in a culture increasingly subsuming individual agency into the language and actions of the war effort. Of course, I do not wish to proclaim Ginsberg a spiritual adept, all the same, insofar as his Buddhism was autodidactic, and often eccentric, through the 1960s and even into the 1970s during his early years with Trungpa. Thus, a vocabulary must be summoned that can think through the cultural tensions of his Buddhism—especially in light of Ginsberg's career-long attention to mechanisms of power and domination at the level of both state and individual. Such a vocabulary also must be adequate to think through the virtues and limitations of his conversion to Buddhism as a Westerner during the nascent period in the development of American Buddhism. Foucault's attention to how "technologies of domination" conflict with the "care of the self" can occupy productively the space between Ginsberg's neoromanticism and the cultural exigencies of his Buddhism.

Indeed, the Senate testimony demonstrates the beginning of a break with romanticism for Ginsberg, a space where romanticism reaches an intractable limit—and a break forecast in "Wichita Vortex Sutra," composed just four months before his testimony and continued later in "Iron

Horse." At one level, his Senate testimony seems simply and self-evidently a confrontation between Ginsberg, as countercultural leader and Senators who represent a ruling establishment elite.[10] Such an emancipatory reading, which Ginsberg himself encourages in his opening confessional remarks, does not fully account for the ways in which state power creates subjectivity and, simultaneously, is threatened by this same creation. A more productive reading of the poet's testimony—one in which Ginsberg is neither fully an orientalist or spiritual adept—might also account for Ginsberg's efforts to deploy the romanticist inheritance of Whitman against what Ginsberg saw as the increasingly sophisticated regulatory mechanisms of the "military-industrial complex." In such context, the Senate testimony, like "Wichita Vortex Sutra" and, later, "Iron Horse," stages Ginsberg's confrontation with the possibility that neoromantic conceptions of the self reach their limit in the U.S. in the mid-1960s. The Senate testimony represents a romantic crisis for Ginsberg, one that he answers with discourse that suggests how technologies of the self—drug use and, eventually, Buddhism—are for him productive means by which to respond to coercive technologies of the state.

As in "Wichita," Ginsberg's Senate testimony is authorized by Whitman's *Democratic Vistas*. Focusing specifically on Whitman's critique of a perceived materialist decadence in late-nineteenth-century U.S. culture—Whitman's own romantic crisis—Ginsberg asserts to the Judiciary Committee that an American subjectivity crafted to resemble "machines" and "impersonal 'objective' figures" threatens to displace Whitman's idealized culture of democratic comradeship, in which "maximum development of individual person" is "to be encouraged" (*United States Senate* 488).[11] In *Democratic Vistas*, Whitman writes that homosocial comradeship, "adhesive love," offers the "counterbalance" that might "offset" an increasingly "materialistic and vulgar American democracy" and produce the culture's "spiritualization" (*Leaves* 770). Where Whitman extolled American literature as the imaginative source of such comradeship, Ginsberg eventually asserted in his testimony that Whitman's "adhesive love" also can emerge from the LSD experience as a communal effort between those taking LSD and those facilitating the experience under controlled circumstances. However, he began his testimony asserting that the power of the transcommunal, individual, romantic, humanist self, as extolled by Whitman and his transcendentalist contemporaries, is that which is most threatened by postwar culture: "I am taking the word from our prophet,

Walt Whitman. This is the tradition of the Founding Fathers, this is the true myth of America, this is the prophecy of our most loved thinkers—Thoreau, Emerson, and Whitman. That each man is a great universe in himself; this is the great value of the America that we call freedom" (*United States Senate* 488). As he invoked the American romantic canon to buttress the authority of his argument that the LSD user should be left alone by the government, Ginsberg also articulated a familiar American romantic crisis: namely, a conflict in which the nationalist literary idealism of American romanticism must contend with the romanticist notion that individual identity potentially transcends nationalism. Thus, Ginsberg's discussion of the LSD experience as an expressivist counterdiscourse to the regulatory speech of the Judiciary Committee actually articulated its own limits in the very space where it sought to be expansive.

Ginsberg reverted to the familiar, for him, language of apocalypticism to articulate a possible, albeit vexed, path out of this romantic crisis. In language that evokes the antagonism toward industrialization that also sparked Anglo-American romanticism, Ginsberg laments a postwar United States in which "the possibility of planetary war and death" haunts American culture "like a Biblical apocalypse." He argues that the United States is a dystopic culture dominated by "a network of electronic communication which reaches and conditions our thoughts and feelings to each other, spaceships which leave earth, loss of our natural green surroundings in concrete cities filled with smoke, accelerating technology homogenizing our characters and experience" (*United States Senate* 488). In "Kaddish," Ginsberg's autobiographical speaker unites with his apocalyptic mother, who destroys imaginative production at the same time that she inspires it; as a figure who resembles the Hindu Goddess Kali, a destroyer-liberator figure in the Hindu pantheon, Naomi represents for Ginsberg both the anxiety of apocalypse and the promise of a new world unveiled in its aftermath.[12] In "Kaddish," the combined Allen-Naomi figuration explores the meaning and value of an apocalyptic state of consciousness that enacts, paradoxically, both the destruction of the self "and what comes after" (*Collected* 209). The city is the redemptive location of this pilgrimage in "Kaddish." However, just five years later, in 1966, Ginsberg no longer codes apocalypse as feminized, positioned ambivalently between destruction and rebirth. Ginsberg's conception of apocalypse is only dystopic during the hearings. Apocalypse, instead, is marked by electronic surveillance, alienation, urban encroachment on the pastoral, and the "homogenizing" of romantic variegation. Ginsberg articulates his lament in terms of romantic pastoral individualism, despite that Buddhist-inspired poems such as "Angkor Wat" and "The Change" portray a struggle with romantic individualism.

At this point in his career, he has reached the limits of a romantic project he is not ready to abandon. During the Senate hearings, he argued that the self is debilitated by its alienation from the community at the same time that it suffers in alienation from what is left of nature. In Ginsberg's words to the Judiciary Committee, the culprit is the "bureaucratic machine" of the technologies of the state that surveils and regulates selfhood, producing its preferred mode of subjectivity rather than inspiring imaginative production in citizens. This "machine," he argued, "reduces our language and thoughts to uniformity, reduces our sources of inspiration and fact to fewer and fewer channels—as TV does—and monopolizes our attention with secondhand imagery—packaged news [. . .] and entertainment hours a day—and doesn't really satisfy our deeper needs for communication with each other" (488). Ginsberg's Manichean duality between technology and romantic humanism during the Senate hearings follows from the crisis of romanticism that produced "Wichita": both the testimony and the poem stage Ginsberg's response in language to the "electronic war" waged by the state.

Both the Senate testimony and "Wichita" are efforts to counter technologies of the state with technologies of the self. In "Wichita," this technology of the self is the embodied mantra, based on conceptions of selfhood that are both mired in self-presence and, in contrast, suffused with shunyata. During the 1966 Senate hearings, Ginsberg's LSD advocacy was framed by an either/or proposition that his use of LSD had been systematic rather than recreational. Whether one actually could use powerful consciousness-altering drugs in such a way is out of the bounds of my rhetorical analysis; Ginsberg likely used drugs both systematically and recreationally but emphasized only the former during the Senate hearings as part of his rhetoric of advocacy. What is more important is how Ginsberg's activist arguments during the Senate hearings are part of his Buddhist-inspired rhetoric of selfhood during this period of his career. Indeed, Ginsberg's LSD advocacy follows from the notion that systematized drug use, rather than recreational use, shapes a conception of the self that might evade governmentality. His testimony both supports and counters his conception of Buddhist subjectivity: the materialist dissolution of subject-object distinctions in Buddhist teachings on shunyata is countered by Ginsberg's insistence in Congress on a boundless American transcendentalist selfhood that is both nationalist and, paradoxically, beyond the constraints of categorical identity.

It would seem that Ginsberg asserts a version of postwar, pastoral romantic subjectivity within a counterdiscourse that, by contrast, would fragment the self, its language, and its trust in the transparency of individual utterances. Buddhist conceptions of the subject in language offer a means by which the poet could negotiate this contradiction. Ginsberg's argument to the Judiciary Committee, along with his crafting of an English-language mantra to end the war in "Wichita," suggests that when neoromantic humanism reaches its limits for him, he fills the gaps with new forms of language (the mantra, as deployed in "Wichita") and action (his focus on the communal aspects of drug use in his Senate testimony) that commingle romantic individuality with performative speech and communal action. The Buddhist notion of the Two Truths is the matrix for Ginsberg's idea that mantra speech is physical language suffused with the metaphysical lineage of past masters who have uttered the same words; thus, it is a matrix, too, for his fusion of materiality and metaphysicality, the quotidian and the magical. The LSD experience also is, for Ginsberg, one that distrusts language and sensation at the same time that it proposes linguistic and sensate materialism as vehicles of redemptive experience. As he described to the Judiciary Committee, "the word 'vision'" is, for him, just another way of articulating that he had "come back to [him]self" (*United States Senate* 490). For Ginsberg, this mode of selfhood as one that redeems as it is recovered is both imprisoning and redemptive:

> Where did I come back from? A world of thoughts; mental fantasies, schemes, words in my head, political or artistic concepts—mostly a world where language itself, or thoughts about reality, replaced my looking out on the actual place I was in, and the people there with me, with all our feelings together. A world where, for instance, you can look at death on television and not feel much or see much, only a familiar image like a movie. (*United States Senate* 490)

The impetus of Ginsberg's later work is to negotiate his distrust of the logos and his belief in an essential, actual place from which one creates a countersubjectivity. Inspired by the enthused contrariety in Blake's prophetic books, especially "The Marriage of Heaven and Hell" and *Milton*,

Ginsberg crafts a poetics in "Angkor Wat," "The Change," and "Wichita" that reflects his nascent Madhyamaka study in the 1960s.[13] Such a conceptual framework is middle-way rather than middling: like the Buddhism that inspires it, Ginsberg's conception of a middle-way is a polyvalent framework that enacts both poles of extremity from which it constructs its middle-way positioning. It is both immanent and transcendent; or, in the language of the Two Truths, it recognizes the oppositional influences of reificatory absolutism and groundless nihilism at the same time that it disavows a commitment to either of these poles.

The technologies of the self of both Buddhism and drug use are, for the poet in the mid-1960s, ways of articulating the desire for romantic transcendentalism and charting the limit, and collapse, of such a conceptual framework. For Ginsberg in the mid-1960s, LSD filled gaps produced by the limits of romanticism, as did Buddhism, in a culture where the pressures of the Vietnam War increasingly overrode the care of the self with a regulatory, surveillant governmentality. Still, Ginsberg's persistent argument at the time that the LSD experience could be coterminous with the meditation experience is a problematic one. Buddhism has no universally identifiable position on psychedelic drugs. Jack Kornfield, one of the most well-known Buddhist teachers in the West, puts the matter simply in a 1996 interview: "Psychedelics are found rarely, if at all, in the Buddhist tradition, and generally would be lumped together in the precepts under 'intoxicants.' [. . .] What points of view we have come from the understanding of Buddhist masters and teachers based on contemporary experience" (34). Although Kornfield is a Theravada rather than Mahayana teacher, his comments in the interview are intended for Western Buddhism at large. The argument in contemporary Buddhist communities for the past forty years over the efficacy or danger of psychedelic drugs—as a possibly useful acceleration of the meditation experience or a potentially fatal shortcut—is not one that will be resolved soon, given the complex, eclectic range of Buddhisms practiced in the contemporary era. Still, a sketch of the disagreement over psychedelic drugs in contemporary Buddhism can illuminate how Ginsberg's position was not revolutionary but instead represented one vector of common debate in the Buddhist community.

In a 1996 poll conducted by the mass-market Western Buddhist magazine *Tricycle*, over 40% of the respondents noted that "their interest in Buddhism was sparked by psychedelics," and 24% said they were "currently taking psychedelics" ("Results" 44). The poll, of course, was a nonscientific sampling. I cite it here, however, because the special section of this issue of the magazine titled "Psychedelics: Help or Hindrance?" represents one of the most significant examples of how the alternative religiosity of the 1960s and 1970s, often fueled by the so-called drug culture, had assimilated by the end of the twentieth century. The *Tricycle* poll offers a reminder on the split over the value of drug use and the limits of drug use in Western Buddhism in the intervening decades since Ginsberg's Congressional testimony. Indeed, even though 59% said that "psychedelics and Buddhism do mix," a full 71% asserted the limits of such use, saying that "psychedelics are not a path but they can provide a glimpse of the reality to which Buddhist practice points." As for this "glimpse," 58% said that "they would consider taking psychedelics in a sacred context." The parameters of this sacred context are not outlined in the poll or its results, however. One of the more succinct accounts of this same ambivalence toward psychedelic drugs is offered by Rick Fields's article in this issue on the history of postwar drug experimentation and Buddhism. Of the effects of psychedelic drugs within the Zen community, Fields writes, "If Suzuki Roshi said (as Gary Snyder told Dom Aelred Graham) that 'people who have started to come to the zendo from LSD experiences have shown an ability to get into good zazen very rapidly,' he also said in New York (as Harold Talbott, Graham's secretary, told Snyder) 'that the LSD experience was entirely distinct from Zen'" ("High History" 50).[14] Fields reports that such a skeptical attitude toward psychedelic shortcuts could also be found in the teachings of Trungpa's Crazy Wisdom school: "Trungpa Rinpoche, for all his outwardly wild nonconventional behavior, was a Tibetan mastiff when it came to practice: your ass was on the line, which meant on the [meditation] cushion" ("High History" 54).

Still, despite the complexities of this ambivalence toward psychedelic drugs in the Buddhist community, it is tempting to examine Ginsberg's drug activism from the same approach that many critics of his Buddhism adopt: namely, discussing Ginsberg's confluence of drug use, drug advocacy, and drug-induced compositional experiments as vectors only of exoticized escapism. Ginsberg's liberationist exhortations make him an easy target—he's the author of much of the mythmaking. Constructions of an orientalized "easy Easternness" or facile, drug-influenced romantic transcendentalism too often can substitute for a nuanced exploration of how Ginsberg's drug use and, especially, his public drug advocacy are incorporated into his visionary poetics. Recent critical discussion of drugs and the literary imagination by Marcus Boon, Sadie Plant, and David Lenson illustrate much of what is at stake in discussions of Ginsberg and drugs—and, specifically, can help construct a vocabulary for understanding how Ginsberg's Senate testimony comes to bear on his poetics of prophecy in the late 1960s and early 1970s. Yet, their readings of what Ginsberg signifies as a literary and cultural figure too often substitute for actual readings of the poems themselves. Boon and Lenson argue that LSD, like Buddhism, is part of Ginsberg's ongoing romantic project to conceive a heroic selfhood that transcends the limiting machinations of Moloch. Boon quotes the famous opening two lines of "Howl" yet offers no textual reading or contextual commentary. These lines, for Boon, are a self-evident reminder of the "outsider mythology" that undergirds the poem, where "the rebellious narcotics user, craving the night again, becomes a *saint*" (Lenson 75).[15] For Plant, the importance of the poem is, simply, that drugs aided its composition. In this way, her remarks on the famous opening lines substitute for a close reading of the poem as a whole; such an approach risks a sloganeering appropriation of the hipster vocabulary of the "angry fix."[16]

In the section that follows, I argue that the literary importance of Ginsberg's narcotics testimony can be found in the collision of romantic and postmodern conceptions of subjectivity and culture. Rather than serve as a vehicle for romanticism, Ginsberg's Senate testimony signals the limits of the poet's neoromantic impulse. His Senate testimony demonstrates that LSD increasingly was a technology of the self articulated in response to technologies of the state and is part of Ginsberg's increasingly materialist emphasis on the "widening" of consciousness, as he remarks in the epigraph to *Kaddish and Other Poems*, an emphasis that becomes paramount in the 1960s from "The Change" onward.[17] Ginsberg's drug use moves from efforts to escape back into the Blake vision and eventually emerges as a materialist response to technologies of the state; Buddhism, too, follows a similar, concurrent path in the poet's work, from autodidactic eccentricities through the 1960s into a materialist emphasis starting especially, as I argue later, in "Mind Breaths."

Romanticism and Legislation

On the surface, it would seem that Ginsberg's articulation of LSD as a mode of widening consciousness is, to echo Tytell, part of the poet's ongoing effort to loosen a culture of containment favored by establishment power in the 1960s. This position would seem to be supported by Ginsberg's initial, deferential tone with the Senators and his eventual marshaling of scientific evidence of the possible positive effects of the drug in his testimony—his effort to situate himself as a well-informed adversary whose efforts to prevent criminalization of the drug are not in the service of recreational use but instead to suggest, in his words, "what kinds of research are possible that might sensibly extend LSD research" (*United States Senate* 501). His appeal to "sensibility" also echoes the appeal to "common sense" in his revisions of "Howl"; his claim that "common sense" determined the important substitution of "hysterical" for "mystical" in the poem's famous opening line (*Howl* 124). Both claims invoke the privileged, populist realm of "common sense," but both exert power by subverting the traditional notion that "common sense" is self-evidentiary. In Ginsberg's poetic prophecies, "common sense" is a "hysterical" sense, a category of understanding in which meaning proliferates rather than admit containment. Indeed, in the Senate testimony, "sensibility" is Ginsberg's word for a position—continued legal research of LSD—that, as I discuss below in the Senators' responses to Ginsberg, was untenable as Ginsberg took his seat before the Judiciary Committee. Thus, a reading that suggests Ginsberg's appearance before the Committee represents the heroic, countercultural hipster positioned against a villainous establishment is one that neglects to account for Ginsberg's own manipulation of subjectivity and governmentality in his response. Ginsberg's language with the Judiciary Committee suggests that for him meaning is dialogic rather than monologic—that "sensibility" is something that can be accessed and manipulated as rhetoric by both counterculture and establishment discourses. Moreover, as discussed earlier, Ginsberg's confessional tone is one that suggests a mutable self neither liberated nor oppressed but instead one that makes knowledge and exploits breaks within circuits of power.

In short, Ginsberg's Senate testimony suggests that the emancipatory potential of Ginsberg's romantic pastoralism, represented for instance in the image of Ginsberg dancing at the Human Be-In, produced new, more complex state oppositional strategies even as its potential waned. Of course, one of the most effective political trends of the 1960s, and one that carried into the 1970s, was not necessarily the rise of the New Left as much as it was, simply, the fashioning of new methods to combat the radical left. Michael E. Staub, for instance, offers the reminder that the sixties represent "a moment when sophisticated anti-Left strategies were already being tested and refined" in law enforcement and the legal establishment and that "these trends intensified at the turn to the seventies" (20). According to Stephen Paul Miller, these strategies owed their increasing success to their strategies of surveillance. Miller observes an emergent culture of surveillance in the 1960s, including electronic eavesdropping and the infiltration of New Left activist groups by police and government agents, which eventually produced a model of governmentality in which political activists were disciplined by their own internalization of surveillance rather than by overt tactical strategies on the part of the state. Commenting on the ongoing effect of self-surveillance into the 1970s, Miller argues that Watergate inaugurated a period when Nixon's "overt surveillance and self-surveillance" created a condition by which U.S. culture virtually "ingested" such surveillance, creating a culture of the 1970s characterized by "a movement from external to internal surveillance" (1). Seen in this context, the language of Ginsberg's appearance before the Judiciary Committee in 1966 mirrors that of "Wichita Vortex Sutra," composed just a month before the hearings. On the surface, it appears to pit the "longhaired" Bard against the black-magic of the government, a battle between the romantic imagination and the industrial forces that seek to contain it. More important, though, the testimony and the poem itself together demonstrate that at this period in Ginsberg's career an antiromantic alternative suggested itself. In "Wichita," this alternative in language takes the form of the mantra, articulated as a materialist, linguistic technology of the self; and during the hearings, Ginsberg creates from the limits of romanticism an alternative conception of identity in which the LSD experience is transvalued, through self-monitored use, into a materialist, chemically produced technology of the self.

In both situations, language is the object over which Ginsberg and the state seek to exert primacy. Staub's reminder on state-counterculture conflict serves as a way of understanding the significance, especially, of language and Ginsberg's appearance before the Senate: "The memory of the sixties (both as historical event and as metaphorical reference point) was, in short, being fought over almost immediately; history was getting rewritten practically as it was happening" (20). In this way, Ginsberg's appearance before the Judiciary Committee is, like "Wichita," an effort both to write the history of the 1960s as it was being lived—to forge a response to what he later would term the "electronic war" in which "Wichita" partakes—and to revise his participation in discourses of romanticism during this period. His effort to "speak" his "lonesomeness" in the poem is, like his confessional language in his Senate testimony, an effort to reinscribe the romantic self in light of the social upheaval and state technologies of power in the period and to revise romantic individualism in terms of Buddhist notions of identity and language.

Indeed, despite his emphasis on romantic individualism in his testimony, Ginsberg's linguistic strategy eventually disavows the self. When asked by Senator Quentin N. Burdick where LSD can be obtained, Ginsberg's response suggests a strategy in which the drug is represented as part of the "common sense" experience of many across the educated middle class but one in which the individual identities of those who take it are fluid and, for purposes of their own protection, even anonymous:

> At the moment I don't obtain it [LSD] myself, so I don't know [where it can be obtained]. In order to speak freely on the subject, I have had to quit all use, because I heard that at one point the Narcotics Bureau was trying to set me up for an arrest. And so I thought if I were going to be able to speak publicly and effect any kind of social understanding of the problem, I had better keep myself out of jail [. . .]. (*United States Senate* 498)

In his opening remarks, Ginsberg framed his discourse as an effort to "talk together" and "make sense" with the Senators (*United States Senate* 487). Ginsberg describes his testimony as public and social rather than individual: language is used for relational ends, and the self is invoked only under the threat of incarceration. Surveillance and discipline are summoned in the testimony not as they would be in romantic discourse, as a means by which language is inhibited, but instead as a way to produce knowledge—as a mode of speech that creates the conditions by which the poet might speak freely in the ritualized arena of the U.S. Senate chambers. Ginsberg's efforts to introduce the testimony of sympathetic scientists suggests, too, that LSD inhabits the space otherwise reserved for romantic individualism. Introduced as exhibit number 76 in the hearings, Ginsberg's self-described "[i]nformal conversations with two dozen M.D.'s who have done clinical experimental & exploratory work with LSD and other Psychedelic chemicals" are deployed to suggest the need for greater research on the subject. At the same time, they invoke the scientific and technological heartlessness of Moloch in the same way that Ginsberg's incorporation of the antipsychiatric movement in "Kaddish" inhabits the authorizing discourses of science in order to empty them of reificatory power and prevent their re-reification. If the romantic poet underwrites his language with scientific discourse, then neither romanticism's traditionally pastoral, pantheistic power nor its conception of a traditionally hostile, absolutist domain of science can claim to be accurate representations of, respectively, heroic or oppositional discourses. Neither poles would truly exist, as Ginsberg's shunyata teaching suggests.

For Ginsberg, of course, desire always is a critical vector of political discourse, and in the Senate hearings, it negotiates romantic pastoralism and contemporary technologies of the self. He explained as much to the Judiciary Committee, invoking some of the ideas about the inspiration of maternal figures in his poetics that he later would develop into the essay, "How *Kaddish* Happened." Describing in his testimony his 1960 experiments in Peru with the psychedelic plant ayahuasca, Ginsberg explained that the plant enabled him to confront repressed psychic material in his relationships with women: "From childhood I had been mainly shut off from relationship with women—possibly due to the fact that my own mother was, from my early childhood on, in a state of great suffering, frightening to me, and had finally died in a mental hospital" (*United States Senate* 490). He continued, his confession of drug use serving a purpose in the making of new knowledge. The "widening of consciousness" occurs not just because of the drug but because of the poet's confessional narration of his experiences with the drug, in the same way that, for Freud, dream work involves not just the analysand's dream itself but also the analysand's narration of the dream after waking:

> In a trance state I experienced [. . .] a very poignant memory of my mother's self, and how much I had lost in my distance from her, and my distance from other later friendly girls—for I had denied most of my feeling to them, out of old fear. And this tearful knowledge that had come up while my mind was opened through the native vine's [ayahuasca] effect did make some change—toward greater trust and closeness with all women thereafter. The human universe became more complete for me—my own feelings more complete—and that is a value which I hope you all understand and approve. (*United States Senate* 490-91)

Ginsberg combines the personal and clinical, describing a "tearful knowledge" of the self as an ambisexual subject, reflecting the unfixed boundaries of desire and subjectivity in poems such as "Love Poem on Theme by Whitman."[18] At the same time, he is speaking in a ritual of power in which he seeks "understand[ing]" and "approv[al]" from a body of legislators. It is a narrative in which desire is both product and producer of knowledge.[19]

What is most important in Ginsberg's testimony, then, is not his mere appearance as countercultural icon but instead his efforts to use the hearings as an opportunity to answer the tactics of state control with the self-knowledge that emerges in the narrativizing of the LSD experience. Ginsberg's testimony represents an important break from romantic conceptions of the self in his poetics; and this break, in turn, enables a more nuanced and paradoxical understanding of selfhood to take a primary role in his Buddhist poetics. The hearings are, to borrow from Foucault, an exercise in "governmentality," where "the technologies of domination of others" make a significant point of contact with the technologies of the self ("Technologies of the Self" 19). As Ginsberg's remarks before the Judiciary Committee demonstrate, the care of the self precedes, for him, knowledge of the self. The poet elevates embodied knowledge to a level equal or superior to knowledge produced by mind. Ayahuasca collapses the distance between himself and others; from here a "tearful knowledge" emerges that is later articulated as a question of power in the ritualized legislative body of the U.S. Senate chambers.

A line might be drawn from "Kaddish" through the Senate testimony, one that includes "Wichita" and anticipates "Iron Horse" and the development of his Buddhist poetics in the early 1970s. Ginsberg, of course, is often perceived as the archetypal counterculture hedonist of the postwar United States; thus, as I discuss in the following chapter, his increasingly serious turn to Buddhism often is perceived as a mode of quietism that dilutes the power of this archetype. Instead, framed within the perspective offered by Foucault's work on the history of sexuality, Ginsberg's project articulates the quite noisy relationship among questions of confession, subjectivity, meaning-making, politics, and desire in postwar U.S. culture. Ginsberg's representations of asceticism in "Angkor Wat," then, would seem more than a gesture of "easy Easternness"; instead it is, as Foucault writes of the history of sexuality, "a question of the relation between asceticism and truth" ("Technologies of the Self" 17). Such a question, indeed, frames both Ginsberg's Senate testimony and his early Buddhist-inspired poetics from "Howl" through "The Change." Foucault's summation of his project on the history of sexuality in "Technologies of the Self" also offers a way to emphasize Ginsberg's career-long emphasis on candor as a political force. Foucault writes, "I conceived of a rather odd project: not the evolution of sexual behavior but the projection of a history of the link between the obligation to tell the truth and the prohibitions against sexuality. I asked: How had the subject been compelled to decipher himself in regard to what was forbidden?" (17). For Ginsberg, candor is the necessary articulation of the truth of the self in a culture that ascribes diminished value to self-knowledge. As Foucault observes, the question of candor is one of the most important to investigate in a culture in which the "decipher[ing]" of the self is part and parcel of the deciphering of the ways in which power circulates; in this way, candor is a mode of speech that can determine where agency is invoked and withdrawn, and that can determine those breaks where agency might proliferate again.

On the surface, the Judiciary Committee is summoning Ginsberg as a countercultural expert but without much desire to deploy his expertise in an effort to forge a mutual "sensibility," as Ginsberg describes his own intentions. However, the Judiciary Committee and Ginsberg ultimately clashed on the role and conception of selfhood in the postwar era: for the senators, knowledge of the self precedes care of the self, while Ginsberg transposes these same priorities, placing care of the self as a primary function that itself can only lead to self-knowledge. I do not mean to suggest that the collective body of the Judiciary Committee constituted a faceless technologized Moloch, as it were. Ginsberg's confessionalism is a rhetorical strategy; his emphasis on psychedelic use among "middle-class people, professional people, and younger people, students" is, of course, a carefully crafted effort to counter the demonization of psychedelics by juridico-medical discourses of criminality and addiction. Ginsberg recasts drug discourse to account for his own educated experimentation and that of the scientific establishment studying LSD—in effect, recasting drug users within a space of "middle-class" decorum that otherwise admits alcohol, nicotine, and caffeine as acceptable drugs used by consumers rather than consumed by "users."

Ginsberg's self-revelatory, confessional tone at the hearings was as much an embodiment of his actual fears as it was a rhetorical device that could be shed when necessary. Asked by Senator Burdick how long he has been "a user," Ginsberg replies: "I have used psychedelic drugs, the varieties, infrequently since about 1952. I am not sure that I enjoy the use of the terminology 'user' because it is associated with dope fiends and dope and drug users." To which Burdick said, "I will just use the word 'used' then" (*United States Senate* 497). Such distinctions were not within the purview of these hearings, where the politics of Ginsberg's literary reputation were portrayed as a matter of national health and security. Noting Ginsberg's "great vogue among our young people," Javits pressed him to state explicitly what his strategies for LSD use and experimentation would be, "because otherwise they [U.S. youth culture] might be misled as to what you are really advising them to do, either by precept or by advice" (*United States Senate* 504). In this instance, Ginsberg's own poetic strategies are turned against him: as a poet-prophet who often stages containment in order to empty gestures of containment of their power to reify, Ginsberg is asked to speak in the language of complicity—in effect, the language of technologies of the state. Ginsberg's testimony focused on personal and scientific experimentation in the service of the care of the self, at times in the language of a Peruvian *curandero* (healer or shaman) and Indian and Buddhist gurus and at other times paraphrasing researchers from the National Institutes of Health. However, Javits now suggested that he speak the logic of legislative language. A figure of the Senate's ritualized, juridico-medico space, Javits said, "I think you ought to state clearly what you have in mind. This is the place to do it" (*United States Senate* 504). Later, he reminded Ginsberg that "you don't have to answer any of our questions which might in your judgment [. . .] incriminate you" (*United States Senate* 506). These remarks serve to remind the poet of the disciplinary language in which any personalized or confessional discourse is framed at the hearings; moreover, Javits's words underwrite his persistent efforts to persuade Ginsberg to reveal what he knows about where LSD is manufactured and to reveal the extent of Ginsberg's public advocacy of the drug.[20] Schumacher writes that Javits "took exception" to Ginsberg's "speaking as if he was an authority and making recommendations to the subcommittee—even if, in fact, [Ginsberg] would not have been invited to testify had it not been believed that he was capable of doing both" (473-74).

Instead, the invitation extended to Ginsberg was not based on his capabilities but on his presence as a counterculture icon. The same ambivalence that Ginsberg was feeling as a public figure—beginning with "Angkor Wat," through his opening to "Wichita" and, later, in poems such as "Ego Confession"—is nurtured by the Senate Subcommittee as a means to extend its surveillance of the drug culture Ginsberg was seen to represent.[21] Ginsberg argued that scientific research of LSD had been "shut off by the Government" and needed to be reactivated (*United States Senate* 509). This response is informed by the direct engagement with governmentality—the "electronic war"—in "Wichita," and, as I discuss in the following chapter, it anticipates "Iron Horse," a poem that confronts the complexities of this break with romantic individualism in the context of Ginsberg's language for desire and sacred experience.

5

Strategies of Retreat

> The writing itself, the sacred act of writing, when you do anything of this nature, is like a prayer.
> —Allen Ginsberg, 1971

Speaking Back to the Conductor

Ginsberg continued to emphasize how language and technology authorize governmentality more than a decade after "Wichita" and his Congressional testimony. In a 1978 interview with Paul Portugés, he asserted that his anti-Vietnam poetry "wasn't about the war" but instead "was about television and war—war as seen, as represented on television, radio, and newspapers [. . .] the *electronic war*" (*Visionary Poetics* 134). "Wichita" constructed a universalized mantra poetics of contestatory "magic." This conflict between magic and materiality, as I have argued, characterized his Senate testimony one month later, when he spoke at the very limit of his romanticist project. There, Ginsberg described drug use as, alternatively, both a pantheistic utopian pastoral refuge from industrialization and a technology of the self that, like Buddhism, detaches the sacred from transcendental discourse and relocates it in the body. Ginsberg's language for subjectivity in his Buddhist poetics borrows from Madhayamaka middle-way teachings to negotiate, however tenuously, the conflicted modes of identity so prominently staged in front of the Judiciary Committee: it produces fissures in the humanist self without debilitating the humanist subject or substituting a fictive discourse of wholeness and referentiality for this fissured self. Yet, as demonstrated in "Iron Horse," completed just months after the Judiciary Committee hearings, Ginsberg's middle-way subjectivity does not always produce a coherent enough self to represent the exigencies of political or religious experience.

What is at stake in Ginsberg's Buddhist poetics after "Wichita" is how a language for sacred experience can assert the authority of the speaking self without surrendering to metaphysics, the standard by which the sacred is most often defined in the West. Where "Wichita" documented Ginsberg's movement westward in the United States and staged his subsequent optimism that wartime language might be repaired, "Iron Horse" is framed instead by Ginsberg's movement back eastward in the United States, his attempt to understand a war that had accelerated since he launched his auto poesy journey. "Iron Horse" mocks the promise of mobility that pervades "Wichita." In "Wichita," the automobile was a means by which a poetry of mobile representation, a language of performativity rather than referentiality, might reenvision a world diminished by the sterile, static language of war. But the Santa Fe train that carries Ginsberg from the West Coast to Chicago in part 1 of "Iron Horse" also transports soldiers just a month into their mobilization. As it props the war effort, mobility in "Iron Horse" produces only belatedness and silence, rather than a prophetic language of immediacy: "Too late, too late / the Iron Horse hurrying to war, / [. . .] I'm a stranger alone in my country again" (*Collected* 445).

Ginsberg turns to Whitman to address this silence and recuperate the consequent otherness it produces. In "Song of Myself," the erotic action of Whitman's twenty-eight bathers invite a twenty-ninth. As Michael Moon writes, Whitman's poem "incorporate[s]" the woman watching the bathing men through her window—she who becomes the twenty-ninth bather—"into the 'fluid' circle" of male homoerotic sexuality represented by the collective twenty-eight bathers.[1] This incorporation occurs, formally, through repetition:

> Twenty-eight young men bathe by the shore,
> Twenty-eight young men, and all so friendly,
> Twenty-eight years of womanly life, and all so lonesome.

> She owns the fine house by the rise of the bank,
> She hides handsome and richly drest aft the blinds of the window.
>
> Which of the young men does she like the best?
> Ah the homliest of them is beautiful to her.
>
> ("Song of Myself" 11.199–205)

Ginsberg recasts the splashed, "sous[ing]" erotic joy of section 11 as sterile warmongering in "Iron Horse."

> Ninety nine soldiers in uniform paid by the Government
>   to Believe—
> ninety nine soldiers escaping the draft for an Army job,
> ninety nine soldiers shaved
>   with nowhere to go but where told [. . .].
>
> (*Collected* 444)

"Iron Horse" suggests that materialist identity and metaphysical self-presence can be negotiated successfully only when the individual prophetic bard of the poems is not isolated from the community for which he speaks. The spiritual crisis of "Angkor Wat," in which the poet is absorbed in solipsistic anxiety, reemerges in "Iron Horse."[2] Rather than speak back to propaganda—as "Wichita" redirects what is "told" in the press and radio—Ginsberg retreats from the very world that inspires "Wichita" and "Iron Horse": "Better withdraw from the Newspaper world / Better withdraw from the electric world / Better retire before war cuts my head off . . ." (*Collected* 446).

Perhaps this withdrawal is precisely the sort of quietism Helen Vendler has in mind in her 1996 *New Yorker* retrospective when she rejects the role of Buddhism in the later poems. Indeed, Ginsberg's withdrawal in "Iron Horse" is forecast at the beginning of the poem in a scene that evokes his 1948 William Blake vision. As documented here and elsewhere, the Blake vision is variously described by Ginsberg as the inaugurating experience of his career as a poet-prophet. Yet, in "Iron Horse," it is recalled and reimagined by the poet as self-absorbed masturbation, where the failure to create a relational rather than singularist wartime language is, for Ginsberg, a failure that comes from the singularity of our conceptions of subjectivity, echoing the solipsistic anxieties that dominate "Angkor Wat." This failure is articulated, as it is in "Angkor Wat," through the speaker's masturbation fantasies. Obsessed by the "mind-soup" anxieties that predicate "Angkor Wat," Ginsberg's speaker in "Iron Horse" opens the poem surrendered "wet handed by meat sex" (*Collected* 311). I have discussed Ginsberg's figural use of masturbation in chapter 2, but its role in the war poetry requires further elaboration, especially insofar as masturbation restages Ginsberg's originary prophetic experience, the Harlem Blake vision. The Blake vision occurred after Ginsberg had been masturbating in his Harlem apartment; as solitary as this scene might be, the experience itself encouraged him to create a common link between himself and the wider world of everyday lived experience. The day of the vision he found himself in a bookstore with other patrons who shared the same common, unified field of perception. As he told Tom Clark in the *Paris Review* interview, Ginsberg, the bookstore clerk, and the customers "all had the consciousness, it was like a great unconscious that was running between [*sic*] all of us that everybody *was* completely conscious" ("Art" 42). Eighteen years after this experience, desire is reduced to sterility on the Santa Fe train in "Iron Horse," and the poet finds himself concealed in his train car asking only, "What can I shove up my ass?" (*Collected* 432). The visionary human connection he felt after the Blake vision, experienced in the wake of masturbation, is reduced to mechanical self-satisfaction in "Iron Horse." Masturbation is disconnected, figurally, from desire in the poem and instead reminds him of the cruel efficiency and violence of the war effort: "Ahh—white drops fall, / millions of children," he writes, then adds, as if ashamed: "Wipe up cream—what if / The Conductor knocked" (*Collected* 433). Ginsberg's career to this point is marked by politically charged confrontations with the Conductor as an emblematic figure of univocal authority voiced in the forms of Blake's Nobodaddy, Moloch, or the U.S. State Department, among others. However, "Iron Horse" opens with the speaker concealing his desire—wiping away spent semen—from the disciplinary gaze of the Conductor who knocks on the other side of the door of the sleeping car. Desire fails to produce an imaginative response to rushing war rhetoric in "Iron Horse," and Ginsberg's attempts to forge intimacy in the poem often result in longing silence or self-obsessive nostalgia.

Even though "Iron Horse" functions as a companion long poem to "Wichita," Ginsberg is less confident in the power of mantric speech, so important in the latter poem, by the time of "Iron Horse." Both "Iron Horse" and "Wichita" are efforts to craft a counterlanguage to wartime discourse—the *"electronic war,"* as Ginsberg has described it—that has authorized violence and muted dissent. Tapevoice language is contrasted with the language of mainstream electronic media and newspapers in both poems; and in "Iron Horse," Ginsberg incorporates overheard conversations by and about soldiers on the train in part 1—then on a bus from Chicago to New York in part 2—with fragmented lyric remembrance of the poet's U.S. travels and more newspaper headlines. Yet, the poetics of possibility evoked by the mantra in "Wichita" is exhausted by the time of "Iron Horse"; Ginsberg's mantric poets becomes in "Iron Horse" a series of frustrated repetitions, suggesting that the pacifist possibility, for Ginsberg, in Buddhism has been exhausted and even reduced to reiteration. Where "Wichita" constructed an English-language mantra to end the war, "Iron Horse" uses English-language repetition to construct a doomed echo of Whitman's twenty-ninth-bather scene from *Song of Myself*. English, it would seem, is no longer an adequate field for the mantra by the time of "Iron Horse": Ginsberg's desire in "Wichita" to "make Mantra of American language now" collapses into reiterative political complaint.

Instead of transforming repetition into the performative mode of mantra speech in "Iron Horse," Ginsberg's language for prophecy repeats but does not reinscribe, as in Ginsberg's exhausted repetition that U.S. soldiers on the train are running a fool's errand:

> Soldiers on this train think they're fighting China
> Soldiers on this train think Ho Chi Minh's Chinese
> Soldiers on this train don't know where they're going
> John Steinbeck stop the war John Steinbeck   stop
>   the war John Steinbeck stop the war.
>   (*Collected* 443)

Earlier in the poem, Ginsberg evoked Yevgeny Yevtushenko's open letter to John Steinbeck disagreeing with the American novelist's support of the U.S. war effort. Yevtushenko's letter is deployed as a counterstatement to the language of military mobilization against which the poem is positioned. However, what once was a belief that the single individual's word could create a countermantra to the "black mantras" of the Johnson administration now has lapsed into a third-generation discourse in which Ginsberg repeats a fellow poet's response to the hawkish views of a novelist with whom Ginsberg had no immediate contact. Rather than perform the illocutionary speech act of mantra-making, this moment of repetition merely utters a declarative complaint: "John Steinbeck stop the war John Steinbeck stop / the war John Steinbeck stop the war."

The impulse to resignify material lived experience as a practice of the sacred seems exhausted by "Iron Horse." Ginsberg's mantric speech in this poem demonstrates that sacred language can thwart itself despite the poet-prophet's intentions otherwise. In contrast to his trust that he can create an English-language mantra in "Wichita," Ginsberg only summons mantric speech once in this poem and in appropriated Japanese rather than original English. This effort to conceive the redemptive mantra speech of "Wichita" without remaking English speech—without, as he says in "Wichita," a voice that "make[s] Mantra of American language now" (*Collected* 407)—is articulated in his incorporation of the Dharani of Removing Disasters, which Ginsberg first encountered in D. T. Suzuki's *Manual of Zen Buddhism* (*Collected Poems* 781). Where "Wichita" constructed a mantra to end the war, "Iron Horse" portrays how "language language / escalating" can drown out the efforts to "remove" this disaster with more language. The speaker utters the Dharani of Removing Disasters, then promptly asserts in English, "The universe is empty" (*Collected* 438). Unlike the casual "Prajnaparamita Sutra over coffee" in "Wichita," which was part of the poet's effort to enact the shunyata qualities of language and from this craft an English-language mantra to end the war, Ginsberg's statement on emptiness in "Iron Horse" functions only as a declaration of faith. The speaker believes the universe is suffused with Buddhist emptiness and has uttered a mantra declaring the same. Yet, unlike "Wichita," the poem does not stage shunyata in its reiterative speech; instead, it stages the failure of pacifistic representation that otherwise would counter the wartime "black mantras" of the Pentagon.

The early masturbation scene leads to a solitude that deprecates the poet's desire to redeem the body rent by war and to redeem his culture's authorizing language for the war. Both body and language unite in this poem, yet their commingling does not produce the redemptive rhetoric of vision that frames Ginsberg's earlier work. As he rests in the "Cabinette in complete darkness," he overhears a solider talking about the night he first took home his girlfriend. This is the sort of heterosexualizing scene that in past poems such as "Love Poem on Theme by Whitman" leads to a consummated ambisexual encounter, or in "This Form of Life Needs Sex," produces an explicit rendering of Ginsberg's maternal fears and procreation anxieties. However, in "Iron Horse," the scene is rendered in the distanced language of eavesdropped, second-hand narrative and with a tone of ennui that recalls the fumbling clerk typist scene from *The Waste Land*. T. S. Eliot's characters lapse into isolation in those very moments they seek sexual community, as do the figures described in the overheard conversation in "Iron Horse":

> [the soldier talked about how he] took off her pants
> and she said that he shd take off his pants
> and he wouldn't take off his pants
> and how they'd have some
> love play, like everybody
> and then, he'd drive her home,
> but when he's out at a bar
> if anybody looks at his girl
> he looks 'em in the eye and snaps his finger & says
> whatter ya lookin like that fur—
> and out in a bar alone,
> anybody's fair game for his love.
> (*Collected* 437)

Sexual possession is not the erotic interplay of dominant and submissive roles, nor are sexed subjectivities invoked in performative language, as in "Please Master." Instead, desire is rendered in this section of "Iron Horse" as a failed effort of heterosexual, masculine hegemony. Hegemony fails without surveillance, and isolation emerges from this solitude: "out in a bar alone, / anybody's fair game for his love."

Ginsberg implies in the next long stanza of the poem that the internalization of the Conductor's disciplinary figuration looms over language as well as the body. Ginsberg pronounces, "Old poetry grows stale, / forlorn, as always forlorn"; it amounts to little more, he says, than "matter-babble behind the ear" (*Collected* 437). Threatened by a Conductor figure against whom Ginsberg agitated throughout his career, the poet now laments a failure to overwrite the language of Cold War containment. Presumably, the old poetry gone stale is his own. The body is threatened by war, and the libido isolated; eventually, language reverts to diatribe and nostalgia, to "matter-babble behind the ear." The difference between performative speech and diatribe in these poems emerges from the role the body plays in them. The emphasis on *forlorn*, its repetition, suggests, too, an echo of one of the most famous uses of the word, in Keats's closing to "Ode to a Nightingale," ostensibly a poem occasioned by anxieties over the diminishment or loss of poetic potency. It would seem, then, that the old poetry Ginsberg wishes to revivify is his own—a statement of regret that his previous insistence on prophetic speech, most recently his construction of an English-language mantra in "Wichita," is now a mere declaration of faith rather than a performative act of linguistic and social renovation.

Ginsberg's English-language mantra in "Wichita" was a means of rescuing the body by repairing the language that authorizes its destruction by sending soldiers to war. Yet, the body reverts to state instrumentalism in "Iron Horse." Ginsberg's ninety-nine soldiers are a debasement of the erotic pleasures of Whitman's twenty-ninth bather at the same time that they invoke the bawdy drinking song, "Ninety-nine bottles of beer on the wall." Whitman's twenty-eight bathers are "all so friendly" in their eroticized intimacy as they splash before the gaze of the woman who will become the phantasmic twenty-ninth ("Song of Myself" 200). The hirsute bodies of Ginsberg's soldiers—"Young fellas that some of them had long hair" (*Collected* 441)—on the train in "Iron Horse" are, in contrast, shaved and berated as part of the process that, rather than eroticize them, disciplines their bodies as it shapes them into instruments of war:

> Ninety-nine soldiers entering the train
>   and all so friendly
>   Only a month
>   hair clipped & insulted [. . .]
>   (*Collected* 440)

The prophetic Bard of "Wichita" uttered his English-language mantra to rescue those "boys with sexual bellies aroused" who were "chilled in the heart by the mailman" delivering draft notices (*Collected* 404). These same figures in "Iron Horse," now mobilized for war, do not recognize that they are instruments of combat, and their lack of self-consciousness creates the despair of the poem. These soldiers "weren't too sad" to enter the train "hair clipped & insulted," because they are "glad going to some electronics field near Chicago / —Been taking courses in Propaganda" (*Collected* 440-41). No wonder, then, that the speaker decries, "Old poetry grows stale" in an environment where tapevoice composition and mantra-making cannot compete with courses in Propaganda offered by a military-industrial complex fighting what the poet terms an *electronic war*. Against systemic schools of propaganda, the poet counters with the

Dharani of Removing Disasters, now reduced to reiteration, and a flat declaration that "[t]he universe is empty." Crucially, the speaker is torn between the complex teachings on emptiness in the Prajnaparamita Sutra and an inability in "Iron Horse" to enact these teachings in a way that would produce a pacifist counterdiscourse more potent than mere "matter-babble behind the ear."

This failure is as much a fault of material resources—the insolvency of poetry against the seemingly limitless economic resources of the Pentagon, in a culture where language is "taxed by [and for] war"—as it is a fault of Ginsberg's inability to distinguish between idealism and materialism. Romantic idealism is at odds with materialist language in "Wichita" and "Iron Horse." Ginsberg combines the two in a reliance on performative language in the former poem but responds to this same conflict in the latter with the suggestion that civilian and wartime language is rent by self-presence. The nondualist language of the performative—where the boundary is blurred between subject and object, frame and edge, meaning and action—coalesces into utterances of nostalgia in "Iron Horse," in which language represents the subject's desire to escape into nostalgia from the terror of war.

For Vendler, the lack of communality in *The Fall of America* poems is precisely the result of the fragmentary nature of their composition, which produces an "avalanche of detail," an exhausting "ardent atlas" of Ginsberg's world (207). Vendler's remarks are true enough. Yet, I am not convinced they go far enough on the question of poetic form. Form is never quite separable from content in "Wichita" and "Iron Horse," and the isolation and exhaustion of "Iron Horse" result from the poet's deliberate representation of exhaustion with his own form, not just, as Vendler implies, from the presence of the form itself. Indeed, by the time the speaker has switched from the Santa Fe train to the bus that will take him from Chicago to New York, he has withdrawn so soundly into nostalgia that representations of the electronic war seem politically unproductive. Nostalgic memories collage on the bus, reconceiving an imaginative, democratically adhesive past; yet they often are addressed to the poet's image of Jack Kerouac rather than to his reader: "Howl for them that suffer broken bone / homeless on moody balconies / Jack's voice returning to me over & over" (*Collected* 451).[3] The speaker claims that Kerouac's voice returns "with prophecy," but by this point in the poem, with the poet urging himself to "withdraw from the electric world" in the midst of the electronic war, the notion that the voice of Kerouac is prophetic in this poem is nothing but a declarative—another statement to be taken on faith rather than enacted in the poem itself. Ginsberg has confronted this issue of faith and prophecy throughout his career as a question of how one distinguishes false from true prophecy. This distinction between false and true prophecy for Ginsberg always has been located in his reliance on language that distrusts its own representational impulses. But such an approach to language is exhausted in "Iron Horse," so that when Ginsberg attempts to empty self-presence from electronic language, the poem lapses into diatribe. Ginsberg energetically indicts governing discourses that propagandize soldiers, the "Grammarschool" that "taught 'em Newspaper Language," and the Safeway market that provides them with *Reader's Digest* (*Collected* 455). What is missing from this indictment, in a poem that otherwise serves as a sequel to the "Wichita" sutra, is a sustained focus on how shunyata might serve as a conceptual framework for an East-West prophetic discourse. To be sure, Ginsberg's image of the constructedness of the evening newscast defamiliarizes the experience of sound, language, and image so that representation and naming are emptied of their reifying context. This is a gesture of shunyata, one that loosens language, sound, and imagery from the moorings that would separate subject from object and, more important for Ginsberg, that would distinguish between citizens and their enemies:

> Cut sound out of television you won't tell who's Victim
> Cut Language off the Visual you'll never know
>   Who's Aggressor—
>   cut commentary from Newscast
>   you'll see a mass of madmen at murder.
> Chicago train soldiers chatted over beer
>   They, too, vowed to fight the Cottenpickin
>   Communists and give their own bodies
>   to the fray.
>   (*Collected* 454–55)

Yet, this distrust of subjectivity created from wartime language is not sustained; it degenerates into dualistic name-calling, with the Bard of "Wichita" and "Iron Horse" caricaturing rather than engaging the language of the black magicians in the Pentagon. Where Lyndon B. Johnson was once perceived as the purveyor of black-magic mantras, his wartime position is now merely metonymized as a black-magic redneck—one who produces from soldiers a "vo[w]" to fight the "Cottenpickin Communists." As discussed in chapter 4, Ginsberg crafted in "Wichita Vortex Sutra" an English-language mantra that would dissolve subject-object distinctions in an illocutionary utterance; yet now, in "Iron Horse," dualist language suggests a failure of the mantric poetics of "Wichita."

Buddhist conceptual frameworks, including the evocations of self and selflessness at the end of "Iron Horse," now depend on referential distinctions between the speaking subject, the Bard, and his distinct enemy, the Pentagon. As the poem closes, the speaker declares that "Buddha's Nameless." This is countered, dramatically, by the final lines of the poem, as the poet returns to a mechanized New York that resembles Moloch and that seems to have no use for the culture of redemption presumed by the invocation "Buddha's Nameless" or by mantric speech itself:

> [. . .] car fumes &
> Manhattan tattered, summer heat,
> sweltering noon's odd patina
> on city walls,
> Greyhound exhaust terminal,
> trip begun,
> taxi-honk toward East River where
> Peter waits working
> (*Collected* 456)

In a sweltering, rusted, nearly oxidized version of contemporary workaday New York, Ginsberg's long poems of linguistic and spiritual mobility, "Wichita Vortex Sutra" and "Iron Horse," end instead with soldiers mobilized—rather than with a mobilization of youth counterculture. They close with contemporary New York City imagined as a terminal space of toil. Desire, represented by Orlovsky, is overcome by labor, the same cultural institution that presumably props the war effort; Ginsberg's embodied poetics of possibility culminates in the simple phrase, "Peter waits working." The prophetic potential of mantric speech, conceived as a way to end the war in "Wichita," is overwhelmed in "Iron Horse" by a combination of the Pentagon's linguistic resources and the poet's own distrust of the power of the mantra.[4] Forecast early in the poem when masturbation replaces human contact, the isolated and singularist speech of the poet serves as a trope for a substitution of the relational, performative utterance of the mantra with referential, singularist language.

Mind Breaths, Speech Breaths

Despite the inability of mantric speech to sustain Ginsberg's conception of the sacred at this point in his career, as seen in "Wichita," the Congressional testimony, and "Iron Horse," Ginsberg does not abandon his Buddhist poetics. Indeed, Buddhism takes on greater urgency in his work soon after his conflicts with the mantra in "Iron Horse." Jay Dougherty has argued that Ginsberg's *Mind Breaths: Poems 1972–1977* inaugurates a "significant thematic shift" in Ginsberg's poetry that has been overlooked, a shift that includes the poet's Buddhism as a significant tendency. Michael Schumacher concurs, asserting that the book "signifie[s] Ginsberg's growing involvement in Buddhism and meditation," and his "most contemplative, introspective volume in a long time" (619). However, Dougherty himself admits that a substantive understanding of Ginsberg's poetry still awaits an exploration of the poet's Buddhist influences. As I have quoted in chapter 1, Dougherty asserts that the poems would "be better understood" if audiences read them "with a knowledge of Ginsberg's Buddhist-Trungpa teachings and vocabulary" (84).

Mind Breaths indeed enacts an important new direction in Ginsberg's work, and this direction is framed by increasingly studious, formal Tibetan Buddhist instruction from Chögyam Trungpa, from whom he took bodhisattva vows in 1972. Ginsberg's Buddhist education becomes formalized once he enters into a guru-student relationship with Trungpa, thus, it is important to examine how this shift from autodidactic to formal education shapes Ginsberg's Buddhist poetics. As he discusses the role of Ginsberg's Trungpa-Buddhism in *Mind Breaths*, Dougherty cautions against Ginsberg's tendency in this volume toward the "declarative" poem, one that does not "offer anything for the reader to grasp onto . . . besides the speaker's declarations"; as such, the success of such poems "depends upon the listener's being sympathetic beforehand to the statements made by the artist" (*Collected* 83–84). These poems risk failure, Dougherty writes, because they prefer "the dogmatic-statement convention of the declarative poem" at the expense of a poetics that would frame "dogmatic-statement convention" with "illustrative context built up around the statements" (*Collected* 83–84). As an example, Dougherty argues that the "Buddhist-Trungpa-related" detail of "Gospel Noble Truths" lacks illustrative context that would resonate with readers who may not feel sympathetic toward Ginsberg's declarations, straight from Buddhism's basic tenets, that "You got to suffer" or "You got no soul." For Schumacher,

Ginsberg's Buddhist-inspired poetic strategies in *Mind Breaths* offer an opportunity to explore the virtues and limitations of the sociopolitical retreat of "Iron Horse." Schumacher asserts that the "introspective works" and "meditation poems" of *Mind Breaths* offer "readers a glimpse of the very human poet in moments of withdrawal from the more familiar prophetic voice" (620).

Two crucial issues emerge from these responses to *Mind Breaths*, and both come to bear on Ginsberg's Buddhist poetics after he begins formal study with Trungpa. First, although Dougherty correctly points up the danger of Ginsberg's declarative tendencies, his response could forestall the exploration of the same Buddhist-inspired poetics that, as his review suggests, is crucial to the book. For instance, Dougherty's discussion of "Gospel Noble Truths" as a declarative poem, quoted above, neglects to mention that the poem encapsulates the Four Noble Truths of Buddhism in its first three stanzas; that lines 13–20 of the poem dramatize Buddhism's Eightfold Noble Path, the core of the fourth Noble Truth; and that, as Ginsberg writes in his 1984 notes to the poem, the final twenty lines of the poem stage "brief instruction for sitting and review of six sense fields" (*Collected* 794).[5] The didactic impulse of these poems warrants further attention as instances of Ginsberg's increasingly formal study of Buddhism. To cite a later example of Ginsberg's didactic Buddhist poetry, "Do the Meditation Rock," from *White Shroud: Poems, 1980–1985,* initially seems like nothing but a passing ditty. However, as in "Gospel Noble Truths," this song undertakes a purpose common to Buddhist texts, containing an entire practice—in this case, Buddhism's Six Perfections, or six sacred practices for attaining enlightenment—in verse form, in much the same way Western prayers accomplish their purposes. The second important issue to reconsider in these critical responses is Schumacher's equation of meditation, introspection, and withdrawal, a commentary that forecasts later critical responses, such as Vendler's in 1996, that describe the poet's Buddhism as a tendency toward increasing "quietism." At this point in his career, Ginsberg confronts questions of withdrawal and quietism that, presumably for readers such as Vendler, would follow from a perception that a Buddhist poetics is predicated only on meditative unity rather than inward-seeking fragmentation. By the publication of *Mind Breaths*, Ginsberg indeed shifts his engagement with governmentality inward. Technologies of the state are at times noticeably absent and at other times subsumed into the individual body-speech-mind of a speaker identified as a Buddhist practitioner, rather than one only inspired by Buddhism. In many of these later poems, he asserts a subjectivity that is simultaneously solid and diffuse; he articulates a humanist subject at the same time that historical particularity and linguistic indeterminacy subvert this same subject. Most of all, mindful of the poet's frustrated conflict with governmentality in the mid-1960s, Ginsberg's Buddhist poetics becomes less trustful of the spoken word if it is vocalized independently of the spoken breath.

From the *Mind Breaths* volume onward, Ginsberg's formal training in Buddhism becomes a central organizing principle in his Buddhist poetics.[6] In this later portion of his career, Ginsberg's ultimate referent for sacred language is his one speech-breath-thought-poetics, introduced as the anchoring, asemantic exhalation *Ah* in *Mind Breaths*. Dougherty and Schumacher correctly infer from these poems that they risk alienating readers with their emphasis on declarative Buddhist statements and potential introspective withdrawal from the public world in which Ginsberg so firmly insinuated himself as a poet-prophet from "Howl" through the poems of the 1960s. However, the poems in *Mind Breaths* continue Ginsberg's experiments with the Buddhist possibilities of the performative utterance in "Wichita Vortex Sutra" and respond to the doomed nostalgia that pervades "Iron Horse." The fatalism of this latter poem is reconceived as Ginsberg fashions himself into somewhat of a good gray poet of American Buddhism. They enact familiar Western notions of Buddhist disengagement and quietism in order to stage a counterdiscourse that recasts common stereotypes of Buddhism in terms of contestatory cultural and linguistic experimentation. Rather than withdraw from the "electric world," they incorporate this world in the ostensibly antidramatic situations of sitting, breathing, and reiterative mantra recitation. They do risk alienating the reader unfamiliar with Buddhism—insofar as they defamiliarize audience expectations for how a reflective, quiet Buddhist experience might be represented.

In poems such as "Thoughts Sitting Breathing," this risk is as much a question of experimental poetic form as it is of Buddhist content. The poem proceeds from what seems a cacophony of Tibetan-English speech, with complex Tibetan Buddhist visualization practices overlaid on the redemptive vocalizations of the poem. Yet, in its insistence on a Tibetan-English collision in language, the poem enacts what Mikhail Bakhtin would term a heteroglossic confluence of languages and cultures. Each strophe-line is introduced by one of the six syllables of the Tibetan Chenrezig mantra,

"Om Mani Padme Hūṃ," the fundamental, most often repeated mantra in Tibetan Buddhism. The mantra, which translates in English to "Hail, Jewel in the Lotus!" is often considered a mantra that encompasses the entire teaching of the Buddha: in some readings, its six syllables at once are considered to represent the Six Perfections of Buddhist practice; in other readings, the syllables are articulated so that they might perform the purification of the six samsaric realms of existence, Buddhism's multiform worlds of suffering beings. Ginsberg's poem dramatizes the latter reading of the mantra. The speaker stages an experience framed by the Tibetan Wheel of Time, which is reproduced as a wood-block rendering opposite the poem in *Collected Poems*. For Tibetan Buddhists, the Wheel of Time portrays the perpetual sufferings of the multiple rebirths of cyclic existence and the corresponding mental states associated, as manifestations of craving, with six particular locations: god realm (pride), angry warrior realm (jealousy), human realm (desire), animal realm (stupidity), hungry ghost realm (poverty), and the varieties of hell realms (aggression). The poem invokes these realms and their circumscribing psychological states in its first section, imagines antidotes to these modes of suffering in the second section, and in its third section, performs the speaker's extrication from cyclic existence, underwritten by the repetition of "free space for Causeless Bliss"—in effect, an English-language mantra *within* the Chenrezig mantra that frames the poem as a whole.

To complicate further the confluence of East and West in the poem, Ginsberg closes with a line that at first glance looks merely scatological but instead invokes the Tibetan Buddhist practice of Tonglen:

> HŪṂ—I shit out my hate thru my asshole, My sphincter loosens the void, all hell's legions fall thru space, the Pentagon is destroyed [...].
>
> (*Collected* 591)

The final HŪṂ section of the poem recalls Tonglen practice, a three-step compassion meditation practice in which the meditator first imagines ingesting, on the in-breath, the suffering of sentient beings, their despair visualized often as black tar or excrement; second, the meditator imagines the release of an antidote for this suffering on the out-breath, usually visualized as the release of medicinal nectar that, as Ginsberg suggests in this poem, can "fix" the "angry brains" of those in hell realms; and the final step is to imagine the release of the original suffering inhaled in step one, usually visualized in terms that suggest excretion, where the sufferings of sentient beings, having entered the crown of the meditator's head, are released through the seat of the sitting meditator. Thus, what seems like an invocation of violence—"the Pentagon is destroyed"—is for the poet a necessary eradication only of what the Pentagon represents for the poet, namely the hatred of the hell realm expressed in the first cycle of repetition of the HŪṂ syllable. This militarized hatred is then purified in the second cycle of repetition, in which the poet calls forth an antidote that echoes the characterization of the protagonists of "Howl": "O poor sick junkies all here's bliss of Buddha-opium, Sacred Emptiness to fix your angry brains" (*Collected* 591). "Howl" once characterized its protagonists as "dragging themselves" through an urban wasteland "looking for an angry fix." "Howl" responded with an antidote of apocalyptic conversationalism, the call-and-response antiphonal of section 3 in Rockland. "Thoughts Sitting Breathing" responds with a dialectic, polyvocal weaving of repeated Tibetan mantra and, as in "Wichita," the poet's repetition of his own English-language mantra. In much the same way Bakhtin has written of the novel, "Thoughts Sitting Breathing" can be characterized as a poem that functions "as a diversity of social speech types (sometimes even diversity of languages) and a diversity of individual voices, artistically organized" (262). To Bakhtin's description one might add the complexities of Tantric visualization practice—all of which combine to demythologize univocal representation. In this way, as Bakhtin writes, "two myths perish simultaneously: the myth of a language that presumes to be the only language, and the myth of a language that presumes to be completely unified" (68). Such myths, for Ginsberg, prop the monovocal, propagandistic language of the Pentagon that circumscribes its excursions into combat. As these myths of language "perish," what remains, as in "Wichita," is a language "taxed" by and for war.

What is changing for Ginsberg is that his Buddhism is becoming increasingly formalized as he studies with Trungpa and takes extended retreats with Trungpa's sangha. As Ginsberg's Buddhist study and practice are formalized in this way, he represents sacred experience in experimental, polyglossic language. Thus, the poem is more than a mere declaration of a particular practice, in this case Tonglen practice. With each line introduced by one of the syllables of the mantra, the poem proceeds in a "diversity of social speech types"—ranging from everyday discourse through the mantra—that subvert even the individual speaker's poetic authority. The translated phrase "Hail, Jewel in the Lotus!" is superimposed over each section of the poem, praising the three jewels of Buddhism as they rise from the muck of *samsara*, the same way the lotus flower rises from darkness instead of sunlight. The logocentric authority of Western prayer is reenvisioned in the context of the situational speech of Ginsberg's mantric poetics. Each syllable enacts the sacred particularity of each of the poem's three sections; each section is suffused with the authority of the translation of the mantra itself; and the final utterances of the poem invoke the specifics of Tonglen practice. Crucially, then, in this collocation of languages, religious traditions, and subjectivities, the speaking self of the poem is emptied of ontological certainty as the poem itself performs the antidramatic process of meditation—of "thoughts" that occur while simply "sitting breathing." These thoughts seem to represent an established, essential self, a pure cause of thought and action; but as Ginsberg stages the matter in heteroglossic form, this ground of subjectivity is as much a fiction as is the essentialist attitude it imputes on its thoughts and actions.[7] "Causeless Bliss," the "fix" of shunyata, emerges in an experimental, dialogic form, embodied and performative, an organic voice, as Bakhtin might describe it, of groundlessness in the polyglossia of the poem.

Rather than just rely on the declarative poem as a response to post-Vietnam scarcity—rather than just declare Buddhist "no-self" as a response to scarcity—Ginsberg performs such an identity, as his speaker's authority is undermined by a heteroglossic confluence of religious authorities. Earlier in his career, he crafted a body of work that stood as a counterdiscourse to hegemonic governmental language; now, the poetry counters the speaker's own tendency to reify identity as univocal "voice." In the title poem of the *Mind Breaths* volume, the dialogism of his Buddhist poetics is embodied in the fluctuations of the spoken breath. The body moves outward in a sacred breath that gathers with it continents of people and their histories. The organization of breath and line mirrors the content of the poem in the act of reading. The travel of the reader's breath in strophes in "Mind Breaths" parallels the travel of the poet's breath, beginning at Trungpa's meditation center in Wyoming and circling the world, returning to the individual poet's opening breath-unit. This breath reaches a crescendo of wind blowing "choppy waters" and "black-green waves" across the globe, finally alighting at the end of the poem, once again in the breath of the individual poet. "Mind Breaths" is structured as a dialectic governed by the body—more specifically, a dialectic of breath. Of course, from the one speech-breath-thought strophes of "Howl" onward, the breath has been critical to Ginsberg's composition process. By the time of "Mind Breaths" and extending the remainder of his career, the importance of the breath is intensified by his Buddhist practice and study with Trungpa's Crazy Wisdom school; and the breath finds language in the articulation *Ah*, an anchoring syllable in his later career. Ginsberg's 1984 annotations to "Mind Breaths" suggest that the *Ah* syllable functions like the seed syllable, or grounding syllable, of a mantra; as a "vocalization" of the "purification of speech," the *Ah* syllable represents a "one syllable summary of the Prajnaparamita Sutra" (*Collected* 791). With the *Ah* articulation, Ginsberg posits a subjectivity that is displaced by every breath at the same time that it is stabilized by what I have described in chapter 4 as the "ritualized spontaneity" of the mantra. Ginsberg's dialectic of breath, his language of ritualized spontaneity, proceeds from personal to global in "Mind Breaths." Eventually, it fuses the two terms into a speaking subject no more solid than any given breath from the poet's nostrils—a subject continually created and re-created within the impermanent framework of a historically contingent body. Breath and body serve as the locus of improvisation and as the steady, anaphoric base of the poem's dialectical movement.

"Mind Breaths" begins by acknowledging its Buddhist intertextual lineage: "Thus crosslegged on round pillow sat in Teton Space." This opening line echoes the standard beginning of Buddhist sutras, when the Buddha's discipline, Ananda, says, "Thus, I have heard." This linguistic convention communicates the relational subtext of the Buddha's teachings; always delivered second-hand, the Buddha's teachings in the sutras are identified as authentic by virtue of their lack of first-person authority. "Iron Horse" encouraged a turn inward that produced self-obsessive, privatized withdrawal from U.S. mass media, the common language of U.S. culture; "Mind Breaths" also turns inward, but the movement of this poem, by contrast, emphasizes an inward-seeking pilgrimage that incorporates Buddhist practice more studiously in Ginsberg's public prophetic voice. Indeed, to further illustrate Ginsberg's return to a public, communal voice, it is important to note that Ginsberg took refuge and bodhisattva vows, formal gestures of commitment to Buddhism, a year earlier with Trungpa. Thus, as nostalgia and escape fail to redeem to country torn by war in "Iron Horse," and in the same year as U.S. disengagement from Vietnam, Ginsberg's title piece for his new volume begins with Ginsberg sitting in meditation with fellow sangha members at Trungpa's dharma center in the Grand Tetons.

The breath, then, functions as mantra-seed syllable and repetitive base for the next several lines of the poem:

> I breathed upon the aluminum microphone-stand a body's length away
> I breathed upon the teacher's throne, the wooden chair with yellow pillow
> I breathed further, past the sake cup half emptied by the breathing guru
> Breathed upon the green sprigged thick-leaved plant in a flowerpot [. . .]
>
> (*Collected* 609)

Ginsberg's opening lines assert a Buddhist poetics that insists on the observational, concrete particulars he learned from reading Williams. As Ginsberg has said elsewhere and as indicated in his introduction to his father's book of poems (discussed in chapter 1), his reading of Williams and his study of Buddhism are interconnected vectors of influence. When asked in 1978 by Portugés about the differences between his Western and Eastern influences, Ginsberg's response reflects a concern with a poetry that combines these influences rather than emphasize their differences. *Samatha* (what Ginsberg translates as "mindfulness") and *vipassana* (translated by Ginsberg as "wakefulness leading to minute observation of detail") are linked by Ginsberg as part of a poetics that combines West and East: "[M]y poetry was always pretty mindful anyway. I always had based it on elements of William Carlos Williams' elemental observations" (Portugés, *Visionary* 148). Extending Williams's poetics further Eastward in "Mind Breaths," Ginsberg blurs the boundary between guru-student and author-reader so that the authoritative locus of the poem is, ironically, the wisp of an individual's breath—the mere wisp, just so, as a catalyst for particularized "elemental" observations. Trungpa may be directing the session, but he is an active participant, not a conventionally disinterested master; he is the breathing guru whose half-empty sake cup sits immobile during his sangha's meditation session.

The natural world, too, is rustled as the poet's breath extends past the meditation hall and is absorbed as wind. The poet's nostrils produce "mountain grass trembling" as his breath leaves behind "the moth of evening beating into window'd illumination." The wind of the poet's breath moves eastward, revealing the natural world to be fragile; even the ancient solidity of the Tetons is softened by the breath, where "snow-powdered crags" are "ringed under slow-breathed cloud-mass white spumes." Each breath disrupts the continuity of human commerce. As a late-autumn breeze through Utah, the breath moves "towards Reno's neon, dollar bills skittering downstreet along the curb" (*Collected* 609). The breath in meditation, then, is not individualistic or withdrawn but is panoramic, even picturesque; and it treats U.S. capitalism as a "skittering" construct, as do earlier poems such as "American Change" and "Death to Van Gogh's Ear."

Yet, the breath, as characterized in "Mind Breaths," may actually be a hindrance to Buddhist practice. The poet's breath risks recapitulating what Trungpa called in a 1974 lecture the "theater" of the self: a "portable stage set that we carry around with us that enables us to operate as individuals" (*Path* 88). According to Trungpa, it is this portable stage set that consecrates the self as an ultimate, essential frame of reference. It is meditation practice, lamas such as Trungpa teach, that exposes this frame of reference as propped by nothing more substantial than a theatrical stage set. The initial conditions of the poet's first exhalation are framed by the safe sanctuary of Trungpa's meditation hall. This safety is relativist, as Trungpa's own teachings at the time on meditation, selfhood, and shunyata suggest. Indeed, the pleasant, late-autumn spectacle of breath and wind in "Mind Breaths" becomes "fall cold chills" and "snowy gales" that promise "a breath of prayer" amid the gust and gale.

If Ginsberg's inward turn in "Mind Breaths" (to borrow a useful phrase from Dougherty) can constitute anything resembling the public prophecy he sought in the 1960s, then it has to overcome the nostalgic impulse of "Iron Horse" and the self-centered quietism that lurks, inevitably, in a poem that begins "crosslegged on round pillow" and separated from the outside world. Generated from this conflict between isolation and intersubjectivity, the picturesque, sacred breath is secularized as it moves Westward:

> a breath falls over Sacramento Valley, roar of wind down the
>   sixlane freeway across Bay Bridge
> uproar of papers floating over Montgomery Street, pigeons
>   flutter down before sunset from Washington Park's
>   white churchsteeple [. . .]
>
>   (*Collected* 609)

"Mind Breaths" revisits the origins of "Howl"—part 1 of "Howl" written at 1010 Montgomery Street in San Francisco—and scatters in an "uproar of papers" and "flutter[ing]" of pigeons the memory of the poem that established Ginsberg's literary reputation. Past Montgomery Street, then on to Hawaii and Fiji, the poet's breath-breeze yields to "trembling wave" in the Pacific Ocean and the aural shock of "foghorn blowing in the China Sea" (*Collected* 610). As if heralded by this foghorn, "torrential rains over Saigon" begin as "bombers float over Cambodia" (*Collected* 610). Thus, the breeze of the poem proceeds just as quickly to its unpleasant antithesis, storms over Saigon and bombers who "float over Cambodia" as if to recapitulate the "slow-breathed cloud-mass white spumes" of the mind no longer comforted by the private, enclosed meditation hall of the poem's opening.

The breath eventually returns to the singular poet, but the end of the poem suggests that the poet's singularity might never be the same. The bombers are "[en]visioned" by Avalokiteshvara, Buddha of compassion, from the "many-faced towers" of Angkor Wat. Under the gaze of these faces of Buddhist refuge in "Angkor Wat," the stormy breath of the poem becomes "a puff" of opium and hashish, then a cloud of "incense wafted under the Bo Tree in Bodh Gaya," the sacred location in Buddhist mythology where the Buddha sat in meditation until he achieved enlightenment. As the breath blows across Europe, it continues to assert its primacy over materialist language. Across "London's Piccadilly beercans roll on concrete neath Eros' silver breast," and "the Sunday Times lifts and settles on wet fountain steps" (*Collected* 610). Through the United States, moving East Coast to West Coast, "the vast breath of Consciousness dissolves," and the epic breath of visionary history returns to a distinct, singular form in Chicago, where, as if facing Moloch once again, "smokestacks and autos drift expensive fumes ribboned across railroad tracks" (*Collected* 611). Distinctions between subject and object are blurred as the breath eventually returns to the Jackson Hole meditation center. Ginsberg writes that "a breath returns vast gliding grass flats cow-dotted into Jackson Hole, into a corner of the plains" (*Collected* 611). Ginsberg's syntax is curiously devoid of signalling punctuation; either the breath returns vast and gliding, or the breath returns—its vastness dissolved over Chicago—over grass flats that are vast and gliding under its breeze. Evasions of grammatical distinction produce a speaking subject who is both distinct and diffuse in his relationship with the outside world. As his breath returns to the meditation center, it is a breath both vast and dissolving in its singularity, both diffuse and self-aware.

The poem ends with another exhalation: "a calm breath, a slow breath breathes outward from the nostrils" (*Collected* 611). Yet, by this point in the poem, this is not the breath of one who in "Iron Horse" would "meditate under a tree" as a means of "retir[ing] before war cuts my head off" (*Collected* 446). Instead, this is a poem in which the act of meditation itself dramatizes the mind *reflecting* on itself, a moment of self-reflexiveness that destabilizes the self as an authoritative, irreducible source of breath. This, then, is the shift inaugurated by the *Mind Breaths* volume and exemplified in its title poem: a shift that places autobiography and formal Buddhist study together at a tense, conflicted center of Ginsberg's prophetic poetry—not just, as Dougherty argues, a shift that takes Buddhism only as a central thematic principle.

That is, Ginsberg's autobiographical poetics is no longer a distinct mode of commentary on the religiosity of his everyday lived experience; instead the autobiographical self is now increasingly the subject of—and more important, the test of—his Buddhist poetics. "Mind Breaths," as such, mimics the progression of Ginsberg's career, from the early Williams-inspired poetics of "The Bricklayer's Lunch Hour," to the "roar of wind" that characterizes "Howl," to a public voice frustrated by war rhetoric into nostalgia, and to a voice that from the scraps and fragments of this nostalgia places itself squarely in the "vision" of Avalokiteshvara and Ginsberg's deepening Buddhist poetics. As one of a community of sangha members, the poet "[b]reathe[s] upon the vase plateglass shining back th' assembled sitting Sangha in the meditation cafeteria" and in doing so produces an exhalation that returns vast and dissolved into the rest of the world—only, paradoxically, to breathe singularly again as a dramatization of shunyata rather than a dramatization of what Trungpa would term the theater of self-obsession. Both body and bodily desire are the sources of delusion and the source (through the body breathing) of the path out of delusion. The poem dramatizes Trungpa's definition of "ordinary mind," a state of basic consciousness—paradoxically both antifoundational and fundamental—in which the mind sees the phenomenal world only as a reflection of itself and, in turn, sees the mind only as a reflection of the phenomenal world. This trick of mirrors, this visual tautology, is for Buddhism a consequence of the Two Truths, in which phenomena are apprehended by a mind that exists as a constructivist essence whose identity is a doubled reflection of absolute and relative realities apprehended, at best, through a representational schema of mirrors rather than experienced as irreducible essence.

Losing It All

Of course, "Mind Breaths" seems at first glance only to be a declarative Buddhist poem. As Dougherty suggests, the entire action of the poem seems to depend upon a reader's a priori acceptance of Trungpa's definition of ordinary mind and the Buddhist emphasis on the sacred nature of breath meditation. As this chapter fills in the gaps of what Dougherty has described as the missing "Trungpa-related detail" in the reader's experience, it also reads Ginsberg's Buddhist poetry beyond the poet's own self-contained Buddhist community—or, to borrow from "Mind Breaths," beyond "the vase plateglass shining back th' assembled sitting Sangha in the meditation cafeteria." Ginsberg fuses song and concentration urged by the Buddhist tripartite path of awareness—body, speech, and mind. For Ginsberg, these three paths to enlightenment are technologies of the self as they are matters of prosody: a fusion of breath (body), mantra (speech), and meditative awareness (mind).

It is important, then, to examine the *Mind Breaths* poems also as experiments in form. Writing under the guidance of a meditating mind is an act of sacred speech for Ginsberg. Because the mantra itself is considered a means by which meditators focus their awareness through repetition, then it follows that the mantra itself, as a reiterative, sacred speech act, is for Ginsberg a moment where the sacred manifests in the otherwise secular location of poetic speech and linguistic repetition. The mantra, then, enacts a poetics that for Ginsberg is sacred in its commingling of Western speech with the focused attentiveness produced by mantric repetition. What Ginsberg describes as Buddhist mindfulness is, too, a matter of poetic lucidity—a mode of clarity that transforms observation into vision. As Ginsberg explains in a 1971 craft interview with the *New York Quarterly*, his practice with mantric speech is for him one more way of "replacing" nineteenth-century English accentual prosody with, in his words, "a much more clear ear" (Allen Ginsberg, interview with Mary Jane Fortunato, et al. 254–55). Ginsberg's interest in the pronunciation of mantric speech, which proceeds from his dilemma in Chicago in 1968, emerges, too, from his interest in what he describes as Sanskrit prosody's "great ancient rules involving vowels and [. . .] great consciousness of vowels or a consciousness of quantitative versification" (254). As he describes later in the *New York Quarterly* interview, in a remark that blurs the boundary between materiality and transcendence in the same way that the "Lord" and "caw" antiphonal of "Kaddish" does, "Writing is a yoga that invokes Lord mind." He adds, noting further that writing is a material speech act made sacred by meditative awareness, "I try to *pay attention all the time.* The writing itself, the sacred act of writing, when you do anything of this nature, is like a prayer" (258; original emphasis). This East-West fusion is articulated more concretely in a 1971 interview with Alison Colbert, when Ginsberg explains his poetics as a threefold "converge[nce]" of tendencies that include Zen practice of "paying complete absorbed attention" to the phenomenal world, Blake's notion "that 'concrete particulars' were the essence of poetry and consciousness observation," and William Carlos Williams's statement of poetics that "all human consciousness depends on direct observation of what's in front of you" (271).[8] Together, writing and meditation are, for Ginsberg, a constitutive sacred practice in which "[t]he act of writing being done sacramentally [. . .] becomes like a meditation exercise which brings on a recall of detailed consciousness that is an approximation of high consciousness. High epiphanous mind" (Interview by Mary Jane Fortunato, et al. 258). Yet, the meditating self, like the secular speaking self of the poems, is empty of a constitutive identity in the work, a significant gesture for a poet whose literary reputation proceeds to a large extent from his self-fashioning as a poet-prophet.

In this way, when the meditating self generates sacred speech at the same time that this self is empty, the poem "'What would you do if you lost it?'" emerges from a context in which Ginsberg's autobiographical *I* comes under greater scrutiny as a sacred fiction of his Buddhist poetics. Ginsberg is interrogating his own attachment to his identity as a poet-prophet, an identity upon which much of his career was built. "'What would you do'" takes its title from a comment Trungpa made in response to Ginsberg's loss of his harmonium in a taxicab. Trungpa's comment suggests, too, that this loss is as much a question of the imagination as it is of the physical harmonium: the poem is framed by any artist's familiar fear of losing it, of the creative block that would prevent the production of new work. The title is syntactically continuous with the first two lines. Together, they convey this fear of loss of imaginative production: "['What would you do if you lost it?'] / said Rinpoche Chögyam Trungpa Tulku in the marble glittering apartment lobby / looking at my black hand-box full of Art" (*Collected* 592). Ornament is everywhere—and not just as a lesson for the disciple Ginsberg, whose use of Trungpa's full title and ironic inverted placement of the honorific Rinpoche suggests that this lesson on reification and attachment is as much the teacher's as the student's. The "black hand-box full of Art" that occasions the poem contained not just the harmonium but also several City Lights publications and a copy of Blake's work, with notes for putting the poems to music. In the 1978 interview with Portugés quoted at the beginning of this chapter, Ginsberg confirms that what is at stake in the poem for him is the necessity of "surrender."[9] In these later poems, Ginsberg is not so much "giving up" the identity of poet-prophet as he is surrendering to a transformation of it necessitated by his Buddhist practice in general and Trungpa's persistent teachings on egoistic self obsessions in particular.

"'What would you do'" is an effort to recalibrate the loud prophetic howl of his earlier career into a negative dialectic of silence and loss:

> Goodbye again Naomi, goodbye old painful legged poet
>   Louis, goodbye Paterson the 69 between Joe Bozzo
>   & Harry Haines that out-lasted childhood &
>   poisoned the air o'er Passaic Valley [. . .]
> Goodbye America you hope you prayer you tenderness,
>   you IBM 135-35 Electronic Automated Battlefield
>   Igloo White Dragon-tooth Fuel-Air Bomb over
>   Indochina [. . .][10]
>
>   (*Collected* 593)

The chant structure of its anaphoric "Goodbye" line-strophes enact the prophetic form he made famous in "Howl," while they submerge this same identification with prophetic representation. The poem waves "Goodbye Heaven, farewell Nirvana, sad Paradise adieu," dramatizing a surrender of his prophetic identity. The poem ends with a reiteration of Ginsberg's apocalypticism, an utterance of "Bom Bom! Shivaye!" which Ginsberg translates in his notes to the poem as the "[m]antra of offering cried out, often at cremation grounds, by cannabis-smoking saddhus to grace a chilam (clay ganja pipe) before inhaling" (*Collected* 594, 790). The poet does leave—and something is lost—in this invocation of the charnel ground. Indeed, as the final line suggest, the poem enacts a mantric poetics of prophecy in order to annihilate the poet's self-representation as a prophet: "None left standing! No tears left for eyes, no eyes for weeping, no mouth for singing, no song for the hearer, no more words for any mind" (*Collected* 594). Ginsberg eventually explains to Portugés that the poem stages a "discoverable" process in which the messianic ego of prophecy is transvalued into a subjectivity that, inspired by the poet's Buddhist study, focuses on "nonattachment to specific facets of the image of myself that I created through my poetry and through my own mind, and to my friends" (interview with Paul Portugés 154). The poem, he says, emphasizes that he is "[l]earning to break those stereotypes, allowing those stereotypes to fall apart naturally" (interview with Paul Portugés 154). What is lost, then, is what the "black hand-box full of Art" represents and what Trungpa seemed to know it represented: the poet's craving of his own continued self-representation as a prophet. The poems of his later career continue to focus on the construction of a language to sacralize the political and social urgencies of the Western prophetic tradition. In this way, a poem such as "'What would you do'" focuses more on a surrendering of the attachment to prophecy—or, better yet, a portrayal of the discoverable pilgrimage whereby the poet might extract himself from this attachment.

"Ego Confession" enacts surrender as a mode of speech in a poem that ostensibly would seem to rage against such surrender. Of course, surrender potentially undercuts the urgency of active self-awareness; or, as Trungpa has warned, "If you meditate long enough, you find out that it's not so pleasant" (*Path* 99). Ginsberg sketches the unpleasant lessons of his own meditation in "Ego Confession." He begins baldly stating, "I want to be known as the most brilliant man in America" and then proceeds through series of strophes anchored by the repetitive *who* of "Howl" but culminating with unexpected humility in the difficult, contradictory truths of his own Buddhist practice. He boasts in "Ego Confession" that his reputation will endure yet admits his legacy is rife with contradiction: at once "unafraid of his own self's spectre" but also "parroting" the teachings of "gurus and geniuses" as if so much "gossip" (*Collected* 623). The poem is constructed as a mock hymn to Ginsberg's self-proclaimed "extraordinary ego." Seen in the context of the "unpleasant" aspect of meditation he was learning from Trungpa—that is, Trungpa's efforts to emphasize the steady, undramatic rigor of meditation as a way of deconstructing Western orientalism—Ginsberg constructs a theater of the self in the poem so that this theater might be dismantled. He asserts that his ego is "at service of Dharma and completely empty" and simultaneously encourages the reader to be skeptical of this, and any, assertion of ego: he proclaims the poem to be nothing more than artifice, a tool by which the poet might "accep[t] his own lie & the gaps between lies with equal good humor" (*Collected* 623-24). Hayden Carruth affirms the complicated tension between boastful assertion and eager surrender in his 1978 review of *Mind Breaths*, asserting that the poem "is a mockery throughout" (321). "Ego Confession" exaggerates at the same time that it contains its maker's regal, expansive fantasies. Eventually, the poem undermines the solidity of the speaking self with its assertions of unfixed subjectivity. As Ginsberg writes, all that remains of desire in the poem is the lie of the imagination's power to create a speaking self; the speaker expresses himself from multiplicitous subject positions that are "[a]ll empty all for show, all for the sake of Poesy" (*Collected* 624).

The anaphoric *who* that opens the poem mocks the self-possessed anger of "Howl," confirming at the level of poetic form that, as Ginsberg has explained to Peter Barry Chowka, the poem is "a great burlesque, a take-off on myself" (Allen Ginsberg, interview with Peter Barry Chowka 388). More specifically, this self-parody of the structure of part 1 of "Howl" suggests that the object of this burlesque is the very public literary figure that "Howl" created: "I want to be the spectacle of Poesy triumphant over the trickery of the world" (*Collected* 623). The idea of shunyata empties language of self-presence and does the same to the identity of the poet who speaks such language. The trickery against which the poet-prophet positions himself produces a counterdiscursive spectacle of poetic language rather than one of logocentric integrity. Thus, the contemporary poet-prophet whose words are circumscribed by Western and Eastern conceptual frameworks is a speaker who "accept[s] his own lie & the gaps between lies with equal good humor," and who writes of "no subject but himself in many disguises" (*Collected* 624). "Ego Confession" departs from the declarative poem insofar as it is a carefully constructed mockery of internalized romantic quest. The poem declares that these deliberate reiterations of selfhood can do the impossible—can hold back the threat to unified selfhood posed by Buddhist teachings on impermanence. The mock form and Buddhist declarative content combine to become, as Carruth would say, "party of the prophesying" (322). The poet-prophet who confesses his ego, then, does not speak in an autobiographical mode that presumes his voice to be a univocal whole. Instead, he speaks from a vantage in which he is "himself in many disguises."

The poem participates in multiple discourses about Buddhism at once, all the while framed by the paradoxical notion that the speaker's "extraordinary ego" is "at service of Dharma and completely empty" (*Collected* 623). On one hand, the poem suggests, to recall Foucault, that the confessional mode is the primary vehicle from which knowledge is made. Yet, from the moment the speaker begins confessing, he actually articulates little but the extraordinary ego fantasies already ascribed to Ginsberg as an outspoken proponent of non-Western religiosity: Ginsberg wishes "to be known as the most brilliant man in America" who "[p]repared the way for Dharma in American without mentioning Dharma." The poem is, as Carruth observes, "a mockery first of the convention of confessional poetry" and "a mockery of the poet himself" (321). More specifically, the poem mocks the poet's status as one of the most recognizable postwar proponents and practitioners of American Buddhism at the same time that it affirms his Tantric Buddhist practice. In noting that the poem's "ego confessions" represent "authentic significations of human spiritual desire," Carruth is affirming the role of Tantric Buddhism in the poem without mentioning it as such (322). As in Tantric practice itself, the poem saturates its assertions in desire made sacred: only through the experience of such saturation can desire be experienced while simultaneously emptied of its mastery.[11]

The poet furiously asserts the self so that he might, in turn, mock confessional poetry: so that he might "accep[t] his own lie & the gaps between lies with equal humor." The title suggests the solidity of the speaking self; and, to be sure, by dint of its confession, the subject reaffirms its ego. However, understood in the context of the confessional nature of Ginsberg's early Senate testimony, where confession is a means of making knowledge about the self, "Ego Confession" instead can be seen as a poem that enacts the Tantric epistemology by which subjects come to know the world by their engagement with the ego, which, in turn, triggers the necessity, in Tantra, of the ego's own undoing. In this negative dialectic, presence is asserted so that its more sustainable absence might become known. The poet asserts a reificatory self that confesses; he does so actually to surrender to the power of the spoken breath—his self "in many disguises," some of which exist in "air-filled" locales beyond the body. The spoken breath responds to the human tendency to reify with an emphasis on the sacred impermanence of the body in Tantric Buddhism. The poem asserts Ginsberg's vanity at the same time that, inspired by Buddhist teachings on the purification of speech, it repudiates the poet's own vanity. Even the body of the poet's own work cannot sustain the strength of its own prophetic declamations: it is, instead, "the spectacle of Poesy" cast against the equally spectacular "trickery of the world." As in earlier work such as "Kaddish," the poet depends on language to articulate apocalyptic consciousness as a double-voice that asserts the ego at the same time that it mocks the extravagance of any such assertion. The poem proceeds from such unravelling contradictory assertions. It depends on an ontological trust in a humanist self often crucial to autobiographical texts; yet, it simultaneously enacts in form and content the spectacular construct, the fictive nature, of this same trust. What is valorized in the poem is not necessarily the ego but instead the knowledge of the ego's impermanence. Moreover, the poem unravels unified conceptions of its form. It is a Western confessional poem that both confesses and mocks its own convention. In doing so, it subverts humanist universalism through both its self-referential artifice of spectacle and its Buddhist-inspired confession of egocentric self-cherishing.

The Self in a Culture of Surveillance

The visionary capabilities of this double-voice reach their limit and strain at this limit in "Mugging," from the *Mind Breaths* volume, in which the speaker invokes mantra speech during a dangerous street assault. The dialogism of "Thoughts Sitting Breathing" becomes in "Mugging" a way of testing one of the most influential of Blake's maxims for Ginsberg: "The eye altering alters all"(485).[12] An autobiographical account of Ginsberg's mugging one block from his own apartment in November 1974, the poem explores the limitations of mantric speech in a world of urban decay and scarcity, the blighted, immigrant Lower East Side of New York in the 1970s. The opening of the poem foregrounds tension between the comforting psychological familiarity of the speaker's neighborhood and a growing sense of urban dislocation the poet feels when he actually *sees* for the first time the degree to which his neighbors have been dislocated by the impoverished youth gangs that control the area. Both the apartment and its surrounding neighborhood are familiar enough to produce a confident conception of agency in the speaker: "Tonite I walked out of my red apartment door on

East tenth street's dusk—/ Walked out of my home ten years, walked out in my honking neighborhood [. . .]" (*Collected* 625). However, as the speaker continues to observe spatial detail, he notes increasing disconnection and deception. The poem takes place during Halloween, yet "under humid summer sky" (*Collected* 625). The poem is framed by illusory signs of identity: the season, late autumn, does not conform to expectations, and the poet himself is walking through an urbanscape where the celebratory deceptions of Halloween still linger. Such illusions are crucial to the poem as a whole, especially as the poem confronts questions of identity and representation important to Ginsberg's Buddhist poetics. The initial moment of the mugging itself is misperceived by the speaker as the erotic attentions of youth; at first, the muggers' advance is represented, mistakenly, as the eroticized "hard boys / Transformed with new tenderness" of poems such as "Come All Ye Brave Boys," also from *Mind Breaths* (*Collected* 637). The youths in "Mugging," of course, are not transformed by lyric tenderness. Ginsberg writes, "As I looked at the crowd of kids on the stoop—a boy stepped up, put his arm around my neck / tenderly I thought for a moment, squeezed harder, his umbrella handle against my skull [. . .]" (*Collected* 625). This misreading of the boy's intent triggers the action of the poem; the boy's friends grab the poet by the arm and trip him. The youths' criminal intent is simply to trip the speaker who, in turn, has tripped himself into believing his own fantasies.

The speaker shouts the mantra "Om Ah Hūṃ" as he falls down. At one level, this response would accomplish little, of course, but to annoy his muggers further. However, as in Chicago in 1968, the mantra functions initially in the poem as song—as reiterative chanting that Ginsberg wants to infuse with the force of calm and quietism. Yet, as Miles observes of the actual mugging that produced this poem, Ginsberg "kept up the continuous chant of 'Om Ah Hūṃ,' thinking that this would calm [the muggers], until they yelled, 'Shut up or we'll murder you!'" (456). These threatening words emerge at the end of section 1, where the poet implores his attackers for equanimity as he continues mantra chanting: "'Om Ah Hūṃ take it easy,'" he tells them (*Collected* 626). Eventually, the mantra that undergirds "Mugging" functions as more than song—it is a concentrated, purposeful chant that functions as a polyvalent speech act. Indeed, of the many contexts in which "Om Ah Hūṃ" is uttered, the mantra often is articulated by Tibetan Buddhists as a blessing for offerings they are making, usually in highly ritualized ceremonies such as pujas.[13] Thus, as the speaker chants

Strategies of Retreat

the mantra, he blesses himself—the self-mocking hero of "Ego Confession"—as an offering to the muggers, even in a setting that acknowledges that the youths he eroticizes now threaten him with violence:

> Have they knives? Om Ah Hūm—Have they sharp metal
> wood to shove in eye ear ass? Om Ah Hūm[.]
>
> (*Collected* 625)

The function of the mantra to undermine belief in an immutable, reified self—by investing the subject's logocentric speech with the sacred performatives once uttered by past masters—is continued in this poem but with the subject dedicating *himself* as an offering to others. The muggers look for money in his socks, and they take his watch. But his satchel of manuscripts is left behind. Section 1 invokes the materiality of Ginsberg's literary reputation as an offering—literally, the commodity value of his manuscripts. Yet, the muggers could not realize the full extent of this potential sacrifice; in suggesting ironically that the muggers have failed, Ginsberg also observes that the mantra itself did not placate them. Thus, his mantra recitation fails, too:

> [. . .] and so they left,
> as I rose from the cardboard mattress thinking Om Ah Hūm
> didn't stop em enough,
> the tone of voice too loud—my shoulder bag with 10,000
> dollars full of poetry left on the broken floor [. . .]
>
> (*Collected* 626)

As quoted in the previous chapter, Ginsberg told Paul Carroll in his 1969 *Playboy* interview that the correction from the audience in Chicago in 1968 made him aware that he had "been using the mantra as song instead of concentration" (92). Mantra chanting fails in "Mugging" because, as he describes earlier in the poem, it is uttered as "shouting," and, at the end of the poem, it is undertaken in a "tone of voice too loud."

Either way, as too-much song or too-loud speech, the mantra also fails to account for the realities of economic deprivation and cultural difference in "Mugging," despite the poem's humorous attempts to point these out. Ginsberg's speaker, absurdly, could not expect muggers looking for cash to realize the value of rare poetry manuscripts or possess the means to fence them. In the same way, he could not expect the mantra to work as a spell amid the dialogic conflict of English, Spanish, and Sanskrit in a neighborhood of first- and second-generation immigrants. It is important to remember Ginsberg's own invocation of—and empathy with—his mother Naomi's fear, upon emigrating from Russia, of the "poisonous tomatoes of America" in "Kaddish," a reference to rumors among the Russian immigrant community that tomatoes were fatal. Misrepresentations of life in the United States are a point of empathy in "Kaddish," but such empathy is absent in Ginsberg's self-dislocated portrayal of the Puerto Rican immigrant community in "Mugging."

It is important to ask, too, what a successful articulation of the mantra would entail. Such a question brings the poem's Buddhist source material into greater relief. If this particular mantra is understood, literally, as the blessing of an offering, then perhaps a successful recitation of the mantra would have resulted, indeed, in the self-sacrificial offering of the poet to the muggers. Such sacrifice is dramatized in one of the most well-known of Buddhist mythic devotional tales, the story of the hungry tigress, part of the Jataka Tales tradition of narratives of the previous lives of the individual who eventually became enlightened as Shakyamuni Buddha. In the tale of the hungry tigress, the Buddha, in a previous incarnation as Mahasattva, son of King Maharatha, sees a starving tigress with her cubs. Driven by compassion for her suffering, Mahasattva literally offers himself to her: he slits his throat so that she might drink his blood and gather enough strength to eat him. At the heart of the tale, for a practitioner such as Ginsberg, lies an important paradox about self-sacrifice, one that resembles (as discussed in chapter 4) the self-immolations of Vietnamese monks in the 1960s. Ginsberg's Tibetan Buddhist study included emphasis on the preciousness of human life, the Perfect Human Rebirth teachings, and, thus, would have precluded the suicidal message of the hungry tigress story. The gore of the myth is intended, of course, to inspire compassion among the faithful—to rehabituate disciples into thinking first about the sufferings of others rather than their own.[14] "Mugging" begins with the suggestion that the poet's mantric speech actually blesses him as a self-sacrificial offering to the muggers. The offering fails, as does the mantra—as does the poet's use of absurdity to recognize economic and social conflict. At the close of section 1, the poet reflects on his own inability to offer himself as, simply, a failed attempt to stop the mugging altogether.[15]

As a poem in which the mantra fails, "Mugging" also tests the limits of visionary language—more precisely, the limits of Blake's maxim that "the eye altering alters all." For Blake as for Ginsberg, the visionary possibility of the eye makes possible the imaginative labor of writing and reading poetry. Such a belief in a visionary poetics of possibility is an inheritance, too, of Ginsberg's teachings with Trungpa, who founded Naropa as part of his belief that all the arts but especially poetry were crucial to the development of Buddhist vision.[16] Thus, at the level of romantic imagination, too, it is significant that Ginsberg closes section 1 emphasizing that the muggers left behind valuable poetry manuscripts. The line is a reminder, of course, that Ginsberg's reputation is large enough by the mid-1970s that his manuscripts indeed would be valuable commodities. As such, it reinvokes Ginsberg's self-consciousness about his public persona and mirrors the self-conscious tension that threads itself from "Kaddish" through "Wichita Vortex Sutra" in the 1960s, including the anxiety of his confessional discourse before Congress in 1966. This final moment in section 1 anticipates the reenvisioning of the poet's public persona in section 2 as, ironically, a vatic poet who cannot see. Framed by the noticeable absence of mantric speech in this section—in contrast to the central importance of the mantra in section 1—the poet investigates the failure of his own vision, along with that of the police and his neighbors, in section 2. In the context of the urban decay of the 1970s and the role of internalized surveillance mechanisms in that decade, Blake's visionary "eye altering" is reconceived as the static eye of state observation.[17]

As in any account of a criminal act, surveillance is a key component in narrating the regulatory ideal of culpability. Ginsberg's description of the neighborhood positions it on the border between the immediate postwar Lower East Side and the scarcity of the 1970s. Noting that he is walking out of his "home [of] ten years," the speaker emphasizes the decay of the neighborhood and the "iron grated" windows of the pharmacy; for him, these sights are associated not with shifting patterns of migration but instead with shifting political events that signify the demise of the left in the 1970s—the mysterious allegiances and activities at the time of Timothy Leary and underground groups such as the Weathermen. Much had changed in this cultural climate since the U.S. extricated itself from Vietnam. Troop withdrawal was, of course, the goal of countercultural activism in the 1960s and early-1970s; however, a national culture of scarcity grew in its place. With rising crime and the continued decay of U.S.

urban centers, surveillance took on a greater role as an industry in the 1970s. As Stephen Paul Miller notes in *The Seventies Now: Culture as Surveillance*, increased surveillance also was a response to crimes in high places, not just in America's cities. Borrowing from Foucault's work on state surveillance and individual complicity, Miller argues that Watergate inaugurated a period in which Richard M. Nixon's "overt surveillance and self-surveillance" created a condition by which U.S. culture virtually "ingested" such surveillance. In this way, Miller writes, the Watergate scandal suggests that 1970s is characterized by "a movement from external to internal surveillance" (1). Considering the importance of the body in Ginsberg's war poetry—both the sexed body and the mangled body, as is the case in Whitman's war poetry—Miller's emphasis on the body politics of surveillance is important to consider in Ginsberg's post-Vietnam poetry: "Body identification tools, which became more available to law enforcement agencies, eventually made it impossible to supply an unidentifiable Vietnam War victim's corpse for the Tomb of the Unknown Soldier" (3). Thus, as Miller observes of a historical moment when the body could be read more easily and categorized and disciplined by law enforcement agencies, "it might be said that advances in ultrasonography made it easier to monitor us from womb to grave" (3).

Written just months after the President Nixon's "overt surveillance and self-surveillance" methods had resulted in the first presidential resignation in the history of the country, "Mugging" is a poem in which vision and surveillance fail to provide justice. The movement toward internalized surveillance described by Miller frames the speaker's failure of vision in the poem. The speaker regains composure at the beginning of section 2 when he recovers the eyeglasses the muggers knocked off him. With the muggers gone, section 2 begins with an emphasis on the poet's ability to see. The urban decay implied in section 1 becomes explicit in section 2 as soon as the poet has regained his eyesight:

> Went out the door dim eyed, bent down & picked up my
>   glasses from step edge I placed them while dragged
>   in the store—looked out—
> Whole street a bombed-out face, building rows' eyes & teeth
>   missing
> burned apartments half the long block, gutted cellars,
>   hallways' charred beams

> hanging over trash plaster mounded entrances, couches &
> bedsprings rusty after sunset[.][18]
>
> (*Collected* 626)

What seemed merely ominous in section 1 is now made real, and horrific, once the poet actually can see at the opening of section 2. The poet's neighborhood is reenvisioned as a scarred body. U.S. culture has "ingested" surveillance into the body politic as a cure that, nevertheless, only worsens corporeal decay. In its description as "charred" with "eyes & teeth missing," it evokes Ginsberg's terrifying vision of Naomi's pathologized body in section 4 of "Kaddish." In contrast to "Kaddish," however, redemption in "Mugging" is a fiction best represented, perhaps, in the poet's description of his community in the immediate aftermath of the mugging. He lives in a rent-controlled apartment while the immigrant community battles landlords, as Naomi's community did a century before. The speaker finally realizes that after ten years, he has become an other in his own community. Even though children "giggl[e]" on the stoops of apartment buildings, he surveys the urbanscape and declares, "Nobody home."

External surveillance fails—the police do nothing—and internal surveillance prevents the neighbors from endangering themselves by volunteering as witnesses. Seen now as an other, the speaker, as a crime victim, is dislocated from the spatializing identity of his own neighborhood. Mantras fail if "song" is separated from "concentration"; and they fail when the external surveillance of neighbors is debilitated as a vision that is just "empty eyed staring afraid" (*Collected* 627). The external mechanism of policing fails to protect the poet's community. Officers help the speaker search for his wallet using a flashlight that is "broken" with "no eyebeam" (*Collected* 627). In an urbanscape where, earlier, he reflected that the political changes of Timothy Leary and the Weathermen might be the result of "F.B.I. plots," discipline is successful only insofar as justice is not. The poet's neighbors have internalized surveillance mechanisms—and who can blame them, terrified of the same gang that mugged Ginsberg—so that self-survival is privileged over community-based justice. They admit to the poet that they know the criminals; but they fear identifying them to the police, based on violent experiences with these criminals who, presumably, live among them. The neighbors add, "Besides we help you the cops come don't know anybody we all get arrested / go to jail I never help no more mind my business everytime" (*Collected* 627). Ginsberg's omission of punctuation suggests speech bristling with anxiety, of course, but the words are delivered, too, in choppy phrases whose hopeless tone suggest a rehearsed utterance, as if the lack of desire to help the police is, indeed, the product of self-surveillance. The speaker closes with thoughts on the consequences of a community that, in effect, polices itself to such an extent that it is beyond the aid of the actual police: "'Agh!' upstreet think 'Gee I don't know anybody here ten years lived half block crost Avenue C / and who knows who?' [. . .]" (*Collected* 627). Of course, the neighbors *do* know each other—they know the criminals well enough to keep quiet, realizing that they will be revictimized if they come forward as witnesses.

Eventually, internalized surveillance in the poem produces a final, lasting image of an "old lady with frayed paper bags / sitting in the tinboarded doorframe of a dead house" (*Collected* 627). It is an image that returns later in his career, in the characterization of Naomi decaying along with her city in "White Shroud," which I discuss in the following chapter. "Mugging" continues one of the concerns of "Kaddish," questioning whether Buddhism, in this case mantra speech, can redeem a decaying material world. I would argue that an important way to approach this conflict is to consider the poem's language alongside Ginsberg's use of mantric speech in "Wichita Vortex Sutra" and, later, his experiments with the mantra at the 1968 Democratic convention. These speech situations suggest that for Ginsberg, the internal surveillance demanded by Buddhist meditation practice must be disengaged from the internalization of state mechanisms of surveillance—from what Foucault would term the process of governmentality. When song is separated from concentration, the mantra risks becoming one more mode of linguistic containment. So, too, when mantric speech is disengaged from poetic vision—as section 1 of "Mugging" is separated from section 2, with the poet's eyeglasses discarded before the muggers take him into an abandoned building—the result is the depredation of the body and the dislocation of the community solidarity. "Mugging" suggests that the *eye altering* does not *alter at all* when the individual is separated from communitarian principles and in contexts where discipline is expected to be internalized.

More important, with his placement of "Ego Confession" and "Mugging" next to each other in the *Mind Breaths* volume (and later in *Collected Poems*), Ginsberg suggests that the eye cannot alter at all if it is governed by an ego allied only with its own stubborn self-presence. *Mind Breaths*, instead, represents a hinge in the poet's construction of a subjectivity that is mindful of both the humanist individualism Ginsberg inherits from British and American romanticism and a postmodern conception of self vigorously asserted and denied in Ginsberg's Buddhist training—a paradoxical fusion of no-self and self, to use conventional rather than philosophical language for Western conceptions of Buddhist subjectivity. Ginsberg implies in a 1992 interview with Peter Money that the eradication of the ego, or the confession of its transgressive presence, is inconsistent with the Tibetan Buddhist conception of Perfect Human Rebirth. Ginsberg says as much in his own notes, suggesting in his response to a 1985 Buddhist lecture that the notion of Perfect Human Rebirth is crucial to the articulation of a conjoined humanist-postmodern poetry. In his notes on Carolyn Gimian's 1985 meditation and elocution lecture, Ginsberg writes that the lecture on Trungpa's notion of mindful elocution challenges students to become increasingly "self-Conscious": "We're different from animals they moo or bark or meow but we have extra faculties . . . so we should be proud of our humanism" (notebooks and journals).[19] Thus, Ginsberg states in colloquial language what the juxtaposition of "Ego Confession" and "Mugging" in *Mind Breaths* demonstrates: namely, that the teachings on nondualism actually restage dualism as a dialectic between ideas of self and no-self, just as these two poems exist, in the *Mind Breaths* volume, as a dialectical pair in which humanist individuality and self-diffusion collide.

Earlier in the same notebook, Ginsberg records a humorous exchange between student and teacher on the subject of nondualism and selfhood. This exchange recalls that in Tantra, the middle-way between self and no-self might be found in a conception of the body as a collection of "participatory capacities" (Weinstone 128). The student, apparently struck by the contradiction between teachings that assert nondualism and those that assert self-consciousness, twice suggests that the self remains as a trace that contradicts assertions of no-self. The teacher's response borrows from the Tibetan consequentalist school of Madhyamaka teaching. In Jeffrey Hopkins's description, the consequentalist attempts "to generate in others an inferring consciousness cognizing emptiness [shunyata]" by focusing on the consequences of perceptions of phenomena (*Emptiness Yoga* 38–39). Thus, in the following teacher-student exchange recorded 29 July 1985 in Ginsberg's notebook, the teacher's answers are an effort to produce "an inferring consciousness" of shunyata in the student:

Q. But isn't there a you?
A. Step out & see if it's drizzling.
Q. But there is an 'I.'
A. We'll have to put you in the shower, fully dressed.
(Notebooks and journals)

The student, concerned that teachings on selflessness were eradicating the ego, seeks to reassert the self; however, the teacher guards against straying from a middle-way path and asserts not the *self*, per se, but the consequences of selfhood—in this case, getting wet. The teacher does not deny the embodied self, which to do so would be to deny the experience of wetness. Instead, the teacher guards against the reification of the self by emphasizing the consequences of selfhood rather than its absolute existence. The placement of "Ego Confession" and "Mugging" next to each other in *Mind Breaths* suggests, I would argue, that Ginsberg is thinking through Trungpa's teachings from the consequentalist school at this point in his career; the poems are placed in the book in such a way that the reified self is asserted loudly in "Ego Confession" while the terrifying consequences of such an assertion—in the form of isolation from an interdependent community, loss of imaginative vision, and fear of loss of life—are articulated in "Mugging."[20]

It would seem Ginsberg wanted it both ways by this period in his career: engaged activist poet and meditative poet in religious retreat from the secular world; romantic humanist self and Buddhist poet unravelling selfhood with performative linguistic strategies suffused with shunyata. The question indeed might be one of *retreat*. Do the poems continue a quietist withdrawal from the political conflict that occasions his work of the 1960s? Or is withdrawal a spiritual strategy—as in meditation retreat, where the Buddhist disciple hones his/her mind for an eventually lucid reengagement with the secular? As often is the case with Ginsberg, it is tempting to think the answer is both the former and the latter and that the wide scope of such an answer is a product of equal parts lucidity and ambivalence. Just so, as the next chapter demonstrates, the challenge for Ginsberg's Buddhist poetics in his later career is to sustain this lucid ambivalence as an adequate response to his fragmenting social, familial, and poetic communities.

6

Language, Dream, Self-(Dis)Closure

> So all of a sudden poets are now confronted by the guys who've got the secrets of the Himalayas! Before, the poets used to deal with Madame Blavatsky, and the Society of the Golden Dawn, and William Butler Yeats, and swami so-and-so who comes over from India. But now the guys who come over are the lamas themselves. [...] And now it's all right here to be confronted.
>
> —Allen Ginsberg, 1979

Beat Nakedness, Crazy Wisdom

On Halloween night, 1976, W. S. Merwin and his companion Dana Naone began the final month of a three-month seminary retreat presided over by Trungpa at the Eldorado Ski Lodge in Snowmass, Colorado. Little has been written about the controversy that emerged from the Snowmass retreat—and what has been published is now out of print—even though by all accounts, the Snowmass incident threatened the stability of Naropa University and burdened Ginsberg, as a Buddhist and poet, into the 1980s. The accounts of Ed Sanders and Tom Clark are the most definitive narrations of the violence at Snowmass, and Michael Schumacher and Barry Miles rely on Sanders's and Clark's books in their Ginsberg biographies.[1] From these published sources, it is clear that both Merwin and Naone were uncomfortable taking part in ritualistic ceremonies that were familiar to Trungpa's students, including Trungpa's heightened emphasis on aggressive and adversarial chant lines.[2] That evening, Trungpa organized a Halloween party as a final night of revelry before his students entered the last month of the retreat, an intensive thirty-day period studying Vajrayana Buddhism. The highly structured format of the three-month retreat required that students demonstrate their commitment to Vajrayana through rigorous teachings and meditation sessions in those two months preceding the final thirty days of Vajrayana. Merwin and Naone were not committed disciples of Trungpa; therefore, they only attended the ceremonial Vajrayana party briefly before retiring to their dormitory room to sleep.[3]

What followed would haunt Merwin, Naone, the American Buddhist community, and Ginsberg himself, even though the poet was not in attendance at the Vajrayana Seminary.

Though interpretations of the actors' motivations vary depending on the source, it is clear that the following occurred. Trungpa ordered that some of the students be stripped of their clothing to teach a lesson on the naked vulnerability of mind required to enter into advanced Vajrayana. He stripped himself, too, and eventually commanded that his "Vajra Guard" strip everyone else in the meditation hall. He ordered student William McKeever to bring Merwin and Naone from their quarters to be stripped. They refused. Their telephone lines were disconnected, and crowds of Trungpa's students gathered in the hallway and the balcony outside their room, effectively trapping Merwin and Naone in their living quarters. Word spread that Trungpa had demanded that the crowd deliver Merwin and Naone to him, no matter the consequences.[4] Incited by this command, the crowd in the hallway broke down the apartment door, and those on the balcony broke the balcony glass door. Protecting himself and Naone with a broken wine bottle, which eventually produced hundreds of stitches in his assailants, Merwin tried to defend against those who had rushed in from the balcony, but the two were outnumbered, with Trungpa's students coming from both the balcony and the broken apartment door. The two were overwhelmed as they realized the greater numbers and force of the crowd. In a 20 July 1977 letter to Sanders's Investigative Poetry Group, Merwin writes that Naone "was shouting, 'Police! Why doesn't somebody call the police?' but they laughed at her, women, too, and Trungpa later mocked her, for that, in one of his lectures" (qtd. in Sanders 85). Merwin and Naone eventually were led back into the meditation hall, where Trungpa's Vajra Guard forcibly stripped them.[5] After their harrowing night, the two met with Trungpa the next day, and based on their wish to finish the Tantric teachings they had begun, Miles writes, Merwin and Naone "made no public statements about their humiliating experiences, but rumor and gossip soon spread throughout the Buddhist and poetry communities" (470).

The Snowmass incident and its fallout are crucial to understanding the shape of Ginsberg's Buddhist poetics in the late 1970s through the death of Trungpa in 1987. Ginsberg was touring with Bob Dylan and the Rolling Thunder Review at the time of the incident occurred. Until 1979, when Ginsberg was interviewed by Clark for a *Boulder Monthly* article on what happened at Snowmass, he managed to avoid being associated with what happened. Yet, as word got around of the incident, contributions to Naropa began to decline, which jeopardized the financial health of the poetics department. Schumacher reports that by early 1979, the "problems at Naropa" stemming from Snowmass produced "severe headaches" and "nightmares" for Ginsberg (*Dharma Lion* 636).

The Snowmass incident caused Ginsberg to question the concept of guru devotion in Tibetan Buddhism. In particular, the Snowmass incident raised doubts for him about Trungpa. In a 4 April 1979 journal entry, Ginsberg represents his growing questions about guru devotion and Trungpa in terms that recall his transference relationships with both his poetic fathers and his spiritual fathers:

> This submission to Trungpa Guru, this Surrender is it correct, a transfer of God failure debasement to a living Being so at least the Adoration Devotion is to a Real Entity not an Image—And Merwin's War is it mine, 'gainst the vulgar drunken Guru Sangha?—Am I a fool? (Notebooks and journals)

Ginsberg realizes he is caught between his sympathy for Clark's investigative reporting—the very candor, advocacy, and activism Ginsberg had supported throughout his career—and his spiritual bond with Trungpa and its attendant hierarchies. Ginsberg notes in a 5 August 1979 journal entry that the stress of the conflict caused writer's block:

> As time's gone on the last two years, the [Snowmass] conflict's crossed my mind every morning on waking, and I've had difficulty knowing

> whether I'm lying to myself to cover Trungpa's Hierarchical secrecy, or lying to Clark in not openly and continuously confronting him in his journalistic spitefulness and intrigue.... This inhibits my working altogether since I don't want to waste my poesy and readers' time on gossip and spite, or exhibit my own confusion [and] anger with [a] phalanx of irritable critics. (qtd. in Schumacher, *Dharma Lion* 646)

Snowmass exerted a significant effect on Ginsberg's poetics, causing him to question whether, as a disciple of Trungpa, he actually had allied himself with "Hierarchical secrecy" against candor—in this case, *candor* as represented both by Clark's efforts as a journalist to uncover the truth of the event and at the same time by Ginsberg's efforts to expose Clark's "spite" in doing so.

The figural nakedness from which Ginsberg had crafted his Beat aesthetic and within which he constructed his literary reputation now was threatened by the coerced, literal nakedness at the center of the Snowmass conflict. Ginsberg's frustrated ambivalence continued into the next year, as demonstrated in a 22 June 1980 journal entry:

> I used to boast no identity! Now why am I stuck with the accusation of a fixed identity as Trungpa's sucker? Am I? [. . .] Why am I torturing myself so? To maintain a public identity? [. . .] Should I renounce Trungpa and retire to my farm? Should I renounce the argument and my public identity altogether and retire to hermitage to mediate 100% till I die into Tibetan Book of the Dead? Who am I? I don't know! Isn't that really good? Or have I lost my nerve? When did I ever think in terms of nerve anyway? Who cares about aggressive Nerve? Who wants Macho Nerve? (qtd. in Schumacher, *Dharma Lion* 649)

What begins, then, as Ginsberg's engagement with the material event of the Snowmass conflict becomes, later, a question of how Buddhism and gender politics can shape subjectivity. His previous assertions of the primacy of an identity based on the groundlessness of shunyata are reduced to mere "boast" in this journal entry. At the same time, he acknowledges that *the recognition of* his lack of knowledge of identity—the possibility that his previous emphasis on shunyata might be mere boast—is itself evidence of spiritual labor. That is, when he asks, "Who am I? I don't know!" he answers, curiously, in the affirmative: "Isn't that really good?" However, at the same time, he questions whether perseverance, one of the Six Perfections he preaches later in his career in "Gospel Noble Truths," is truly one of the Buddhist *paramitas* (perfections) or just, reductively, a question of a hegemonic version of masculinity—of "Macho Nerve."

In some ways, these issues of identity are not engaged fully in Ginsberg's work until his final volume, in the poem "Is About." They are significant at this stage of his career, however, as the 1970s lead to the 1980s because they illustrate how the scandals of Trungpa's community would affect Ginsberg's construction of subjectivity in his Buddhist poetics. Thus far, in exploring identity (and identity-lessness) in Ginsberg's Buddhist poetics, I have traced the effects of his relationship with his father, especially Ginsberg's inheritance of a Judaic tradition and a poetic lineage from Louis; of his early autodidactic study of Buddhism as this study comes to bear on his poetics of anxiety in the early 1960s; of his experiments with the mantra in his construction of a conjoined East-West language for prophecy that might respond to the Vietnam War and contribute to the drug-decriminalization movement of the 1960s; and of Ginsberg's performative mantric poetics amid the political withdrawal and post-Vietnam scarcity of the 1970s. However, as my opening discussion of the Snowmass incident might demonstrate, this chapter will engage biography with more critical emphasis than other chapters have. The reason is simple. Ginsberg's withdrawal after "Iron Horse"—his literary withdrawal in the poem and his literal withdrawal to his Cherry Valley, New York, commune—produces a greater autobiographical urgency in his work from the *Mind Breaths* volume onward. At this same time, his literary reputation is shaped increasingly by autobiographical narratives inspired by his Buddhist practice, accounts that, too, are important as literary strategies in his construction of a poetics that stages and critiques subjectivity from a Buddhist frame of reference. Most of all, Ginsberg's concerns over the Snowmass conflict and his corresponding guilt as a peer of Merwin's and a student of Trungpa's were just as often played out in public forums as they were in the poetry itself. The matrix of this guilt, as I discuss later in this chapter in readings of his most significant dream poems of the period, can be traced to an intersection of his early family memories and his Buddhist study and practice.

Dislocating Oedipus

As dream-texts that emerge from the context of Ginsberg's Buddhist practice, "White Shroud" and "Black Shroud," both published in the 1986 collection *White Shroud: Poems, 1980–1985*, offer a landscape from which to explore the growth and, at times, delimitation of the poet's mind during a period in which he was haunted by the Snowmass incident. Moreover, as poems that engage Ginsberg's relationship with his mother, both poems function as coda to "Kaddish," further exemplifying Elise Cowen's remark, quoted in note 19 for chapter 4, as she finished the typing of his "Kaddish" draft, that Ginsberg was not yet "done with" Naomi (*Journals: Early Fifties, Early Sixties* 269). Ginsberg was a prolific recorder of his own dreams, and his journals demonstrate that dream recollection offered one more way of dramatizing Buddhist subjectivity in the composition process. Gordon Ball identifies the most prominent recurring motif as "room dreams" and usefully taxonomizes eleven features of such dreams in *Journals: Early Fifties, Early Sixties* (xxvi). Ginsberg's disorientation in these dreams also mirrors feelings in dreams recorded by his father. Louis experienced a recurrent dream in which he was lost in the Newark suburbs. He could not find his car, and he was without his wallet or keys. In this dream, he eventually finds a dime and locates a phone booth, but the phone swallows his dime without making the call. As Ball explains, this recurrent dream makes it into Louis's poetry (xxv).[6] In Louis's dream, as in many of his son's room dreams, he feels "a sense of amnesia and an anxious, confused struggle to return to a place the dreamer was certain he had only just left"—an experience similar to the descriptions of realms in the wandering Bardo state of the Tibetan Buddhist afterlife (xxv–xxvi). This conjunction of sleeping, dreaming, and death commingles the "gross" (materialist) and "subtle" (shunyata) truths of Tibetan teaching on the Two Truths. As the Fourteenth Dalai Lama explains, the sleeping, dreaming, and dying processes are taught as interrelated manifestations of the sacred in Tibetan Buddhism. He writes that Tibetan Buddhist tradition believes that each process "results in a shift of consciousness from gross to subtle" (qtd. in Varela, 43–44).[7] In this way, Ginsberg's Naomi dreams that become "White Shroud" and "Black Shroud" are informed by understandings of subjectivity and desire that commingle East and West at the same time that they echo and revise "Kaddish." These poems, too, continue the inward pilgrimage of the *Mind Breaths* volume, creating a continuous poetic narrative of the interiority of the poet's meditative practice from the early 1970s through the 1980s.

Ginsberg opens "White Shroud" with a series of five heroic couplets that, as an overture and argument for the poem, imply that referenceless produces a feeling of dissolution that eventually sustains the poet. He is "[l]ooking for my ancient room" with a "feeling in my heart of doom." In this mental space of referencelessness, Ginsberg uncovers "my mother saner than I" who "[l]aughs and cries She's still alive" (*White Shroud* 47). Of the biographical context of "White Shroud," Schumacher writes, "Even as he approached his sixth decade, [Ginsberg] was plagued—at least in his sleep—by feelings of guilt and ambivalence" surrounding the circumstances of Naomi's institutionalization and death (*Dharma Lion* 673). As Ginsberg reached his sixties, "Kaddish" still was not the final word on his relationship with Naomi.[8] "Kaddish" redeems Naomi through the Western form of the elegy and the poet's own Buddhist-inspired revision of the Kaddish prayer. In turn, "White Shroud" redeems the poet, the son himself, as it constructs a narrative in which Naomi's insanity, portrayed in "Kaddish," is instead a product of the social neglect from which contemporary homelessness emerges. Naomi's portrayal as a ragged homeless woman driven to insanity by sociocultural neglect continues the emphasis in "Kaddish" on Naomi's debilitating treatment in state psychiatric settings. Inspired by the postwar antipsychiatry movement, Ginsberg dramatizes the extent to which Naomi's mental condition was worsened by the psychiatric community's treatment of her. In this way, "White Shroud" enables the poet to reenter the drama of his relationship with his mother in a public context that foregrounds wish fulfillment without relegating dream-work to a privatizing gesture.[9] Even at the end of the poem, when Ginsberg's dream-reunion with his mother is displaced into his relationship with Peter Orlovsky, the focus of the poem is both biographical and historical: equipped with just the most basic facts of Ginsberg's public life, especially his queer activism, readers are encouraged to see that the traditional Oedipal entry into desire is reversed, proudly, by Ginsberg, so that his dream reunion with his mother wakes him into his desire for Peter. The Cold War discourse of "momism," in which excessive attention on sons by mothers was considered by American psychoanalysis as a cause of male homosexuality, is articulated in "White Shroud," as in "Kaddish," so that it might be emptied of its cultural authority. In "Kaddish," momism is engaged in order to redeem Naomi's frame of reference in a culture that pronounces her only ill; the same occurs in "White Shroud" to redeem her son's frame of reference.

Gilles Deleuze and Félix Guattari offer a useful language for understanding this convergence of vision, desire, and madness. Among the most challenging and experimental writers to emerge from the postwar anti-psychiatry movement and the revolutions of 1968, Deleuze and Guattari theorize that when the Oedipal model is integrated into lived experience, violence and fascism are internalized by individuals in order to fit themselves to this model. Deleuze and Guattari counter with the *schizoid* as a conceptual framework for resistance to normative Oedipalized identity formation; and in their *Anti-Oedipus: Capitalism and Schizophrenia*, they declare—with hope—that "literature is like schizophrenia" (133). With such hope, they turn to the outlaw and experimental traditions in U.S. and European literature for their own anti-Oedipal models, writers such as Samuel Beckett, Henry Miller, and Ginsberg, whose "Kaddish" is quoted without attribution in the book. Seen from the perspective of Deleuze and Guattari's work, "White Shroud" and "Kaddish" denaturalize Cold War momism to redeem not just son's and mother's ways of seeing but also the very productions of their desire in history. This process admits of Oedipus only so that he might be historicized and chased from the stage.

As in "Kaddish," the son's subjectivity in "White Shroud" is delimited by his urban experiences in New York. Yet, as a poem that engages the dislocated subjectivity Ginsberg inherits from Buddhism, the poem's urbanscape is both real and imaginary, both materialist and reference-less. The five couplets that open the otherwise narrative poem explain that the poet is "summoned from [his] bed / To the Great City of the Dead." The poem opens in the passive voice, suitable for dream narrative, with the speaker asserting that "I found myself again in the Great Eastern Metropolis." Ginsberg's passive voice locates the speaker in medias res—ostensibly in the dynamic framework suggested by the couplets that precede the poem, yet with the bewildered, hesitant pitch of a dreamer thrust into a disjunctive psychic landscape. Significantly, insofar as the setting is the poet's psyche, the setting of the poem is not named as New York but is the Great Eastern Metropolis of his imagination. This is a collaged city, a product of New York in 1983, when the poem was composed, and the New York recalled and rendered in "Kaddish." The poet eventually places himself more specifically under the El train's iron support beams in the Bronx of his youth. Walking with David Dellinger, one of the Chicago Seven war activists, the speaker sees a vision of Buba, Ginsberg's grandmother tormented by Naomi in "Kaddish," now melancholy, eating and spilling crumbs in bed "abandoned in Old Folks House." Yet, this is a wish fulfillment of family stability. When he sees Buba alone and muttering to herself, the speaker imagines himself as a force of recuperation in his trouble family: "I realized I could find a place to sleep in the neighborhood, what / relief, the family together again, first time in decades!" (*White Shroud* 47). Yet, the speaker's sense of place is stabilized as soon as his family appears. The poem, as wish fulfillment during a period when Ginsberg's Buddhist community is collapsing because of Snowmass, dramatizes a sane, structured family life absent in "Kaddish."

The speaker's dream continues the impulse of "Kaddish" to revise an anxious childhood with the wisdom of age. "Kaddish" asserts the power of elegiac language at the same time that it distrusts language altogether in the poem's final two sections. In contrast, "White Shroud" elegizes the poet's own damaged childhood, when Ginsberg was forced to serve as caretaker for his mother in his adolescence, a situation best dramatized in the "Madness Highway" section of "Kaddish," documenting his childhood bus ride with Naomi to a rest home in Lakewood, New Jersey. As if revisiting the anxious mobility of "Kaddish"—walking the pavements of New York in combined Naomi-Allen form or traveling with Naomi to Lakewood, his father often absent—Ginsberg recreates his childhood in "White Shroud" as a phantasy of restful domesticity:

> [. . .] my own hot-water furnished flat to settle in,
> close to visit my grandmother, read Sunday newspapers
> in vast glassy Cafeterias, smoke over pencils & paper,
> poetry desk, happy with books father'd left in the attic,
> peaceful encyclopedia and a radio in the kitchen.
>
> (*White Shroud* 47)

The bourgeois setting of the dream is complete when the father's absence is asserted. The poet's imagination reaches fruition at his writing desk "with books father'd left in the attic." Of course, Louis is present as much as he is absent, insofar as the attic can serve as a cipher for the poet's mind—for Louis's influence as father and fellow poet on his son.[10] However, "father'd" is as much a contraction of the phrase "father had" as it is of the word "fathered." Thus, Ginsberg revisits his familiar procreation anxieties from his poems of the 1960s and reimagines these as an Oedipal triumph: these may be the books *father had* left in the attic, but they, too, are Louis's *fathered* books—his offspring—now adopted by the son who has assumed the role of father. Ginsberg's midlife potency is represented in redemptive, communitarian terms—but in a manner that suggests, in its play with language, that the son has assumed the father's Oedipal subject position. Ginsberg is the agent of familial solidarity, the only person presumably capable of bringing the family together again.

A major point of convergence between "Kaddish" and "White Shroud" is the speaker's insistence that Oedipalized accounts of identity formation must be critiqued and revised to account for multiplicitous vectors of desire. For instance, the Oedipalized incest narrative in "Kaddish" leads in a direction that differs significantly from the traditional Freudian model, in which the son's and father's competition for the mother ends with the father victorious, internalized within the son's psyche.[11] Read in the context of Deleuze and Guattari's "schizoanalysis," where a language of unconscious flow reimagines the idealism of Oedipal representation, this internalization—or as Deleuze and Guattari describe it, this "oedipalization"—fails for Louis in "Kaddish." The incest narratives of the poem fail to force the Oedipalization of the young Allen; to borrow from Deleuze and Guattari, this failure is a symptom of what psychoanalysis itself fails to imagine—the breakdown of the archetypal, Oedipalized "holy family" that sustains psychoanalytic methodology. By the end of the poem, Louis reestablishes himself in Paterson, as the traditional Oedipal father might. Yet, as I have discussed in *"Strange Prophecies Anew,"* he does not do so as a patriarch. While still supporting Naomi financially, he remarries and takes a "grimy apartment in negro district" (219). Louis's "reestablish[ment]" occurs outside the territory of Oedipus—in this case, outside the communities of the white, normative middle class and beyond the normative boundaries of Cold War social and cultural arrangements—which, in turn, disrupts the white, patriarchal power of the postwar territory of the holy family.

It would seem that in "White Shroud," Ginsberg crafts a traditional Oedipal model of identity formation, imagining a lineage of influence from Louis to his son that displaces Louis's role as the person who "father'd" this same influence. This standard psychoanalytic narrative, with its ontological trust vested in Oedipus, is disrupted in the poem. Indeed, Ginsberg's recall of Louis's fathering his intellectual and artistic tradition forecasts that "White Shroud" eventually, and with some guilt, will continue to rewrite the narrative of forced Oedipalization that "Kaddish" also revises. The speaker is dissatisfied with and even skeptical of his own Oedipalized fiction. His attitude toward his own dream fantasy shifts. He describes his wish fulfillments as a "picture cavalcade," a source of "amuse[ment]" in which he "strayed too long" (48). He emphasizes again his sense of dislocation, interjecting an abrupt question that distinguishes the living from the objects of their phantasy, the dead. "Where was I living?" he asks and later asserts, "The Dead look for a home, but here I was still alive" (48).

The aphoristic quality of this statement lingers into the next section of the poem, where Ginsberg encounters Naomi, a "shopping-bag lady" who lives in an alley. Framed as it is by the poem's sharp distinction between its homeless dead and its dislocated living dreamers, the visit with Naomi is marked by conditionality even in its most declarative moments. Descriptions of Naomi are uttered simultaneously as realist narrative and as artifice, as in the elegiac spirit of "Kaddish"; thus, the shock of the real evoked in "White Shroud" must always contend with the trace of artifice that remains from "Kaddish." Encountering Naomi straightaway in "White Shroud," the speaker notes, "She looked desolate, white haired, but strong enough to cook and stare" (48). This moment serves as an intertextual echo of some of the most distressing memories depicted in "Kaddish": when Naomi claims to keep company with and to cook for God and the debilitating effects of her stroke that occurred during her institutionalization. As Naomi speaks of her meals with God in "Kaddish," she makes debased dinners for her son, who explains, "I can't eat it for nausea sometimes" (219). Yet, by the end of the poem, when Naomi experiences "that dark night on iron bed by stroke when the sun gone down on Long Island," Ginsberg imagines her vision as a Gnostic "nightmare" produced by "divided creation," a discourse that reimagines the context of her institutionalization as an immanent and transcendent narrative of coercion, one in which the Gnostic creation mythos deterritorializes prophetic language (225).

Ginsberg's Buddhist practice displaces his Gnostic sympathies, and these signifiers of revulsion and revolutionary language reappear in "White Shroud," suggesting that this later poem is an effort to revisit Naomi's effect as a debilitating and inspiring force in the poet's efforts to craft a language for the sacred in his work.[12] His revision of the Oedipalized holy family, in turn, reenvisions the way language represents the holy. Revisionary language in both poems is circumscribed by a reenvisioning of maternal representation. As in "Kaddish," the poet is both afraid of and inspired by the materiality of his mother's body: she is both an ambisexual Naomi with "a long black beard around the vagina" and the prophetic maternal figure "from whose pained head" the poet "first took vision" (223). Before he even sees her as Naomi, this old woman the speaker meets in "White Shroud" is "strong enough to cook and stare"; yet, the speaker claims he might not "take vision" from this "pained head" because she repulses him, just as Ginsberg, too, is repulsed by his mother's femininity in "Kaddish." In "White Shroud," the woman in the alley suffers from "tooth troubles," her teeth "ground down like horse molars"; when she opens her mouth, she "display[s] her gorge" (48). Her gum disease, the "hard flat flowers rang[ing] around her gums," even recalls the apocalyptic impulse of "Kaddish," in which New York is a redemptive space for his pilgrimage with his mother, and the city is "a flower burning in the Day" (*White Shroud* 49; *Collected* 209). Ginsberg's earlier efforts to reenvision the Oedipal narrative in "White Shroud" only recircumscribe the speaker within what Deleuze and Guattari describe as the inexorable territoriality of the Oedipal holy family. The transgressive potential of his impulse to assume Louis's fathering role is diminished once the poet decides he has "strayed too long amused in the picture cavalcade," thereby producing sharp distinctions between the homeless dead and the rootless living. These distinctions, I would argue, effectively disengage the poet from the homeless bag lady who eventually is revealed to be Naomi. The poet's displacement of his father in the Oedipal drama is an effort to reinscribe the decay of sickness, aging, and death as, instead, revivifying female-coded representations of agency—just as in his earlier poem "This Form of Life Needs Sex," when the speaker seeks a "woman Futurity" to reproduce "[his] own cockbrain replica Me-Hood" to evade death (*Collected* 284). Yet, in "White Shroud" he cannot displace his feeling that he continues to be "horrified a little," nor can he fully answer his baffled question of "who'd take care of such a woman" (*White Shroud* 48).

Of course, in this section, the poet reveals that "such a woman" is his own mother. This revelation anticipates the role that guilt will play in the poet's efforts to rewrite his relationship with Naomi in the antimetaphysical, even anti-Oedipal, language of the sacred that emerges from his Buddhist practice. Thus, the moment the speaker realizes that the shopping-bag lady is his own mother, he represents her in his dream as a force that "mock[s]" him. Her first words are harsh representations of Ginsberg's childhood efforts to caretake her through her mental illness and of the lingering effects of his authorization of her institutionalization and lobotomy:

> 'I'm living alone,
> you all abandoned me, I'm a great woman, I came here
> by myself, I wanted to live, now I'm too old to take care
> of myself, I don't care, what are you doing here?'
> *(White Shroud* 49)

The language is the familiar disjointed Naomi-speak of "Kaddish," with Naomi's abrupt syntactical shifts and continued assertions the she is a great woman. Yet, they demonstrate a break between "Kaddish" and "White Shroud." This time, the poet can reenvision Naomi's illness not just as a redemptive condition but also in a manner that might redeem the poet himself from his own guilt: "Those years unsettled—were over now, here I could live / forever, here have a home, with Naomi, at long last [. . .]." The line break suggests the fulfillment of a death wish, of the end of desire; the same is true of the following line, when the speaker describes the pilgrimages of both poems as a "search [. . .] ended in this pleasant way" (*White Shroud* 49). The end of desire, then, is represented when the poet chooses to make a home for himself in an urban landscape he has deemed earlier, the Great City of the Dead.

Yet, what is at stake in the poem is not just the speaker's return to his dead mother in the dream—though, of course, this return is crucial to the emotional resonance of the poem, rewriting the abject loss of Naomi in "Kaddish" as an idealist domestic reunion in "White Shroud." Instead, the poem suggests a return to the very Oedipal model that it, along with "Kaddish," seemed determined to revise. Seeing his dead mother alive, the speaker proclaims that he has found a home. The wandering-room dreams are over—his "apartment dreams, old rooms I used to live in, still paid rent for, / key didn't work, locks changed, immigrant families occupied / my familiar hallway lodgings [. . .]." The room dreams as ciphers for the wandering Bardo state are bracketed off so that the poet might accept his identity as one that is rent of its dislocated subjectivity. He is the Bardo wanderer who finally finds a home and settles, dead, into its extranatural security. Indeed, as the dream moves to an end, Ginsberg represents himself as nurse and caretaker to the extent that even his most egoistically bound activities, his literary reputation, are undertaken in the service of his mother's health and domestic security: "I can cook and write books for a living, / she'll not have to beg her medicine food, a new set of teeth / for company, won't yell at the world, I can afford a telephone [. . .]" (*White Shroud* 49). The lines are written as subordinating clauses separated by commas, but they actually read on the page as long paratactic statements. Ginsberg's phrasing, then, suggests that the act of reenvisioning the sacred must occur at the grammatical level, too: the boundary-making capability of the sentence-level clause is asserted so that it might be subverted as paratactic flow. His desire for his mother, in the same way, unsettles the traditional Oedipal model with its assertion of flow—of a desire that resists the territorializations of waking life as they are represented in the content and the grammar of its expression.[13]

These poems are an effort to continue the work of Ginsberg's early, Reichian analysis: that is, they craft a theory of subjectivity that is Western in its invocation of Oedipus and Eastern in its Tantric revision of the Oedipal holy family. This new subject, Ginsberg's Tantric Oedipus, valorizes desire in language that asserts constraint only so that such constraint might be engaged by the body in its dislocation of Oedipal territorialization. Deleuze and Guattari ask, with their usual (affected) bitter humor, whether theorists of representation and the psyche should "suppose that some tolerate oedipalization less well than others?" (*Anti-Oedipus* 123). The question, of course, is a fait accompli. The difference for Deleuze and Guattari is the difference between psychotics and neurotics—of "[t]hose on whom the Oedipal imprint does not take [psychotics], and those on whom it does [neurotics]" (*Anti-Oedipus* 124). Ginsberg's early correspondence, especially his efforts to save money for psychoanalysis, suggest that as a young poet, he might have found more allegiance with neurotics, those, in Deleuze and Guattari's words, "who tolerate [Oedipal identity-formation] and are even content with it and evolve within it" (*Anti-Oedipus* 124). Ginsberg's early correspondence shows the extent to which he was, at the least, "evolv[ing] within" Oedipal identity formation, even if he was growing discontented with Oedipalization itself. In an 11 March 1947 letter to Wilhelm Reich, for instance, asking for advice on with whom to begin analysis, he writes, "My main psychic difficulty, as far as I know, is the usual Oedipal entanglement" (qtd. in Miles 95). He praises Burroughs's psychoanalysis of him from September 1945 to June 1946 as well intentioned but causing heightened "neurosis" (qtd. in Miles 96). However, this characterization changes by the time of "Howl," as Ginsberg's critique of subjectivity is dramatized in the figure of the hysterical male who does not entirely fit the regulatory boundaries of hegemonic masculinity: the "secret heroes" of "Howl" who are "starving, hysterical, naked"—not, as in the earlier version of the poem, "starving, mystical, naked." Taking on the female-coded word "hysterical," Ginsberg adopts the psychotic's undomesticated language and, as Deleuze and Guattari would it, the psychotic's "loss of reality." The poet's reenvisioning of selfhood and gender as multiplicitous and multiplying is a form of mobility that, for Ginsberg, enacts the sacred. It threatens dominant heteronormative territorialities, too, as in "Howl," when "hysterical" protagonists in mystical ecstasy "let themselves be fucked in the ass by saintly motorcyclists, and screamed with joy" (*Collected* 128).

Some of us, then, do "tolerate oedipalization less well than others." Indeed, "White Shroud" suggests that the speaker's Oedipalization, his "father'd" moments in the poem, actually produce a critique of Oedipalized subjectivity. They create a Queer Oedipus from which the poet first reunites with his mother in a dream union that dissolves his ego and then wakes to reassert his union with his life-partner, Peter Orlovsky.[14] Ginsberg shifts to a final section of the poem in which the speaker awakens in Boulder, reacquaints himself with his surroundings, and announces that he has come back "from the Land of the Dead to living Poesy." Crucially, his waking is represented as a return to language, "to living Poesy"; the poem is its own self-reflexive reminder of the power of language to reimagine the formation of subjectivity. He writes that upon waking he composed "this tale of long lost joy, to have seen my mother again!" In the subsequent lines, he explains that he went downstairs to see Peter "when the ink ran out of my pen." The internal rhyme, "again/pen," recalls the opening couplets of the poem, when the poet's quotidian dream setting was transformed into a heroic Great City of the Dead, reminding readers of the extent to which dream-work depends upon the waking efforts of the conscious mind. Yet, at first glance, the closing of "White Shroud" seems particularly antidramatic. Ginsberg's speaker has run out of ink; he goes to the living room, where he finds Peter watching the morning weather report on television. The speaker's actions that follow nevertheless suggest that this otherwise mundane domestic scene is charged with questions of desire, language, and imagination: "I kissed him & filled my pen and wept" (*White Shroud* 50). This final moment of the poem revivifies the speaker; he fills his pen and regains potency—not potency in the service of sexual conquest or even in this case in the service of writing. Instead, he is reinvigorated so that he might sit and weep. The tears suggest a dramatic wish fulfillment carried from dream-work into waking life. The speaker's wish indeed has been fulfilled in this dream, his "tale of long lost joy, to have seen my mother again!" He has accomplished what "Kaddish" did, creating a poem of family romance that resists Oedipalization—yet in "White Shroud," the reunion with his mother reinforces his union with Peter. As a critique of subjectivity, then, "White Shroud" rewrites Freud's Oedipal narrative so that successful negotiation of the Oedipal family occurs within a queer imperative.

For Ginsberg, this queered Oedipal narrative also carries with it a significant Buddhist impulse. In his *Gay Sunshine Interview* with Allen Young, Ginsberg describes his relationship with Peter as a "marriage" of "two merged souls" whose marital vows resemble bodhisattva vows. He explains to Young that their "vow was that neither of us would go into heaven unless we could get the other in—like a mutual Bodhisattva's vow" (23). Thus, in "White Shroud," his relationship with Peter is a figure (despite Peter's own bisexuality) for his Queer Dharma practice.[15] As often is the case with Ginsberg, Buddhist influence is commingled with that of Blake; Ginsberg describes their marriage vow as "a limited version of that [the bodhisattva vow], the vow to stay with each other to whatever eternal consciousness: him with his trees bowing, me with Blake eternity vision." Ginsberg's 1973 interview with *Gay Sunshine* anticipates how his study of Buddhism influences his incorporation of desire and family romance in his work. During this period, Ginsberg had just begun teachings with Trungpa, and his dharma practice still reflect the ambivalence of its autodidactic roots: first, he describes his marriage vow with Peter as "like a Bodhisattva vow"; later, he describes them as "a limited version," an "intuitive" version, of the bodhisattva vow. But at the same time, he claims that their vow not to "go into heaven" without the other is "actually the Bodhisattva's vow," which he paraphrases as:

> Sentient beings are numberless, I vow to enlighten them all. Passions are numberless, I vow to quench them all, cut them all down. The nature of the dharma, the doors of nature are endless, I vow to enter every single one of them. Buddha path very high and long and endless—vow to follow through all the way—Buddha path infinite, limitless, vow to go all the way through. (qtd in Young 23-24)

It is important to note that Ginsberg's paraphrase of the bodhisattva vow's comments on passion—as something to be "quench[ed]"—is articulated in the same context in which he describes the sexual component of his relationship with Peter, especially Ginsberg's own sexual needs, which, as Schumacher has noted, exceeded Peter's. What is important here is not that Ginsberg discusses sexual desire in the same breath in which he discusses the cessation of desire. Ginsberg confronts questions of desire in the interview in terms that reflect his study of Tantric Buddhism, where, as I have written earlier, desire is embraced as part of the practitioner's efforts not to become attached to his/her own cravings. "Passions" eventually are "quench[ed]" as they are engaged. Of his marriage vows with Peter and their relationship with Buddhist ethos, Ginsberg explains, "We had the understanding that when our (my particularly) erotic desire was ultimately satisfied by being satiated (rather than denied), there would be a lessening of desire, grasp [sic], holding on, craving and attachment." From this lessening of attachment to desire by the engagement of desire, Ginsberg says "ultimately we would be delivered free in heaven together" (qtd. in Young 23).

Professionalizing Karma

The "Kaddish" story cycle is incomplete without what Ginsberg describes as the "Karma nightmare" narrated in "Black Shroud" (70). The poem opens in Ginsberg's hotel during a visit to China, with the poet in the bathroom vomiting a chicken sandwich he had eaten on moldy bread. This moment in China recalls Ginsberg's account of his mother's violent physical illness in "Kaddish":

> One night, sudden attack—her noise in the bathroom—like croaking up her soul—convulsions and red vomit coming out of her mouth—diarrhea water exploding from her behind—on all fours in front of the toilet—urine running between her legs—left retching on the tile floor smeared with her black feces—unfainted [. . .].
>
> (*Collected* 218)

Naomi is "unfainted," denied what would seem a merciful loss of consciousness. This language is revisited in "Black Shroud" as Ginsberg portrays guilt over what he denied her by authorizing the lobotomy.[16] Ginsberg returns to bed in the narrative, but Naomi follows him to his sleep and dreams, as does the "Kaddish" bathroom scene. She appears in the dream on all fours, just as in "Kaddish"; and her screams resemble a "croaking up [of] her soul," as they do in "Kaddish." Echoing the final hospital visits of "Kaddish," Ginsberg renders the figure of Naomi in "Black Shroud" with death rattles "convuls[ing]" through "her living body" (69).

More important, these continuities of "Kaddish" reenvision Naomi's mental illness. By the time of "Black Shroud," twenty years past the composition of "Kaddish," Naomi's relationship to her son as caretaker is still marked with ambivalent mother-son feelings and distrust for the medical establishment. Early in the poem, "Black Shroud" reconceives Naomi's schizophrenic paranoia as both an imagined condition and one caused by the very medical treatment prescribed as its cure. She is retching at the toilet, and Ginsberg observes, "Some electric current flowing up her spine tortured her, / foot to scalp unbearable, some professional advice / required quick action [. . .]" (69). This moment recalls what Naomi describes in "Kaddish" as the "3 big sticks" that she believed were placed inside her back as surveillance mechanisms by her doctors. These sticks, however imaginary, of course did torture her; Ginsberg's focus on electric current and professional advice reminds readers, too, of the pain his mother suffered during electroshock treatment. The torment also is Ginsberg's own, as he recalls in "Kaddish," narrating his walks through Greystone Hospital while his mother was "taking Shock":

> On what wards—I walked there later, oft—old catatonic ladies, gray as cloud or ash or walls—[. . .] and the wrinkled hags acreep, accusing—begging my 13-year-old mercy—
> 'Take me home'—I went alone sometimes looking for the lost Naomi, taking Shock—and I'd say, 'No, you're crazy Mama,—Trust the Drs.'—[. . .]
> (*Collected* 216)

With the doctors' authority underwritten by their signatory title—"the Drs."—this moment in "Kaddish" emphasizes the burden placed on the young Ginsberg, whose "13-year-old mercy" is inadequate to the task of saving a mother who represents, ambivalently, both "crazy Mama" and one of the "wrinkled hags acreep" who "accus[e]" at the same time that they "be[g]" that he rescue them from the hospital.

Ginsberg crafts a break with this ambivalence in "Black Shroud." Invoking the need for professional advice, he takes quick action—and summarily beheads his mother at the bathroom sink. Of course, this action is a figure for Ginsberg's authorization of Naomi's lobotomy. In exploring the importance of Ginsberg's restaging of Naomi's lobotomy in the poem, it is important to note that Ginsberg's identification with Naomi in "Black Shroud" recalls and revises such identification in "Kaddish."

"Black Shroud" invokes this identification to engage the delimiting guilt, as opposed to Wordsworthian growth, of the poet's mind. The reversed hierarchical arrangement in "Kaddish," where Ginsberg serves alternately as child-caretaker and Oedipalized son, is destabilized in "Black Shroud": Ginsberg finds himself sick at the toilet, this time recalling the emotionally crippling scene from his childhood narrated in "Kaddish." Having become Naomi, this act of empathy allows him, finally, to engage the question of guilt over her lobotomy.

By mistakenly admitting foul food into his body, the poet causes the illness from which he creates an identification with his mother; this identification admits into his dream the drama of his mother's lobotomy and his role therein. Thus, Ginsberg stages the larger question about his judgment on Naomi's body, the lobotomy authorization, only by assuming a lack of good judgment about his own body. Observing food consumption and digestion as social acts, William Ian Miller suggests that the mouth and anus are linked in a relationship of "ingress" and "egress" whose consequences bear relevance on psychic judgment as well as physical health. Miller writes that the task of the mouth "is to admit things and make the final judgment about their swallowability. The anus is not at risk from so many sources. While a multitude of taboos rank the food substances that enter the mouth, those substances are all leveled by the time they are expelled at the anus" (98–99). Not so in "Black Shroud," where Ginsberg admits that his illness—his "wave of nausea, bowels and bladder loose"—was caused by eating greasy chicken on moldy bread: an admission of lack of judgment, just as the poem itself questions the poet's judgment to authorize his mother's lobotomy (69). The anus, often dramatized in Ginsberg's work as a locus of sexual pleasure, serves here as, in Miller's words, a "democratizer" that "not only levels foods, but reminds us [. . .] that we the eaters of that food are not immune to its leveling powers" (99). As in "Angkor Wat" and "The Change," anxiety is constitutive with desire and pleasure. His first line after beheading Naomi in the dream is a simple question that is as much about the dream as about the lobotomy: "What had I done, and why?" (69). Brought to the level of Naomi by his poor judgment in eating greasy food on moldy bread, the poet brings himself, in dream, to engage one of the most important moments, next to Snowmass, of inhibiting guilt in his work.

Ginsberg first assumes responsibility for the action but then declares it a mistake undertaken as a response to the professional advice of doctors, an approach that continues the antipsychiatric theme that suffuses "Kaddish." The poet's guilt over his mother's lobotomy is dramatized in the dream in the rash, barbaric act of beheading his mother; yet, the apparent haste with which Ginsberg beheads Naomi in the dream is also the result of his trust in the medical profession. For Ginsberg, "following the doctors' rules" is part of the problem, as is his own erroneous diagnosis. At once afraid to look at her head, which he compares to Medusa's, and also aware that she, nevertheless, finally seems at peace, he questions whether her illness was the result of "neural agony" at all:

> Why'd I do it so abrupt
> without consulting the World or the rest of the family—
> Her look at last so tranquil and true made me wonder
> why I'd covered her so early with black shroud.
> Had I been insane myself and hasty?
>
> (*White Shroud* 69–70)

In this passage, Ginsberg continues the anxieties over family life and the sacred that extend from "Kaddish" into "Angkor Wat" and "The Change." He revisits issues of divine madness from "Kaddish" and thereby questions the relationship between neural agony and spiritual truth, as dramatized in Naomi's "look at last so tranquil and true." He questions, too, whether the white shroud of his own elegizing impulse has, evidenced by the lobotomy order, always been a black shroud enacted by a poet self-described as possibly "insane myself and hasty" (*White Shroud* 70).[17]

As the poet mulls his own queries about the nature of insanity and medical treatment, the poem shifts from the scene of Naomi's beheading to his cousin Joel's wedding reception. At the reception, Ginsberg confesses, albeit clumsily, to his mother's beheading. Epistemological questions of truth and madness that once seemed indeterminate in the poem are now portrayed as stable, even hardened, by the time the poet confesses: his admission of guilt comes "too late to undo confession and truth," even though those around him try to cover up his guilt with recourse to the legal staff that now accompanies the "fortunate contract" of his recently published *Collected Poems*. As a sequel, then, to "Kaddish" and "White Shroud," "Black Shroud" also undermines the elegizing efforts of those poems. This poem elegizes someone the poet murders in a dream, thus seemingly rendering its elegizing impulse fraudulent. To complicate matters further, the poem then draws on Ginsberg's literary reputation in a self-reflexive attempt to subvert its own confession, with the poet protected by the lawyers of his new publishing house. Yet, the party guests' appeal to lawyers is, for the poet, "too late for me / to undo the murder of my mother, I must confess, I had / confessed, too late to undo confession and truth" (70). Subjectivity is framed by familial desire and the self-knowledge enacted by confession; at the same time, such knowledge is fragile and not worthy of trust because its articulation is destabilized the moment it is voiced.

The complexity of the speaker's confession here, I would argue, cannot be separated from the poet's Buddhist practice. At the time of the poem's composition, Ginsberg's Buddhism was still marked by guilt and ambivalence over the way he handled the Snowmass incident, which troubled Naropa University into the 1980s. In the opinion of many associated with Naropa, including Ginsberg, one of the more significant ways in which the Snowmass incident shadowed Naropa's growth in the 1970s and 1980s was the 1977 rejection of the Naropa's application for a grant from the National Endowment for the Arts (NEA). Public records are not available to document the reason for the rejection, first in February and then again in April after the application was resubmitted. According to Ed Sanders, rumors existed about whether Naropa had met the procedural qualifications for the grant itself; it was unclear whether the application conformed to the basic criteria of NEA fundable categories or whether it was just poorly written.[18] According to Merwin's 20 July 1977 letter to the Investigative Poetry Group, Ginsberg asked Merwin to intervene with literary-board director Leonard Randolph on the NEA rejection. Ginsberg requested Merwin's help because he suspected that the grant was rejected "because of the board's having heard of the Hallowe'en party events at seminar. The board evidently thought they'd happened at Naropa" (qtd. in Sanders 80). Eventually, Merwin did speak with Randolph by telephone, explaining to him that the Merwin incident happened at Trungpa's seminar retreat and not at Naropa Institute proper.[19] Ginsberg himself was among those who believed that, at the least, the Snowmass incident severely damaged Naropa's professional reputation. As Schumacher reports, the "damage" from the Snowmass incident was "inestimable, but there is no question that it was very real" (*Dharma Lion* 650). Trungpa's sexual harassment of Naone was worsened by his race-baiting of her, as an Asian woman involved with an Anglo man. Trungpa was drunk that night, and the Buddhist community knew him as an alcoholic. Therefore, it should come as no surprise that with Trungpa's erratic and dangerous behavior, the Buddhist community was beginning to suggest that Trungpa was a cult leader, especially in the wake of the 1978 People's Temple suicides. Schumacher observes that "there is little doubt that, in light of the negative publicity coming out of Naropa and [Ginsberg's] continued support of Trungpa, a portion of the poetry community had lined up against [Ginsberg] in a battle that reached beyond a small Buddhist community in Boulder" (*Dharma Lion* 650).

"Black Shroud" enacts Ginsberg's struggle with professionalization that emerges from the Snowmass incident at three levels: the professionalized hierarchies of the medical profession, of the literary community, and of Trungpa's Buddhist community. As Deleuze and Guattari argue in *A Thousand Plateaus*, professionalization is a consequence of a "territorialization of functions" (321). This "territorial refrain" threatens to produce a static condition of being in which the particularities of human activity occur narrowly only in one bounded territoriality; this condition is static insofar as "the same activity cannot be performed" except by specialized—professionalized—agents (321). Such a condition threatens, moreover, the deterritorializing imperative of Ginsberg's revisionary spiritual poetics. Ginsberg's anxiety over what happened with Merwin is a dilemma borne of his desire to follow the rules Trungpa laid down for Vajrayana practice—influenced by the need, as Trungpa saw it, to shake the human self of its tendency to reify—and his liberal humanist impulse to defend Merwin against Trungpa's Buddhist establishment. In a 1979 interview with Tom Clark for *Boulder Monthly*, later reprinted in Clark's *Great Naropa Poetry Wars*, Ginsberg identifies most of all with the professionalized hierarchy represented by Trungpa. When asked about Naone's cries to "Call the police!" as she was forcibly stripped by the Vajra Guard, Ginsberg replies:

> In the middle of that scene, to yell 'call the police'—do you realize how *vulgar* that was? The Wisdom of the East was being unveiled, and she's going, 'call the police!' I mean, shit! Fuck that shit! Strip 'em naked, break down the door! Anything—symbolically! I mentioned privacy before—the entrance into Vajrayana is the abandonment of all privacy. And the entry onto the Bodhisattva path is totally—you're saying, 'I no longer have any privacy ever again.' (60)

Schumacher's observation of Ginsberg's comments is apt: "Of all the statements made by Ginsberg during the course of the interview, this one would be the most damaging" and was the one he regretted most (*Dharma Lion* 639).[20] This was a statement that only "supplied more grist for the gossip mill," Schumacher writes, instead of "clarifying, or maybe even defusing, the bad feelings toward Trungpa" (*Dharma Lion* 639). What was at stake was not so much the accuracy of Ginsberg's remarks; indeed, Vajrayana practice does call to question liberal humanist notions such as privacy. Instead, critics rightly noted the contradiction that Ginsberg, as a politically engaged poet, could suspend his understanding of power relations so that the forcible stripping of a woman by a group of uniformed men led by a spiritual figure—what Merwin considered a "psychic rape"—could be described instead as simply the "unveil[ing]" of the "Wisdom of the East."[21]

A split between professionalization and individual human agency, so important in "Black Shroud," is critical in Ginsberg's response to the interview with Clark. Ginsberg's 10 March 1979 letter to Merwin, reprinted in *The Great Naropa Poetry Wars*, suggests, too, that Ginsberg's guilt originates from his split between his simultaneous loyalty to the professionalized Buddhist establishment—represented by Trungpa's controversial Crazy Wisdom techniques in teaching shunyata—and humanist individualism. "My main shame," he writes to Merwin, "is in having discussed your situation in public (re the Seminary conflict) when you've had the delicacy to leave the situation ripen on its own without aggression on your part" (69).[22] Ginsberg confesses later in the letter, "Through my own ineptness the disrelation between yourself and the local Trungpa Buddhist scene has been exacerbated" (69). For Ginsberg, the conflict, as in "Black Shroud," is one resulting from his self-professed shame at an inability to reconcile cultural forces of professionalization with his belief in the individual integrity of the humanist subject. Thus, as in Ginsberg's own poetry, the Snowmass incident demonstrates a lasting conflict for the poet between singularity and diffusion. The "Karmic nightmare" of Snowmass included Ginsberg's ambivalence about his authorization of his mother's lobotomy and about the lasting effects on the Naropa poetic community of his authorization of Trungpa's teachings.

An Elegy for "What It's All About"

As dream poems composed by a poet such as Ginsberg who placed a high emphasis on his dream-life in his journals, "White Shroud" and "Black Shroud" offer insight into the ways in which the unconscious residue of the poet's waking life comes to bear on the constructions of selfhood in his Buddhist poetics. Moreover, the psychic fragmentation that characterizes all the categories of Ball's taxonomy of Ginsberg's room-dreams suggests that such dreams (dis)locate in the poet's body the fusion of transcendence and immanence that is so important to Ginsberg's Buddhist poetics. It is useful to note that Ball's discussion borrows from the language of the teachings of the Trikaya, or "three bodies of the Buddha," in Tibetan Buddhism, where the *dharmakaya*, known as the Buddha-body, is its highest incarnation. The body of the Buddha is manifest nondualistically in a shunyata form as the dharmakaya—divine while also, paradoxically, emptied of essentialist identity. Ball argues that Ginsberg's room-dreams represent "the plane of material existence which the separated entity [Ginsberg himself in his dreams] may wander around looking for, bewildered, trying to get back in emotionally, unwilling to give up or let go and enter Dharmakaya" (*Journals: Early Fifties, Early Sixties* xxvi). Ginsberg himself notes that the significance of what Ball describes as the "referenceless disorientation" of these dreams is situated in questions of death and impermanence. Such dreams, Ball says, are "not very dissimilar to actual life feelings in the sense that we die every day, or change—that is, continuous change—we die every day and leave our rooms and bodies behind and our minds behind" (*Journals: Early Fifties, Early Sixties* xxv, xxvii). Ball's remarks and Ginsberg's response together confirm that simultaneous assertions of singularity and diffusion are a crucial collocation in the language for subjectivity Ginsberg shapes from his Buddhism. This poetics is framed most of all by the emphasis on impermanence—"continuous change"—vital in the Tibetan wheel of life, the famously iconographic image of the same figural dying "every day" that Ginsberg emphasizes in his discussion of Ball's taxonomy. As discussed in chapter 5, the wheel of life image is so important to Ginsberg that he reproduces it in *Collected Poems* opposite "Thoughts Sitting Breathing," his heteroglossic blur of secular speech and sacred speech, in which the power of the speaker's cravings are undercut, cyclically in time, by the authority of mantric speech.

In Ginsberg's Buddhist poetics, this combination of singularity and fragmentation—of selfhood and self-diffusion—occurs at the edge of representation, where, as Dick Hebdige has described, representation serves both the limitation and proliferation of meaning. As much as this approach might contribute to the inward pilgrimage of the *Mind Breaths* volume and to the dream excursions "White Shroud" and "Black Shroud," it also risks a self-canceling gesture, as in the language of "On Cremation of Chögyam Trungpa, Vidyadhara," from Ginsberg's next volume, *Cosmopolitan Greetings: Poems 1986–1992*. Faced with the death of Trungpa in 1987, Ginsberg responds with a poem that intensifies the authority of the speaking subject at the same time that it seems to diminish the linguistic authority of mantra chanting to banal reiteration. "On Cremation" emphasizes the limitations of language while also acknowledging the power of language to provide narratives, however fictive, of consolation or redemption. Between the poles of reiteration and innovation—between Ginsberg's tense engagement with song and concentration—the poem acts as a statement of Buddhist poetics, functioning as an elegy to Trungpa as it dramatizes the heightened, imaginative perceptions of its speaker in the act of elegizing. Where the goal of a traditional Western elegy is consolation through language that reaffirms metaphysical authority, consolation in this Buddhist elegy might best be expressed as a representation of the mind in an intensified condition of awareness, proof in the poem that the guru's lessons on meditation and perception have been put into practice after his/her death.[23]

Just so, "On Cremation" threatens to continue Ginsberg's alienating tendency toward what Jay Dougherty has called the "declarative poem." "On Cremation" restages Trungpa's cremation at his Buddhist center, Karme-Chöling, in a series of long, chanting breath-lines anchored by the phrase "I noticed." The poem offers as its illustrative context the past body of Ginsberg's work and influence, specifically his impulse toward anaphoric, mantra-chant phrases anchoring list–catalogue lines. Like "Ego Confession," "Mugging," and "Thoughts on a Breath," this poem could alienate the reader who has little or no knowledge of the guru-student relationship in Tibetan Buddhism. Each line accelerates in an accumulating catalogue demonstrating the virtues and limitations of Trungpa's legacy, from the suspicious "ticket takers" and "guards in Khaki uniforms" gathered that day at Karme-Chöling to the "all-pervading smiles & empty eyes" of mourning students filling the center's parking lot.[24] As Ginsberg earlier told Portugés, his Buddhist poetics owes much to Williams's "elemental observations" (*Visionary Poetics* 148). If truly "no ideas" exist "but in things," then the poet's means of observing these things take center stage in "On Cremation." The poet's ability to notice—to perceive—is as important as any observation dramatized in the poem itself.

The guru's legacy, after all, lives on after death in the abilities of his/her students. Thus, the turning point of the poem arrives in the shortest, most clipped breath-line of the poem, after a series of long, chanting breath-lines catalogue the mourners' arrival and the preparation of the corpse, ending with the direct statement: "I noticed the Guru was dead" (*Cosmopolitan Greetings* 25). As profound as the cremation ceremony might be for Trungpa's students, Ginsberg describes his observation as more of a glimpse or glance, a merely "noticed" situation rather than the eschatological metamorphosis of consciousness one might expect upon the death of a venerated guru. The poem reconceives the most profound visions as images subject to the transitory attention span of passing frames of reference. The cremation of Trungpa produces a "rainbow round the sun" witnessed by all the mourners and, according to Stephen T. Butterfield, "the sign and seal of a great teacher" in Tibetan Buddhist tradition (151). Yet, the rainbows are, crucially, no more or less a part of the poet's hierarchy of vision than anything else he notices. The mundane and the apocalyptic flit past the speaker's consciousness with equal claims to transience, perhaps the most significant elegizing gesture a student might make for his/her guru: "I noticed food, lettuce salad, I noticed the Teacher was absent, / I noticed my friends, noticed our car the blue Volvo, a young boy held my hand" (*Cosmopolitan Greetings* 26). As in one of his earliest poems, "The Bricklayer's Lunch Hour," Ginsberg risks banality in "On Cremation," and this risk precisely is what sustains the poem. So, too, does he take this risk in "Mugging," in which the repetition of mantras would seem to Westernized ears a pale response to predatory muggers who have dragged the poet into an abandoned building.

What Dougherty describes as "Ginsberg's Buddhist-Trungpa teachings and vocabulary" deserves further attention, however. For Trungpa, an acknowledgement that passing thoughts are hierarchized by the rational mind is the first step to enacting, through meditation, a nonhierarchical vision in one's daily life. As discussed in chapter 5, subjectivity is, in Trungpa's Buddhist teachings, constituted by conceptual and linguistic frames of reference that constitute what he terms a "theater" of the self— "portable stage set that we carry around with us that enables us to operate as individuals" (*Path* 88). The mind, Trungpa argues, is suffused with shunyata and, therefore, is nothing but a theater of passing performance; it is the practitioner's task to inhabit this theater and empty its essentialized identity through meditation and, in the case of this poem, through the performative speech of mantric poetics. Such distrust of the human tendency toward hierarchization indeed is crucial to all forms of Buddhism, not just Trungpa's, and is the core teaching of the Prajnaparamita Sutra. Thus, a banality of vision actually elegizes the dead guru in "On Cremation"; it confirms that the guru's teachings carry on substantively in his/her students. With each utterance of "I noticed," the absent guru is made present.

As Dougherty implies, approaching Ginsberg's later work mindful of his Buddhism imposes vexing complications. That is, in Ginsberg's later poetry, song and concentration may be as much matters of urgent aesthetic concern as they are a lax conflation of each other—in the same way that his self-identification in "Kral Majales" as a "Buddhist Jew" induces much the same sense of inspiration and burden. To further complicate critical reception of Ginsberg, his later poetry seems to borrow ambivalently from both the postmodern avant-garde and from traditional humanism, emphasizing intersubjective relationships in which language mediates the boundaries between absence and presence while valorizing individualist presence itself. The limit and possibility of this strategy are most pronounced in "Is About," from his final volume, *Death and Fame: Last Poems, 1993-1997*. In "Is About," the relationship between words and what they represent is first staged as an expression of postmodern banality: where referents once redemptively enacted what they represented, as in his performative incorporation of the mantra, representation in "Is About" only serves to sustain and justify its own reiterations. The poem begins with a series of abstract generalizations, each of which proffers the idea that meaning is nothing but a chain of abstract equivalencies that can be brokered equally by commodified or sacred language. In its lack of concrete particularity, the chant-phrase "is about" produces an endless repetition of abstraction that erases the particulars of difference. Ginsberg would seem to violate the poetics of one of his primary influences, Ezra Pound, who once famously counseled poets to "go in fear of abstraction." At first glance, "Is About" stands as an anomaly in a career devoted to particulars, as best seen in "Kaddish," where a "release of particulars" enables redemptive candor (*Collected* 214). After seven lines of commutative generalization in "Is About," the speaker steps back as if to correct himself: "Russia is about Tzars Stalin Poetry Secret Police Communism barefoot in the snow / But that's not really Russia it's a concept" (*Death* 27). The real Russia, presumably, is to be found in particulars, not in unpunctuated lists of nouns that elide any notion of difference. Yet, the speaker returns straightaway to "is about" reiterations: "A concept is about how to look at the earth from the moon / without ever getting there" (*Death* 27). In this instance, the moon is the primary frame of reference for a chain of conceptualizations that threaten the imagination's ability to "make it new." From the vantage of abstraction—from the poet's perch on the moon—the speaker chants a perspective that "is about love & Werewolves, also Poe," combining ideas in such a way that the act of their fusion is foregrounded at the expense of the ideas themselves. Thus, one can "look at the earth from the moon / without ever getting there." The poem no longer functions as an occasion for meaning-making; instead, it seems to be a confined space where meaning is delivered in the form of banal postmodern equivalencies that are "about" looking but never really seeing.

Yet, the chant repetitions of the poem offer a reminder that postmodernism is more than just a celebration of pop idioms and instead can represent a vibrant avant-garde counterforce, as the Language movement's most politicized practitioners argue. It is important to remember Bruce Andrews's argument that avant-garde poetics restages the dominance of "established sense & meaning" precisely in order to disrupt its "reign" (31). Ginsberg's "Is About" can be seen as a dramatization of Andrews's remarks, an occasion when "[w]riting's method . . . can suggest a *social* undecidability, a lack of successful *suture*" (Andrews 31). Instead of lapsing into banality, the chant-phrase "is about" sutures undecidability in order to burst its seams, restages commodified speech in order to disrupt its reign. Eventually, the poem suggests that the "is about" mantra chant is a trick of artifice: "Everything is about something if you're a thin movie producer chain-smoking muggles" (*Death* 27). If one indeed is a narcoticized Hollywood producer—where "muggle" is slang for a joint—then truly "[e]verything is about something," and the rich and variegated world can be understood (and this same understanding summarily shelved) by chanting the commutative phrase "is about." Just as repetitious language forms can combine breath, body, and mind in a sacred mantra speech, they also can underwrite a world of packaged and commodified ideas in which human language is a source of plunder, where "[c]ommunication is about monopoly television radio movie newspaper spin on Earth, i.e. planetary censorship" (*Death* 27). The "is about" mantra is exhausted in the poem at the moment that its power to territorialize audiences with banality is vocalized, an instance in which speech empties commodified language from within by performing, rather than overtly countering, the force of banal utterance.

The final lines of "Is About" reenvision the reductive mantra of the entire poem—the "language abused," as in "Wichita"—and declare that this mantric poem is a call to further concrete action and not a mere collection of abstract statements. The speaker asks, "Do you care? What are you about / or are you a human being with 10 fingers & two eyes?" (*Death* 28). If subjectivity is produced and confined by language, then, for Ginsberg, the only locus of prophetic change might be the individual body, down to its "10 fingers & two eyes." The final question of the poem asserts humanist confidence in both the subject who speaks the poem and in his readership. Ginsberg suggests a unified voice that "cares what it's all about" can emerge from the constraining chains of signification that frame the poem; furthermore, the first step in caring "what it's all about" involves dismantling the entire notion that "[e]verything is about something" and instead localizing a fixed language for subjectivity in the individual body. Eventually, the poem asserts that the act of being "about" something is contrary to *being* in itself: one is either "about" something, or one is a flesh-and-blood human individual "with 10 fingers & two eyes."

The ending of "Is About" presumes an ontological commitment that situates Ginsberg in a curious position in debates over language and subjectivity in contemporary poetry. As much as Ginsberg's mantric poetics might be described by the vocabulary of postmodernism favored by the Language movement and its constellation of post-Language descendants, "Is About" suggests, nevertheless, that Ginsberg keeps a neoromantic humanism in the offing as a form of spiritual pastiche, combining Judeo-Christian teleology with Buddhist shunyata. As a Madhyamaka practitioner, Ginsberg crafts a middle-way in "Is About" that represents, to borrow from Vernon Shetley's discussion of Language poetry and New Formalism, an effort to forge a poetics of both "lucidity" (concentration) and "lyricism" (song). Incorporating Charles Altieri's work on contemporary poetics, Shetley adapts Altieri's use of the terms *lucid* and *lyric* to name "institutional alignments" in the debate over forms of the genuine in contemporary poetry: the Language movement is aligned with critical theory, itself an extension and revision of Enlightenment lucidity; New Formalism, on the other hand, takes shape from humanist conceptions of selfhood, privileging lyricism "against the skeptical ironies of a 'lucid' literary theory" (Shetley 18–20). Of course, Ginsberg is an unlikely figure in a discussion of authenticity that combines New Formalist and Language poetry. As Shetley writes, Ginsberg "is practically the Devil himself in New Formalist demonology" (158). Ron Silliman has described Ginsberg as a "directly (and positively) felt" influence on Language poetry, and for Silliman, "Wichita" is the "defining text" of this influence.[25]

Even though Ginsberg's construction of sacred speech reflects poststructuralist thought in his Buddhist poetics, his belief in a primal form and meter from which authentic subjectivity can emerge resembles claims for language and subjectivity made in New Formalist poetics. Indeed, Dana Gioia's remarks on poetic form and primal language can function as a Western equivalent of Ginsberg's interest in the Hindu Gayatri meter. Privileging the legacy of inherited Western forms, Gioia writes that poetry shares a premodern cultural space with "religion, history, music, and magic. All were performed in a sacred, ritual language separated from everyday speech by its incantatory metrical form" (33). Given that lyricism predates writing, Gioia argues, it follows that "[b]efore writing, the poet and the poem were inseparable, and both represented the collective memory of their culture" (33). It would seem imprecise to cast Ginsberg as a New Formalist "Devil" when he, too, claims an archetypal authenticity—a "universal meter," no less, but of Eastern rather than Western origin—in which poet, poem, and audience are inseparable in a mantric poetics that sparks the "same *affects* or emotions" in poet and reader alike (interview with Michael Aldrich 36). I do not mean to imply for a moment that Gioia and Ginsberg are unproblematically kin. I would argue, instead, that our terms for describing debates over poetic language and subjectivity need to be recast to account for variations such as Ginsberg's. Perhaps Annie Finch's suggestion of "multiformalism"—a term that encompasses traditional, avant-garde, and non-Western poetic forms—can contribute a useful critical vocabulary. For Finch, an emphasis on a multiformalist poetics would draw "critical attention to forms from other than European traditions as well as to the procedural and other forms used by 'experimental' poets" (xiii).

It is not just the allure of contemporary tendency toward postmodern fragmentation that leads me to argue that Ginsberg's Buddhist poetics eludes a firm placement in one particular movement or in either conceptual pole of East or West. Nor is my intent to disguise middling undecidability as middle-way rhetoric. Instead, the evasions of fixed designation that mark his Buddhist poetics demonstrate the extent to which his work proceeds from the energetic confluence of body, speech, and mind emphasized in his Buddhist study and practice—a confluence of individual self-diffusion and, paradoxically, individualism. For Ginsberg, the breathing body is the teleological source of the spoken line and operates as a mode of containment for the spoken line; the spoken line proceeds, by contrast, to unravel the ontological certainty of the speaking self in linguistic forms of indeterminacy whose roots extend from contemporary postmodernism through the sources available to Ginsberg as a serious student and practitioner of Tibetan Buddhism. Ginsberg's tension between song and concentration so pronounced, for instance, in Chicago in 1968 informs a continuing effort throughout his career to incorporate Buddhism in the construction of an authentic language for subjectivity. This language negotiates oppositional tendencies in which the "authentic" is framed in contemporary critical and poetic discourse, collapsing the boundaries between its conception as either an attractive fiction or a neoromantic, transcendental ideal.

7

On the Devotional

Thus far, I have explored Ginsberg's Buddhism while resisting the urge toward a strict taxonomy. Still, inspired by Ginsberg's remarks in his 1988 essay "Meditation and Poetics," I have traced his spiritual poetic strategies to three tendencies, introduced in chapter 1: a poetics of memory (what he terms in the essay "recollection or mindfulness"), of representation (what he terms "experiments with language and speech"), and of containment (what he terms "experiments with forms"). In order to maintain the linearity necessary for a scholarly study while swerving, still, from a rigid paradigmatic approach, I have discussed his Buddhist poetics within the framework of his changing conceptions of the self, where subjectivity is constructed and experienced in recollection, linguistic representation, and linguistic containment. I have examined the psychospiritual origins of Ginsberg's Buddhist poetry (chapter 1); his initial experiments in a poetry of the sacred that continue and revise his earlier self-fashioning as a poet-prophet, and how these experiments construct a Queer Dharma that energizes his continued production of Buddhist-influenced poetry (chapters 2 and 3); his emphasis on how hybrid East-West mantric language forms seek to redeem wartime culture by commingling the secular concerns of poetry with Buddhist sacred practice (chapters 4 and 5); and his efforts to reanimate his Buddhist practice and its paradoxical accounts of human subjectivity at the same time that such practice was threatened by both singularist withdrawal and cultural professionalization in the final decades of his career (chapter 6).

As much as this is a book energized by the recent emergence of Beat Studies in literary criticism, it was not conceived as a book on the Beats.[1] Studies of Beat Buddhism are necessary, as recent anthologies might suggest. Carole Tonkinson's *Big Sky Mind: Buddhism and the Beat Generation* collects Beat Buddhist poetry in one location with an important contextualizing introduction by religious scholar Stephen Prothero. More recent anthologies synthesize the Buddhist-inspired poems of Beat Generation writers within a larger Buddhist context that includes the eclectic range of poetries of the last decades of the twentieth century—a period in literary history characterized by its own "glossolalia" of poetic forms, to borrow liberally from Robert S. Ellwood's description of 1960s religiosity (6). These collections include Gary Gach's *What Book?! Buddha Poems from Beat to Hip-Hop* (1998); Kent Johnson and Craig Paulenich's *Beneath a Single Moon: Buddhism in Contemporary American Poetry* (2001); Ray McNiece and Larry Smith's *America Zen: A Gathering of Poets* (2004); and Andrew Schelling's *Wisdom Anthology of North American Buddhist Poetry* (2005).

I've called this chapter "On the Devotional," a title that might seem strange considering that the idea of the devotional has received little space thus far in the book. Indeed, its only mention is in chapter 6, where the principle of guru-devotion in Tibetan dharma comes under fire as a hierarchical religious ideal that would seem squarely at odds with North American conceptions of civil liberties and individual civic freedom. I've said little about Buddhist devotion in general—its ritual practices, the historical lineage of teachings on the subject, or its primary texts—though when I discuss the religiosity of Buddhism, it would seem that devotion deserves more attention as a practice of the sacred. On one hand, I have been silent in this regard because the devotional in Buddhism looks so different than it does in the West. As a Buddhist, one is devoted to an ongoing mindfulness of the tactile materiality of the everyday world—its shunyata or codependent arising—as a mode of the sacred rather than to an transcendental Godly presence to whom one devotes oneself as a worshiper. Buddhism teaches that a devotion to the long-term well-being of others arises from a devotion to the shunyata experience. Ginsberg's explorations of Buddhist philosophy and his poetry of political activism speak, respectively, to these questions of shunyata and compassion (also known in its Sanskrit form as "bodhicitta"). Perhaps I've focused on devotion in the ways that former Zen and Tibetan monk Stephen Bachelor sees Buddhism, as a philosophy rather than religion. In his effort to wrest contemporary Western Buddhism from what he perceives as an overdependence on ritual religiosity, Batchelor argues for a Buddhism devoted, simply, to the increased clarity of human experience, even if the expressions of such experience—memory, language, forms of expression—are themselves fragmented rather than self-evidently lucid and even though they often defy the same representational schemas in which they partake. Batchelor's emphasis on "[a]n agnostic Buddhist vision of a culture of awakening" depends on a conception of individual heroic imagination that resembles the same Blakean Poetic Genius that so soundly inspired Ginsberg (114). It is a conceptual framework in which, to recall Blake's *Jerusalem*, the individual Buddhist practitioner must create a system or be enslaved by another's orthodoxies. It follows, then, that with the power of the romantic imagination set as a devotional ground, the medium for Batchelor's "agnostic Buddhist vision of a culture of awakening" is the artist rather than the priest. "Dharma practice," he writes, "is more akin to artistic creation than technical problem solving" (103).

Whether or not Batchelor has served as the unconscious ground for my own conception of the devotional in this study, I do wish to linger on his emphasis on the imagination. Following Jerome McGann's cautions on reading with a "romantic ideology," I have attempted to trace Ginsberg's neoromantic impulse—his debt to British and American romantics, especially to Blake and Whitman—while not reading his poetry myself as a romantic. With this continued resistance to a romantic-critical reading, I would like to explore the traces of romantic imagination that persist in my discussion thus far of Ginsberg's Buddhist poetry. These traces, I would argue, can offer a starting point from which to consider further the relationship between Buddhism and contemporary American poetry.

In short, these traces can build a bridge between Ginsberg's particular "Buddhist poetics" and the conception of what general shape a Buddhist poetics might take in the contemporary West. In his introduction to the 2003 version of the influential annual volume *The Best American Poetry* that he guest-edited, Yusef Komunyakaa names, with some hesitance, experimental or avant-garde forms of poetry as "exploratory" modes. His effort to eschew the more common term *experimental* in favor of *exploratory* is, in the context of his essay, an effort to distinguish those poetics that, for him, truly experiment with new ways of seeing the world from those whose disruption of syntax and meaning only constitute "a poetry that borders on cultivated solecism" (11). I do not wish to quarrel too much with Komunyakaa on his position—after all, an introduction such as the one in *Best American Poetry* is as much an effort to describe the poems chosen by the guest editor as it is an effort to stake a claim for the guest editor's position in debates on contemporary canon formation. All the same, I do wish to recuperate Komunyakaa's term "exploratory" from its rhetoric of exhaustion in his essay so that the word might be used as a term of art rather than a term of derision, one that describes a mode of experimental poetics that can include the impulse of contemporary Buddhist poetry in the United States. The word *exploratory* is more useful, I would argue, as a descriptive rather than qualitative account of how the rise in American Buddhism affects contemporary U.S. poetry. Borrowing from Ginsberg's own terminology, in which sacred (or for him "real" poetry) is "a 'process,' or experiment, a probe into the nature of reality and the nature of the mind," I would argue that the place, however tenuous, from which to read Buddhist-inspired poetry in the contemporary United States is one characterized by a vocabulary of process or experiment. It is a location from which the poet undertakes what could be called the exploratory. It is indeed the place that admits and sometimes embraces the experimentation that Komunyakaa warns could veer into "cultivated solecism," but it retains, nevertheless, the humanist spirit of the postwar era of witness and experience that Komunyakaa extols in his reading of the 1960s and 1970s as "an era that praised content and the empirical" (12).

It would seem that Ginsberg's exploratory urge is refracted through his humanism—the same collocation of formal poetic strategies I describe in the previous chapter, which tries to find a home, however curiously, where poets such as Dana Gioia and Ginsberg can both reside. Is this point of contact between humanism and experimentalism a space from which a Buddhist poetics might emerge? I would hope that a book such as this can begin such a dialogue among poets, literary scholars, and Buddhist scholars. Such discussion, too, might rejuvenate psychoanalytic literary criticism in the same way that, for example, the work of Jeremy Safran and Mark Epstein have reenvisioned psychotherapeutic practice from a Buddhist perspective.[2] Of course, in claiming an exploratory voice for a Buddhist middle-way between, say, Gioia and Ginsberg, I do not mean to claim that such a poetics only can be undertaken by U.S. Buddhists. The range of Buddhist-inspired poets extends beyond strict Buddhist adherents. I would suggest that the appellation *Buddhist practitioner* is itself an unproductive biographical standard against which to measure this sort of exploratory poetics. Indeed, in a 2003 Stanford University Poetics Seminar on Buddhism and contemporary American poetry titled "Practitioners of Reality," Michael McClure affirms that no such thing as an American Buddhist poetry can exist if such a poetry is described as one that depends on an author who represents him/herself as "committedly a Buddhist." McClure offers a reminder that Buddhist poetic strategies can be deployed as often by those poets who identify as Buddhist practitioners and those who, like himself, might compose a Buddhist-inspired book "because it is new to me and I want to experience it and experiment with it" ("Practitioners"). Fischer, a poet and Zen priest, strikes a similar note at the 2003 seminar when he cautions that a poetics of Buddhism is one that resonates from an author's textual strategies as much as his/her individual religious commitment—and that the latter might serve as an inhibiting force if emphasized too greatly. He begins with gentle self-mockery:

> Now that I'm a Buddhist poet, I should now write a Buddhist poem. I think that [attitude] would be the death of everything, and I think of poor Mr. Hopkins who wrote wonderful poetry but suffered a lot because trying to make it all fit into Christian doctrine I think is a very hard, nervous-making doctrine [. . .] and I don't want to suffer like that. I just want to write. In my life [as a Zen priest], my Buddhist practice is front and center, so I just assume that writing is about that. ("Practitioners")

Fischer's later emphasis on the distinction between secular writing and writing that "is about" Buddhism echoes what I would estimate is the main argument of this book: his remarks reaffirm Ginsberg's commentary on Buddhist writing as simply that which stages the mind "prob[ing] into nature"—a recasting, as I have argued earlier, of Komunyakaa's exploratory mode as a mode that mirrors Buddhist epistemological concerns. A Buddhist poetics, Fischer says, is "not about one's own feelings"; moreover, "it doesn't privilege one's own biography or feelings or thoughts or emotions" as they take place in a "special moment" of the experience of "transcendence or beauty." Instead, Fischer posits that a Buddhist-inspired composition process is one in which the poet "in the moment of writing" is "trying to investigate what's going on without a preconception of what that is—whether it's a Buddhist preconception or any other preconception.

[. . .] That may be the Buddhist part: that one is an open field looking at what's real and with writing investigating what's real" ("Practitioners").

Where Fischer's words seem to affirm the Buddhist poetic lineage that Ginsberg himself traces, too, back to Charles Olson's composition by field metaphor, Leslie Scalapino, during this same seminar, reconceives this field as one that resembles both the groundlessness of shunyata—grounded, that is, in the fluctuations of dependent co-arising—and of postmodern conceptions of language and being. Commenting on the linguistic influence of Philip Whalen's Buddhist poetry, she implies that the particular field of Buddhist composition is one framed, however tenuously, by a paradoxical melding of groundlessness and ground that resembles the Two Truths:

> Words do have referents, but these referents have no substance to them, being themselves merely label entities that depend on other label entities in a giant web where the only reality is the interrelatedness of the entities. There's no real substratum to this, and the only existence that things can be said to have is a very weak conventional one that is reflected in the patterns of interconnection—that is, in the usage of language. What emerges is a picture of a world of elements in freefall. Because they all fall at the same rate, however, there is the appearance of solidity but in fact there is no stable substratum on which they all rest. ("Practitioners")

Given the comments, above, of McClure, Fischer, and Scalapino, one might conclude that if one takes as a starting point a Buddhist ethos of inward-seeking process, experiment, or exploration, one might see that the phenomenological "probing," as Ginsberg would term it, of Buddhist poetics is not markedly different from the epistemological groundless ground of contemporary postmodernism.[3] Such probing can be seen in the work of McClure's collection of poems in *Plum Stones: Cartoons of No Heaven*, which takes Buddhism as its overt subject matter and point of influence, or in Scalapino and Marina Adams's *The Tango*, which explores sacred experience as a form of phenomenological otherness in its fragmentary excursions into the linguistic and gestural figurations of Tibetan Buddhist monks at the famous Sera Monastery in Tibet. In different ways, as a mimetic negotiation of the ever-fluctuating centers of Buddhist conceptions of self and nature (McClure) and as an attempt to enact the process of Buddhist phenomenology (Scalapino), these books introduce ways in which Buddhist thought and practice are indebted to the experimental impulse of postmodern poetry while they reanimate this impulse by transvaluing secular fragmentation as a process of sacred, phenomenological exploration.

Ginsberg has been among perhaps the most vocal of post–World War II poets to claim a place for Buddhism that might be both humanist and experimental/postmodern. I have kept alive this divide between the humanist and postmodern throughout this book, only so that I might reaffirm that Ginsberg's work with Buddhism is a point of humanist-postmodern contact where this divide seems artificial. I might seem to have taken liberties with Gioia's formulations by yoking his humanism with Ginsberg's, but I do not do so without precedent. In his own discussion of Gioia as a champion of the New Formalist movement, Kevin Walzer reminds readers that Gioia's argument that New Formalism turns from high culture to popular culture can be seen as a rejection of master narratives that resembles the postmodern turn. Working from the definition of Expansive poetry as a mode that subsumes both New Formalist and New Narrative urges, Walzer argues, "Expansive poetry is a manifestation of poetic postmodernism described by Jameson—though Gioia would likely not describe Expansive poetry as 'the random cannibalization of all the styles of the past'" (16). Still, Walzer's sense of postmodernism can be reductive, as in his comment that one of the "key assumptions" of postmodernism is "that the Western tradition must be deconstructed," which oversimplifies the role of the "construct" in *deconstruction* and twines postmodernism and deconstruction in a one-to-one relationship of mutual inclusivity (22). I turn to Walzer here, as I turned to Shetley in chapter 6, to demonstrate that the seemingly oppositional poles of the debate, the humanist urge and the postmodernist urge, rest in positions staked across a porous boundary. Despite my own tendency, too, toward postmodern readings, I find that as I read the "Buddhist part," as Fischer might say, of Ginsberg's poetry, I see both the groundless ground of "elements in freefall" (Scalapino) and an effort to combine this freefall and its sacred particularity into an abiding concern for individual and shared human experience that we might call humanism. I have used the word *humanism* throughout this book mindful of both its romanticist context as a central force in the construction of a culture of redemption and its contemporary critical-theoretical context as a term that, at its worst, can mystify reactionary cultural policy. I also have kept in mind Lisa Ruddick's crucial cautions against knee-jerk reactions to humanism in her essay on the shape of contemporary literary studies, "The Near Enemy of the Humanities Is Professionalism." Ruddick, reflecting on her scholarship in humanism and the politics of culture, revives the Tibetan Buddhist concept of the "near enemy"—a point of moral confusion where, the Tibetan tradition teaches, "any virtue has a bad cousin, a failing that closely resembles the virtue and can be mistaken for it." She argues that an attachment to the "near enemy" of humanism, the fear of corrosive middle-class quietism, has undermined the abilities of scholars to discuss humanism in ways that might breach the conventional divide between it and postmodernism. In such confusion, "the near enemy of the heart is the human heart as envisioned by a Victorian sentimental ideology," and "the near enemy of the feeling of shared humanity is a bourgeois humanism that says we are all exactly the same." In short, I have attempted to revive a humanism for Buddhist poetics that does not claim universalism, what Jacques Lezra has described in a different context as the need for a "reparticularized or resensualized" language for what we call "human" (85).

I would suggest that forms of the genuine in U.S. Buddhist poetics—in an era where, as I discuss in chapter 6, the genuine is continually both asserted and denied—commit themselves to the experience of a freefall of language and vision inspired by shunyata teachings, with a belief in a reparticularized or resensualized human experience that does share, as Buddhism teaches, general experiences and desires expressed in the Four Noble Truths without lapsing into hegemonic universalism (the experience of suffering; the causes of such suffering; an awareness of the path out of suffering; and the ability to undertake, through meditation practice, this path out of suffering). What seems clear is that the commitment of U.S. poetry has shifted to include language and form as more than stylistic concerns but as ontological imperatives. Those who identify with New Formalists, or with new poetries indebted to the earlier Language movement, propound a conception of ontological trust—a poetics based in a continual reenvisioning of forms of the genuine. Yet, this shift has occurred in a era dominated by postmodern embrace of the groundlessness of language and form—as infinite chains of signification or as forms of historical continuity that can be recovered—an embrace of localism and particularity that departs from the conventional Western metaphysical scene of devotion.[4] These responses, of course, are not necessarily Buddhist in spirit, nor should they be. All the same, they share the *groundless ground* of Buddhist epistemology, an impulse to make meaning, in form and content, in what Buddhism would term a necessary coexistence of relative and absolute truths. This book has examined how Ginsberg's particular Buddhist poetics developed within his enthused clash of romantic, modern, and postmodern revolutions of subjectivity. The conceptions of selfhood produced from such collisions were, for Ginsberg, equally solid and fragmentary; they were as trustworthy as a breathing body and as diffuse as its spoken breaths. This book suggests that such collisions, too, are points of contact for poets and scholars to consider how a Buddhist poetics for the contemporary West might emerge from what disappears in this clash—what Ginsberg has dramatized in "Mind Breaths" as the indeterminate breath that nevertheless "breathes outward from the nostrils."

Notes

Works Cited

Index

Notes

Preface: Four Faces of Ginsberg's Buddhism

1. Chapters 5 and 6 of this book examine Ginsberg's self-questioning in his journals and the texts of the poems themselves of his Buddhist commitment. Michael Schumacher's *Dharma Lion* is a useful biographical source, too, for examining the inconsistencies in Ginsberg's Buddhist practice. A more recent biographical collection of anecdotes on this subject is Sam Kashner's 2004 memoir *When I Was Cool: My Life at the Jack Kerouac School*. As I argue in my preface and, I hope, as I demonstrate in this book, Ginsberg's struggles with Buddhism should not be seen as a negation of his commitment to Buddhist practice but instead as a reaffirmation that Buddhism is, indeed, a lifelong practice and that the fits and starts of a Buddhist's commitment to the path are part and parcel of that person's individual path itself.

2. The bodhisattva vow is one of the most serious commitments to Buddhism that a lay practitioner can make. The practitioner vows to continue taking rebirth as a bodhisattva, a saint-like being with a devotion to continued altruistic rebirths until all sentient beings attain enlightenment. Ginsberg describes the motivation behind taking the bodhisattva vow as the "ideal" of Buddhist practice. The vow serve as "a compass point or a direction or an indication of desire [to be a bodhisattva], and a vow to go in that direction" ("Kerouac's Ethic" 367).

3. Ben Giamo offers the important reminder that "[a]lthough Kerouac always had a devotion for the Cross, and was throughout his life preoccupied with the crucifixion of Christ, his later years (from 1960–1969) signal a far more unmitigated attachment to the sorrows and sacrifices of Jesus" (198). One of the standards by which a commitment to Buddhism often is measured is the degree to which the Buddhist practitioner formalizes his/her practice in study with a spiritual teacher. In this regard, too, Kerouac's Buddhism differs dramatically from Ginsberg's, even as Kerouac was Ginsberg's first Buddhist teacher. "Whether out of extravagant pride or utter faith in self-reliance," Giamo writes, "Kerouac's unwillingness to submit himself to a master that would guide his Buddhist quest (as Ginsberg, Snyder, and Whalen had done) reflects [Kerouac's] inability to decenter the self, to put it in the hands of another" (199).

4. From the vantage of Tibetan Buddhism, the Vajrayana tradition is a subset of the Mahayana tradition. Ginsberg studied Mahayana texts and practiced Mahayana Buddhism. Within the Mahayana, he concentrated on the Tantric practices of Vajrayana.

5. Tantra is a group of techniques and beliefs in Buddhism and Hinduism that take the potentially debilitating cravings of human desire and incorporate these cravings into systematic spiritual practices.

6. In chapter 2, I note Ginsberg's influence on American Buddhism, as seen through the eyes of Gehlek Rinpoche. Still, it is important to note the degree to which American Buddhism has grown in and of itself, as the result of immigration practice and the expanded availability of Buddhist teachers in the United States. As Richard Hughes Seager concludes in *Buddhism in America*, "During the last forty years, Buddhism in the United States has been transformed from the religion of a relatively small number of Asian Americans and an esoteric preoccupation of a much smaller European American avant-garde into what amounts to a mass movement" (232). In *American Buddhism: Methods and Findings in Recent Scholarship*, Christopher S. Queen notes that by the turn of the twenty-first century, roughly 1.6% of the U.S. population was Buddhist. Nearly 25% are Buddhist converts, such as Ginsberg, and 75% are immigrants who brought their Buddhist practice with them to the U.S. (xv). This number of Buddhists in the U.S., less than 2%, is not enormous, which could suggest that Seager's comments exaggerate the case. Still, Seager's report is influenced less by the numbers of actual Buddhists in the United States than by the staggering growth of Buddhism here over the past four decades. Charles S. Prebish's account of the emergence of Buddhism in the U.S. is useful here. Writing about the definitive text on Buddhist membership in America, Don Morreale's *Complete Guide to Buddhist America*, Prebish quotes Morreale's 1997 report that roughly 2% of Buddhist centers had been founded between 1900 and 1964. Prebish writes that by 1975, "the number of centers had increased fivefold" (48). This number doubled between 1975 and 1984 and again doubled between 1985 and 1997 (48).

1. Ginsberg's Spiritual Fathers

1. Rodden's focus on what he terms *reputation formation* depends on a complex relationship of factors that are useful, too, in reading Ginsberg's reputation: authorial self-fashioning, audience reception of the work itself, and audience response to the public figure of the artist in the historical moment in which the particular work is received.

2. I use *orientalism* throughout this book in terms of Edward Said's formulation, where Western whites construct a passive, idealized version of the East as part of larger colonizing gestures in which the East is object of the subjugating gaze of the West. The initial allure of Ginsberg's Buddhism might indeed be

termed orientalist in this regard. He found in Buddhism a heterogeneous space for the imagination that he could appropriate for his own political and artistic activities. Such is the orientalist gesture—much like Norman Mailer's racially insensitive use of the word *hip* in his 1957 essay "The White Negro." Still, as I argue in this book, orientalism cannot fully account for the nuances of Ginsberg's twenty-five years of formal Buddhist practice. On one hand, to be sure, Ginsberg's Buddhism might be seen to perpetuate the idea of countercultural religiosity as ahistorical; yet, on the other hand, as I discuss throughout this book, Ginsberg often deployed Buddhism as a means of reenvisioning postwar materialist, political-power structures. A central organizing principle of this book is that Ginsberg's maturation as a Buddhist poet draws paradoxically from both orientalist and revolutionary energies. Robert Bennett's observation of the Beats in general can serve, too, as a more specific commentary on Ginsberg's Buddhism. Simply put, Beat counterculture "was less revolutionary than it thought but more powerful than its harshest critics contend" (182).

3. For more on Buddhist practitioners from Judaism, see Roger Kamenetz, *The Jew in the Lotus: A Poet's Rediscovery of Jewish Identity in Buddhist India*. Kamenetz's discussion of Ginsberg's Buddhism emphasizes that the matrix of the poet's quarrel with his birth faith is at the level of religious language (237). On the question of authentic appropriations of Buddhism, it is important to note that Ginsberg's effort to engage himself in an authentic Buddhist practice parallels the struggles of American Buddhism to set its own standards for authenticity—and that Ginsberg's effort is, in no small measure, an influence on American Buddhism. Even the phrase *American Buddhism* is itself a contested linguistic formulation within the diverse Buddhist communities of the U.S., some of whom favor a conservative approach that would drop the *American*, and others arguing for a Buddhism that adapts itself to Western culture in the same way that Buddhism historically allowed itself to be adopted by its many host countries in its roughly twenty-five-hundred-year history. See Richard Hughes Seager, as well as Charles S. Prebish, for more on the divergent varieties of Buddhist experience in the United States.

4. I recognize the risks in citing Fields's *How the Swans Came to the Lake* in this discussion of authenticity. When Fields's book was published first in 1981, it was considered a comprehensive account of American Buddhism. Through its two subsequent editions, its value has been reconsidered in terms of the diverse Buddhisms brought to the United States after immigration from Asia was reexpanded by the Immigration Act of 1965. As Seager explains, Fields's book is significant in its "account of how a generation of cultural revolutionaries in search of alternative spirituality found their way to Buddhism"; in this way, *How the Swans Came to the Lake* offers "countercultural Buddhists a sense of their own indigenous Buddhist lineage" even if it does not fully account for the

variations of immigrant Buddhisms (x). Despite the risk of working with Fields in this discussion of authenticity, I refer to him in this context because his book is the definitive account of that "generation of cultural revolutionaries in search of alternative spirituality" in which Ginsberg is a primary figure.

5. I will discuss the Two Truths in depth in chapter 3. For introductory purposes, it is important to note that the Two Truths doctrine is a principle by which an "absolute truth" of sacred experience coexists, however paradoxically, with the equally important "relative truth" of material, embodied experience. The latter truth might simply be defined as quotidian, sensory experience. However, the former truth is complex. It is commonly translated as an absolute or subtle truth, but both translations can be misleading because both suggest the revelation of a solid, metaphysical presence. Instead, the presence of absolute truth can be measured by its metaphysical absence: it is, instead, the experience of *shunyata*, or "emptiness," in which all phenomena exist in a state of "interdependent arising," also termed "dependent co-arising." For the Buddhist practitioner, the interplay of both truths—their interdependence, or co-arising—is as important as either of them in separation.

6. Earlier in the essay, Ginsberg asserts that contemporaneous Buddhist language such as "Take a non-totalitarian attitude" or "Express yourself courageously" offer useful analogues with "Bohemian art of the twentieth century" (264). While I do not mean to dismiss the slang interplay of Ginsberg's hipsterisms, I also do not want to pretend that the same language that would resonate in the early postwar period of American Buddhism might do the same in the first decade of the twenty-first century. One of the reasons Trungpa might be described as "Tibetan Buddhism's most influential teacher in the West" (Coleman 93) is his unique talent for speaking the language and customs of those in the counterculture seeking alternative religiosity in the late-1960s and 1970s. Seager makes the case perhaps more directly, noting Trungpa's "reputation for his ability to present the essence of traditional Buddhist teachings in a way that addressed the needs and aspirations of western students" (250). In this way, Ginsberg's terminology, such as his use of "hanging loose," is not just an awkward linguistic artifact but instead encodes in language the nascent American Buddhist culture that Trungpa and his students were creating within the ranks of Vietnam-era alternative religiosity.

7. Of course, this line echoes, too, Blake's direct quotation from Numbers in his preface to *Milton*, Blake's own major text of prophetic influence. As this book discusses later, Blake's influence on Ginsberg is not limited to literary history; he is a precursor poet for Ginsberg's Buddhist verse. Blake, echoing Numbers, insists on a community where "all the Lords people were Prophets." As his prophecies demonstrate, Blake's conception of a prophetic community is one where selfhood is destabilized by a conception of language and identity that is

fluid and relational rather than univocal. See also Mark Bracher, *Being Form'd: Thinking through Blake's "Milton"*; Nelson Hilton, *Literal Imagination: Blake's Vision of Words*, and my discussion in *"Strange Prophecies Anew."* Ginsberg continues Blake's insistence on a prophetic poetry of mediated subjectivity and, guided by the Buddhist notion of *shunyata* (emptiness), emphasizes that such a conception of identity is a manifestation of the sacred. Hence the importance for Ginsberg in the *Morning in Spring* introduction of describing his father's lyric epiphanies in terms of both a Kabbalistic conceptual framework and of the definitive Buddhist sutra on shunyata, the Prajnaparamita Sutra.

8. However, just two years earlier, in a letter to his son that comments on Ginsberg's 1969 *Playboy* interview, Louis praises the same syncretic religious idealism for which he takes his son to task in the 1971 feature by Gefen. Louis in a 30 March 1969 letter to his son writes, "By the way, I liked your statement in your *Playboy* interview that 'by the holy spirit I mean the recognition of a common self in all of us and our acceptance of the fact that we are all the same one'" (Ginsberg and Ginsberg, *Family Business* 290). Louis then offers a logical extension of the *Playboy* interview remarks, suggesting an affirmation rather than revision of his son's religiosity: "What is Holy? That which unites the souls of men. Roman Rolland declared, 'One never knows where one begins and where one ends'" (Ginsberg and Ginsberg, *Family Business* 290). These remarks are striking because they demonstrate how the vectors Zionism takes in the late-1960s affected both Louis's and Allen's relationships with Judaism and with each other. Foremost, of course, it is crucial that Louis's "correction" of his son's Buddhism occurs in the *Jerusalem Post Magazine*, while his solidarity with his son's syncretism takes place in private correspondence. It becomes clear in their correspondence that Louis's Old Left values within which Ginsberg was raised have been transformed by post–World War II Zionism as it is assimilated in the United States and framed by the Holocaust. After World War II, the father began to embrace what Ginsberg saw as political quietism, especially with regard to Middle East politics. As Ben Lee argues, Ginsberg at this same time saw the trajectory of American leftism trumping the concerns of Jewish assimilation (372).

9. Although Louis's account of audience reaction to these joint readings is touched by (understandable) paternal idealism, his remarks on the audience suggest that he, too, favors a relationship between young poets and their precursors that is relational rather than competitive: "Sometimes when we finish reading, we hug each other, and the whole audience gets up and applauds" (qtd. in Gefen 9). Louis's need to emphasize that the audience of "Hippies and their fathers" has rewarded the father-son hug with applause suggests the importance of relational influence on the two poets and implies that their joint readings reverse the traditional model of Oedipal competitiveness and usurpation between father and son.

10. In a 24 January 1968 letter to Ginsberg attached to a clipping of the article, Bishop explains that he wrote the piece but removed his byline because of a personal reference to himself that he included in the article.

11. I use the word *guru* here mindful of its often pejorative usage in contemporary dismissals of what has come to be called "New Age" religiosity in the U.S. The term *guru* is apt, however. The word translates from Sanskrit as "teacher" in English. *Guru* is the word used in some American Buddhist communities, including those in which Ginsberg practiced, to mean, simply, a teacher of Buddhism. Of course, *guru* has come to connote in popular culture a word that only befits so-called New Age practice rather than reflect its discursive function in the twenty-five-hundred-year-old lineage of one the five major religions of the world.

12. Ginsberg's Buddhist notes suggest that the collision of Louis's Hebraic influence with his son's Buddhism enables Ginsberg's spiritual questing; however, his Buddhism is as much a revision of Hebraic ontological certainty as it is of monotheism. Even in this regard, Ginsberg's language for the sacred borrows from that of family romance and familial caretaking. In Ginsberg's notes to a 1985 Buddhist lecture, titled in his notebook as "Theism & Non-Theism," Ginsberg observes that the difference between Hebraic monotheism and Buddhist non-theism can be framed in terms of parent-child relations: "Theism—worshipping external agent. Worshipping external agent[—]maybe you're looking for your babysitter [w]ho hides in outside world or part of family" (Notebooks and journals). Ginsberg later adds that to "[c]ure symptom (of babysit?)" produced by theism "one needs to develop some meditative experiences." Ginsberg's notes suggest a line of thinking in which Buddhism helps overthrow an "external agent," Yahweh, once an object of worship by the child. More intriguing, however, Ginsberg's parenthetically asserts, then immediately questions, "babysit[ting]" as a pathological symptom of theism. At this advanced stage of his career—and nine years after Louis's death—parent-child relations and his own Buddhist practice are still a complicated commingling of burden and influence. Such a complex relationship with authority should come as no surprise, given the guru-student transferential relationship Trungpa encourages with Ginsberg and how this relationship contributes to the vexing questions of guru devotion Ginsberg faced after the 1976 Snowmass incident at Trungpa's Vajrayana seminary, detailed in chapter 6. Ginsberg's Buddhist notebooks are quoted with permission of the Department of Special Collections, Stanford University, and the Allen Ginsberg Trust.

13. Ginsberg's incorporation of Williams as a poetic father and literary correction to Louis's influence is documented, too, in Michael Schumacher's account of the young Ginsberg's early literary encounters with Williams. In his introduction to *Family Business*, Schumacher reports that the literary competition in the Gins-

berg family was between Louis and the new poetic father Williams rather than between Louis and Allen: "According to Edith Ginsberg [Louis's second wife], Louis was pleased that a poet of Williams's reputation had befriended his son, although he was slightly put off when Williams would visit and he and Allen would huddle together in Allen's room, excluding Louis from their conversation" (xxvi). Ginsberg's introduction to *Morning in Spring* begins with this same exclusionary gesture, appropriating Williams's rejection of the young Ginsberg's work as a way of framing Ginsberg's own rejection of Louis's poetry—but only insofar as this appropriation might later in the essay bring Louis figurally back into the literary conversation between Ginsberg and Williams. That this literary conversation is figurative, even strained at times, in the *Morning in Spring* introduction serves as a reminder of the ambivalent influence of Louis on Ginsberg's development as a poet. Later in this chapter, I discuss how Ginsberg's relationship Louis can be read, too, as a figure for his relationship with Buddhism.

14. Ben Lee describes how such a conception of aesthetic authority also can function as a formal, stylistic device. Writing of Ginsberg's use of anaphora in "Howl," Lee explains that in addition to establishing "prophetic momentum" from line to line, anaphora serves as "a figure of return that troubles linear progression and confuses origins by insisting on starting over, again and again, seemingly at the same place (the 'who') but always with a difference (the predicate)." Anaphora, then, is a trope for Ginsberg's conception of literary influence and historicity—where each new generation emerges from a dialectic of both continuity and revision. At the same time that the poem delineates the "actions, attitude, and suffering" of its protagonists in their historical moment, Lee argues that "the form of the poem leads us to wonder when exactly—and with whom—these actions and attitudes originate." Lee concludes, "Through force of repetition [. . .] the relative pronoun 'who' becomes interrogative, and the form of Ginsberg's poem subtly undermines the notion that generations break away cleanly, defining themselves through their clear difference from the past" (383).

15. Louis recognizes, too, the dual purpose of his son's introduction, as both a quarrel with and promotion of *Morning in Spring*. In an undated letter to his son [ca. June 1970], Louis writes of the introduction to his book, "I resent the slight blemish of your attribution of the word 'anachronism'" but adds later, "the rest of your Introduction, especially Part II, with its touching, emotional love for me and its high praise of my lyric perfection, *dissolves* your word 'anachronism.'"

16. Even Ginsberg's first meeting with Trungpa, famously recounted in interviews over the years, is framed by his relationship with his biological father. He met Trungpa in 1971 on a Manhattan street corner, stepping in front of the cab Trungpa was hailing so that Louis might have the taxi instead. In a 1976 interview with Peter Barry Chowka, Ginsberg stated simply, "I stole [Trungpa's] taxicab; my father was ill and I wanted to get my father off the street" (381).

17. In this 7 July 1969 letter, Ginsberg affirms to Louis that "as perfect as many of the poems are it [*Morning in Spring*] should have a publisher." He apologizes for not involving himself previously in efforts to find a publisher: "I'm sorry I never intruded before but I didn't think I should (reverse nepotism) but the quality of the poems outweighs other thoughts, & the shame that you're not enjoying their publication shames me [. . .]." In the standard Oedipal narrative of the anxiety of influence, Ginsberg would compete to overthrow his strong, precursor poet-father. Instead, he expresses "shame" that heretofore he has done nothing to aid his father's publication efforts—that he has not contributed to a model of influence based on relationality rather than competition. He closes with a promise to help get the poems published. Indeed, as an earlier letter to Ginsberg from Louis suggests, this model of influence has been a strong presence for the two, despite Ginsberg's anxieties about "reverse nepotism." In this letter, from 30 May 1969, Louis discusses with his son the difficulties of getting *Morning in Spring* accepted for publication. He eventually concludes, "Maybe by now I have enough exposure, thanks, in parts, to you, to have my book given consideration (*Family Business* 290). It is important to emphasize, then, that even before Ginsberg explicitly begins to advocate for publication of *Morning in Spring*, his literary reputation alone furthered a conception of influence that proceeds as much from negotiated human relationships as from Bloomian competition.

18. The claim for Trungpa's access to Absolute Truth produces the authoritarian excesses that nearly brought down Naropa University (then Naropa Institute) in 1976, which I discuss further in chapter 6.

19. See page 4 of an undated draft copy titled "Allen Ginsberg, Comments on *First Thoughts, Best Thoughts*." Also see page 4 of an earlier (also undated) draft copy titled "Comments on *First Thoughts, Best Thoughts*." Ginsberg's own attacks on the academy from "Howl" onward are marked by an oppositional tendency to embrace opportunities to read at colleges and universities and, whenever possible, to shape the reception of Beat Generation literature within the academic literary establishment. His eventual chairpersonship of the poetics department at Naropa and successful efforts to win accreditation for the school, along with his eventual distinguished professorship at Brooklyn College at the end of his career, suggest that Ginsberg's relationship with the academy is both skeptical and accommodating, despite his adversarial statements otherwise over the years.

20. Because Ginsberg's early Buddhism was autodidactic, and his practice thereby eccentrically individualized until he met Trungpa, a word of clarification is necessary about exactly what form of Buddhism Ginsberg primarily practiced. The Tibetan Mahayana Buddhism that Ginsberg studied and practiced during the last three decades of his life was a form of the Madhyamaka (translated as "middle way"), or Centrist, philosophical school. The Madhyamaka is one of the dominant schools of Buddhism imported to the West, and its basic principles

were compatible with Ginsberg's exploration of the "middle way" in his early, self-generated Zen studies, even if the Tantric rituals and practices of Tibetan Madhyamaka often differ greatly with Zen. Unless noted otherwise, subsequent references to Buddhism in this book refer to the Tibetan traditions that governed Ginsberg's Buddhist practice for most of his life.

21. Trungpa's authoritarian excess is well documented. Trungpa's successor, Osel Tenzin (Thomas Rich), promiscuously slept with students and, in one of the most appalling breaches of spiritual ethics in the postwar era, did so when he knew he was infected with HIV. Several of these students contracted the virus from him. Ginsberg's notebooks and correspondence from this period demonstrate an effort to protect Trungpa's Vajradhatu organization from the stigma of Osel Tenzin's actions while imploring the organization's senior students to recognize explicitly that Osel Tenzin's moral authority as a religious leader had been destroyed as a result of his actions. During this period, Ginsberg left the Vajradhatu organization for Gehlek Rinpoche's Jewel Heart Sangha. In a discussion that otherwise praises Trungpa's deft abilities to engage Buddhist practitioners no matter what level of their practice, Buddhist scholar Charles S. Prebish offers the reminder that those outside Trungpa's circle of students could be justifiably skeptical: "Trungpa's well-publicized reputation and unpredictability seemed to require at least a bit of caution from all who had not known him previously" (159–60). Perhaps the most extended account of Trungpa's teaching methods is Stephen T. Butterfield's *The Double Mirror*. A poet and former member of Trungpa's sangha, Butterfield takes the lama to task for his authoritarianism, yet does so from the informed perspective of one who studied and practiced the Crazy Wisdom tradition and admits that the so-called craziness of the wisdom promulgated by Trungpa might be both "a form of spiritual materialism and a means for cutting through spiritual materialism." In chapter 6, I discuss how poet W. S. Merwin's terrifying experience with Trungpa unsettled the Naropa community and, eventually, affected Ginsberg's poetics through the late 1970s and early 1980s. As my exploration of the Merwin-Trungpa incident will demonstrate, Trungpa's methods themselves could be coercive and authoritarian, even though they were conceived in sympathy with the anti-authoritarian urgency of late 1960s and early 1970s Western youth culture.

22. See accounts of Ginsberg's psychoanalysis in Barry Miles's and Schumacher's biographies. See also James Breslin, "The Origins of 'Howl' and 'Kaddish.'"

23. Commenting on Ginsberg's *Morning in Spring* introduction, Breslin concludes that from "Howl" onward, Ginsberg "take[s] up his father's medium of communication (poetry) and, declaring it hollow and dead, transform[s] it by infusing it with the hallucinatory visions and human vulnerability of his mother" (417).

24. As I will discuss in chapters 2 and 3, notions of shunyata (emptiness) in the traditions in which Ginsberg studied and practiced render even this notion of "Buddha mind or true nature" to be materially unfixed and ontologically uncertain. Jack Engler argues that, as a representation per se and given the dualistic nature of language, "Buddha mind" carries with it a potentially vexing trace of ontological independence. Engler offers the useful reminder that "Buddhist analysis says, in effect, you cannot appropriately represent yourself to yourself as independently existing. If you do, there are serious consequences for your own mental health, and if you act out of this belief you will cause harm to others" (52). Engler's key word, of course, is "appropriately." As I have discussed earlier, the tenuous issue of representation in Buddhism—especially self-representation—is significant to understanding Ginsberg's Buddhist poetics. In the poet's insistence that a Buddhist poetics is an extension of Pound's dictum that poets engage "direct treatment of the thing," he explains that "the thing[s]" of such "direct treatment" include the mind itself in the process of understanding itself. As a way of thinking through this often vexing issue of representation in Buddhism, it is useful to visit briefly a commonly cited difference between the Tibetan Madhyamaka school and Mind-Only school. Both posit the mind as the locus of being—as that which constructs being and its subsequent projection of itself into the material world. However, *mind* is an irreducible frame of reference in the Mind-Only school. For the Prasangika Madhyamaka school, the lineage with which Ginsberg's primary teachers identified, *mind* can be the object of its own perception, even though the mind is considered to be suffused with shunyata—that is, considered to be empty of essentialized existence. The predictable problem, of course, is that such ideas must be represented in language—especially complex for poetic language, where meaning proliferates rather than suffers containment. The realization of shunyata, an enlightenment experience or *satori* experience, can only be represented; thus, a poem at best can dramatize second-handedly, the process by which such experience may be enacted. This quarrel with representation is a crucial element of Ginsberg's Buddhist poetics, as I discuss, especially, in chapter 4.

25. I will discuss in chapter 2 how the intersection of desire and the sacred is deployed by Ginsberg in the construction of a Queer Dharma. As he says to Clark in the interview quoted in this chapter, discussions of religious devotion must "be done really delicately" because of the way they are shaped by desire (53). At this juncture, however, it is important to acknowledge that Ginsberg's response to Clark is consistent with the Tibetan Buddhist position that progress on the path to enlightenment is hastened when the practitioner recognizes that religious devotion is shaped by and can shape desire. As Jeffrey Hopkins has noted, such an approach to sacred experience actually is for Tibetan Buddhism a means of decreasing attachment to desire. Hopkins writes of Tibetan Buddhist approaches

to desire: "Through desirous activities such as gazing at a loved one, or smiling, embracing, or engaging in sexual union, a pleasurable consciousness is produced; it is used to realize the truth of the emptiness of inherent existence [shunyata], whereby desire itself is undermined" ("Compatibility" 377). These remarks by Hopkins—the Dalai Lama's main English translator from 1979–1989—reinforce the notion that the multiplication rather than repression of desire is crucial in Tantric Buddhism. Moreover, as I will explore in more detail in chapter 2, these remarks demonstrate that Tantric Buddhism's lack of a strict prohibition against sexual expression suggests, too, a potential equivalence in the role played by both heterosexual and homosexual desire in the Tantric tradition. Though the sacred wisdom for which Ginsberg aims may have been Crazy Wisdom, its foundation was anything but crazy for him: unlike traditional and mainstream Western religious practices in the postwar era, Buddhism was compatible with the poet's homosexual identity.

26. As discussed earlier in this chapter, the post-Trungpa scandals in Trungpa's Vajradhatu organization suggest that Tilopa's initial teachings that "enlightenment [is] identical with sex and aggression" (Finn 110) could be fatal if seen as a pedagogical archetype.

2. Queer Dharma, Anxiety, and Fantasy in "Angkor Wat"

1. In *Naked Angels: The Lives and Literature of the Beat Generation*, Tytell writes that early in his career, Ginsberg "was particularly attracted to Zen, comparing its impact to Carl Solomon, seeing that its essence was to exhaust words so as to see the world new" (99). Writing in the *New Republic* in one of his earliest attacks on Beat literature and culture, Norman Podhoretz describes Buddhist influence on Beat Generation literature as only exoticized rebellion. Michael Rumaker's review of "Howl," a year after the poem was published, frames the sort of argument that typifies most critical rejections of Ginsberg's Buddhism. Rumaker asserts that the poem fails precisely because Ginsberg's incorporation of Buddhism "corrupts" the genuine "anger" in the poem. Much later in Ginsberg's career, in Helen Vendler's forty-year *New Yorker* retrospective of the poet published in 1996, Ginsberg's Buddhism is described as a poetics of "quietism," one that fails because it "would turn every phenomenon into illusion" ("American X-Rays" 89).

2. Unless otherwise indicated, subsequent citations from Ginsberg's poetry until *White Shroud* are from *Collected Poems, 1947–1980*.

3. This spiritual crisis in Ginsberg's Buddhism, as I will argue later in this book, begins with "Angkor Wat" and continues through "Wichita Vortex Sutra" and "Iron Horse." Only when Ginsberg begins his studies with Trungpa in the 1970s does he create a more stable Buddhist practice, one that Gehlek Rinpoche eventually heralded in his eulogy to Ginsberg: "the actual Dharma

practice which affects millions of people's lives, he [Ginsberg] made possible to take root, through all these efforts that he made" (301).

4. Ginsberg implies that the individual's physical action of taking refuge in the Three Jewels is adumbrated by the physical experience of the temple of Angkor Wat itself. The notion that the sacred physicality of objects might be incarnated in the body is suggested, too, by the sacramental architectural planning of the Angkor Wat complex. Eleanor Mannikka describes the crucial "geophysical location" of Angkor Wat as an intersection of divinity and materiality: the Angkor temples were conceived as "spiritual, political, cosmological, and astronomical or geophysical centers" (9). Indeed, Mannikka cites Alice Boner's translation of eleventh-century Orissa, India, architect Rāmacandra Kaulācāra as proof that early Asian temple architecture is meant to reflect cultural beliefs in divine architectural models. Kaulācāra proclaims that a divine Creator "lays out the plan of the universe according to measure and number. [. . .] He is the prototype and model of the temple builder, who also unites in his single person, the architect, the priest, and the sculptor" (qtd. in Mannikka 8–9). It should come as no surprise, then, that Ginsberg's physical place of refuge in this poem is one whose cultural history presumes, as does the poem, a physical sanctuary that blurs the boundary between human and divine.

5. *Vipassana* itself translates as "insight." Depending on the Buddhist tradition in question, vipassana can be defined as a method that leads to insight or as simply the resulting insight that comes from direct, experiential meditation practices. Buddhadāsa Bhikku's definition can offer common ground: vipassana is "meditation for the sake of insight into impermanence, unsatisfactoriness, and not-self" (39).

6. As Gordon Ball explains, Ginsberg's travels in Europe during 1957 and 1958 included reading and study in Surrealism and meetings with noted Surrealists and Dadaists. Ginsberg's experiences in Europe at this time contributed to his treatment of madness in "Kaddish" as both a dangerous condition and a means of resistance to postwar rational consciousness. However, the most direct influence of Ginsberg's experiences with the Surrealist avant-garde occurred two years before "Kaddish," in the poem "At Apollinaire's Grave" (1959), which elegizes the prewar European avant-garde at the same time that it hails a revivifying experimentalism in Ginsberg's contemporaries. The poem invokes Guillaume Apollinaire as Ginsberg's Surrealist muse; as if anticipating the fusion of Surrealist form and geopolitical content in "Angkor Wat," Ginsberg defines the urgency of his muse as both a personal and historical response to U.S. militarism. Apollinaire's "madness is only around the corner and Genet is with us stealing books / the West is at war again and whose lucid suicide will set it all right [?]" (*Collected* 180). But just as Surrealist technique risks self-obsession in "Angkor Wat," the speaker of "At Apollinaire's Grave" never leaves Père Lachaise cemetery

itself. The poem ends with an elegiac collage of disjunctive images—a burning cigarette sends the poet's book in flames, an ant crawls on him, he *feels* a tree growing—and, as in Shelley's "Adonais" and Whitman's "When Lilacs Last in the Dooryard Bloom'd," the speaker becomes the subject of his own elegy. He is trapped in a graveyard despite the redemptive potential summoned by the elegiac voice: "I am buried here and sit by my grave beneath a tree" (*Collected* 182). Amid the cultural urgency that frames the poem and triggers the invocation of the muse, the speaker never leaves the place of the dead. He buries himself with them instead.

7. My subsequent references to Ginsberg's notes to the poem are taken from this edition of "Angkor Wat" rather than the Fulcrum Press edition.

8. In *Articulate Flesh: Male Homo-Eroticism and Modern Poetry*, Gregory Woods asserts that this uneven meeting between spontaneous composition and the discipline of Buddhism produces theoretical inconsistencies in Ginsberg's sexual politics. Yet, Woods suggests that improvisatory technique is not incompatible with theories of power, whether such theories are intended to explain cultural, religious, or sexual power relations. In my examination of the composition process of "Wichita Vortex Sutra" in the following chapter, I discuss how theory and praxis—forethought and improvisation—can combine with coherence in Ginsberg's Buddhist poetics. Spontaneity and political engagement are not necessarily mutually exclusive for Ginsberg.

9. For Gregory Woods, the policeman fantasy of "Angkor Wat" is an expression of democratic comradeship, a direct engagement with Whitman's homosocial nationalist ideal. Woods argues, "If police activity is one of the most visible signs of the loveless state of the USA, then the ideal vision of a changed nation must include some change in the role of the police" (199). Woods usefully emphasizes the association of policing and sexual asceticism in Ginsberg's work, isolating important examples in poems such as "American Change," "Kaddish," and "Death to Van Gogh's Ear!" Not surprisingly, then, Ginsberg's speaker in "Angkor Wat" is confused and unsettled by the authority of religious teachers who preach asceticism in response to his appetites. After all, asceticism would seem at odds with Whitman's ideology of democratic adhesion. However, for Whitman, masturbation runs counter to a romanticist, sexualized political economy based on male comradeship. As David S. Reynolds has noted, the sexual "intensity" of masturbation passages in poems such as "Song of Myself" (section 28), "The Sleepers," or "Spontaneous Me" is accompanied by "elements of the moralistic language" of mid-nineteenth-century "purity reformers" (199–200). In a poem such as "I Sing the Body Electric," with its specularized, anatomistic catalogue of the sexualized human body, Whitman describes masturbators as "those who corrupt their own bodies," a practice that leads them to "conceal themselves" (5). The act of concealing precludes the political possibility of Whitman's vision of

democratic comradeship. The poem, too, stages an eroticized touch between two human bodies at the end of its sexually evocative catalogue, suggesting, I would argue, that the spiritual culmination of his embodied political and poetic project emerges not in masturbatory solitude but instead in "[t]he curious sympathy one feels when feeling with the hand the naked meat of the body" (158).

10. See also Robert K. Martin's assessment of sex, sexuality, and politics in "Howl" in *The Homosexual Tradition in American Poetry*.

11. For the term *Queer Dharma*, I am indebted to Winston Leyland's anthology of the same name, *Queer Dharma: Voices of Gay Buddhists*.

12. Hopkins's authority as a gay Buddhist scholar is augmented by his role as the main English translator from 1979 to 1989 for the Dalai Lama, the leader of the Tibetan government-in-exile and the spiritual head of the Gelugpa sect of Tibetan Buddhism (the school to which Ginsberg's final teacher, Gehlek Rinpoche, belonged). Still, the Dalai Lama himself, as perhaps the most widely recognized of all contemporary Buddhist leaders, has delivered contradictory messages on Buddhism and homosexuality over the years that would have troubled Buddhist practitioners such as Ginsberg. On one hand, in his role as a global political figure, the Dalai Lama has spoken forcefully in favor of gay civil rights; on the other hand, as a Buddhist lama, he has said that Buddhism must adapt to the historical and cultural norms of each different country in which it is practiced, whether such norms embrace or are hostile toward sexual equality. It is important to remember that even though the Dalai Lama is seen by Tibetan Buddhists as a living embodiment of Buddhahood—as a reborn figure of Avalokiteshvara, the Buddha of compassion—his authority is not an immutable one for Buddhists. As Hopkins has said, the Dalai Lama "doesn't have the authority to make broad edicts. He's not like the Pope in that respect" (qtd. in Conkin 353). In a 1997 meeting in San Francisco with gay Buddhist leaders and human rights activists, the Dalai Lama noted that "no single person or teacher can redefine [Buddhist] precepts. I do not have the authority to redefine the precepts, since no one can make a unilateral decision or issue a decree. Such a redefinition can only come out of sangha discussions within the various Buddhist traditions" (qtd. in Conkin 354).

13. The depth of Whitman's influence can be seen, too, in Ginsberg's enthusiastic prose criticism of the poet. See especially the essays, "On Walt Whitman, Composed on the Tongue, or, Taking a Walk through Leaves of Grass" and "Whitman's Influence: A Mountain Too Vast to Be Seen." Yet, this enthusiasm often produces selective readings of influence. In the latter essay, Ginsberg praises "Passage to India" as a poem that "predicted a meeting of Eastern and Western thought in our twentieth century" (332). However, Ginsberg's important emphasis on the East-West convergence in "Passage to India" neglects the bewitching role of technology in the poem and does not mention how Whitman's adoration of technology is part of the poetic manifest destiny that praises, too, the eventual

consumerist culture that Ginsberg himself, as an activist, seeks to transform. Ginsberg, of course, creates a Whitman specifically suited for his own work. In "Whitman's Influence: A Mountain Too Vast to Be Seen," Ginsberg asserts that he takes up Whitman's contrariety with vigor in his Buddhist poetics as a paradoxical "pragmatic transcendentalism" that is "flavor[ed]" with the materialism of "meditation practice in American poetry as we approach the second millennium's end" (332–33).

14. Brian Docherty argues that the Whitman theme in question in Ginsberg's poem instead echoes lines 11–20 of Whitman's "The Sleepers." Docherty's point is well taken: these lines in "The Sleepers" establish a ghostly speaker whose movement from one occupied bed to another might be recast in Ginsberg's poem as a figural expression of polyamorous sexuality. However, the explicit circulation of desire in "Love Poem on Theme by Whitman"—the poem's floating corporeality and ambiguously embodied subject positions—most resembles the oscillating, and at times displaced, pleasures of section 11 of "Song of Myself." The greater influence, then, would seem to be "Song of Myself." The opening line of Ginsberg's poem borrows from "Song of Myself," lines 818–19, section 33: "I turn the bridegroom out of bed and stay with the bride myself, / I tighten her all night to my thighs and lips." During cross-examination of his witness testimony at the Chicago Seven trial in 1969, Ginsberg attests to the significance of "Song of Myself" in the composition of "Love Poem on Theme by Whitman." Asked by prosecuting attorney Thomas Foran to read his poem and comment on its religious importance, Ginsberg offers his own critical commentary on its sexual content: "Walt Whitman is one of my spiritual teachers and I am following him in this poem, taking off from a line of his own ["Song of Myself," lines 818–19] and projecting my own actual unconscious feelings, of which I don't have shame, sir, which I feel are basically charming actually" (Ginsberg, "Chicago Seven" 242). The effect of this influence, he proclaims in court, is meant to be charming. Still, the differences between the two poems are important and are emphasized herein as a way of considering the development of Ginsberg's Buddhist poetics in the mid-1960s. For Whitman, the lines in section 33 stage a sexually unbound but heterosexually coded embodied spiritual vision. But for Ginsberg, as I discuss later in this chapter, these "actual unconscious feelings" empty heteronormative sexuality of its authority by commingling polymorphous bodies whose ecstasies are experienced as conditions that resist delimitation by any particular gender coding.

15. At first glance, this seems a liberatory poem in which the clothing of convention is shed in favor of a shared and vulnerable freedom. Yet, a note seems required here on vexing critical response to the trope of nakedness in Beat literature. A common romantically coded critical reading might posit polysexual experience in and of itself as the liberating alternative to postwar sexual convention, as in the

readings of Beat nakedness most widely visible in Tytell's foundational *Naked Angels*. Even Woods, whose readings of Ginsberg's homoerotic poetry often suggest sophisticated narratives of the relationship among, sex, power, and politics, seems guided by an enthusiastic romantic ideology wherein unmitigated freedom from repression follows straightaway from Beat nakedness. For instance, in his discussion of "Television Was a Baby Crawling toward That Deathchamber," Woods argues that sexual openness in Ginsberg's work successfully resists a "virtual synonymity of repression and oppression" (204). For the Beats, Tytell argues in *Naked Angels*, "Nakedness signified rebirth, the recovery of identity" (4). However, as I argue herein, the physical fact of nakedness does not necessarily presage liberation—nor, despite Woods's remarks, does sexual expression necessarily relieve oppression—no matter how many bodies might be entangled, however pleasurably, on the bed. The ending of "Love Poem on Theme By Whitman," with its emphasis on its naked protagonists as lonely, wandering ghosts, suggests that, for Ginsberg, the trope of nakedness was as complex as any other conceit in his poetry; identity was no monolithic construct waiting to be recovered under the same sheets that just as easily might enforce its re-covering.

16. See also Robert K. Martin's commentary on "A Supermarket in California," in which he argues that the dream vision of the poem "is marred by guilt (or fear)—'followed in my imagination by the store detective'—and [. . .] does not assuage Ginsberg's sense of himself as an isolated outsider" (167).

17. Ginsberg's note to this line suggests that his endnotes are a form of literary parenting. The line referenced is line 24 of "Howl," where Ginsberg's most important visionary and romantic sources are proclaimed as an instance in the exhortative lineage of those "who studied Plotinus Poe St. John of the Cross telepathy and bop kabbalah because the cosmos instinctively vibrated at their feet in Kansas." Speaking as if to nurture an upcoming generation of visionary poets, Ginsberg explains in his notes to the line, "Overt intention of this mystical name-dropping was to connect younger readers, Whitman's children already familiar with Poe and Bop, to older Gnostic tradition."

18. Later in his career, in his practice of Tibetan Tantra, he works with more ease in this contradictory space of discipline and desire. For instance, as I discuss in detail in chapter 6, "On Cremation of Chögyam Trungpa, Vidyadhara" elegizes Ginsberg's late Tibetan guru in a compendium of observations that privileges rather than disciplines the proliferating associations of the desiring mind. (*Vidyadhara*, which literally translates from Sanskrit as "wisdom-bearer" is an honorific for a realized master in Trungpa's Crazy Wisdom tradition.) Everything the poet notices at the cremation ceremony is represented as sacred vision—including the absence of the teacher in the presence of the funeral pyre, the teacher's legacy signified by a rainbow that appeared in the sky that day, the particulars of their postceremony meal, and a boy Ginsberg took back to

his motel with him that day after the ceremony. Yet, the multiplicitous paths of desire so important to later poems such as "On Cremation" produce paralysis in "Angkor Wat" and lead the poet-prophet to proclaim, "I am Coward in every direction" (*Collected* 313). Ginsberg's remark is as much about conceptual direction as spatial direction. The Ten Directions is a Buddhist idiomatic phrase that represents the eight ordinal points of the compass, with "above" and "below" added as sacred markers of direction. In Ginsberg's linguistic formulation, his self-assertion of cowardice, then, is a collection of spatial, spiritual, and mental locations from which he cannot hide.

19. As Schumacher's and Miles's biographies report, Ginsberg went through such a tortured period of doubt in his early adulthood that in 1953, he followed an analyst's advice to date women as an effort to "cure" homosexuality. "Angkor Wat" demonstrates that such doubts were part of Ginsberg's early development of a Buddhist poetics.

20. The phrase, of course, comes from Michel Foucault's important work on the care of the self. "Technologies of the self" are among four vectors of behavior inherited from Greco-Roman culture that, according to Foucault, serve as "techniques" for human beings to create, structure, and transform identity. Such technologies "permit individuals to effect by their own means or with the help of others a certain number of operations on their own bodies and souls, thoughts, conducts, and ways of being, so as to transform themselves in order to attain a certain state of happiness, purity, wisdom, perfection, or immortality" ("Technologies" 18). One way to measure the difference, for Ginsberg, between drug use as a technology of the self or as mere recreation is to explore the poet's efforts, documented most of all in his 1966 LSD testimony before the U.S. Senate, to approach drug use with rational diligence. Such deliberation is a hallmark of those techniques that structure identity transformation, for Foucault, insofar as they "impl[y] certain modes of training and modification of individuals, not only in the obvious sense of acquiring certain skills but also in the sense of acquiring certain attitudes" ("Technologies" 16). As discuss later, especially in chapter 4, these "certain skills" and "certain attitudes" by which Ginsberg frames drug use—the desire for an altruistic expansion of consciousness through methodical practice of drugs and meditation on the body—become the same skills and attitudes he acquires as a student within the systematic Tantric structures of Tibetan Buddhism.

21. Buddhist hell-realm cosmology is beyond the scope of this book. However, it is important to note here that, according to these teachings, Devadatta was headed for a rebirth—whether physical, psychological, or both—where the agonies that awaited him resembled what Western Judeo-Christian culture terms "hell." Thus, *hell* is the common translation for such teachings on Buddhist rebirth. Buddhism posits the existence of innumerable hell spaces, whether

physical or psychological, hence the term "hell realm" is preferred to "hell." The Buddha could not save even his cousin Devadatta because in the conceptual framework of Buddhism, each person is responsible for his/her own salvation through compassionate karmic actions and the purification of past karma extended back through multiple lifetimes. Devadatta's salvation does occur in the Lotus Sutra but only as the Buddha's foretelling of the fruits of Devadatta's good karma in a previous life—an earlier rebirth when he was Shakyamuni Buddha's teacher himself.

22. *Mudras* are sacramental gestures in Tantric Buddhism. They are specific hand gestures within what is for Buddhism a semiotics of the body in which each gesture proceeds from a complex body-speech-mind signification system.

3. The Two Truths of "The Change"

1. Subsequent references are to the 2001 HarperCollins edition of the interview.

2. Portugés's efforts to frame the poem in terms of the sutra are important, and I wish to build my discussions upon them. Our approaches to the poem differ, however, on the metaphysical issue of exorcism. At the same time that Portugés emphasizes issues of metaphysicality, he also asserts in contrast that the influence of the Satipatthana Sutra suggests that the poem, like the sutra that influences it, encourages the Buddhist practitioner "to stop desiring transcendence, to stop conjuring up ideas of a blissful other world, to accept the human form and its natural process of decay" (96).

3. As I discuss in chapters 4 and 5, the performative is a preferred speech act in Ginsberg's Buddhist poetics. The performative is useful in finding a vocabulary to explain in materialist terms the magical connotations of the mantra. Also, performative speech collapses the distinction between subject and object in language; in turn, it distorts tense by erasing time distinctions between utterance and action. Thus, the performative can function as the materialist staging of mystical incantation. For Ginsberg, performative language asserts a religiosity that, as he describes in an 18 May 1956 letter to Richard Eberhart, frames his desire to represent "mystical mysteries in the forms in which they actually occur here in the U.S. in our environment" (*Howl* 152).

4. Charles D. Orzech explores the conflict between Buddhist prohibitions against murder and suicide and the numerous instances of self-sacrifice in Buddhist Jataka tales, apocryphal stories that narrate Siddhartha Gautama's multiple lives before he was born as the historical Buddha. Orzech concludes that "in the case of self-sacrifice the Buddhist seeks to imitate the Buddha but is paradoxically forbidden to do so" (146). As to the figural dimensions of these monks' suicides, Liz Wilson describes self-immolation as an "offering of oneself" whose political spectacle also is meant to teach the shunyata experience of selfhood. She

writes that "this dramatic form of self-destruction may be understood as both a sacrificial act in which one willingly offers oneself to the flames and as a form of teaching in which one proclaims one's lack of essential nature in a wordless display of evanescence" (30). In chapter 6, I discuss further the Jataka and their teachings on self-sacrificial offerings as they come to bear on Ginsberg's poem "Mugging."

5. This representation of the father as paternal not patriarchal mirrors Ginsberg's construction of familial poetic influence, discussed in chapter 1 as a relational rather than competitive paradigm.

6. This focus on rebirth and the instability of consciousness—often described as Buddhism's idea of an illusory self—could lead just as easily to self-negation without the guiding conceptual framework of the Two Truths. Such an approach risks more than just privatizing self-abnegation: for an avowedly politicized poet such as Ginsberg, the negation of selfhood would suggest political silence. The ego exists in Buddhism, and Ginsberg understood this. Ego is part of the individual practitioner's exploration of mind. If, as the Four Noble Truths teach, a path indeed exists out of suffering, such a path cannot be traversed without a subject—however provisional, contingent, and perhaps illusory—who can launch him/herself on such a path, and without objects that themselves are indeterminate and vulnerable to transformation. Indeed, without the Two Truths, some of the most important teachings in the Tibetan Buddhism that Ginsberg practiced, such as the teaching on Perfect Human Rebirth, would not be part of the Tibetan canon. According to Perfect Human Rebirth teachings, no living creatures are better suited to receive and practice dharma than human beings. Such an approach to human possibility would be debilitated from the start if both guru and student could not at the least agree that a human being *existed*, albeit indeterminately, within the admittedly groundless, for Buddhism, environment in which the teaching itself takes place. See also the work of Buddhist scholars such as David Loy, Roger R. Jackson, and Jay L. Garfield, who argue for the compatibility of contemporary postmodern notions of subjectivity with the necessary, for Buddhism, collision of absolutism and relativism in the theory of the subject that undergirds the Two Truths.

7. The speaker's movement in "The Change" recapitulates a similar movement from isolation to community during Ginsberg's 1948 Blake vision. He initially experienced the vision masturbating alone in his room. Then he rushed out the fire escape and knocked on the window of the women who lived next door, but he only managed to frighten them. Still experiencing the vision in solitude, Ginsberg eventually went to the Columbia University bookstore, where he found himself in the midst of what seemed to be an ecstatic community, a visionary company of fellow ordinary consumers. His sense of separate, solitary self-identity collapsed as he blurred the conceptual distinctions between himself

and others. As he described to Clark in the *Paris Review* interview, the bookstore clerk, the customers, and Ginsberg himself "all had the consciousness, it was like a great unconscious that was running between [*sic*] all of us that everybody *was* completely conscious" ("Art" 42). In my reading of "Iron Horse" in chapter 5, I discuss further the significance of masturbation and the Blake vision in Ginsberg's effort to craft a relational rather than singularist poetics.

8. The antagonist is not always Yahweh, of course, though metaphysics often is a major element of the conflict. Ginsberg famously tropes absolutist governmental authority by literally demonizing it as a mode of metaphysical wickedness, as in "Pentagon Exorcism." This trope is discussed in greater detail in chapter 4, in my reading of "Wichita Vortex Sutra."

9. As Gehlek Rinpoche, Ginsberg's final teacher, describes it, hungry ghosts "are normally said to have eighteen knots in the throat, that's why they can't eat. It's not that they're poor, many of them are extremely wealthy, much richer than Rockefellers. [. . .] But they can't use their wealth, it is useless for them" (177). A secular analogue for this myth can be found in the vocabulary of Gilles Deleuze and Félix Guattari. In books such as *Anti-Oedipus*, especially, Deleuze and Guattari discuss how capitalist culture transforms humans and their desires into "desiring machines," perpetually desirous but insatiable creatures "territorialized" by the very insatiability that drives them.

10. As Woods asserts, reiterations of the phrase "Please master" dramatize the difficulty of ascribing fixed names such as "dominant" or "submissive" to the sexual partners in the poem. The phrase, instead, allows sexual power to circulate between both partners. When the phrase is spoken by the slave as a means of asserting power, it highlights, too, the oscillation of subject positions between the two parties. Used as an "imperative" by the slave, the phrase "Please master" creates an occasion in which "[t]he slave-as-master orders the master-as-slave to carry out the actions which will supplement the multiplicity of their roles" (Woods 208–9).

11. Ginsberg's possible use of *black* as a signifier for *debased* is an extension of Beat exoticizing of the African experience in America. Ginsberg's "negro streets at dawn" in "Howl" appropriate Beatness as a colonizing sobriquet for the African American experience in the same way that Norman Mailer later appropriates blackness as a signifier for "hip" in his essay "The White Negro." Such ahistorical use of color representations that in U.S. culture evoke racially racial power inequities are later, for Ginsberg, part of the Tibetan Tonglen practice, a meditation in which the practitioner imagines absorbing the evils of the world, signified by black tar, and bestowing on the world a healing nectar that is colored white.

12. Portugés argues that these words reference "the worm of death in Blake's 'The Sick Rose'" (*Visionary Poetics* 97). Yet, the worm in "The Sick Rose" is

primarily a devouring presence, whereas the speaker in "The Change" likens himself with a worm because he himself is stalked and eventually devoured by the relentless metamorphotic impulse of the poem. David Erdman's textual notes for Blake's poem "The Fly" suggest that Blake, too, had in mind something altruistic rather than devouring for the worm image that eventually makes it into "The Marriage of Heaven and Hell." Erdman notes that Blake deleted the following stanza from "The Fly":

> The cut worm
> Forgives the plow
> And dies in peace
> And so do thou
>
> (Blake 794)

The worm, then, is not a symbol only of death in this instance. The death of the worm actually is an ancillary component of something more important for Blake—its Messianic capabilities for forgiveness. This gesture of forgiveness influences "The Change," especially as it is made physical in the text's culminating Abhaya Mudra.

13. These moments of self-abnegation also forecast Ginsberg's insistence on the scatological in so many poems from his final volume, *Death and Fame: Last Poems, 1993–1997.* In such work, Ginsberg acknowledges that his reputation as a contemporary Whitman-inspired poet of the body is, like any other aspect of the politics of literary reputation, a construction. These poems demonstrate through the body's wasting away that he always has celebrated a historicized body rather than one propped by fantasies of the irreducibility. Thus, Ginsberg's scatological work represents a larger gesture that celebrates the full *and* fulsome body, its impermanent passing, in language of abjection. See especially poems from *Death and Fame* such as "Here We Go 'Round the Mulberry Bush," "Excrement," "Bowel Song," "Hepatitis, Body Itch . . . ," "Scatological Observations," "I have a nosebleed . . . ," and "This kind of hepatitis can cause ya."

14. See also Ginsberg's notes in *Collected Poems* on his 1973 poem "Mind Breaths" and my commentary on the poem in chapter 5.

15. See also Ben Lee, who describes Ginsberg's incorporation of mass travel as a form of leftist populism. Lee argues that the "lost past" of Ginsberg's Old Left childhood is recuperated in his poetry "through images of automobiles and trains, connecting industrial production and working-class employment with Beat romanticizations of American machinery in endless motion along the roads and tracks of town and country" (375). Lee's remarks can forecast my arguments in the following two chapters about Ginsberg's struggles to convey a coherent politicized Buddhist speech in his road poems "Wichita Vortex Sutra" and "Iron Horse."

4. Language and the Limits of Romanticism

1. In a journal entry dated 7 June 1980, Ginsberg transcribes a dream that demonstrates the extent to which he, too, questioned his understanding of the mantra in the 1960s. Lineated in his journal as a poem draft, the dream transcription begins as Ginsberg finds himself in a cafeteria on the Naropa campus interviewed by television reporters:

> [. . .] talking with C.B.S. reporters from the
> Investigation Committee of Dharma and
> they did want to know once & for all
> of my proclivity for Mantra chanting in the Sixties.
>
> (Notebooks and journals)

Ginsberg confesses, "I felt shabby about my position & / was being accused of abusing OM mantra & / others for politics & vanity." The CBS reporters are a screen for Ed Sanders's Investigative Poetry Group, which had recently published its research on the Snowmass incident at Chögyam Trungpa's 1976 Vajrayana retreat (discussed in chapter 6). More important, this dream suggests that Ginsberg was haunted later in his career by regrets over the eccentricities of his early dharma practice, even as the dream simultaneously confirms the importance of such practice to his construction of a poetics of prophecy:

> The question was, did I not degrade and
> vulgarize the Goteric & use of mantra
> yoga by my loose & ignorant handling of
> the sounds & tradition? & wasn't this a
> False Prophet attitude, and shouldn't that
> be shown up to the general public, and wouldn't
> I please go burn in some hot or freeze in
> some cold hell? Wasn't that the least justice?
>
> (Notebooks and journals)

He responds to his own question with a new stanza that indicates the inadequacy of historical reflection to represent the particularities of an individual's suffering: "Vanzetti went to the electric chair bravely, / according to the snide book I looked / at before sleeping last night." Ginsberg, of course, would be mindful of the critical charge, discussed in chapters 1 and 2, that his Buddhist practice is inauthentic. Framed by his admission of a possibly "loose & ignorant" fusion of East and West, Ginsberg's dream dramatizes his fear that his Buddhist poetics might amount to nothing but a "False Prophet attitude" (Notebooks and journals).

2. See also the poem "Kral Majales" (1965), where Ginsberg refers to himself as a "Buddhist Jew," a statement that could be seen as self-evasive, a hesitation to commit fully to either Hebraic or Buddhist tradition, precisely the sort of

dabbling that might impel audiences to ask, "Will you please stop playing with the mantra?" "Kral Majales" instead is one of the few poems after "Kaddish" that maneuvers between both traditions. The poem dramatizes Ginsberg's search for a middle-way, a "mid Heaven," as he describes it, of poetic speech and cultural practice that would combine seemingly dichotomous religious and political traditions rather than choose only one or disengage from both. "Kral Majales" was written after Ginsberg had visited Cuba and the Eastern bloc in search of an alternative to Western capitalism. During this trip, he was expelled from Cuba and then from Czechoslovakia by each country's secret police. Composed on his return flight to England, the poem takes shape in a middle ground, in airspace between East and West, "on a jet seat in mid Heaven," as the poet searches in poetic language for a third term between the poles of capitalism and communism.

3. Schumacher argues that "Kaddish" emerged from Ginsberg's experiences with colonialism in Tangiers in 1957 and was possibly the poet's response to his own admission to Kerouac that "Howl" "seemed to be an inadequate statement in comparison to the worldwide plight of the masses" (253). As such, "Kaddish" inaugurates Ginsberg's earliest conscious efforts toward crafting a public voice sufficient to represent emergent post–World War II counterdiscourses to a prevailing Cold-War culture of consensus. Yet, the poem is spoken with what later readers might call the confessional voice, something Ginsberg himself admits in his essay, "How *Kaddish* Happened": "I realized ["Kaddish"] would seem odd to others, but *family* odd, that is to say, familiar—everybody has crazy cousins and aunts and brothers" (345). Still, "Kaddish" is not marked by the tension between public and private language that dominates "Howl," and as such, "Kaddish" inaugurates a particularly public phase of Ginsberg's poetics, a phase that continues from "Angkor Wat" and "The Change" through his Senate testimony.

4. As I discuss in chapter 2, Ginsberg's simultaneous embrace of and withdrawal from Whitman are not isolated to "Wichita," despite the central place of Whitman in Ginsberg's career. Of course, Whitman's abiding faith in U.S. industry is nowhere more empty than in Ginsberg's Moloch. Yet, Whitman's influence on Ginsberg is overstated if examined only in terms of the ecstatic political potential, for Ginsberg, of adhesive and amative desire, described in *The Fall of America* epigraph and reinscribed in "Wichita" as a poetics of holding one's lover "breast to breast on a mattress." As much as Ginsberg and Whitman share a desire to heal a platonic split between body and soul, Whitman's transcendentalist impulse is continually revised in Ginsberg's work, from the materialist language for prophecy of "Kaddish" and the contestatory reenvisioning of "Love Poem on Theme by Whitman," through Ginsberg's increased incorporation of the antimetaphysical conceptual framework of Buddhism throughout his career.

5. See also Ginsberg's letter to Richard Eberhart, 18 May 1956, in which he describes "Howl" as an attempt to reenvision mystical experience as common,

concrete experience: "I am paying homage to mystical mysteries in the forms in which they actually occur here in the U.S. in our environment" (*Howl* 152).

6. This visionary voice inscribed within a materialist environment echoes the Blakean vortex in "Wichita." Blake's vision of a world where conversations with God take place in a person's own house is materialist in its own right, insofar as houses signify states of consciousness in Blake's work, and "All deities," for Blake, "reside in the human breast" (38).

7. See also Ginsberg's interview by Alison Colbert for the *Partisan Review*, in which he states that the cosmologies of India and the West "converge in their origin. They come from the same Garden of Eden, or the same Middle Eastern source" (265). In this interview, Ginsberg constructs a common originary lineage for Eastern and Western conceptual frameworks through a syncretic fusion of Gnostic Christianity, pre-Socratic philosophy, Blakean poetics, and Hindu and Buddhist phenomenology. As I argue in chapter 5, Ginsberg's references to such a lineage throughout his career enable him to craft a Buddhist poetics that is mindful, paradoxically, of both Western ontology and, as he describes it to Colbert, "Buddhist maya," the illusory, imputed nature of the presumably stable self of ontology.

8. Indeed, such a relationship between confession and self-knowledge exists for Foucault even at the level of etymology: "The evolution of the word *avowal* and the legal function it designated is itself emblematic of this development: from being a guarantee of the status, identity, and value granted to one person by another, it came to signify someone's acknowledgment of his own actions and thoughts" (58).

9. Ginsberg's rhetorical strategy, asserting the LSD experience to be a sacramental one, reflects a Western discursive history in which hallucinogenic drugs are described by users in the vocabularies of religious experience. David Lenson's skepticism toward such discourses usefully counters their emancipatory optimism. Still, Lenson seems more focused on exposing Ginsberg's religiosity as an "acid Orientalism" rather than on actually studying the texts and contexts that produce Ginsberg's religious sensibility (146). Of Ginsberg's efforts to transform U.S. culture through controlled LSD use, Lenson writes that Ginsberg's "persona is grounded in Whitman's individualism but attenuated by the peppering of Oriental lingo that dislodges it from the America it is always driving across" (154). Ginsberg's effort in "Wichita" to invoke and revise Whitman while reconceiving the mantra suggests that, at the very least, the "Oriental lingo" with which Ginsberg frames his political advocacy might be the result of a carefully conceived—though at times eccentric, as a result of its autodidactic roots—effort to forge a Buddhist poetics capable of intervening in U.S. culture, rather than a mere "peppering" of language that "dislodges" itself from its culture.

10. See, for instance, Schumacher's description of Ginsberg's testimony as a heroic "work of art," in contrast to Schumacher's representation of a Senatorial establishment predisposed to ignore the poet's "tightly constructed summary of his personal history of drug use, his own scholarship on LSD, and his recommendations for its future in the country" (471).

11. For more on Whitman's political crises in the Civil War and postbellum United States, see Timothy Sweet, *Traces of War: Poetry, Photography, and the Crisis of the Union* and Betsy Erkkila, *Whitman the Political Poet*.

12. Ginsberg's recreation of Kali in the *Indian Journals* (1962), later revised as "Stotras to Kali Destroyer of Illusions" for the collection, *Planet News* (1963), represents Kali, who perpetually dances on the skulls of newborns in Hindu iconography, as a cosmic figure whose dance is both ecstatic revelry and an anxious, threatening shake. In "Stotras to Kali Destroyer of Illusions," Kali is the annihilating mother of "Kaddish" (Naomi "of the hospitals" whose mental illness frightens the young Ginsberg) and a revivifying maternal source of prophetic consciousness in "Kaddish" (Naomi "from whose pained head" the young Ginsberg "first took vision").

13. The limitations of language are, of course, significant in the prophetic tradition in which Ginsberg places himself. Of his influences, perhaps Blake is the most self-reflexive in engaging this problem. In *Jerusalem*, Blake describes English as "the rough basement," where language is a "stubborn structure" of "dumb [speechless] despair" (38: 58–60). Rather than retreat into silence at the inability of material language to convey visionary experience, Blake confronts this conflict between immanence and vision with a preference for a language of contrariety in the prophetic books.

14. As Fields notes, part of the difficulty in identifying a Buddhist position on the intersection, if any, between the LSD experience and the meditation experience is the tendency in Buddhism to be skeptical of the human tendency to reify such experiences, a skepticism Ginsberg did not adopt until years after his Blake vision. Fields writes, "More than most spiritual paths, Buddhism tends not to be very impressed by 'experiences,' be they spiritual or psychedelic" ("High History" 54).

15. As I have discussed in *"Strange Prophecies Anew,"* these famous first lines also can be read in terms of Ginsberg's revisions of the poem. Ginsberg's important substitution of "hysterical" for "mystical" changes the entire tenor of the poem, suggesting that juridico-medico discourse cannot be extricated from mystical or transcendentalist discourse in Ginsberg's construction of a language for prophecy.

16. At the same time, the works of both Boon and Plant are valuable in their efforts to trace the cultural work of texts, such as "Howl," that represent the

drug experience, and also of texts that attribute drug use as a significant locus of inspiration. My remarks in this chapter, instead, emphasize what is lost when their discussion does not account for Ginsberg's drug use both as an artist and self-fashioned activist. Both writers are usefully skeptical of the dualistic separation, for instance, between materialism and transcendentalism in such works. Boon suggests that for all of the facile constructions of drug use as romantic efforts to transcend the self, literature of the drug experience at the same time articulates a skeptical counterdiscourse toward transcendentalism. For Boon, the "transcendentalist impulse" of "drug literature" is perhaps most visible "in its negation or absence," an approach that reenvisions transcendentalism in ways that resemble the fused immanent-transcendent mode of representation that marks Ginsberg's language for prophecy in poems such as "Howl," "Kaddish," and "The Change"—an approach that, for Boon, "integrate[s] transcendental experience within the realm of the possible" (11–12). Plant eschews a close reading of "Howl" in favor of a discussion of the way the drug discourse of the poem is appropriated in the culture at large. Plant's commentary usefully examines how literature of the drug experience intervenes in Western constructions of subjectivity—and how such literature contributes to the history of ideas at the same time that it is often submerged, nearly made invisible, within this same history. Taken together, Boon and Plant offer a valuable context for how Ginsberg's drug experimentation and his testimony as such before Congress can be seen as decisive breaks with conventional notions of the drug experience as a transcendentalist one.

17. Ginsberg's suggestion of a religious history in which LSD opens the mind to a transcendentalist consciousness is worthy of debate, of course. Yet, it seems more productive to study how Ginsberg's belief in religious and at times transcendentalist representation during a period of increased government surveillance of drug users reveals the juridico-medico boundaries of his work and in so doing complexifies the religious and political boundaries of subjectivity in his spiritual poetics. Lenson's discussion of LSD, in contrast, conflates the metaphysical and the religious. Moreover, Lenson's resistance to the religiosity of the 1960s is striking precisely because his work seems so interested in denigrating the postwar turn to the East without a sense of philosophical or historical context. Dismissing Eastern religiosity in the 1960s as "pseudo-Oriental cant," Lenson argues that a "rhetoric of Easternization" prevents an understanding of the psychedelic experience that can extend beyond the 1960s. Lenson is correct to resist the "romantic ideology," as Jerome McGann might describe it, that would take the drug experience of the 1960s as a heuristic for that same experience in the following decades. Still, like the very "easy Easternness" he seeks to refute, Lenson speaks of Eastern philosophy and religiosity as a monolith—one in which any interest by Westerners smacks of orientalism. Such an approach, of course, forecloses

the possibilities of cultural change within religious communities and suggests that the religious community into which one is born brands the self with such religion essentially. Lenson writes that the continued use of Eastern terminology to describe the LSD experience is "remarkable considering the diminution of Western interest in Buddhism since the 1960s and 1970s, and that LSD use, despite mythology to the contrary, seems not diminished significantly since that supposed heyday" (143). Lenson fails to account for the historically documented growth of Buddhism in the U.S., which, as I have discussed earlier in this book, has been part of the framework of American religiosity since the early twentieth century and which has grown dramatically since the 1960s.

18. In his interview with Allen Young of *Gay Sunshine*, Ginsberg portrays this particular experience with LSD in terms of queer identity rather than asserting, as Timothy Leary did, that Ginsberg's experience was a heterosexualizing one. In remarks that echo queer denaturalization of heterosexuality in "Love Poem on Theme by Whitman," Ginsberg explains, "When Leary was looking around for information and rationalization on LSD, I told him that it would probably loosen up some of the blocks in homosexuality. The reverse is true, too: it would probably loosen up some of the blocks in heterosexuality, which it's notorious for doing" (Ginsberg, interview with Allen Young 36). In *Guys like Us*, Davidson emphasizes these sexual fissures in the postwar avant-garde as forces that both enable and constrain the production of politically active art: "What remains constant within the largely male forums within which the avant-garde was debated was that the structure of homosocial relations, genitalized or not, often undergirds the production of new art forms and practices, even though that structure is often at odds with the liberatory sexual ethos that articulates those practices" (29). Jeffrey B. Falla explores this conflict as a consequence of Beat disruptions of heteronormativity that "threatened to expose the nonmateriality regarding categories of sexual identity, that, in effect, the construction of sexual identity as categorical standards inevitably consists of no one" (54).

19. See also his journal note from late November 1961, written while influenced by opium, in which desire and drugs produce self-knowledge in a space private and, because of its singularity, necessarily nonconfessional. In this entry, he reflects on how his relationship with his mother affected his relationship with other women in his life: "And Elise [Cowen] said, '[Y]ou haven't done with her, yet?' after typing the mss. of *Kaddish*. I'm attracted to intellectual madwomen" (*Journals: Early Fifties, Early Sixties* 269).

20. As Schumacher notes, the poet's self-proclaimed "paranoia" was well grounded. Returning to New York in June 1965, a month after his Czech expulsion, Ginsberg was strip-searched at the airport for drugs: "While he waited, [Ginsberg] stole a peek at some documents on a table, which noted that his 'files' had been reactivated and Peter Orlovsky's were still active. 'These persons are

reported to be engaged in smuggling narcotics,' one of the documents read" (449). Schumacher writes that as early as 1961, when the Drug Enforcement Agency began a file on Ginsberg, the poet had been under periodic surveillance. These files also contained information on the influence of Ginsberg in the shaping of desire and sexuality in the public imaginary: "[D]ifferent government agencies were also interested in [Ginsberg's] sexual behavior, which some officials believed to be threatening [. . .]" (Schumacher 624).

21. To borrow again from Rodden's work on Orwell and literary reputation, the subcommittee's nurturing of Ginsberg's ambivalence is an effort to shift what Rodden terms the "reception scene" from the literary institutional space to the locale of governmentality.

5. Strategies of Retreat

1. See also Moon, *Disseminating Whitman: Revision and Corporeality in "Leaves of Grass."*

2. Helen Vendler has argued that *The Fall of America* poems (into which "Iron Horse" was later added by Ginsberg when he complied his *Collected Poems*) are characterized by "the disappearance or exhaustion of long-term human relations" (Review 206). Vendler asserts that these poems attempt to evade rationality and are predicated upon improvisation and simultaneity; she argues that these early efforts to swerve from the limitations of representation by Ginsberg do not sustain their multivocal intentions. Both "Wichita" and "Iron Horse" were not part of the original volume of *The Fall of America*. But in *Collected Poems 1947–1980*, they are added to *The Fall of America* sequence to fill conceptual "gaps," as Ginsberg describes it, in the original publication history of his work (xix). Given the primary roles of Buddhism and pacifism in these two poems, their addition to *The Fall of America* sequence circumscribes his socially engaged Buddhist poetry of the mid-1960s with the epic authority of the long poem form.

3. I return to Whitman's concept of democratic adhesion to emphasize the masculine-coded frame that underwrites political triumph and failure in Ginsberg's work. See also Davidson's *Guys Like Us*, which discusses how homosocial bonding in the Cold War era and especially among writers of the San Francisco Renaissance allowed for the expression of queer identity at the same time that it reinforced its continued submergence. For more on the gendered political limitations of Beat bohemia, see Nancy M. Grace and Ronna C. Johnson's *Girls Who Wore Black: Women Writing the Beat Generation.*

4. My reading of the end of "Iron Horse" differs from that of Terence Diggory in his important essay "Allen Ginsberg's Urban Pastoral." The differences in our readings seem matters of emphasis rather than questions of accuracy. Diggory reads the poem in the context of the urban pastoral as it is framed by Vendler and James L. Machor, and in doing so, he argues that the ending is a hopeful return

for the poet to "his ordinary self" (114). I would argue that the poem indeed presages such a return but one that does not occur until the later poems of the *Mind Breaths* volume. If "Iron Horse" is read in the linguistic and Buddhist context of its companion road pilgrimage, "Wichita Vortex Sutra," the poem seems to continue rather than revise the industrial urbanscape metonymized elsewhere as Moloch—as seen in the failure of language, especially of mantra speech, to redeem this landscape and the fragmented wartime language that represents it.

5. These "six sense fields" in Buddhism consist of the five senses and what is for the West the addition of the activities of the mind as the sixth sense, as in Ginsberg's addition of the line, "Think what you think" (*Collected* 641).

6. True to such an extent that just three years later, in an interview with Peter Barry Chowka, Ginsberg explains that he was beginning to move in a "direction" that would communicate Buddhism through poetry, extending his prophetic voice more conspicuously into a language that would even eschew West for East (Allen Ginsberg, interview with Peter Barry Chowka 379–80).

7. As further evidence of the poem's heteroglossia, Ginsberg's translation of the mantra is only one of many possible forms of expressing it. His Sanskrit version also is translated as "Om Mani Padme Hung." Ginsberg's translation of the mantra itself adds another dimension to the poem's dialogic impulse to welcome counterstatements within its own discursive field. His decision to break the final three syllables as "PA"/"DMI"/"HŪṂ" instead of the traditional "PAD"/"MI"/"HŪṂ" (or "PAD"/"ME"/"HUNG") suggests, too, that in the absence of many Tibetan teachers in the early 1970s, questions of authoritative spelling and translation in American Buddhism were as unsystematized as in the early stages of any language or cultural tradition.

8. The exact quotation from Blake should be "minute particulars," not "concrete particulars."

9. Portugés asked Ginsberg if he had "given up [his] 'prophetic, messianic identity.'" Ginsberg replies, "Yeah, that's lost, and I could give up my harmonium. I mean, it would be bad if the harmonium was just another prop, a crutch." Portugés aptly describes this process of loss as one of surrender, as in "letting go of ego completely." Although Ginsberg expresses discomfort at the use of the word *surrender*, he nevertheless admits, "Yeah, that's the word. I haven't thought of it much in those terms" (*Visionary Poetics* 153).

10. "Dragon-tooth" and "Fuel-Air Bomb" are the names of weapons used by the United States to destroy above-ground tracts of land and underground Viet Cong hideouts. "Igloo White" was itself a weapons program, one that, as Ginsberg explains in his notes to the poem, was designed "to destroy supply trucks and people moving down Laotian Ho-Chi-Minh jungle train" (*Collected* 789). As Paul N. Edwards explains of Igloo White, which ran from 1967 to 1972, the success of this weapons program was exaggerated by the U.S. government. According to

Edwards, the claims for Igloo White's success depended on compliant reporters "dazzled" by the technologized machinations of war (3). He argues that in its reliance on expensive warfare technology and its deceptive self-assessments of success, "Operation Igloo White's centralized, computerized, automated method of 'interdiction' resembled a microcosmic version of the whole United States approach to the Vietnam war" (4).

11. See also Weinstone's discussion of Tantra and poststructuralism, where, building on Loy's work with Buddhism and poststructuralism, the body is a potentiality that engages the world textually and physically. For her, Tantra is a form of "postdeconstruction" that entails "learning to recognize the body's incorporations, including those occasioned by trauma and pleasure, as *participatory capacities*" (128; original emphasis).

12. Ginsberg appropriated this line as the title of the first poem he composed after the 1948 Blake vision. Ginsberg referred to this idea from Blake frequently in interviews, and the line itself also is reproduced as the title of Louis Simpson's chapter on Ginsberg in his *A Revolution in Taste: Studies of Dylan Thomas, Allen Ginsberg, Sylvia Plath, and Robert Lowell.*

13. "Om Ah Hūṃ" also serves as the opening to the Padmasambhava mantra, which would have been one of the most important mantras in Ginsberg's dharma practice when he was a student of Trungpa. The mantra, "Om Ah Hūṃ Vajra Guru Padma Siddhi Hūṃ," translates in English as: "I invoke you, Vajra Guru, Padmasambhava, by your blessing may you grant us ordinary and supreme realization."

14. See also Rafe Martin's *Hungry Tigress: Buddhist Myths, Legends, and Jataka Tales.* In his commentary on the "extremity" of the myth of the hungry tigress, Martin points up the formalized narrative patterns of this tale as characteristic of a "classic" Jataka that attempts to represent the idealized, therefore unrepresentable, "pure compassion" of the mind of a bodhisattva. As such, the traditional reception of the hungry tigress myth is, as I mention above, "*not* to recommend that we should literally offer our bodies to tigers." Instead, Martin argues, the narrative finds its place among all traditional Jataka, as tales that "dramatize Equality and give life to an awareness of the ultimate worth of each living thing—even of something which may directly threaten our own self-interest and safety" (224).

15. One additional source for the poem from Buddhist mythic literature might be the story of a famous crisis of faith experienced by Shariputra, one of the Buddha's legendary disciples. As explained in the Padmakara Translation Group (an organization started by Trungpa) edition of Shantideva's *Way of the Bodhisattva*, Shariputra is visited by a demon who sets out to test his commitment to the Buddha's teaching. The demon asks Shariputra to give him his right hand. Shariputra amputates his right hand and gives it to the demon with his left. The

demon refuses it, however, because it was offered to him with Shariputra's *left* hand, an impolite gesture in ancient India. The commentary to this edition of Shantideva's text notes, "At this point, it is said that Shariputra lost hope of ever being able to satisfy the desires of beings, and turned from the Mahayana to pursue the path of arhatship [enlightenment]" (198).

16. See also Robert E. Goss, who describes Trungpa's fused secular-Buddhist Shambhala training program as an effort "to bring 'art to everyday life'" (219).

17. The actual events that occasioned the poem also demonstrate that they threatened the poet at the same time that they enhanced his reputation. Miles reports that Ginsberg sold "Mugging" to the *New York Times* "for seven times the amount the kids had stolen from him" (457). In this discussion of the poet's Buddhism, it is significant that Ginsberg sold this poem that commingles victimization with mantric discourse to the largest-circulation newspaper in the United States, based in New York, which was experiencing such economic decline that it nearly declared bankruptcy in 1975. The poet, then, offers his ego as sacrifice at the same time that he seeks the ego's proliferation, in the form of survival and monetary gain.

18. I have discussed thus far the importance of vision to the poem—how the poem tests Blake's maxim "The eye altering alters all." Ginsberg's revisions to the poem suggest that in its original draft form, the poem emphasized instead the speaker's victimization and, simply, his need to see the muggers arrested. The original draft of the opening two lines of section 2 appears as follows, from the poet's 10 December 1974 journal entry: "Went out the door in shock, who can I talk to catch the mean thieves?—/ The whole street like a bombed out face, building eyes empty & rows' & with eyes teeth rows missing" (notebooks and journals). Of course, it should come as no surprise that signifiers of vision from the final draft are absent and that the original focus of this draft is on victimization and justice, on "catch[ing] the mean thieves." The speaker, after all, is Ginsberg himself, and he was victimized and did want to catch the muggers. The revision could seem insignificant solely for its irony: Ginsberg the poet who demonized state authorities now seeks the aid of these same authorities. I cite this revision, however, to demonstrate further that as he drafted and revised the poem, he shifted its emphasis from a story about a mugging to an allegory of failed vision.

19. As Ginsberg uses the word in this instance, "pride" is not inconsistent with humility. In Buddhist teachings on Perfect Human Rebirth, the practitioner is encouraged to recognize his/her "humanism" so that it might be deployed in the service of dharma. What distinguishes humans from animals in this teaching is the ability of the former to practice Buddhism, to seek the realization of shunyata, and to engage the Eightfold Noble Path for the sake of other sentient beings (human and animal).

20. The political implications of consequentalist teaching are staged further in "Who Runs America?" also from the *Mind Breaths* volume. Staging the interconnectedness of war and leisure economies in the United States, this poem suggests Ginsberg's emergence from the crisis of nostalgia that marks "Iron Horse." "Who Runs America?" is a companion poem to "Mind Breaths" in which oil sardonically replaces breath as a source of sacred gusting. Oil is the logos of American thought and action. Where Whitman once articulated a unifying "word over all" to mark the country's recovery from the Civil War and its eventual emergence as an industrial power, Ginsberg's contestatory version replaces the word with oil: "Oil brown smog over Denver / Oil red dung colored smoke / level to level across the horizon" (*Collected* 628). In a culture of scarcity—with gas lines forming across the United States—this dystopian reenvisioning of Whitman's optimism as *oil over all* is for Ginsberg a suggestion that one person's ego confession might be writ large into the same such confessions of an entire country. Eventually, as a counterdiscourse to the returning exhalation of "Mind Breaths," the oil that in this instance is emitted by the United States returns as a corrosive force that "spills onto Santa Barbara beaches from / Standard of California derricks offshore" (*Collected* 628).

6. Language, Dream, Self-(Dis)Closure

1. See Sanders, ed., *The Party: A Chronological Perspective on a Confrontation at a Buddhist Seminary*, and Clark, *The Great Naropa Poetry Wars*. Clark's book reproduces important primary sources from the local Boulder media, and Sanders's account is especially useful in its effort to maintain distanced reportage.

2. In his 20 July 1977 letter to Sanders's Investigative Poetry Group, students who had taken Sanders's Investigative Poetry seminar at Naropa, Merwin reminded the group that Trungpa was aware that Naone and he were not committed fully to the Tantric tradition. He wrote that they "were only in a limited sense students of Trungpa's" (qtd. in Sanders 82). Their concerns with the violent imagery in the chanting were not just the result of their pacifism but also were expressed in a wider context that, he writes, included their concerns about Trungpa's apparent lack of ecumenical religious spirit. He explained that "at our one private meeting with [Trungpa] before the party we had spoken of our objections to the blood-thirsty nature of some of the chants, and more particularly to his increasingly frequent and heavy sneers at other religious and contemplative traditions" (qtd. in Sanders 82).

3. In a 20 July 1977 letter to the Investigative Poetry Group, Merwin wrote that Naone and he "were members of no group in [Trungpa's] organizations, had taken no vows at all with him, [and] had made no promises to obey him." He added, "One of the assumptions of the seminary was a much older involvement

with Trungpa and his methods, and a far less questioning commitment to them than we, in fact, had" (qtd. in Sanders 82).

4. According to Merwin's 20 July 1977 letter, word was passed through the crowd "that Rinpoche had sent an order to bring us down 'at any cost'" (qtd. in Sanders 84). The account of Jack Niland, one of those in attendance at the seminary, confirms Merwin's narrative. Niland remembered Trungpa telling the students, "I want you to realize that I'm really going to insist that Merwin come down here no matter what, or what it takes" (qtd. in Sanders 41). Some of the students resisted, but, as Niland observed, Trungpa insisted that Merwin and Naone be brought to him: "They went down and told Rinpoche, Merwin's barricaded himself and there is no way to break down the door, can't we drop it? Rinpoche says, break through the plate glass window" (qtd. in Sanders 42).

5. As Naone explained in a 25 July 1977 letter to the Investigative Poetry Group, all but one of the Vajrayana students stood by passively as she and Merwin were stripped by Trungpa's Vajra Guard:

> Guards dragged me off and pinned me to the floor. I could see William [Merwin] struggling a few feet away from me. I fought, and called to friends, men and women, whose faces I saw in the crowd—to call the police. No one did. Only one man, Bill King, broke through to where I was lying at Trungpa's feet, shouting, 'Leave her alone' and 'Stop it.' Trungpa rose above me, from his chair, and knocked Bill King down with a punch, swearing at him, and ordering that no one interfere. (qtd in Sanders 91)

Another of Trungpa's students, Dennis White, tried to persuade Trungpa to stop the attack, Naone wrote "but Trungpa told him to shut up" and White's protestations ended there (qtd. in Sanders 91).

6. See also Louis Ginsberg's "Nightmare" in his *Collected Poems*: "Yet what could I do / When this coin clicked lost? No dial tone sang hope. / I saw that the phone was dead. And was I, too?" (295).

7. These remarks occur in the context of Varela's discussion of how neuroscientific and Buddhist theories of the mind and sleep "can modify each other" (43).

8. Schumacher states that even though the confessional aesthetic of "Kaddish" suggests that "Ginsberg might have exorcised the demons of his youth," it is "obvious from 'White Shroud' and a number of journal entries written throughout his life [that] Ginsberg had never fully come to terms with his relationship with his mother or with his feelings of culpability connected to the final years of her life" (*Dharma Lion* 673). This latter point, Ginsberg's authorization of Naomi's lobotomy, euphemistically phrased as the question of "culpability connected to the final years of [Naomi's] life," is engaged more substantively in my discussion, later in this chapter, of "Black Shroud."

9. Of course, while the confessional mode of "Kaddish" emphasizes private family drama, the poem also directly engages the Ginsberg family's immigrant background within early-twentieth-century, left-wing Jewish communities of the northeastern United States. Naomi's fears of Hitler, for instance, are represented more than just as the private terrors of her mental illness. As Scott Herring explains, "Naomi is not just a victim of mental disease but is a Cassandra figure, an unheeded prophet. By making her a seer ('from whose pained head I first took Vision'), the poem again participates in the evolving tradition of literature about the Holocaust, in which the unheeded warning has become a kind of topos" (548). Herring's reading of the poem leads him to conclude, correctly, that "Ginsberg too carefully fuses the family's disaster to a global one" for the poem to be considered only an elegizing chronicle of Naomi's illness (550). As Herring notes, Naomi came to the United States in 1905 from the western Russian town of Nevel—her family fleeing a pogrom. The town was occupied by the Nazis in 1941, and by the fall of that year, the German army destroyed the Jewish ghetto in Nevel as a response to arson attacks that it had attributed to forces within the ghetto itself (554–55).

10. The title of Louis's first book of poems, *The Attic of the Past* (1920), figures, too, in his dual presence-absence in this scene.

11. See also James Breslin, "On the Origins of 'Howl' and 'Kaddish.'"

12. Just as important, too, in this reenvisioning of Naomi is Ginsberg's title "White Shroud." In "Kaddish," Ginsberg rewrote the Hebrew Kaddish prayer that had been denied Naomi at her death, as is well known by critics. He could not be there for her funeral, so he contributed an English-language revisionary burial prayer after the fact. The title of "White Shroud" itself suggests Ginsberg's continued interest in revisiting the scene of Naomi's burial, this time to bury her in the white shroud that in Jewish tradition is worn by all the dead, rich or poor, to signify their equality in the eyes of God. Both efforts are important actions by Ginsberg to reenvision his "transgressive" mother—mentally ill and communist during the mid-century Red Scare, also unkempt and psychologically battered—as a redemptive religious figure. With Naomi's grave revisited twice, first for the revisionary Kaddish prayer and then for the burial in white shroud, Naomi's burial becomes both an elegiac ritual of mourning and of the recovery of artistic imagination. As Helen Vendler argues of Ginsberg's elegiac impulse in the poem, the "Muse, so helpless in 'Lycidas' [. . .] has moved into a position of power here, appearing as a 'Communist beauty, Russian-faced (in defiance of American fears in the fifties of both Russia and Communism)" (*Soul Says* 12). In this way, "Kaddish" functions, in Vendler's words, as a "reversed Pietà," one in which "we see not the mother holding the broken body of the son, but the son holding the broken body of the mother" (*Soul Says* 9).

13. As Deleuze and Guattari explain of the loss of reality suffered by the schizophrenic—their model of the transgressive subject territorialized in psychoanalysis and capitalism—this condition might not be "the effect of the schizophrenic process, but the effect of its forced oedipalization, that is to say, its interruption." Deleuze and Guattari's vocabulary can be useful in explaining Ginsberg's assertion and revision of the Oedipal model from "Kaddish" through "White Shroud" and "Black Shroud" and in his prose and correspondence. They write that the bounded, singularist standards of the Oedipal drama in psychoanalysis are "not an abstract operation"; instead, they are "imposed on the psychotic" in a circulation of power "for the sole purpose of assigning the *lack* of this organization in the psychotic, in his very body" (*Anti-Oedipus* 123).

14. Biography and textuality collide, messily, in the question of sexual identity and Ginsberg's relationship with Peter Orlovsky. As described in interviews, Peter's sexuality is less defined than Ginsberg's. Schumacher notes the "many times when Peter resented Allen's sexual demands, many times when Peter yearned for a conventional relationship with a woman." Schumacher concludes that "Peter was—and always would be—primarily heterosexual" (*Dharma Lion* 677).

Of course, Schumacher's focus on the sexual details of their relationship tells readers quite a bit about the nature of their commitment to each other. Still, such a focus on sexual practice as a constitutive component of subjectivity calls to mind the complaints Foucault raises in his work of how confession *produces* being, often at the subject's peril in cultures, such as ours, where the knowledge of one's sexual identity becomes reified as a normalizing cipher for one's subjectivity. The public persona constructed by Orlovsky and Ginsberg was that they lived as a gay couple; this persona, moreover, eventually was inextricable from Ginsberg's literary reputation as a gay American Buddhist poet. Schumacher writes that Ginsberg "was aware that, as public figures, he and Peter had become living symbols of homosexual marriage, and since living such a life in public was still a relatively new idea, [Ginsberg] felt a certain responsibility to those who might try to emulate him" (*Dharma Lion* 675–76). Thus, his relationship with Orlovsky proceeded from competing notions of subjectivity: the private one of a marriage half-fulfilled emotionally and sexually and the public one, suitable to Ginsberg's self-representation as a media figure and poet-prophet, in which the two were archetypes for gay marriage. A comprehensive account of Orlovsky and Ginsberg's life together is found in Bill Morgan's biography, *I Celebrate Myself: The Somewhat Private Life of Allen Ginsberg*.

15. Keeping in mind Ginsberg's remarks in *Gay Sunshine Interview*, much the same can be said about the poet's Queer Dharma in the poem "Dream," from his final volume, *Death and Fame: Last Poems, 1993–1997*. Composed eight days before his death, the poem dramatizes a dream of the poet's pregnancy and his

consequent worry—"half grateful, half appreciative"—that he would not be able to care for the child adequately while suffering from hepatitis C. His relationship with Peter, circumscribed as it is by marital vows and bodhisattva vows, creates the conditions by which the child can be raised. "A glow of happiness next morn," Ginsberg writes of the now absent "mystic baby," adding that the dream of the child and the sustenance of his vows with Peter together create "a warm glow of pleasure half the day" (97).

16. Schumacher describes Ginsberg's guilt over what he denied Naomi in terms of death and rebirth, issues that became central to Ginsberg's Buddhist practice. Recreating Ginsberg's interior monologues about the lobotomy over the years, Schumacher writes, "Carl Solomon had once suggested that lobotomy was a painless form of suicide. If that obliteration of consciousness was a form of death, what was [Ginsberg's] ordering the lobotomy of his mother? Was it murder? And what did it say about [Ginsberg], the obvious product of his mother's body and spirit? What did it suggest about his own mind?" (*Dharma Lion* 674).

17. See also Schumacher's discussion of the lobotomy authorization. He writes that Ginsberg "had signed the legal documents permitting [the lobotomy] only after a soul-searching period that found him considering his own feelings about the nature of insanity and unconventional behavior" (*Dharma Lion* 674). Schumacher only discusses briefly the question of guilt in the poem and dismisses "Freudians" who would "have a field day interpreting the significance of the mother-son relationship and speculating on the meaning of [Ginsberg's] violent termination of Naomi's life" (*Dharma Lion* 675). This dismissal might seem unusual, given that the poem is steeped in many of the same intimacies of familial desire that are crucial to psychoanalysis. As I have discussed earlier, in chapter 1, a neglect of the psychoanalytic frame of Ginsberg's familial relationships is also a neglect of Ginsberg's own documented interested in reenvisioning psychoanalysis as a spiritual pilgrimage. Still, despite Schumacher's hesitation, his remarks are useful in demonstrating the correspondence between Ginsberg's agony at making the lobotomy decision and the representation of this agony in dream-images in "Black Shroud."

18. Referring to his interview with William Matthews, then a member of the NEA literary board, Randy Blair writes: "Though Matthews does not clearly remember the application[,] he suggested that it may have simply been badly written and that at any rate it was unclear in reference to NEA funding categories" (qtd. in Sanders 63). However, Matthews also argued "that the board members 'are not stupid,' and are not deceived by a well-written proposal when a less polished one contains a better idea . . . the board members to a certain extent learn to discount and not be impressed by a simply well-written proposal" (qtd. in Sanders 63). In an interview for Sanders's study, Ginsberg asserted that the composition of the NEA application form "was all right"; but he added, "it wasn't

quite as pure as [the NEA] needed" (64). Leonard Randolph, then director of the NEA literary board, stated simply that the application was considered on its merits and that the application itself "was technically fine" (qtd in Sanders 64).

19. Randolph's questions for Merwin, as reported in the 20 July 1977 letter, suggest that the distinction between Naropa and the seminary indeed was not clear to the NEA literary board. Merwin writes that Randolph "asked whether there was a relation between the seminary and Naropa" and "whether the Kerouac School was independent of Naropa"(Sanders, *Dharma Lion* 81). Randolph's line of questioning suggests that the NEA was concerned with the possible connections between Trungpa's seminary, as the location where the Merwin incident occurred, and Naropa, the institutional body requesting grand funding. Still, as the matter is represented in Merwin's letter, this line of questioning does not necessary lead to the conclusion that the possible connection between the seminar and Naropa resulted in the rejection of the grant. Indeed, in Randy Blair's account of his interview with Matthews, he concludes that Matthews "does not think that the Merwin incident was a major deciding factor in the vote" (qtd. in Sanders 64). Instead, according to Matthews, what was more important was that Naropa's application did not distinguish itself as a request distinctly suited for the funding categories typical of successful NEA applications.

20. As Schumacher reports, and Ginsberg's correspondence confirms, Ginsberg regretted these remarks and planned to excise them before the interview was published. Ginsberg said they had agreed that he would see the interview draft before it was published and that he would have the right to make corrections. According to Clark, no such agreement had been made. Whether or not such an agreement existed, the account of their interview by Sam Kashner suggests that Ginsberg considered his initial remarks to Clark carefully: "Peter [Orlovsky] sang to himself, but in a very loud voice, while Allen spoke softly into Tom's tape recorder in the living room, driving Tom crazy by making him turn it off and on every few minutes, while Allen considered what he wanted to say, 'for posterity'" (287).

21. Randy Blair writes, from his Investigative Poetry Group notes, "According to an interview with William Matthews, Merwin and Naone went directly to Matthew's [sic] house in Boulder after the seminary. Merwin was angry, considering the incident a form of psychic rape, a total invasion of personal privacy, which Merwin has a strong desire to protect" (Sanders 56–57).

22. Of Merwin's "delicacy to leave the situation ripen on its own without aggression," see his 20 July 1977 letter to the Investigative Poetry Group, in which he states: "We'd come to study the whole course; we'd taken it (as [Trungpa] knew) seriously; we wanted to finish what we'd begun, and not be scared off. The last lap, about to begin, was the famous Tantric teachings." Speaking also about the subject of obedience within Trungpa's Buddhist hierarchy as it affected

his and Naone's decision, Merwin explains, "We said that if we stayed, it would be with no guarantees of obedience, trust, or personal devotion to [Trungpa]. He said alright; so did we, and we shook hands. No apology on either side" (Sanders 56).

23. See also Vendler's 1995 discussion (also quoted earlier in note 12) of "Kaddish" as a "reversal of the cultural icon we call the pietà" (*Soul Says* 9). This cultural "reversal" extends, too, into her discussion of Ginsberg's Buddhist reenvisioning of elegiac form in the poem: "A traditional Western elegy would end the double apotheosis [of Naomi, spiritually and physically]. But Ginsberg [...] gives his elegy a less transcendent Buddhist end, in which human experience, however full, is finally both spiritually and physically obliterated" (*Soul Says* 14).

24. The significant role of the Vajra guard in subduing and stripping Merwin and Naone at Snowmass understandably produced significant criticism of the Trungpa's bodyguards. Schumacher writes, "The Vajra guard, [Trungpa's] group of private bodyguards, had a paramilitary look to them that made some people uncomfortable"; and as a result, by 1978, at the time of the People's Temple suicides in Guyana, "Rightfully or otherwise, the word *cult* slipped into conversations about Trungpa's Buddhist group" (*Dharma Lion* 633).

25. See Ron Silliman, "Ginsberg@Center?".

7. On the Devotional

1. Evidence of growing interest in Beat Studies as a field can be found in the increase in individually published books, articles, and symposiums and in the recent formation of the Beat Studies Association, an international affiliation of Beat scholars. As a study specifically focused on Ginsberg's particular Buddhist poetics, this book also is indebted to the work of previous scholars of the Beat Generation's arguably most well-known Buddhist practitioners, Jack Kerouac and Gary Snyder. Kerouac and Snyder are mentioned briefly in this work, where their eccentric (Kerouac) and sustained (Snyder) Buddhism might bring into relief the movement of Ginsberg's own Buddhist practice.

2. See Jeremy Safran, *Psychoanalysis and Buddhism: An Unfolding Dialogue* and Mark Epstein, *Thoughts Without a Thinker: Psychotherapy from a Buddhist Perspective*.

3. I do not mean postmodernism in its diachronic sense, as simply poetry after high modernism. Instead, I mean postmodernism as an aesthetic strategy that emphasizes the constructedness of phenomena and the eschewal of organizing master narratives; and a strategy that, moreover, in its synchronic framework can be traced in the West as far back as the pre-Socratic philosophers and in the East to the ancient Buddhist master Nagarjuna, a forefather of Buddhist philosophy in India and Tibet. Much, of course, has been written on the synchronic possibilities of postmodernism, but for more on the synchronic, East-West cross-cultural

resonance of postmodern thought, see David Loy, "The Clôture of Deconstruction: A Mahāyāna Critique of Derrida," and Roger R. Jackson, "In Search of a Postmodern Middle."

4. Even Walzer's book, which aims to elevate the aesthetic currency of Expansive forms, concedes that the standard by which one measures such currency often is the dominance of the postmodern aesthetic.

Works Cited

Allen Ginsberg. Dir. Lewis MacAdams and John Dorr. Lannan Literary Videos, 1989.
"Allen Ginsberg with R. D. Laing." *Writers in Conversation*. London: ICA Video, 1984. Anthony Roland Collection of Films on Art, 1989.
Andrews, Bruce. "Poetry as Explanation, Poetry as Praxis." *Politics of Poetic Form: Poetry and Public Policy*. Ed. Charles Bernstein. New York: Roof, 1990. 23–43.
Austin, J. L. *Philosophical Papers*. Oxford: Oxford UP, 1979.
Bakhtin, Mikhail. *The Dialogic Imagination*. Austin: U of Texas P, 1981.
Ball, Gordon, ed. Introduction (reader's guide). *Journals: Early Fifties, Early Sixties*. By Allen Ginsberg. New York: Grove, 1977. xiii–xxx.
Batchelor, Stephen. *Buddhism without Beliefs: A Contemporary Guide to Awakening*. New York: Riverhead, 1997.
Bate, Walter Jackson. *The Burden of the Past and the English Poet*. New York: Norton, 1972.
Bennett, Robert. "Deconstructing and Reconstructing the Beats: New Directions in Beat Studies." *College Literature* 32.2 (Spring 2005): 177–84.
[Bishop, Gordon.] "Louis and Allen Ginsberg Read Poetry at Rutgers." [Passaic, NJ] *Herald-News* 20 Jan. 1968: 11.
Blake, William. *The Complete Poetry and Prose of William Blake*. Ed. David V. Erdman. New York: Doubleday, 1988.
Bloom, Harold. *The Anxiety of Influence: A Theory of Poetry*. New York: Oxford UP, 1975.
Boon, Marcus. *The Road of Excess: A History of Writers on Drugs*. Cambridge: Harvard UP, 1992.
Bracher, Mark. *Being Form'd: Thinking through Blake's "Milton."* Barrytown: Station Hill, 1985.
Breslin, James. "The Origins of 'Howl' and 'Kaddish.'" *Iowa Review* 8.2 (Spring 1977): 82–108. Rpt. in Hyde 401–33.
Brooks, Eugene. Introduction. "Paterson's Principal Poet." *The Collected Poems of Louis Ginsberg*. Orono, ME: Northern Lights, 1992. 23–35.
Buddhadāsa Bhikku. *Mindfulness with Breathing: A Manual for Serious Beginners*. Trans. Santikaro Bhikku. Boston: Wisdom, 1997.

Butler, Judith. *Gender Trouble: Feminism and the Subversion of Identity.* New York: Routledge, 1990.

Butterfield, Stephen T. *The Double Mirror: A Skeptical Journey into Buddhist Tantra.* Berkeley: North Atlantic, 1994.

Cabezón, José Ignacio. "Homosexuality and Buddhism." Leyland 29–44.

Carruth, Hayden. "Chants, Oracles, Body-Rhythms." *New York Times Book Review* 19 Mar. 1978: BR4. Rpt. in Hyde 231–23.

Carter, David, ed. *Spontaneous Mind: Selected Interviews, 1958–1996.* New York: Harper, 2001.

Chögyan Trungpa Rinpoche. *Crazy Wisdom.* Boston: Shambhala, 1991.

——— *First Thought, Best Thought: 108 Poems.* Boulder: Shambhala, 1983.

———. *The Path Is the Goal: A Basic Handbook of Buddhist Meditation.* (Transcription of 1974 lectures.) Ed. Sherab Chödzin. Boston: Shambhala, 1995.

Clark, Tom. "The Art of Poetry VIII." Interview with Allen Ginsberg. *Paris Review* 10 (Spring 1966): 13–55. Rpt. in Carter 17–53.

———. *The Great Naropa Poetry Wars.* Santa Barbara: Cadmus, 1980.

Coleman, James William. "The New Buddhism: Some Empirical Findings." Williams and Queen 91–99.

Conkin, Dennis. "The Dalai Lama and Gay Love." Leyland 351–56.

Davidson, Michael. *Guys Like Us: Citing Masculinity in Cold War Poetics.* Chicago: U of Chicago P, 2004.

———. "Technologies of Presence: Orality and the Tapevoice of Contemporary Poetics." *Sound States: Innovative Poetics and Acoustical Technologies.* Chapel Hill: U of North Carolina P, 1997. 97–125.

Deleuze, Gilles, and Félix Guattari. *Anti-Oedipus: Capitalism and Schizophrenia.* Trans. Robert Hurley, et al. Minneapolis: U of Minnesota P, 1983.

———. *A Thousand Plateaus: Capitalism and Schizophrenia.* Trans. Brian Massumi. Minneapolis: U of Minnesota P, 1987.

Diggory, Terence. "Allen Ginsberg's Urban Pastoral." *College Literature* 27.1 (Winter 2000): 103–18.

Docherty, Brian. "Allen Ginsberg." *American Poetry: The Modernist Ideal.* Ed. Clive Bloom and Docherty. New York: St. Martin's, 1995.

Dougherty, Jay. "From Society to Self: Ginsberg's Inward Turn in 'Mind Breaths.'" *Sagetrieb* (Spring 1987): 81–92.

Edwards, Paul N. *The Closed World: Computers and the Politics of Discourse in Cold War America.* Cambridge: MIT, 1996.

Ellwood, Robert S. *The Sixties Spiritual Awakening: American Religion Moving from Modern to Postmodern.* Rutgers: Rutgers UP, 1994.

Engler, Jack. "Being Somebody and Being Nobody: A Reexamination of the Understanding of Self in Psychoanalysis and Buddhism." Safran 35–79.

Epstein, Mark. *Thoughts without a Thinker: Psychotherapy from a Buddhist Perspective.* New York: Basic, 1995.

Erkkila, Betsy. *Whitman the Political Poet.* New York: Oxford UP, 1989.

Falla, Jeffrey B. "Disembodying the Body: Allen Ginsberg's Passional Subversion of Identity." *Interdisciplinary Literary Studies: A Journal of Criticism and Theory* 3.2 (Spring 2002): 49-65.

Fields, Rick. "A High History of Buddhism." *Tricycle: The Buddhist Review* 6.1 (Fall 1996): 45-58.

———. *How the Swans Came to the Lake: A Narrative History of Buddhism in America.* 3rd ed. Boston: Shambhala, 1992.

Finch, Annie. Introduction. *After New Formalism: Poets on Form, Narrative, and Tradition.* Ed. Finch. Ashland, OR: Story Line, 1999. xi-xiii.

Finn, Mark. "Tibetan Buddhism and a Mystical Psychoanalysis." Safran 101-15.

Foucault, Michel. *The History of Sexuality, Volume I: An Introduction.* New York: Vintage, 1980.

———. "Technologies of the Self." *Technologies of the Self: A Seminar with Michel Foucault.* Ed. Luther H. Martin, et al. Amherst: U of Massachusetts P, 1988. 16-49.

Gach, Gary. *What Book?! Buddha Poems from Beat to Hip-Hop.* Berkeley: Parallax, 1998.

Garfield, Jay L. *Empty Words: Buddhist Philosophy and Cross-Cultural Interpretation.* New York: Oxford UP, 2002.

Gefen, Pearl Sheffy. "My Son the Guru. My Father the Poet." *Jerusalem Post Magazine* 9 July 1971: 8-11.

Gehlek Rinpoche. *Odyssey to Freedom.* Transcription of 1997 lectures. Ann Arbor: Jewel, 1999.

Giamo, Ben. *Kerouac, The Word and the Way: Prose Artist as Spiritual Quester.* Carbondale: Southern Illinois UP, 2000.

Ginsberg, Allen. *Ankor Wat.* Photographs by Alexandra Lawrence. London: Fulcrum, 1968.

———. "The Art of Poetry VIII." Interview with Thomas Clark. *Paris Review* 10 (Spring 1966): 13-55. Rpt. in Carter 17-53.

———. "Chicago Seven Trial Testimony." *Chicago Trial Testimony.* San Francisco: City Lights, 1975. Rpt. in Carter 200-42.

———. *Collected Poems, 1947-1980.* New York: Harper, 1984.

———. "The Complete Naropa Lectures of Allen Ginsberg." Unpublished. Allen Ginsberg Papers, M0733. Department of Special Collections, Stanford University Libraries, Stanford, CA.

———. "Confrontation with Louis Ginsberg's Poems." Introduction. *Morning in Spring and Other Poems.* By Louis Ginsberg. New York: Morrow, 1970. 11-20.

———. "Contemplation on Publications." *Allen Ginsberg: An Annotated Bibliography, 1969–1977.* Ed. Michelle P. Kraus. Metuchen, NJ: Scarecrow, 1980. Rpt. in Morgan 211–13.

———. *Cosmopolitan Greetings: Poems 1986–1992.* New York: Harper, 1994.

———. *Death and Fame: Last Poems, 1993–1997.* New York: Harper, 1999.

———. *Howl: Original Draft Facsimile.* Ed. Barry Miles. New York: Harper, 1986.

———. *Indian Journals: March 1962–May 1963.* San Francisco: Haselwood and City Lights, 1970.

———. Interview with Alison Colbert. "A Talk with Allen Ginsberg," *Partisan Review* 38 (1971): 289–309. Rpt. in Carter 259–72.

———. Interview with Clint Frakes. 15 July 1991. in Carter 532–45.

———. Interview with Ekbert Faas. "Allen Ginsberg." *Towards a New American Poetics.* Santa Barbara: Black Sparrow, 1979. 269–88. Rpt. in Carter 355–62.

———. Interview with Mary Jane Fortunato, Lucille Medwick, and Susan Rowe. "Craft Interview with Allen Ginsberg." *New York Quarterly* 6 (Spring 1971): 12–40. Rpt. in Carter 245–58.

———. Interview with Michael Aldrich, et al. "Improvised Poetics." *Composed on the Tongue: Literary Conversations, 1967–1977.* San Francisco: Grey Fox, 1980. 18–62.

———. Interview with Michael Goodwin, Richard Hyatt, and Ed Ward. "Q: How Does Allen Ginsberg Write Poetry? A: By Polishing His Mind." *City Magazine* 13–26 Nov. 1974: 30–34. Rpt. in Carter 363–76.

———. Interview with Paul Carroll. *Playboy* April 1969: 81–92, 236–44.

———. Interview with Paul Portugés and Guy Amirthanayagam. "Buddhist Meditation and Poetic Spontaneity." *Writers in East-West Encounter: New Cultural Bearings.* Ed. Amirthanayagam. New York: Macmillan, 1982. Rpt. in Carter 398–418.

———. Interview with Peter Barry Chowka. "This Is Allen Ginsberg." *New Age Journal* Apr. 1976. 22–28. Rpt. in Carter 377–97.

———. Interview with Peter Money. "An Interview with Allen Ginsberg." *Provincetown Arts* 8 (1992): 92–96.

———. Introduction. *First Thought, Best Thought: 108 Poems.* By Chögyam Trungpa. Boulder: Shambhala, 1983. xi–xviii.

———. *Journals: Early Fifties, Early Sixties.* Ed. Gordon Ball. New York: Grove, 1977.

———. *Journals: Mid-Fifties, 1954–1958.* Ed. Gordon Ball. New York: Harper, 1995.

———. "Kerouac's Ethic." *Un Homme Grand.* Ed. Pierre Anctil, et al. Ottawa: Carleton UP, 1990. Rpt. in Morgan 358–73.

———. "Meditation and Poetics." *Spiritual Quests: The Art and Craft of Religious Writing.* Ed. William Zinsser. Boston: Houghton, 1988. Rpt. in Morgan 262–73.

———. "On Walt Whitman, Composed on the Tongue, or, Taking a Walk through *Leaves of Grass.*" *Walt Whitman, The Measure of His Song.* Ed. Jim Perlman, Ed Folsom, and Dan Campion. Minneapolis: Holy Cow! 1981. 329–52. Rpt. in Morgan 285–331.

———. Notebooks and journals. Unpublished. Allen Ginsberg Papers, M0733. Department of Special Collections, Stanford University, Stanford, CA.

———. "Reflections on the Mantra." *Back to Godhead* Dec. 1966: 5–9. Rpt. in Morgan 148–50.

———. *White Shroud: Poems, 1980–1985.* New York: Harper, 1986.

———. "Whitman's Influence: A Mountain Too Vast to Be Seen." *Sulfur* 31 (Fall 1992): 229–30. Rpt. in Morgan 332–33.

Ginsberg, Allen, and Louis Ginsberg. *Family Business: Selected Letters between a Father and Son.* Ed. Michael Schumacher. New York: Bloomsbury, 2001.

Ginsberg, Louis. *The Collected Poems of Louis Ginsberg.* Orono, ME: Northern Lights, 1992.

———. *Morning in Spring and Other Poems.* New York: Morrow, 1970.

Gioia, Dana. "Notes on the New Formalism." *Can Poetry Matter? Essays on Poetry and American Culture.* Saint Paul: Graywolf, 1992. 31–45.

Goddard, Dwight, ed. *A Buddhist Bible.* Trans. Bhikshu Wai-tao. Thetford: Dutton, 1938. Boston: Beacon, 1994.

Goss, Robert E. "Buddhist Studies at Naropa: Sectarian or Academic?" Williams and Queen 215–37.

Grace, Nancy M., and Ronna C. Johnson, ed. *Girls Who Wore Black: Women Writing the Beat Generation.* Rutgers: Rutgers UP, 2002.

Hassan, Ihab. "Allen Ginsberg." *Contemporary Literature, 1945–1972: An Introduction.* New York: Ungar, 1973. 102–4.

Hebdige, Dick. "Even unto Death: Improvisation, Edging, and Enframement." *Critical Inquiry* 27.2 (Winter 2001): 333–53.

Herring, Scott. "'Her Brothers Dead in Riverside or Russia': 'Kaddish' and the Holocaust." *Contemporary Literature* 42.3 (Fall 2001): 535–56.

Hilton, Nelson. *Literal Imagination: Blake's Vision of Words.* Berkeley: U of California P, 1983.

Hopkins, Jeffrey. "The Compatibility of Reason and Orgasm in Tibetan Buddhism: Reflections on Sexual Violence and Homophobia." *Que(e)rying Religion, A Critical Anthology.* Ed. Gary David Comstock and Susan F. Henking. New York: Continuum, 1997. 372–83.

———. *Emptiness Yoga: The Tibetan Middle Way.* Ed. Joe B. Wilson. Ithaca, NY: Snow Lion, 1995.

Hyde, Lewis, ed. *On the Poetry of Allen Ginsberg*. Ann Arbor: U of Michigan P, 1984.

Jackson, Peter A. "Male Homosexuality and Transgenderism in the Thai Buddhist Tradition." Leyland 55–90.

Jackson, Roger R. "In Search of a Postmodern Middle." *Buddhist Theology: Critical Reflections by Contemporary Buddhist Scholars*. Ed. Roger R. Jackson and John Makransky. London: Routledge, 2000. 215–46.

Jarraway, David R. "'Standing By His Word': The Politics of Allen Ginsberg's Vietnam 'Vortex.'" *Journal of American Culture* 16 (Fall 1993): 81–88.

Johnson, Kent, and Craig Paulenich. *Beneath a Single Moon: Buddhism in Contemporary American Poetry*. Boston: Shambhala, 2001.

Kalupahana, David J. *A History of Buddhist Philosophy: Continuities and Discontinuities*. Honolulu: U of Hawaii P, 1992.

Kamenetz, Roger. *The Jew in the Lotus: A Poet's Rediscovery of Jewish Identity in Buddhist India*. San Francisco: Harper, 1994.

Kashner, Sam. *When I Was Cool: My Life at the Jack Kerouac School*. New York: Harper, 2004.

Komunyakaa, Yusef. Introduction. *The Best American Poetry 2003*. Ed. Komunyakaa. Series ed. David Lehman. New York: Scribner, 2003. 11–21.

Kornfield, Jack. Interview with Robert Forte. "Domains of Consciousness: An Interview with Jack Kornfield." *Tricycle: The Buddhist Review* 6.1 (Fall 1996). 34–40.

Lee, Ben. "*'Howl' and Other Poems*: Is There Old Left in These New Beats?" *American Literature* 76.2 (June 2004): 367–89.

Lehman, David. Rev. of *Ankor Wat. Poetry* 114 (Sept. 1969): 403–5. Rpt. in Hyde 192–94.

Lenson, David. *On Drugs*. Minneapolis: U of Minnesota P, 1995.

Leyland, Winston, ed. *Queer Dharma: Voices of Gay Buddhists*. San Francisco: Gay Sunshine, 1998.

Lezra, Jacques. "Unrelated Passions." *differences* 14.1 (Mar. 2003): 74–87.

Loy, David. "The Clôture of Deconstruction: A Mahāyāna Critique of Derrida." *International Philosophical Quarterly* 27 (Mar. 1987): 59–80.

Machor, James L. *Pastoral Cities: Urban Ideals and the Symbolic Landscape of America*. Madison: U of Wisconsin P, 1987.

Mannikka, Eleanor. *Angkor Wat: Time, Space, and Kingship*. Honolulu: U of Hawaii P, 1996.

Martin, Rafe. *The Hungry Tigress: Buddhist Myths, Legends, and Jataka Tales*. Cambridge, MA: Yellow Moon, 1999.

Martin, Robert K. *The Homosexual Tradition in American Poetry*. Austin: U of Texas P, 1979.

McClure, Michael. *Plum Stones: Cartoons of No Heaven*. Oakland, CA: O, 2002.

McNiece, Ray, and Larry Smith. *America Zen: A Gathering of Poets.* Huron, OH: Bottom Dog, 2004.

Miles, Barry. *Ginsberg: A Biography.* New York: Harper, 1989.

Miller, William Ian. *The Anatomy of Disgust.* Cambridge: Harvard UP, 1998.

Miller, Stephen Paul. *The Seventies Now: Culture as Surveillance.* Durham: Duke UP, 1999.

Moon, Michael. *Disseminating Whitman: Revision and Corporeality in "Leaves of Grass."* Cambridge: Harvard UP, 1991.

Morgan, Bill. *I Celebrate Myself: The Somewhat Private Life of Allen Ginsberg.* New York: Viking, 2006.

———, ed. *Deliberate Prose: Selected Essays, 1952–1995.* New York: Harper, 2000.

Newland, Guy. *Appearance and Reality: The Two Truths in the Four Buddhist Tenet Systems.* Ithaca: Snow Lion, 1999.

Orzech, Charles D. "'Provoked Suicide' and the Victim's Behavior: The Case of the Vietnamese Self-Immolators." *Curing Violence.* Ed. Mark I. Wallace and Theophus H. Smith. Sonoma, CA: Polebridge, 1994. 137–60.

Plant, Sadie. *Writing on Drugs.* New York: Picador, 1999.

Portugés, Paul. "Allen Ginsberg's Paul Cézanne and the Pater Omnipotens Aeterna Deus." *Contemporary Literature* 21 (Summer 1980): 435–49.

———. *The Visionary Poetics of Allen Ginsberg.* Santa Barbara: Ross-Erikson, 1978.

"Practitioners of Reality." Symposium with Norman Fischer, Michael McClure, and Leslie Scalapino. Stanford University. 15 Mar. 2003.

Prebish, Charles S. *Luminous Passage: The Practice and Study of Buddhism in America.* Berkeley: U of California P, 1999.

Queen, Christopher S. Introduction. Williams and Queen xiv–xxxvii.

"Results from the Tricycle Poll: Help or Hindrance." *Tricycle: The Buddhist Review* 6.1 (Fall 1996): 44.

Reynolds, David S. *Walt Whitman's America: A Cultural Biography.* New York: Random, 1995.

Robinson, James Burnell. "The Lives of Buddhist Saints: Biography, Hagiography, and Myth." *Tibetan Literature: Studies in Genre.* Ed. José Ignacio Cabezón and Roger R. Jackson. Ithaca: Snow Lion, 1996. 57–69.

Rodden, John. *George Orwell: The Politics of Literary Reputation.* New Brunswick, NJ: Transaction, 2002.

Ruddick, Lisa. "The Near Enemy of the Humanities Is Professionalism." *Chronicle of Higher Education* 23 Nov. 2001: B7.

Rumaker, Michael. "Allen Ginsberg's 'Howl.'" *Black Mountain Review* (Fall 1957): 228–37. Rpt. in Hyde 36.

Safran, Jeremy. *Psychoanalysis and Buddhism: An Unfolding Dialogue.* Boston: Wisdom, 2003.

Sanders, Ed, ed. *The Party: A Chronological Perspective on a Confrontation at a Buddhist Seminary.* Woodstock, NY: Poetry, 1977.

Scalapino, Leslie, and Marina Adams. *The Tango.* New York: Granary, 2001.

Schelling, Andrew. *The Wisdom Anthology of North American Buddhist Poetry.* Boston: Wisdom, 2005.

Schumacher, Michael. *Dharma Lion: A Critical Biography of Allen Ginsberg.* New York: St. Martin's, 1992.

———. Introduction. *Family Business: Selected Letters between a Father and Son.* Ed. Schumacher. New York: Bloomsbury, 2001. xxi–xxx.

Seager, Richard Hughes. *Buddhism in America.* New York: Columbia UP, 1999.

Shantideva. *The Way of the Bodhisattva [Bodhicharyavatara].* Trans. Padmakara Translation Group. Boston: Shambhala, 1997.

Shetley, Vernon. *After the Death of Poetry: Poet and Audience in Contemporary America.* Durham: Duke UP, 1993.

Silliman, Ron. "Ginsberg@Center?" Discussion of American Poetry Group (CAP-L). 8 Sept. 1995. <http://homepages.packet.net/schaeff/capl/log9509.gz>. (This link is no longer available; however, Silliman's 8 Sept. 1995 remarks can be accessed, as of the publication of this volume, at the Internet Archive, <http://web.archive.org/web/20010513012838/myweb.packet.net/schaeff/capl/welcome.html>.)

Simpson, Louis. *A Revolution in Taste: Studies of Dylan Thomas, Allen Ginsberg, Sylvia Plath, and Robert Lowell.* New York: Macmillan, 1978.

Skerl, Jennie, ed. *Reconstructing the Beats.* New York: Palgrave/Macmillan, 2004.

Staub, Michael E. "Setting Up the Seventies: Black Panthers, New Journalism, and the Rewriting of the Sixties." *The Seventies: The Age of Glitter in Popular Culture.* Ed. Shelton Waldrep. New York: Routledge, 2000. 19–40.

Stepanchev, Stephen. *American Poetry since 1945: A Critical Survey.* New York: Harper, 1965.

Sweet, Timothy. *Traces of War: Poetry, Photography, and the Crisis of the Union.* Baltimore: Johns Hopkins UP, 1990.

Tonkinson, Carole, ed. *Big Sky Mind: Buddhism and the Beat Generation.* New York: Riverhead, 1995.

Trigilio, Tony. *"Strange Prophecies Anew": Rereading Apocalypse in Blake, H. D., and Ginsberg.* Madison, NJ: Fairleigh Dickinson UP, 2000.

Tweed, Thomas A. *The American Encounter with Buddhism, 1844–1912: Victorian Culture and the Limits of Dissent.* Bloomington: Indiana UP, 1992.

———. "Night-Stand Buddhists and Other Creatures: Sympathizers, Adherents, and the Study of Religion." Williams and Queen 71–90.

Tytell, John. *Naked Angels: The Lives and Literature of the Beat Generation.* New York: McGraw, 1976.

United States Senate. Special Subcommittee of the Committee on the Judiciary. *The Narcotic Rehabilitation Act of 1966.* 89th Cong., 2nd sess. Washington: GPO, 1966.

Varela, Francisco J., ed. *Sleeping, Dreaming, and Dying: An Exploration of Consciousness with the Dalai Lama.* Boston: Wisdom, 1997.

Vendler, Helen. "American X-Rays: Forty Years of Allen Ginsberg's Poetry." *New Yorker* 4 Nov. 1996: 98–102.

———. "Frank O'Hara: The Virtue of the Alterable." *Frank O'Hara: To Be True to a City.* Ed. Jim Elledge. Ann Arbor: U of Michigan P, 1990. 234–52.

———. Rev. of *The Fall of America. New York Times Book Review* 15 Apr. 1973: 1. Rpt. in Hyde 203–9.

———. *Soul Says: On Recent Poetry.* Cambridge: Harvard UP, 1995.

Walzer, Kevin. *The Ghost of Tradition: Expansive Poetry and Postmodernism.* Ashland, OR: Story Line, 1998.

Weinstone, Ann. *Avatar Bodies: A Tantra for Posthumanism.* Minneapolis, U of Minnesota P, 2004.

Whitman, Walt. *Leaves of Grass.* Ed. Michael Moon, Sculley Bradley, and Harold W. Blodgett. 2nd ed. New York: Norton, 2002.

Whittemore, Reed. "From 'Howl' to OM." *New Republic* 25 July 1970: 17–18. Rpt. in Hyde 200–202.

Williams, Duncan Ryūken, and Christopher S. Queen, eds. *American Buddhism: Methods and Findings in Recent Scholarship.* Richmond, Great Britain: Curzon, 1999.

Wilson, Elizabeth. *Bohemians: The Glamorous Outcasts.* New Brunswick, NJ: Rutgers UP, 2000.

Wilson, Liz. "Human Torches of Enlightenment: Autocremation and Spontaneous Combustion as Marks of Sanctity in South Asian Buddhism." *The Living and the Dead: Social Dimensions of Death in South Asian Religions.* Ed. Wilson. Albany: State U of New York P, 2003. 29–50.

Woods, Gregory. *Articulate Flesh: Male Homo-Eroticism and Modern Poetry.* New Haven: Yale UP, 1987.

Young, Allen. *Gay Sunshine Interview.* Bolinas, CA: Grey Fox, 1974.

Young-Eisendrath, Polly. "Transference and Transformation in Buddhism and Psychoanalysis." Safran 301–18.

Zweig, Paul. "A Music of Angels." *Nation* 10 Mar. 1969: 311–13. Rpt. in Hyde 195–99.

Index

Adams, Marina, 192
Aldrich, Michael, 91, 97, 98
Altieri, Charles, 184
American Buddhism. *See* Buddhism, Western
Andrews, Bruce, 183
"Angkor Wat" (Ginsberg), xiii, 30–47, 50–61, 64, 66, 71, 73, 76, 81, 82–83, 90, 94, 101, 105, 106–7, 114, 116, 138, 174–75, 209n. 3, 221n. 3; and apocalypse, 60–61; and the body, 37–38, 40–47, 51, 59–60, 65–66, 69, 70, 72, 74, 75, 78, 79, 83–84, 211n. 9, 215nn. 18, 19; and Dadaism, 43; and literary collage, 30, 36, 37, 40–47, 60; mantric poetics of, 81–82, 86; and masturbation, 60, 71, 72, 120; as spiritual confession, 66–67, 120–21; and Surrealism, 40–45, 58–59, 210–11n. 6; and the Vietnam War (*see also* Vietnam War), 40–43, 59–60, 72, 81–82
Angkor Wat temples (*see also* "Angkor Wat"), 30, 31, 36, 37–38, 41, 44, 46, 56, 57, 59, 60, 138
Ankor Wat (Ginsberg) (Fulcrum Press edition), 35, 36–37, 57, 69–70
Apollinaire, Guillaume, 60
Auden, W. H., x
Austin, J. L., xvi, 88, 89

Bachelor, Stephen, 189
Bakhtin, Mikhail, 131, 133, 134, 179, 227n. 7
Ball, Gordon, 161, 179, 210n. 6
Baraka, Amiri, 59–60
Bate, Walter Jackson, 12
Beat Studies, xv, xvii, 188, 236n. 1
Beckett, Samuel, 163
Bennett, Robert, 201n. 2
Black Mountain school, 10

Blair, Randy, 234–35n. 18, 235nn. 19, 21
Blake, William (*see also* Ginsberg, Allen, Blake vision of), xi, 10, 11, 90, 142, 227n. 8; concept of Poetic Genius, 68, 189; influence on Ginsberg's Buddhist poetics, 20–21, 35, 39, 63–64, 66, 68–69, 79, 82–83, 93, 96–97, 99–100, 106–7, 141, 146, 150, 153, 171, 202–3n. 7, 222nn. 6, 7, 223n. 13, 229n. 18; Nobodaddy figure, 68, 74, 83, 121; Urizen figure, 74
Blake, William, works: annotations to Bishop Watson's *An Apology for the Bible*, 93; "The Fly," 219n. 12; *Jerusalem*, 189, 223n. 13; "The Marriage of Heaven and Hell," 78, 82, 106–7; *Milton*, 11, 94, 106–7, 202–3n. 7; "The Sick Rose," 218–19n. 12; "A Vision of the Last Judgment," 68, 69, 83
Blavatsky, Helena Petrovna (Madame Blavatsky), 32, 156
Bloom, Harold, 12, 15–16
Boner, Alice, 210n. 4
Boon, Marcus, 109, 223–24n. 16
Bracher, Mark, 203n. 7
Breslin, James, 207nn. 22, 23
Brooklyn College, xiii, 206n. 19
Buddhadāsa Bhikku, 210n. 5
Buddhism (*see also* Ginsberg, Allen, Buddhism of): bodhisattva ideal, 78; and contemporary U.S. poetry, 189–95; Crazy Wisdom (*see also* Chögyam Trungpa Rinpoche, and Crazy Wisdom), xi, 209n. 25; Eightfold Noble Path, 130, 229n. 19; Four Noble Truths, 41, 57, 84, 130, 194, 217n. 6; guru-student relationship (Tibetan Buddhism), x–xi, 18, 25–27, 54–55, 129, 136, 158, 180–81, 188, 204nn. 11, 12; and homosexuality (*see*

249

Buddhism (*continued*)
  also Ginsberg, Allen, and homosexuality), 31, 46–47, 208–9n. 25, 212n. 12; and hungry ghosts, 74–75, 218n. 9; Jataka Tales, 149, 216–17n. 4, 228n. 14; *lam rim* (Tibetan Buddhism), xii, xiii; Mahayana, xii, 18, 89, 107, 200n. 4, 206–7n. 20; Middle-Way school (Madhyamaka), xvi, 4, 19, 73–74, 95, 107, 118–19, 154, 184, 185, 206–7n. 20, 208n. 24; and nihilism, 68, 70, 71, 74, 82; Perfect Human Rebirth (Tibetan Buddhism), 149, 154, 217n. 6, 229n. 19; and poststructuralism, xv, 89, 93–94, 99, 192, 194–95, 228n. 11; and the postwar counterculture, 3–4, 32, 33–34; and psychedelic drugs, 107–8; and psychoanalysis (*see also* Ginsberg, Allen, and psychoanalysis), 18, 25–29, 169, 190; refuge prayer of, 5, 8, 30–32, 35, 38, 52–53, 69, 79, 210n. 4; *shunyata* (emptiness), 16, 39, 41, 57, 70, 78, 93–94, 105–6, 113, 123, 125, 127, 134, 139, 154–55, 159, 161, 178, 181–82, 184, 188, 192, 194, 202n. 5, 203n. 7, 208n. 24; Six Perfections, 130, 132, 159–60; Tantric, xii–xiii, 16–17, 21–22, 23, 26, 28, 43, 46, 55, 68–69, 72, 145, 146, 154, 169, 172, 200n. 4,5, 207n. 20, 208–9n. 25, 215n. 20; Tonglen practice (Tibetan Buddhism), 132–34, 218n. 11; the Two Truths, 6–7, 16, 18–20, 68, 69–71, 73–74, 79, 80–81, 83–84, 106, 139–40, 161, 192, 202n. 5, 217n. 6; Vajrayana, xii, 18, 157, 177, 178, 200n. 4; vipassana, 38, 40, 136, 210n. 5; Western, xv, 4–5, 22, 31–32, 33, 40, 102, 107–8, 131, 157, 188, 190–91, 200n. 6, 201n. 3, 202n. 6, 204n. 11, 225n. 17; Zen, 21, 25, 34, 39, 43, 108, 141, 207n. 20
Burdick Quentin, 112, 115–16
Burroughs, William S., 17, 18, 22, 169
Butler, Judith, xvi, 49
Butterfield, Stephen T., 22, 181, 207n. 21

Cabezón, José Ignacio, 46
Carroll, Paul, 85–86, 148
Carruth, Hayden, 144, 145
Cassady, Neal, 75–76
"Change, The: *Kyoto-Tokyo Express*" (Ginsberg), xiii, 35, 36, 41, 42, 61, 62–84, 90, 93, 94, 101, 105, 106–7, 114, 174, 175, 218–19n. 12, 221n. 3; and Blake vision (*see also* Ginsberg, Allen, Blake vision of), 64–65, 66, 68, 71–72, 73, 77–78, 80, 82–83, 217–18n. 7; and the body, 47, 62, 63, 65, 68–84; and Hinduism, 77, 78; and language, 58, 62, 65–66, 67, 72, 78–81, 83–84, 216n. 3, 224n. 16; mantric poetics of, 81–82, 86; and masturbation, 71, 72; and mudras, 81–82, 216n. 22, 219n. 12; and sadomasochism, 75–76; and the Satipatthana Sutra, 66, 67–68, 70, 73, 74, 76–77, 78, 90, 109, 216n. 2; and *shunyata* (*see also* Buddhism, *shunyata*), 70–71, 77, 78; as spiritual confession, 66–67; and the Two Truths (*see also* Buddhism, the Two Truths), 70, 71, 72–73, 74, 76, 79, 80–81, 83–84; and the Vietnam War (*see also* Vietnam War), 67–68, 72, 77, 81–82
Chögyam Trungpa Rinpoche (*see also* Ginsberg, Allen, Buddhism of, as student of Chögyam Trungpa Rinpoche), 137, 140, 156, 180–82, 202n. 6; Crazy Wisdom and, x, xi, xii, 21–22, 23, 108, 135, 178, 207n. 21, 214–15n. 18; excesses of, x, 176–77, 207n. 21, 209n. 26; and Naropa University (*see also* Naropa University), 27–28, 150; poetry of, 10, 17–20; Shambhala teachings of, xiii, 229n. 16; and Snowmass scandal, 26–27, 157–60, 176–78, 204n. 12, 206n. 18, 230n. 2, 230–31n. 3, 231nn. 4, 5, 235–36n. 22, 236n. 24
Chowka, Peter Barry, 144, 227n. 6
Clark, Tom (Thomas), 26–27, 63–64, 74, 121, 156, 157, 158–159, 177, 178, 208n. 25, 230n. 1, 235n. 20
Claudel, Paul, 18
Colbert, Alison, 141, 222n. 7
Cowen, Elise, 161, 225n. 19
Creeley, Robert, 19

Dadaism, xi, 42–43, 210–11n. 6
Das Thakur, Sitaram Onkar, 53–56, 57
Davidson, Michael, 88, 95, 97, 225n. 18, 226n. 3
Deleuze, Gilles, xvi, 162–63, 165, 167, 169–70, 177, 218n. 9, 233n. 13
Dellinger, David, 163

Diggory, Terence, 226–27n. 4
di Prima, Diane, 3
Docherty, Brian, 213n. 14
Dougherty, Jay, xi, 2, 129, 130, 131, 137, 139, 140, 180, 181, 182
Dylan, Bob, 158

Eckman, Frederick, 47
Edwards, Paul N., 227–28n. 10
Eliot, T. S., x, 9, 18, 34, 124
Elwood, Robert S., 31, 32, 188
Engler, Jack, 208n. 24
Epstein, Mark, 190
Erdman, David, 219n. 12
Erkkila, Betsy, 223n. 10

Falla, Jeffrey B., 225n. 18
Ferlinghetti, Lawrence, 3
Fields, Rick, 5, 22, 32–33, 108, 201–2n. 4, 223n. 14
Finch, Annie, 185
Finn, Mark, 26, 27–28, 29, 209n. 26
Fischer, Norman, 191–92, 193
Foucault, Michel, 100, 102, 151; and confession, 100–101, 102, 111–12, 115, 116, 145–46, 222n. 8, 233n. 14; governmentality, concept of, 87, 105, 107, 114, 118, 130–31, 153; technologies of the self, concept of, 102, 103, 105, 107, 114, 115, 118, 130–31, 140, 215n. 20

Gach, Gary, 188
Garfield, Jay, xv, 217n. 6
Gehlek Rinpoche (see also Ginsberg, Allen, Buddhism of, as student of Gehlek Rinpoche), xii, 209–10n. 3, 218n. 9
Giamo, Ben, 199n. 3
Gimian, Carolyn, 154
Ginsberg, Allen: Blake vision of (see also "Change, The: *Kyoto-Tokyo Express*"; "Iron Horse"), xiv, 11, 12, 20, 32, 35, 36, 62, 65, 69, 71–72, 77, 80, 81, 82–83, 86, 101, 120–21, 217–18n. 7, 223n. 14, 228n. 12; and Chicago Democratic National Convention (1968), 85–86, 91, 147, 148, 153, 186; and Chicago Seven trial, 100, 213n. 14; drug use of, 57, 58, 59, 62, 74, 77, 81, 82–83, 88, 100–117, 118, 160, 215n. 20, 222n. 9, 223–24n. 16, 225n. 19, 225–26n. 20; and Gnosticism, 166, 214n. 17, 222n. 7; and heterosexuality, 48–53, 55, 56, 71, 72, 80, 113–14, 123–24, 164, 170, 213n. 14, 225n. 18, 233n. 14; and homosexuality, 23, 31, 33, 45–53, 55–56, 59, 60, 71, 72, 79–82, 113–14, 123, 147, 148, 162, 170–72, 187, 208–9n. 25, 212n. 12, 213n. 14, 213–14n. 15, 214n. 16, 215n. 19, 225n. 18, 233n. 14; literary reputation of, 1, 3–4, 17–18, 19, 89–90, 96, 108–9, 110, 114, 115–17, 124–25, 131, 135, 141, 143–44, 145, 148, 150, 155, 160, 168, 175–76, 206nn. 17, 19, 219n. 13, 226n. 21, 229n. 17, 233n. 14; poetry readings with father (Louis Ginsberg) (see also Ginsberg, Louis), 13–14, 203n. 9; and postmodernism (see also Buddhism, and poststructuralism), 109, 154, 182–86, 192, 193, 195; and psychoanalysis (see also Buddhism, and psychoanalysis), 22–29, 169, 207n. 22, 233n. 13, 234n. 17; romanticist influence of (see also Ginsberg, Allen, Buddhism of, as revision of poet's romanticism), 7, 20, 87–88, 100, 103–5, 109, 110, 111, 118, 126, 144, 150, 155, 184–85, 186, 189, 195; Snowmass scandal and (see also Chögyam Trungpa Rinpoche, and Snowmass scandal), 26–27, 156, 157, 158–60, 161, 164, 174, 176–78, 204n. 12, 220n. 1; as teacher, xiii, 38–39, 65, 66; testimony before United States Senate, 100–117, 118–19, 129, 145, 150, 221n. 3, 222n. 10, 224n. 16; travel to Cuba, 45, 221n. 2; travel to Czechoslovakia, 45, 221n. 2, 225–26n. 20; travel to India, 45, 53–54, 62–64, 74, 82–83
Ginsberg, Allen, Buddhism of: as autodidactic, xii, 33, 35, 43, 58, 86, 102, 160, 206–7n. 19, 222n. 9; and bodhisattva vows, xii, 129, 135, 171–72, 199n. 2, 234n. 15; and the Cold War, 34, 98; and experimental poetry, 10–12; and Dadaism (see also Dadaism), 42–43; and Hinduism, xiv, 1, 31, 33, 34–35, 45, 54–56, 77, 85–86, 88, 89, 97–98, 104, 185, 222n. 7, 223n. 12; and humanism, xiv, 7, 97, 119, 131, 146, 154, 155, 178, 182, 184, 190, 193–94, 229n. 19; and Judaism, 1–2, 12–14, 20, 23, 34, 51–52, 58, 73, 79, 81, 84, 95–96, 160, 182,

Ginsberg, Allen, Buddhism of (*continued*) 184, 204n. 12, 220–21n. 2; and language, 8–9, 34, 37–47, 54–55, 88–89; mantric poetics of (*see also* "Angkor Wat"; "Change, The: *Kyoto-Tokyo Express*"; "Iron Horse"; "Wichita Vortex Sutra"), xiv, 54, 81–84, 86–90, 98–100, 121, 131–34, 135–36, 140–42, 147–50, 152–53, 160, 180–84, 185–86, 187, 220n. 1; and Modernist poetry, 5–11, 195; notes by Ginsberg on Buddhist teachings, 22, 154–55, 204n. 12, and orientalism, 3, 33–34, 103, 108–9, 114, 200–201n. 2, 222n. 9; and psychoanalysis (*see also* Buddhism, and psychoanalysis; Ginsberg, Allen, and psychoanalysis), 27–29; as quietism, 114, 120, 130, 131, 137; refuge prayer (*see also* Buddhism, refuge prayer of), 34–37, 69–70, 76, 79; as revision of poet's romanticism (*see also* Ginsberg, Allen, romanticist influence of), 87–88, 99, 100, 102, 105–7, 111–14, 155, 195; as student of Chögyam Trungpa Rinpoche, x–xi, xii, xiii, 2, 4, 9, 14, 17, 21–22, 26–29, 55, 102, 129, 130, 133, 134, 135–37, 139, 141–44, 150, 154–55, 158–60, 171, 177–78, 180–82, 186, 205n. 16, 214–15n. 18, 228n. 13; as student of Gehlek Rinpoche, xii, xiii, 4, 14, 17, 55, 186, 200n. 6, 207n. 21; and subjectivity, 19, 36–37, 41, 57–58, 61, 73–74, 76–77, 79, 89, 100, 105–7, 118–19, 131, 137–40, 143–46, 153–54, 155, 159–61, 163, 176, 178–80, 181, 184–86, 187–88, 195, 217n. 6; and Surrealism (*see also* "Ankgor Wat," and Surrealism; Surrealism), 40–45

Ginsberg, Allen, works: "America," 47; "American Change," 137, 211n. 9; "Angkor Wat" (*see* "*Angkor, Wat*"); "At Apollinaire's Grave," 210–11n. 6; "Black Shroud," 160–61, 172–76, 177–79, 180, 231n. 8, 234n. 17; "Bowel Song," 219n. 13; "The Bricklayer's Lunch Hour," 139, 181; "The Change: *Kyoto-Tokyo Express*" (*see* "*The Change:* Kyoto-Tokyo Express"); *Collected Poems, 1947–1980*, 35, 37, 57, 69–70, 79, 130, 132, 135, 153, 175, 179, 226n. 2; "Come All Ye Brave Boys," 147; "Confrontation with Louis Ginsberg's Poems" (intro. to L. Ginsberg's *Morning in Spring*), 11–17, 24, 25, 136, 203n. 7, 205nn. 13, 15, 207n. 23; *Cosmopolitan Greetings: Poems, 1986–1992*, 180; *Death and Fame: Last Poems, 1993–1997*, 26, 182, 219n. 13, 233–34n. 15; "Death to Van Gogh's Ear!" 137, 211n. 9; *Deliberate Prose: Selected Essays, 1952–1955*, 34; "Do the Meditation Rock," 130; "Dream" (from *Death and Fame*), 26, 233–34n. 15; "Ego Confession," 116–17, 143–46, 148, 153, 154, 155, 180; "Excrement," 219n. 13; *The Fall of America: Poems of These States, 1965–1971*, 92, 126, 221n. 4, 226n. 2; "Footnote to Howl," 56; "Gospel Noble Truths," 129, 130, 160; "Guru Om," 55; "Hepatitis, Body Itch . . . ," 219n. 13; "Here We Go 'Round the Mulberry Bush," 219n. 13; "How *Kaddish* Happened," 113, 221n. 3; "Howl" (*see* "Howl"); *Howl and Other Poems*, xii, 1, 24; "I have a nosebleed . . . ," 219n. 13; "I Love Old Whitman So," 48; *Indian Journals*, 33, 54, 55, 65, 223n. 12; intro. to Chögyam Trungpa Rinpoche's *First Thought, Best Thought: 108 Poems*, 17–20, 25, 206n. 19; "Iron Horse (*see* "Iron Horse"); "Is About," 160, 182–84; *Journals: Early Fifties, Early Sixties*, 161; "Kaddish" (*see* "Kaddish"); *Kaddish and Other Poems*, xii, 1, 87, 109; "Kerouac's Ethic," 34, 36, 37; "Kral Majales," 84, 95–96, 182, 220–21n. 2; "Love Poem on Theme by Whitman," 47, 48–50, 51, 80, 114, 123, 213n. 14, 213–14n. 15, 221n. 4, 225n. 18; "Many Loves," 75; "Meditation and Poetics," 5–11, 29, 187, 190; "Mind Breaths," 87, 109, 134–40, 195, 230n. 20; *Mind Breaths: Poems, 1972–1977*, 2, 129–30, 131, 134, 139, 140, 144, 146, 147, 153–54, 160, 161, 179–80, 227n. 4, 230n. 20; "Mugging," 146–54, 155, 180, 181, 217n. 4, 229nn. 17, 18; "On Cremation of Chögyam Trungpa, Vidyadhara," 87, 180–82, 214–15n. 18; "On Walt Whitman, Composed on the Tongue, or, Taking a Walk Through *Leaves of Grass*," 212–13n. 13; "Pentagon Exorcism," 218n. 8; *Planet News: 1961–1967*, 35, 223n. 12; "Please Master," 75–76, 124,

218n. 10; "Reflections on the Mantra," 88–89; "September on Jessore Road," 24; "Scatological Observations," 219n. 13; "Stotras to Kali Destroyer of Illusions," 223n. 12; "Sunflower Sutra," 90; "A Supermarket in California," 47, 48, 214n. 16; "Television Was a Baby Crawling toward That Death Chamber," 214n. 15; "This Form of Life Needs Sex," 44, 47, 50–51, 53, 72, 123, 167; "This kind of hepatitis can cause ya," 219n. 13; "Thoughts on a Breath," 180; "Thoughts Sitting Breathing," 131–34, 146, 179, 227n. 7; "'What would you do if you lost it?'" 141–43; "White Shroud," 153, 160–72, 178–79, 180; *White Shroud: Poems, 1980–1985*, 130, 161; "Whitman's Influence: A Mountain Too Vast to Be Seen," 212–13n. 13; "Who Runs America?," 230n. 20; "Wichita Vortex Sutra" (*see* "Wichita Vortex Sutra)

Ginsberg, Louis (father) (*see also* Ginsberg, Allen, poetry readings with father; Williams, William Carlos, as poetic mentor to Ginsberg), 1, 22–24, 26, 28, 142, 161, 164–65, 203n. 9; 205n. 16, 231n. 6; as poetic mentor to Ginsberg, xv, 11–20, 23, 24, 27, 29, 160, 164, 204–5n. 13, 206n. 17; as spiritual mentor to Ginsberg, xiii, 11–17, 27, 29, 160, 203n. 8; 204n. 12.

Ginsberg, Louis (father), works: *The Attic of the Past*, 232n. 10; *Morning in Spring*, 12, 15, 17, 18, 24, 25, 203n. 7; 205n. 13; 205n. 15; 206n. 17; "Nightmare," 161, 231n. 6

Ginsberg, Naomi (mother), 1, 13, 23, 38, 50, 56, 77, 96, 104, 142, 149, 152, 153, 161–71, 172–76, 223n. 12, 232n. 9, 232n. 12; lobotomy of, authorized by Allen Ginsberg, 167–68, 173–75, 231n. 8, 234nn. 16, 17

Gioia, Dana, 185, 190, 193

Goddard, Dwight, 57–58

Goss, Robert E., 229n. 16

Grace, Nancy M., 226n. 3

Guattari, Félix, xvi, 162–63, 165, 167, 169–70, 177, 218n. 9, 233n. 13

Gunn, Thom, 47

Hassan, Ihab, 47

Hebdige, Dick, 98, 179

Herring, Scott, 232n. 9

Hilton, Nelson, 203n. 7

Hopkins, Gerard Manley, 191

Hopkins, Jeffrey, 46, 154, 208–9n. 25, 212n. 12

Housman, A. E., 16

"Howl" (Ginsberg), ix–x, xiii, xiv, 11, 26, 33, 35, 36, 38, 45, 52–53, 56, 59, 114, 133, 134–35, 139, 143, 144, 169–70, 205n. 14, 206n. 19, 209n. 1, 212n. 10, 214n. 17, 221n. 3; and apocalypse, 57, 60; and the body, 64; and industrialization, xvi, 74, 76, 94, 98, 109, 112–113, 121, 138, 227n. 4; and language, 34, 37, 66, 77, 80, 87, 90, 98, 110, 221–22n. 5, 223n. 15, 224n. 16; origins of, 90, 138; and prophetic poetry, lineage of, 63, 64, 86, 131, 142

"Iron Horse" (Ginsberg), 60, 84, 100, 102, 114, 119–28, 129, 135, 137, 139, 160, 209n. 3, 226n. 2, 226–27n. 4, 230n. 20; and Blake vision, 120–21; and the body, 123–25; failed vision of, 60, 120–21, 123, 127, 128, 130, 131; and language, 121–23, 124, 126–28; mantric poetics of, 122–23, 127–28, 131; and masturbation, 60, 120–21, 128; and propaganda, 94, 125–26; and romanticism, 102–3, 117; and *shunyata* (*see also* Buddhism, *shunyata*), 126–127; and Vietnam War (*see also* Vietnam War), 119, 120, 121–27, 135

Jack Kerouac School of Disembodied Poetics (*see also* Naropa University), 13, 29, 235n. 19

Jackson, Peter A., 46

Jackson, Roger R., 217n. 6, 237n. 3

James, William, 9

Jameson, Fredric, 193

Jarraway, David R., 88

Javits, Jacob, 101, 116

Johnson, Kent, 188

Johnson, Lyndon, 91, 93, 94, 96–97, 122, 127–28

Johnson, Ronna, 226n. 3

"Kaddish" (Ginsberg), xiii, xiv, 11, 33, 35, 36, 38, 40, 50–53, 56, 149, 150, 153, 175, 182, 211n. 9, 221n. 2, 232n. 9; and anti-

"Kaddish" (Ginsberg) (*continued*)
psychiatry, 112–13, 162–63, 165, 167, 173, 175; and apocalypse, 57, 60, 104, 146, 167; "Black Shroud," influence on, 161–62, 172–73, 174, 231n. 8; and the body, 64, 152; and Ginsberg's Buddhist poetics, development of, 45, 114, 236n. 23; father's (Louis Ginsberg) influence on, 12–13, 17; Ginsberg's international travel, influence on, 59, 210n. 6, 221n. 3; and language, 34, 37, 66, 77, 90, 96, 141, 146, 224n. 16; origins of, 90, and prophetic poetry, 2, 63, 64, 86, 166–67, 221n. 4, 223n. 12; "White Shroud," influence on, 161–62, 164, 165–68, 171, 232n. 12;
Kamenetz, Roger, 201n. 3
Kashner, Sam, 199n. 1, 235n. 20
Keats, John, 7, 10, 124–25
Kerouac, Jack, 5, 17, 18, 19, 126–27, 236n. 1; as Ginsberg's first Buddhist teacher, xii, 34, 36–37, 199n. 3
King, Bill, 231n. 5
Komunyakaa, Yusef, 189–90, 191
Kornfield, Jack, 107
Kyger, Joanne, 63

Language movement, contemporary U.S. poetry, 6, 7, 97–98, 183, 184–85, 194
Lawrence, Alexandra, 35
Leary, Timothy, 150, 152, 225n. 18
Lee, Ben, 203n. 8, 205n. 14, 219n. 15
Lehman, David, 40, 41–42, 43, 58–59
Lenson, David, 109, 222n. 9, 224–25n. 17, 225n. 18
Levertov, Denise, x
Leyland, Winston, 212n. 11
Lezra, Jacques, 194
Lowell, Robert, x
Loy, David, xv, 89, 94, 217n. 6, 228n. 11, 237n. 3

MacAdams, Lewis, 39
Machor, James L., 226–27n. 4
Mailer, Norman, 201n. 2, 218n. 11
Mannikka, Eleanor, 210n. 4
Martin, Rafe, 228n. 14
Martin, Robert K., 47, 212n. 10, 214n. 16
Matthews, William, 234n. 18, 235n. 21

McClure, Michael, 191, 192
McGann, Jerome, 189, 224n. 17
McKeever, William, 157
McNamara, Robert, 96
McNiece, Ray, 188
Merwin, W. S., xv, 156, 157, 158, 160, 176, 177, 178, 207n. 21, 230n. 2, 230–31n. 3, 231nn. 4, 5, 235nn. 19, 21, 235–36n. 22, 236n. 24
Miles, Barry, xi, xvii, 12, 62, 63, 67, 82, 147, 157, 158, 207n. 22, 215n. 19, 229n. 17
Miller, Henry, 163
Miller, Stephen Paul, 111, 151
Miller, William Ian, 174
Money, Peter, 154
Moon, Michael, 119, 226n. 1
Morgan, Bill, 34, 233n. 14
Morreale, Don, 200n. 6

Nagarjuna, 70, 236n. 3
Naone, Dana, xv, 156, 157, 158, 176, 177, 178, 230n. 2, 230–31n. 3, 231nn. 4, 5, 235n. 21, 235–36n. 22, 236n. 24
Naropa (Buddhist master), 27–28, 29
Naropa University (formerly Naropa Institute), xii, xv, 27–28, 29; Snowmass scandal, 26, 27, 156–57, 158, 176, 177–78, 235n. 19
New Criticism, 2, 24
New Formalism, 184–85, 193, 194
Newland, Guy, 71, 73, 84
Niland, Jack, 231n. 4
Nixon, Richard M., 111, 151

Objectivist poets, 39
Olcott, Henry Steel, 32
Olson, Charles, 10, 192
Orlovsky, Peter, 17, 43, 54, 128, 162, 170, 171–72, 225–26n. 20, 233n. 14, 233–34n. 15, 235n. 20
Orzech, Charles D., 216n. 4

Paulenich, Craig, 188
People's Temple, 177, 236n. 24
Plant, Sadie, 109, 223–24n. 16
Podhoretz, Norman, 5, 209n. 1
Portugés, Paul, 38, 47, 62, 63, 65–66, 67, 70, 73, 77, 82, 118, 136, 143, 180, 216n. 1, 218–19n. 12, 227n. 9

Pound, Ezra, 8, 9, 10, 182, 208n. 24
Prebish, Charles S., 200n. 6, 201n. 3, 207n. 21
Prothero, Stephen, 188

Quang-Doc, Thich, 68 (*see also* Vietnam War, Vietnamese Buddhist monks, self-immolation protests of)
Queen, Christopher, 200n. 6
Queer studies, 48

Randolph, Leonard, 176, 235nn. 18, 19
Reich, Wilhelm, 169
Reynolds, David S., 211–12n. 9
Reznikoff, Charles, 39, 66
Rich, Adrienne, xvi
Robinson, James Burnell, 54
Rodden, John, 1, 200n. 1, 226n. 21
Roth, Paul, 51
Ruddick, Lisa, 193–94
Rumaker, Michael, 209n. 1

Safran, Jeremy, 190
Said, Edward, 200–201n. 2
Sanders, Ed, 156, 157–58, 176, 220n. 1, 230n. 1, 234–35n. 18
San Francisco Renaissance, 10
Scalapino, Leslie, 192, 193
Schelling, Andrew, 188
Schumacher, Michael, xi, xvii, 24, 43, 62–63, 67, 82, 85, 99, 129–30, 131, 156–57, 158, 162, 176, 177–78, 199n. 1, 204–5n. 13, 207n. 22, 215n. 19, 221n. 3, 223n. 10, 225–26n. 20, 231n. 8, 233n. 14, 234nn. 16, 17, 235n. 20
Seager, Richard Hughes, 32, 200n. 6, 201nn. 3, 4
Shelley, Percy Bysshe, 16, 211n. 6
Shetley, Vernon, 184–85, 193
Silliman, Ron, 185, 236n. 25
Simpson, Louis, 228n. 12
Smith, Larry, 188
Snyder, Gary, 3, 32, 63, 108, 199n. 3, 236n. 1
Staub, Michael E., 110–11
Stein, Gertrude, 10
Steinbeck, John, 122, 123
Stephchanev, Stephen, 47
Surrealism (*see also* "Angkor Wat," and Surrealism), xi, 40–45, 210–211n. 6

Suzuki, D. T., 123
Sweet, Timothy, 223n. 11

Theosophical Society, New York, 32
Tonkinson, Carole, 188
Trungpa. *See* Chögyam Trungpa Rinpoche
Tweed, Thomas A., 32
Tytell, John, 5, 33, 34, 47, 109–10, 209n. 1, 214n. 15
Tzara, Tristan, 43

Untermeyer, Louis, 14

Vendler, Helen, 120, 126, 130, 209n. 1, 226nn. 2, 4, 232n. 12, 236n. 23
Vietnam War (United States) (*see also* "Angkor Wat," and Vietnam War; "The Change: *Kyoto-Tokyo Express*," and Vietnam War; "Wichita Vortex Sutra," and Vietnam War), 33, 38, 39, 40, 59, 68, 90, 91, 92–93, 94–97, 99, 107, 126, 138, 142, 150–51, 160, 227–28n. 10; Vientamese Buddhist monks, self-immolation protests of, 68, 149

Walzer, Kevin, 193, 237n. 4
Weathermen, 150, 152
Weinstone, Ann, 17, 154, 228n. 11
Whalen, Philip, 192, 199n. 3
White, Dennis, 231n. 5
Whitman, Walt, x, 7, 11, 38, 45, 47, 52, 90, 93, 151, 189, 219n. 13, 223n. 10; as figure Ginsberg revises, 20, 49–51, 53, 87, 92, 221n. 4, 222n. 9; influence on Ginsberg's Buddhist poetics, 20, 51, 53, 56, 100, 103–4, 119–20, 212–13n. 13, 214n. 17, 226n. 3
Whitman, Walt, works: "Beat! Beat! Drums!," 92; *Democratic Vistas*, 91–92, 103; "I Saw in Louisiana a Live Oak Growing," 48"; "I Sing the Body Electric," 97, 211–12n. 9; "Passage to India," 92, 212–13n. 13; "Reconciliation," 92, 230n. 20; "The Sleepers," 211n. 9; 213n. 14; "Song of the Banner at Daybreak," 92; "Song of Myself," 48–49, 50, 119–20, 122, 125, 213n. 14; "Spontaneous Me," 211n. 9; "Trickle-Drops," 48; "When Lilacs Last in the Dooryard Bloom'd," 211n. 6

255

Index

Whittemore, Reed, 33–34, 40–41, 45, 53, 74
"Wichita Vortex Sutra" (Ginsberg), 27, 42, 53–54, 55, 84, 87–100, 102, 106–7, 114, 116, 117, 119, 120, 126, 150, 209n. 3, 221n. 4, 226n. 2, 227n. 4; and the body, 60, 87, 90, 94–95, 99, 125; composition process of, 95, 97–99, 211n. 8; and history, evasions of, 90–91, 99–100, 111–12; and improvisation, 97–99; and language, 60, 87, 91, 95, 98, 118, 121–23, 125, 126, 127–28, 131, 133, 184, 185; and magic, 96–97, 99, 118; and mythology, 91; mantric poetics of, 90–91, 96–97, 99–100, 105–106, 121–23, 125, 128, 129, 131, 133, 153, 184, 222n. 9; and race, 76, 99–100, 218n. 11; and romanticism, 102–3, 105, 106, 111; and *shunyata* (*see also* Buddhism, *shunyata*), 93–94; as sutra, 90–91, 93; and Vietnam War (*see also* Vietnam War), 88–100
Williams, William Carlos: influence on Ginsberg's Buddhist poetics, 38–39, 66, 136, 139, 141, 180; as poetic mentor to Ginsberg, xv, 9, 14, 15, 16, 204–5n. 13
Wilson, Elizabeth, 5–6
Wilson, Liz, 216–17n. 4
Woods, Gregory, 41, 211nn. 8, 9, 218n. 10
Wordsworth, William, 3, 174

Yeats, William Butler, 156
Yevtushenko, Yevgeny, 122
Young, Allen, 171, 225n. 18, 233n. 15
Young-Eisendrath, Polly, 25

Zukofsky, Louis, 39, 66

Tony Trigilio is the associate chair of the English department at Columbia College Chicago, where he teaches courses in literary studies and poetry. He is the author of *"Strange Prophecies Anew": Rereading Apocalypse in Blake, H.D., and Ginsberg*, which examines poetry and prophecy, and of *The Lama's English Lessons*, a collection of poems.